Leadership Decapitation

Studies in Violence and Terrorism
EDITED BY MIA BLOOM

Leadership Decapitation

STRATEGIC TARGETING OF TERRORIST ORGANIZATIONS

Jenna Jordan

STANFORD UNIVERSITY PRESS
Stanford, California

Stanford University Press
Stanford, California

© 2019 by the Board of Trustees of the Leland Stanford Junior University. All rights reserved.

No part of this book may be reproduced or transmitted in any form or by any means, electronic or mechanical, including photocopying and recording, or in any information storage or retrieval system without the prior written permission of Stanford University Press.

Printed in the United States of America on acid-free, archival-quality paper

Library of Congress Cataloging-in-Publication Data
Names: Jordan, Jenna (Jennifer Elaine), author.
Title: Leadership decapitation ; strategic targeting of terrorist
   organizations / Jenna Jordan.
Other titles: Violence and terror (Stanford, Calif.)
Description: Stanford, California : Stanford University Press, 2019. |
   Series: Sudies in violence and terror | Includes bibliographical
   references and index.
Identifiers: LCCN 2019009121 (print) | LCCN 2019011745 (ebook) | ISBN
   9781503608245 (cloth ; alk. paper) | ISBN 9781503610675 (ebook)
Subjects: LCSH: Terrorism—Prevention.
Classification: LCC HV6431 .J674 2019 (print) | LCC HV6431 (ebook) | DDC
   363.325/16—dc23
LC record available at https://lccn.loc.gov/2019009121
LC ebook record available at https://lccn.loc.gov/2019011745

Cover design: Andrew Brozyna
Typeset by Newgen in BemboAR Rmnosf 10/13.5 Points

Contents

	Acknowledgments	*vii*
1	Introduction	1
2	A Theory of Organizational Resilience	22
3	Hypotheses on Leadership Decapitation	47
4	Is Leadership Targeting Effective?	62
5	Hamas: Bureaucracy, Social Services, and Local Support	93
6	The Shining Path: The Organization and Support of a Left-Wing Group	124
7	Al-Qaeda: Religious Ideology and Organizational Resilience	151
8	Conclusion	181
	Appendix	*197*
	Notes	*203*
	Bibliography	*231*
	Index	*249*

Acknowledgments

I could not have completed this book without the support and guidance of so many wonderful people. It is with great pleasure that I have the opportunity to thank them here. Robert Pape inspired me to study terrorism and guided me in the development of this project. Bob helped me to grow as an academic, and his support was unwavering. He was patient, encouraging, and above all, he taught me to believe in myself. I would also like to thank John Mearsheimer who taught me to think critically, ask clear questions, and realize my value as an academic. Charles Lipson provided wonderful support and excellent comments on all stages of the project. Charles Glaser encouraged me think critically and analytically. It is from Bob, John, Charles, and Charlie that I developed a passion for International Relations. I also want to thank Mia Bloom, who has been a wonderful mentor and true friend. She has encouraged and supported me in so many ways. She helped me through periods of doubt and struggle in completing this manuscript, while offering constant feedback and unending friendship. From Mia I have learned that academic research can truly have real-world implications.

I am profoundly grateful to all of my friends and colleagues for comments and on this project. At the University of Chicago, I was very lucky to have developed a rigorous and supportive community. I would like to thank Zeynep Bulutgil, Jon Caverley, Alex Downes, Anne Harrington, Anne Holthoefer, Matt Kocher, Adria Lawrence, Chad Levinson, Jennifer London, Chris MacIntosh, Emily Meierding, Michelle Murray, Nuno Monteiro, Harris Mylonas, Sebastian Rosato, John Schuessler, Duncan Snidal, Frank Smith, Keven Ruby, Lora Viola, and Joel Westra. They asked hard questions and gave great advice. A special thanks to

Jennifer London for editing anything and everything. Kathy Anderson facilitated the entire process and helped me to navigate along the way.

I have been fortunate to have a supportive academic community. My colleagues at the Sam Nunn School of International Affairs at the Georgia Institute of Technology—Anjali Bohlken, Mariel Borowitz, Scott Brown, Alberto Fuentes, Claire Greenstein, Maggie Kosal, Dalton Lin, Mike Salomone, and Adam Stulberg—have all provided invaluable feedback on this project. I am particularly appreciative for many long conversations with Larry Rubin and Rachel Whitlark, who read numerous drafts and offered extensive comments. Vince Pedicino and Marilu Suarez have helped me endlessly. I would also like to thank Victor Asal, Steven Barela, Risa Brooks, Shana Cohen, Julie Chernov, Martha Crenshaw, Audrey Kurth Cronin, Christine Fair, Michael Freeman, Mohammed Hafez, Patrick Johnston, Michael Kenney, Peter Krause, Avery Plaw, Bryan Price, Jacob Shapiro, Jim Walsh, Brian Williams, and Will Moore who all offered feedback and helpful suggestions that have had an important impact on my research. Their research has inspired me and shaped my thinking about this topic. My apologies to those I have forgotten to mention.

I am thankful for the amazing students at Georgia Tech. I could not have completed the research for this book without help from my incredible research assistants, Dan Brady, Elizabeth Clark, Zale Clay, Noah Crafts, Elizabeth Cupido, Sarah Drummond, Nathan Fisher, Amy Hartman, Grainne Hutton, John Krzyzaniak, Yuanyuan Lin, Jash Padhiar, Zack Shephard, Will Thomas, Bryn Thornburgh, Jesse Turcotte, and Tammy VuPham.

I received generous financial and institutional support from the Smith Richardson Foundation, the University of Chicago, and the Ivan Allen College of Liberal Arts at the Georgia Institute of Technology. These generous contributions afforded me the time and resources necessary to complete this project. I would also like to thank Ethan Bueno de Mesquita at the Harris School of Public Policy Studies at the University of Chicago for offering me a research position. It was a rich learning experience, and it allowed me the time to research and write.

I have also been fortunate to have presented this research at the Program on International Politics, Economics, and Security and the Program on International Security Policy at the University of Chicago, the Triangle Institute for Security Studies, the MIT Security Studies Program, the Institute for Security and Conflict Studies at George Washington University, the University of Notre Dame, the International Center for the Study of Terrorism at Pennsylvania State University, Emory University, and the Atlanta International Club. I am thankful for the participants at these workshops and seminars who provided me with excellent and helpful suggestions, challenging questions, and critical feedback. I thank the anonymous reviews who provided valuable feedback on the manuscript. I am indebted to editor Alan Harvey and assistant editor Leah Pennylark for the opportunity to publish this book. They were extremely patient and instrumental in helping me finish this process.

Finally, I owe an enormous amount of gratitude to my family. Jenirose Friedkin, my sister and best friend, can always bolster my confidence and make me laugh. Her puns give me life. She has been there for me always, unconditionally. Rob Campbell has been a constant source of support. He has tirelessly listened to many complaints and endless iterations of this book over the years, offering good advice and a critical eye. His help and care has allowed me the opportunity to research, write, and teach. I would not have been able to finish this without him. A special thanks to John and Ruth Campbell for their love and support, and for never asking me why this has taken so long. Conversations with John provided the foundation for this book's theoretical framework. He has read countless drafts, edited my writing, and offered sage advice throughout the years. John has made my thinking, theories, and research sharper and more focused. I would also like to express my love and thanks to Adrienne Erlick and Lowell Sigmund, who kept me laughing and traveling all along the way. I profoundly thank my father, David Jordan, for his unconditional love, encouragement, advice, and support. He has taught me independence, acceptance, and how to believe in myself and others. The memory of my mother, Beverly Jordan, inspires me daily to be a better person. Finally, I dedicate this book to my son Isaiah, who has had to hear a lot about terrorism. His positivity inspires me daily. He has brought so much joy and love to my life, and for that, I am most grateful.

Leadership Decapitation

1

Introduction

It is just after 11 p.m. on May 1, 2011. Two Blackhawk helicopters carrying twenty-three Navy Seals from the US Naval Special Warfare Development Group, also known as DEVGRU or Seal Team 6, leave Jalalabad airfield in eastern Afghanistan. Fifteen minutes later, the team crosses into Pakistani airspace. Five minutes from Osama bin Laden's compound in Abbottabad, Chalk One, the team in Helicopter One, prepares to fast-rope into the compound. The pilot begins to lose control of the helicopter, and it goes down. The assaulters from the Seal team exit the helicopter, jumping about six feet down to the ground. The compound is dark; the power seems to be out.

The team blasts a hole in the gate of the compound's inner wall and moves inside. They approach the guesthouse, reach a locked door, and blow it open. As they charge the door, the team receives fire from an AK-47. They fire back and call for al-Kuwaiti, bin Laden's courier, to come out. The door opens a crack and al-Kuwaiti's wife comes out carrying a child, followed by three children. She tells the Seal team that they have shot her husband. The Seals find al-Kuwaiti's body and enter the main building, meeting up with a second Seal team that is already inside the building on the first floor. The Chalk One team exchanges fire with al-Kuwaiti's brother and wife, killing them both.

The two teams then move through a metal gate blocking the entrance to the second floor. Bin Laden's twenty-three-year-old son, Khalid, who is armed with an AK-47, fires at them. At least two Seals fire back and kill Khalid. Both teams move up to the third floor. Three of the five adult males suspected to be in the compound are still alive. Bin Laden is next.

The Seals blast through another metal door to a staircase leading to the third floor. Their point man sees a man, presumed to be bin Laden, peeking out from a bedroom and fires two shots at him. They enter the room and see two of bin Laden's wives. Amal al-Fatah, his fifth wife, is yelling, and afraid that she will charge, one of the team members shoots her in the calf. The point man grabs the women and pushes them to the side of the room. A second Seal enters the room and shoots an unarmed bin Laden (capturing or detaining bin Laden had not been seen as an option; the risk of him escaping in a hostile country had been judged to be too great).[1]

The first phase of the operation, from crash-landing the helicopter to killing bin Laden, has taken eighteen minutes. During the next twenty minutes, four men begin the intelligence-gathering process, collecting flash drives, CDs, DVDs, and computer hardware. The files would reveal that bin Laden was far more involved in the operational aspect of al-Qaeda's activities than previously assumed. In fact, he had been involved in a number of plans targeting the United States.

The killing of Osama bin Laden is arguably one of the most significant moments in US counterterrorism policy. Shortly after assuming office in January 2009, President Barack Obama directed his new secretary of defense, Leon Panetta, to make "the killing or capture of bin Laden the top priority of our war against al-Qaeda, even as we continued our broader efforts to disrupt, dismantle, and defeat his network."[2] Just after the raid, in his speech to the nation on May 2, 2011, Obama stated, "The death of bin Laden marks the most significant achievement to date in our nation's effort to defeat al-Qaeda."[3]

Immediately after bin Laden's death, leaders, policy makers, and analysts argued that the organization would be crippled. Bruce Riedel, a former Central Intelligence Agency (CIA) officer and analyst at the Brookings Institute's Saban Center, argued that, "the death of bin Laden is a very severe blow for al-Qaeda. And it comes at a particularly bad time for al-Qaeda."[4] Given the revelation after the raid that bin Laden had maintained an operational role within the organization, it is unsurprising that policy analysts assumed his capture would devastate the group's operational capacity. Obama was more cautious in his assessment, arguing that bin Laden's death would not mark the end of the US counterterrorism effort and that al-Qaeda was likely to continue pursuing attacks against the United States. The administration continued, and increased, its targeting policies. In a May 2013 address to the National Defense University, President Obama announced that instead of conventional military action, targeted operations to dismantle terrorist networks would be a critical aspect of the administration's counterterrorism strategy. The administration stated a preference for capturing terrorist leaders; however, where this was either not possible or posed considerable risks, as was the case with bin Laden, they argued that targeted killings should be employed. These speeches highlight the tension between the belief that decapitation is an effective counterterrorism policy and the acknowledgement that groups such as al-Qaeda or the Islamic State of Iraq and Syria (ISIS) are likely to continue carrying out terrorist attacks.

States can employ a number of different tactics to defeat and degrade terrorist organizations, including brute force, repression, regime change, negotiations, undermining of support, ideological change, cutting off of finances, and leadership targeting. While all of these measures have been used, leadership decapitation or leadership targeting, which refers to the arrest or killing of a group's leadership, has become the primary tool in current counterterrorism strategies. The targeting of terrorist leaders has increased substantially since the attacks of September 11, 2001. It was listed first in the priorities of action in the 2006 National Strategy on Combating Terrorism,[5] a document framed in terms of countering a broader ideological threat. By 2011, the National Strategy for Counterterrorism was focused less on a strategy of regime change in countries in which terrorist activity emerged and more on the importance of undermining al-Qaeda's operational capacity. It argued that the threat of terrorism could be eliminated through weakening, disrupting, and degrading al-Qaeda and its affiliates. While the 2011 strategy did not highlight the tactical choices necessary to achieve its broader goals, it argued that US efforts in Afghanistan and Pakistan had destroyed much of al-Qaeda's leadership and thus substantially weakened the organization. Released just after the death of Osama bin Laden, the document claimed that the group was struggling and faced significant organizational challenges, likely undermining its ability to adapt and evolve.

Terrorist leaders can be targeted in a number of different ways: by strikes fired from aircraft or unmanned aerial vehicles, raids, or the use of special operations forces to capture or kill them. While bin Laden was killed during a raid carried out by US Navy Seals and Abu Muhammad al-Adnani, a leader of ISIS in Iraq, was killed by an air strike, drone strikes have become one of the primary means by which the United States targets leaders. They have a much smaller footprint than a ground invasion and are unlikely to be seen as an occupation. Drone strikes also are considered to be more accurate, result in fewer civilian casualties, and as less likely to cause radicalization, all of which increase the likelihood that decapitation will remain a widely used tactic.[6] Most of the strikes in Pakistan, Yemen, and Somalia were against lower-level operatives rather than the upper leadership. While the majority of drone strikes have been carried out in Yemen and Pakistan, the United States has also carried out strikes in Afghanistan, Iraq,

Somalia, and Syria, with an increasing number targeting ISIS and al-Qaeda operatives in Iraq and Syria.

The frequency with which the Obama administration used predator air strikes against militants in Yemen and Pakistan demonstrates the prevalence of the belief that targeting leaders is a strategic move and that drone strikes are a low-cost delivery system that minimizes the risk of civilian casualties while precipitating organizational decline. Beginning in 2008, the Obama administration significantly increased the number of drone strikes used to target both high- and lower-level operatives.[7] In a few prominent examples, Abu Umar al-Baghdadi, leader of the Mujahideen Shura Council, which later became the Islamic State of Iraq, and Abu Ayyab al-Masri, leader of al-Qaeda in Iraq, were both killed in drone strikes in April 2010 in Iraq. Ilyas Kashmiri, reportedly a senior member of al-Qaeda and the operational commander for Harakat-ul-Jihad al-Islami (HuJI), an Islamist organization largely active in Pakistan, Bangladesh, and India, was killed in a drone attack in South Waziristan on June 3, 2011. Anwar al-Awlaki, a Yemeni-American cleric linked to a number of terrorist plots in the West, was killed in Yemen on September 30, 2011, by a Hellfire missile fired from an American drone.[8] In June 2012, Abu Yahya al-Libi, al-Qaeda's deputy leader, was killed in a CIA drone strike in Pakistan; he was highly experienced and served an important operational function within the organization, and his death was seen as a significant blow to an already weakened al-Qaeda.[9] On August 22, 2011, Atiyah Abd al-Rahman was reportedly killed in a drone strike in Pakistan;[10] he was believed to be al-Qaeda's second highest leader and a key link between bin Laden and lower-ranked members of the organization. On June 12, 2015, the leader of al-Qaeda in the Arabian Peninsula, Nasir al-Wuhayshi, was killed by a drone strike in Yemen. While policy makers predicted that these attacks would result in substantial organizational weakening and operational degradation, these groups remain active, and in some cases have become even more so.[11]

Decapitation is a visible counterterrorism measure that can make a fearful domestic audience feel secure in the belief that their government is winning the war on terrorism and willing to act to keep them safe. The Israelis have utilized this as a powerful tool. Leadership targeting[12] can also appeal to the public's sense of justice and retaliation. For example, scholars have claimed that even though targeting Hamas leaders has neither weakened nor destroyed the group, it appeals to the public's sense of revenge and justice and enhances the perception of government strength.[13] In his May 2, 2011 address, Obama stated that "justice has been done." After his announcement of the death of bin Laden, crowds formed outside the White House to celebrate.

While it is clear that a large number of attacks against leadership have been successful in killing their intended targets, there is considerable debate regarding the effectiveness of decapitation in destabilizing terrorist groups, as well as its legality and morality.[14] Some academics, analysts, and policy makers have found evidence that it is effective, reducing a group's operational capacity and frequency of attacks, hindering its organizational cohesion, and forcing leadership underground. Others have found that it is ineffective and can have counterproductive consequences, including an increase in retaliatory attacks, a surge in attacks to signal that the group has not been weakened, or an increase in the targeting of civilians as a tactic.[15] Further, the death of terrorist leaders can trigger new attacks, either in retaliation or to signal that a group is still strong. Often, groups will call upon their followers to avenge the death of a particular leader, resulting in attacks both claimed and unclaimed.

Despite continued debate over its ability to destabilize and weaken a terrorist group, policy makers continue to argue that targeting leaders is an important part of US counterterrorism policy. For example, immediately following the death of Abu Musab al-Zarqawi, who was killed on June 7, 2006, by a US air strike in Iraq, President George W. Bush announced that al-Qaeda had been dealt a "severe blow." After the death of al-Masri on April 18, 2010, the Obama administration announced that al-Qaeda had suffered a "major setback." The day after bin Laden's death, President Obama stated:

> For over two decades, bin Laden has been al-Qaeda's leader and symbol, and has continued to plot attacks against our country and our friends and allies. The death of bin Laden marks the most significant achievement to date in our nation's effort to defeat al-Qaeda.[16]

The state department echoed this assessment in the 2011 Country Reports on Terrorism: "The loss of bin Laden and these other key operatives puts the network on a path of decline that will be difficult to reverse."[17]

Analysts have also predicted that leadership targeting will weaken ISIS. For instance, Abu Muhammad al-Adnani, believed to be the second most important leader of ISIS after Abu Bakr al-Baghdadi, was killed by an air strike in Aleppo, Syria, in August 2016. One of the group's longest-serving top commanders, al-Adnani was a spokesperson in charge of ISIS's operations outside of Syria and Iraq and was responsible for the recruitment of foreign fighters. Thomas Joscelyn, a senior fellow at the Foundation for Defense of Democracies and senior editor of *FDD's Long War Journal*, states that al-Adnani was one of the group's most senior officials, and probably the most visible.[18] His death was considered by analysts and policy makers to be a major blow to the organization.[19] Adam Deen, a senior researcher at the Quilliam Foundation, said that ISIS would be "scrambling to find a replacement."[20] He argued that the group was dependent upon personality cults and the charisma of its leaders, and as such, the death of a figure such as al-Adnani would be destabilizing.

But in the months after the assassination, ISIS continued to gain new recruits, hold territory, and carry out attacks. Prior to his death, al-Adnani had stated that while ISIS may experience periods of weakening, the movement is more than its capacity to control territory. It is built upon its beliefs and ideology. He states, "O America. Would we be defeated and you be victorious if you were to take Mosul or Sirte or Raqqa? Certainly not! We would be defeated and you victorious only if you were able to remove the Koran from Muslims' hearts."[21] This statement reflects one of the theoretical arguments advanced in this book—that the ideology of ISIS or al-Qaeda is not dependent upon leadership, or even territorial control. Rather, ideology, organizational structure, and local support have contributed to their ability to withstand the loss of their leaders.

Al-Qaeda Central and its affiliates suffered periods of decline, but bin Laden's death did not fatally harm the organization. Ayman al-Zawahiri assumed the leadership of al-Qaeda in June 2011, and the group has continued to franchise with the growth of more affiliates, many of which, such as al-Qaeda in the Arabian Peninsula, continue to operate. ISIS has also undergone a large number of attacks on its leadership since the summer of 2014. While the organization has experienced significant setbacks in its territorial control in Iraq, this is not likely the result of its leaders being killed.

Attacks against al-Qaeda and ISIS show no sign of abatement. It is thus essential to evaluate whether decapitation is an effective strategy, and to examine its potential consequences. To address these concerns, this book poses the following question: Does leadership decapitation work? The primary goal of this book is to determine whether it is a successful counterterrorism policy and to account for the variation in its efficacy, both theoretically and empirically. In doing so, the book will examine the conditions under which decapitation is more or less likely to result in organizational decline and degrade a group's operational capacity. To do this, I created a dataset that examines 1,276 instances of leadership targeting against terrorist groups from 1970 to 2016.[22] Figure 1.1 displays the number of both arrests and killings of terrorist leaders from 1970 to 2016. While there has been a decline over the past few years, this trend is unlikely to reverse itself in any considerable way. This issue is even more salient given US and international efforts to target ISIS leaders.

In order to develop counterterrorism policies that undermine and weaken terrorist organizations, it is essential to identify whether our policies are likely

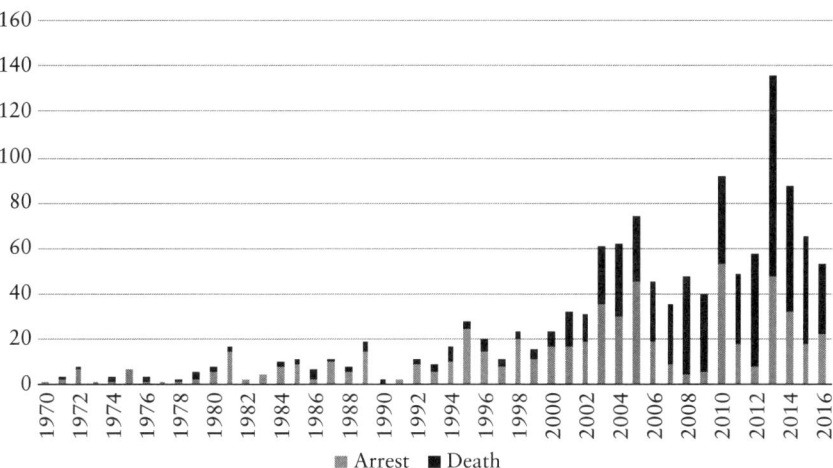

FIGURE 1.1 Leadership targeting, 1970–2016

to be effective. If decapitation is unlikely to weaken a terrorist organization or is likely to result in adverse consequences for the types of organizations the United States is currently targeting, then it is essential that counterterrorism policy be rethought.

The Argument and Method

This book aims to identify and explain why decapitation works in some cases and not in others. To account for this variation, I argue that a group's susceptibility to leadership targeting is a function of three factors: (1) organizational structure, (2) popular support, and (3) group type or ideology.[23] Leadership decapitation is unlikely to result in the demise of groups that are highly bureaucratized, have high levels of popular support, or are driven by a religious or separatist ideology. Leaders matter less under these conditions, and their removal can often have adverse consequences such as retaliatory attacks or an overall increase in the frequency of attacks. This is the case because, first, bureaucratized terrorist groups are diversified, have a clear division of administrative responsibilities and functions, follow rules and procedures, and are thus more likely to withstand the sudden removal of a leader or leaders. Smaller and younger organizations are less likely to be bureaucratized and are thus more likely to succumb to attacks on their leadership. Second, group type is an important factor in resilience to leadership attacks. Islamist, religious, or separatist groups should be more resilient to targeting efforts because their ideology does not depend upon the leader for its articulation; it is often deeply engrained within the group or the local community.[24] As a result, these groups often have more popular support, further increasing their resilience. Third, communal or popular support is essential for the provision of resources and potential recruits necessary for a terrorist group to sustain itself and carry out activity. It provides the basis for group legitimacy, which can increase an organization's efficiency and resilience. Popular support is essential to a terrorist group's ability to maintain organizational strength and capacity following an attack on its leadership.

The efficacy of decapitation can be evaluated in a number of different ways. Decapitation can result in organizational weakening, degradation, or complete defeat. Alternatively, targeting efforts can strengthen a group by enhancing its resolve or bolstering support and sympathy from local communities or the larger international community. In some cases, leadership targeting has been effective and has resulted in the decline of an organization. In other cases, it has not only been ineffective but has actually emboldened terrorist organizations. This book examines trends in decapitation to account for whether and when it is an effective counterterrorism strategy.

The database created for this study indicates that, overall, decapitation is not an effective strategy. First, it does not increase a group's mortality rate and does not result in a significant decline in organizational activity. In other words, groups that have experienced decapitation are no more likely to "die" or end than those that have not had their leaders killed or arrested. While certain types of organizations may have a longer or shorter life span in general, decapitation does not have a statistically significant impact on a group's survival. Second, the statistical analyses identify the conditions under which decapitation is more or less likely to result in a decline in activity and a group's life span, accounting for variation in its success. In certain cases, decapitation can result in a decline in a terrorist group's activity. However, the data reveals that larger, older, Islamist, and separatist groups are less likely to fall apart or experience a decline in activity than other groups—and against the most active organizations, decapitation actually results in an *increase* in activity. In addition, organizations in more autocratic countries or those with a higher GDP had a higher rate of decline. Taken together, the data demonstrates that while decapitation can be effective in certain cases, overall, it does not shorten a group's life, decrease its activity and lethality, or bring about its demise, and this is particularly true for certain types of organizations.

Definitions and Scope

There has been ongoing discussion in the literature regarding the meaning of the term *terrorism*.[25] The words *terrorism* or *terrorist organization* are laden with emotion and political biases and are subject to multiple understandings. As a result, there is little agreement over a clear and precise definition of terrorism. Even within the US government, there are multiple definitions, with each definition reflecting an agency's priorities. For example, the US Department of State defines terrorism as "premeditated, politically motivated violence perpetrated against noncombatant targets by subnational groups or clandestine agents, usually intended to influence an audience,"[26] while the Federal Bureau of Investigation calls it "the unlawful use of force and violence against persons or property to intimidate or coerce a government, the civilian population, or any segment thereof, in furtherance of political or social objectives,"[27] and the Department of Homeland Security and the Department of Defense define it as "the calculated use of unlawful violence or threat of unlawful violence to inculcate fear; intended to coerce or to intimidate governments or societies in the pursuit of goals that are generally political, religious, or ideological."[28]

In a large and comprehensive study of terrorist definitions, Alex Schmid looked at over one hundred definitions of terrorism in an attempt to find a broad and widely acceptable definition.[29] He identified twenty-two different frequently cited definitional elements. In an early influential study of terrorism, Walter Laqueur recognized the challenges in finding a clear and precise definition, and concluded that terrorism is the illegitimate use of force to achieve a political objective by targeting innocent people.[30] Bruce Hoffman argues that terrorism is political in its aims, violent or threatens violence, designed to have psychological impacts beyond the target, perpetrated by a nonstate entity, and conducted by either an organization, an individual, or a group of individuals.[31] He concludes that terrorism is "the deliberate creation and exploitation of fear through violence or the threat of violence in the pursuit of political change."[32] Following Hoffman's definition, this book defines terrorism as violence, or the threat of violence, directed against civilians and used by a nonstate actor in the pursuit of a political goal. The term *political* can encompass a wide range of phenomena, such as the establishment of a religious state, revolution, autonomy, independence, societal change, or even maintenance of the status quo.[33]

Hoffman argues that while terrorism is difficult to define, it is important to distinguish it from other kinds of violence.[34] Specifically, he argues that there is an important distinction between terrorist and insurgent organizations.[35] Unlike insurgent groups, Hoffman argues that terrorist groups

> do not function in the open as armed units, generally do not attempt to seize or hold territory, deliberately avoid engaging enemy militant forces in combat, are constrained both numerically and logistically from undertaking concerted mass political

mobilization efforts, and exercise no direct control or governance over a populace at either the local or national level.[36]

However, these categories are not entirely clear, and there is considerable overlap. For example, some large terrorist groups have features of insurgent organizations and are able to hold considerable amounts of territory or engage with military forces, while other organizations that engage in terrorist activity do not possess characteristics of insurgencies.

This distinction between defining a group as terrorist or insurgent can have implications for understanding theory, policy, and the specific nature of the threat they pose. Moghadam, Berger, and Beliakova argue that there is a tendency to label insurgent groups as terrorist, and this labeling has political implications. They conclude that it is more accurate to call groups insurgent, given that most of the terrorist groups they examined attacked civilians in addition to government, military, and police targets.[37] They argue, "It is also important to note that seeing terrorism as an insurgency-related phenomenon will require governments to adjust their counterterrorism policies to better handle the cultural peculiarities of insurgencies."[38] Obscuring this difference could undermine counterterrorism policies by overlooking the many different means by which terrorist groups attempt to achieve their goals.

Many organizations can be classified as both terrorist organizations and insurgent organizations as many insurgent groups have also used terrorism as a tactic. This book includes insurgent organizations that have used terrorism as a tactic in pursuit of their goals, such as Chechen separatists, Sendero Luminoso (the Shining Path), and the Armed Islamic Group of Algeria (GIA). Some of the groups in the analyses have characteristics of insurgencies, while others are smaller, with little to no territory or governance capabilities, and have relied primarily on the use of terrorist tactics.

The statistical analysis in Chapter 4 conducts separate analyses on the largest and most active groups, which are often considered to be insurgent organizations. Moreover, the exclusion of insurgent groups that do not use terrorism should not impact the validity of the findings. Moghadam, Berger, and Beliakova argue that in practice, most insurgent groups use terrorism as a tactic. Focusing exclusively on insurgent organizations, however, would eliminate a large number of organizations that have been subject to attacks on their leadership. Furthermore, there is something distinct and meaningful about a group's decision to employ terrorism. While acknowledging that it is important to use the label of "insurgent group," Moghadam, Berger, and Beliakova acknowledge that the label "terrorist" is still useful because once a group decides to engage in violence against civilians, "it crosses a certain moral threshold that sets it apart from other groups."[39] Given these concerns, this project includes both terrorist groups that do not have characteristics of insurgencies and insurgent groups that target civilians in acts of terrorism in addition to other means. This book recognizes that insurgency is an important category, and thus draws upon literature on both terrorism and insurgencies.

The data utilized for this book covers the period between 1970 and 2016. Three case studies—on Hamas, the Shining Path, and al-Qaeda—are used as a way to examine the theory of organizational resilience and evaluate the statistical results. These cases were chosen for a number of reasons, notably because they offer regional and temporal variation as well as variation in group goals. Hamas has been one of the most frequent targets of decapitation, sustaining nearly thirty years of targeting efforts. There is currently a significant amount of debate surrounding this tactic's efficacy, yet it continues to be treated as an efficient means by which to undermine Palestinian terrorist groups. The case study on the Shining Path is a hard test for the book. At the time of its demise, it was a large and older organization, which should have increased its resilience to targeting efforts. However, earlier instances of leadership decapitation were not effective against the Shining Path; it was not until the arrest of its leader in 1999 that organizational activity significantly declined. As a result, this chapter offers within-case variation in the efficacy of decapitation against the Shining Path. I argue that it was susceptible to organizational destabilization due to the lack of support inherent to ideologically driven terrorist organizations; support for the organization changed over time and can thus account for the disparity in the effectiveness of leadership decapitation against the Shining Path. Finally, al-Qaeda has been a frequent and continued target of leadership attacks, along with ISIS, so it is important to understand the impact this targeting has had on al-Qaeda's activity in order to assess the impact of past and future counterterrorism policies.

Research on Leadership Decapitation

There is considerable disagreement over the ability of decapitation to bring about organizational decline. Much of the extant research focuses on either anecdotal evidence or quantitative analysis and fails to develop a theoretical explanation to account for variation in the efficacy of leadership targeting. Early research on state coercion sparked an important debate regarding the effectiveness and the legality of leadership targeting.[40] In a study of the coercive ability of air power, Colonel John Warden argues that leadership is a critical element in "determining a nation's will to fight."[41] He claims that in modern times, command and control have become so important that decisively removing a leader can be damaging, particularly to a nation's ability to direct war efforts. Warden finds that while capturing or killing a state leader is difficult, it can induce the command structure to make concessions. While this work has contributed to the debate about decapitation as a counterterrorism strategy, the conclusions were deduced primarily from evidence on targeting state leaders. In contrast, Robert Pape responds to Warden's claim and argues that leadership targeting is not likely to result in successful coercion for three reasons:[42] (1) it is hard to find individuals and kill leaders,[43] (2) the death of a leader during war often brings less policy change than expected, and (3) in most states, succession is unpredictable. Pape concludes that while decapitation can temporarily disrupt terrorist operations, it rarely leads to long-term gains.[44]

Stephen Hosmer has also examined whether targeting state leaders has an effect upon the ability of the United States to "shape the policy and behavior of enemy states and other hostile actors."[45] Examining twenty-four cases of leadership targeting, Hosmer concludes that they are rarely successful: "An examination of past cases shows that direct attacks on leaders rarely produce wanted policy changes, often fail to deter unwanted enemy behavior, sometimes produce harmful unintended consequences, [and] frequently fail to kill the leader."[46] While this early research focuses primarily on operations against state leaders, it underscores the importance of determining whether a leader's removal actually impacts a group's operational capacity.

Quantitative Research on Decapitation

A newer wave of research on targeting is more quantitative in its approach. Much of this literature is optimistic about the ability of targeting to reduce levels of violence or to negatively impact a group's life span.[47] Bryan Price and Patrick Johnston conducted two of the most robust and comprehensive quantitative analyses of leadership targeting to date.[48] Price analyzes 204 instances in which the top leader was either captured or killed and determines the mortality rate of 207 terrorist organizations from 1970 to 2008.[49] He also records another 95 incidents in which the leader stepped down, was expelled from the group, died of natural causes, or entered into political processes or ceasefire agreements with the government. He codes a group as having ended or "died" if it failed to carry out a violent attack in two years, and uses the group's last attack as its end date. His analysis reveals that, controlling for other factors, decapitation increases the mortality rate of terrorist organizations. Decapitated organizations are 3.6 to 6.7 times more likely to end than those that have not undergone decapitation.[50] Second, he finds that terrorist groups with allies are more likely to end than those competing with rival groups. Third, older organizations have a lower mortality rate; once an organization passes a twenty-year threshold, decapitation has little if any effect.[51] Fourth, while all three methods of decapitation (capturing, killing, or capturing and then killing the leader) increase the mortality rate of organizations, they are statistically indistinguishable from one another. Fifth, any type of leadership turnover, such as a leader resigning or being ousted from the group, increases group mortality. Finally, nationalist groups are more resilient than religious groups following decapitation. While this is one of the most comprehensive studies on leadership targeting, the data is limited in time and scope.

Price argues that for targeting to be successful, leaders must be important to the success of the organization and leadership succession must be difficult. He distinguishes between values-based and profit-based organizations and argues that because terrorist groups are violent, clandestine, and values based, leadership succession is particularly difficult.[52] First, values-based organizations, which have a harder time articulating their ideology than profit-based ones, require that their leaders have unique skill sets, such as the ability to provide transformative leadership that appeals to followers' emotions and values. Price notes, "Transformational leaders, therefore, seek to create significant change in the behavior and belief systems of their followers, often encouraging personal sacrifice to achieve goals that benefit the team, group, or organization."[53] Profit-based organizations, in contrast, are able to provide monetary incentives, which makes attracting recruits and planning succession easier. Second, violent organizations are frequently led by charismatic leaders and tend to be more cohesive than non-values-based organizations. Third, nonviolent organizations "depend upon conventional forms of authority to ensure compliance from their subordinates,"[54] while the nature of violent, clandestine organizations makes them more dependent upon leaders who are less likely to institutionalize their operations for both strategic and personal reasons, further complicating succession. Fourth, Price argues, leaders in values-based organizations are responsible for framing or creating their groups' ideology. As a result, removing leaders may result in instability, particularly if the group has not undergone the routinization of charisma. While Price offers one of the few extant theoretical explanations for leadership decapitation, his model does not account for variation in the effectiveness of leadership targeting. His theory treats all terrorist organizations as values based, thus overpredicting the occurrence of success.

In another influential quantitative study of leadership targeting, Patrick Johnston uses regression to determine the effect of leadership decapitation on counterinsurgency outcomes and dynamics using two measures. The first measure is war termination and success, and the second measure is the conflict dynamic, which focuses on lethality and insurgent-initiated incidents. His study concludes that decapitation decreases the intensity and frequency of militant attacks, increases the chance of war termination, and raises the probability of government victory.[55] Two key findings emerge from his analysis. First, the impact of removing insurgent leaders may be larger in older campaigns, supporting his hypothesis that decapitation could "help break the morale of insurgencies that have been engaged in long, often difficult campaigns."[56] Second, killing leaders is likely to be more effective than capturing them. He concludes that while decapitation can be effective, it is more likely to help counterinsurgency operations as part of a larger campaign strategy. His study also examines the relationship between the efficacy of decapitation and the following variables—whether a group is identity based or ideological, a group's age, whether the leaders was arrested or killed, and whether the insurgency was center seeking. While most of the variables were not statistically significant, he found that killing leaders is more effective than capturing them, and that the impact of removing leaders in longer campaigns is greater.

Finally, Johnston answers an important question that has not been explored in current studies of decapitation: What are the consequences of failed decapitation attempts? Johnston argues that "decapitation attempts fail more often than they succeed, and these outcomes are uncorrelated with key observable variables. As a result, failed attempts provide an ideal set of counterfactual observations that enable identification of leadership decapitation's causal impact."[57] In order to answer this question, his study assesses the impact of both successes and failures on counterinsurgency outcomes. Using failed attempts as a control for successes, he is able to identify whether successful versus failed decapitation attempts have an effect on the outcome and dynamics of insurgent campaigns. The findings of this analysis suggest that "successful leadership removals, not blowback from failed attempts, drive the effect of leadership decapitation."[58] This finding challenges the argument that failed attempts at targeting leaders may negatively impact a government's chance of defeating insurgencies.

Johnston's findings have provided more nuance to the debate about the impact of decapitation, but there are a few limitations to his study. First, his analysis focuses only on insurgent campaigns, which excludes many organizations that have engaged in terrorist activity. Second, focusing exclusively on top leaders could bias the results in favor of success, especially for insurgent organizations, in which the top leader may play a more critical role.[59] Current targeting policies are not only directed at top leaders. The United States targets many mid- and upper-level leaders, and the inclusion of these instances is important. I expect that there is a difference between targeting top and lower-level leaders within an organization. Third, it is important to know whether many upper echelon leaders were targeted prior to the death or capture of the top leader. Finally, the dataset focuses on campaigns between 1975 and 2003. While this is a sufficiently long time period in which to analyze the life span and activity of insurgent organizations, by excluding the time period after 2003, the dataset is missing a considerable number of targeting efforts, both successes and failures. Many instances of decapitation that occurred after 2003 have not resulted in organizational death or a substantial weakening of the group. Further, while Johnston's statistical findings are robust and important, his article lacks a theoretical discussion of decapitation. It does not provide an explanation for why decapitation is effective and how it can affect a group's operational capacity. More importantly, these findings do not provide insight into when states should or should not target terrorist organizations.

In another, smaller analysis, Langdon, Sarapu, and Wells examine nineteen groups and thirty-five cases of decapitation in order to determine whether an organization had disbanded, divided, or radicalized after its leader's death.[60] Four key findings emerged from this research. First, a majority of organizations were unchanged by leadership decapitation, and none of the groups had radicalized after the removal of their leaders. Second, internal disputes prior to leadership crises made groups more likely to splinter after decapitation, and hierarchically structured organizations were better suited to deal with leadership setbacks. Third, religious organizations had rarely disbanded, because they provide a strong source of group cohesion. Finally, Langdon, Sarapu, and Wells claim that groups that rely heavily on a leader's teachings are more likely to survive. However, their dataset was small and included only groups with one leader. Moreover, as their study was not limited to terrorist organizations, it is difficult to apply these findings to counterterrorism trends more broadly.

Aaron Mannes examines seventy-one terrorist groups and sixty cases of decapitation.[61] To assess effectiveness, the study compares terrorist activity in the period before and after a terrorist attack. While he leaves out organizations with under a hundred members, in order to exclude groups that committed fewer than ten attacks, he includes small groups that committed highly significant operations, such as Aum Shinrikyo. Most of the results are not statistically significant, but Mannes finds a decline in the number of terrorist incidents in the five years after a leadership attack. However, he claims that killing a religious organization's leaders rather than arresting them causes them to become more deadly, and concludes that in these cases decapitation may be counterproductive.[62] Mannes's study is too limited in scope to make concrete claims regarding the effectiveness of leadership decapitation. Had he included smaller organizations, his results might have been dramatically different. Finally, he selects only groups that had been targeted; to determine whether decapitation is an effective strategy, it is necessary to compare the rate of decline and activity to organizations that have not been targeted.

In a more recent study on decapitation, Tominaga looks at whether leadership targeting has deterred militant operations. This is a novel approach to understanding the efficacy of targeting. He argues that targeting the leadership of one group warns other groups that they too could be targeted. Through quantitative analyses, Tominaga found that targeting deterred operations in nontargeted groups, and that this effect is strongest when there are alliances between the organizations.[63]

Arguments on Resilience

Many of the quantitative studies on leadership targeting lack a theoretical explanation to account for variation in its efficacy. In the remainder of this section, I examine extant theoretical arguments on the efficacy of leadership decapitation that can offer insight into the susceptibility of organizations to leadership removal. These arguments have influenced and informed the theory of organizational resilience presented in this book.

Leadership. Leaders are often seen as critical in creating and maintaining organizational strength and cohesion, and a leader's function or role can explain when decapitation is most likely to weaken an organization. Price's study, discussed earlier in this chapter, offers a theory of organizational resilience based on the value of leadership to an organization's operations. Michael Freeman also highlights the importance of a leader's role in accounting for the efficacy of decapitation. He argues that terrorist groups face collective action problems and that charismatic leaders can overcome these obstacles by motivating individuals to commit violent acts for the good of the leaders, rather than for their own benefit. Leaders can also inspire individuals "through the articulation of an ideological vision."[64] Accordingly, the likelihood of targeting efficacy can be determined by whether leaders hold an operational or inspirational role;[65] organizations in which the leader has both key operational and inspirational roles are the most likely to fall apart after decapitation. Although organizations with charismatic leaders tend to be susceptible to leadership attacks, Freeman claims that, over time, they can become more institutionalized and their leaders more resilient.

Intelligence. A second set of studies has focused on how critical information can be obtained during the capture of terrorist leaders. Targeting operations can result in the discovery of organizational documents revealing information about group activity. The Italian capture of Red Brigade leaders led to information that was used to dismantle the organization.[66] During the arrest of Abimael Guzmán, leader of Sendero Luminoso, authorities found documents that resulted in the arrest of other Sendero members.[67] Documents obtained during the arrest of Basque Homeland and Freedom (ETA) leader Francisco Múgica Garmendia revealed that the organization was far more sophisticated than authorities had previously thought.[68]

Furthermore, arrested leaders can provide intelligence about locations, capabilities, personnel, and operations that sheds light on a group's organizational structure, complexity, or even potential activities.[69] Cronin notes, "Interrogating leaders often provides valuable intelligence on the rest of the group. In an ideal world, arresting and prosecuting terrorist operatives is the optimal solution."[70]

Disruption. There are others who contend that either arresting or killing leaders will cause a significant amount of organizational chaos, disrupting a group's operational capacity.[71] Daniel Byman argues that to avoid detection, terrorist organizations must frequently hide, change locations, and engage in behavior that makes communication difficult.[72] These operational problems are further compounded when leaders are targeted. When leaders spend time trying to avoid detection and maintain secrecy, they have less time available to plan attacks, which could decrease the frequency of attacks and perhaps their lethality. As Carvin notes, "keeping leaders on the run is a major advantage."[73]

Public Opinion. Social preferences toward violence have an effect upon the willingness of terrorist groups to use suicide terrorism.[74] Support for violence can encourage terrorist groups to carry out more violent campaigns. Mia Bloom examines the relationship between communal support and the occurrence of suicide terrorism. She argues that suicide terrorism provides radical groups with an opportunity to increase their share of the political market as a function of competition among militant groups. When societies support killing civilians, terrorist groups have an incentive to adopt such measures.[75] Terrorist organizations care about social approval and want to be seen as legitimate in order to increase their status relative to other groups. Similarly, Risa Brooks argues that "the militant's home constituency forces militants to adhere to societal norms about how violence is used."[76] Society's tolerance for violence can influence physical security, intelligence, and defensive resources that can help to conceal militants,[77] as well as the provision of key resources necessary for building organizational infrastructure.

Organizational Structure. Other studies have looked at the relationship between organizational structure and group stability.[78] Much of this work argues that decentralized organizations are harder to destabilize than hierarchical ones.[79]

Marc Sageman claims that, given the structure of such networks, leaders may not be the appropriate target of counterterrorism forces. In a 2004 study of the global Salafi jihad, Sageman argues that social networks provide a way for isolated and alienated individuals to join a community. The social bonds created within these communities can foster ideological commitment and encourage would-be militants to join jihadist movements. The decentralized and local nature of these groups makes them difficult to target. Instead, he argues, it is necessary to identify key hubs within the organization, individuals who often are not the group's top leaders.[80]

Similarly, Cronin argues that while decapitation can be an effective strategy, "Past experience with terrorism indicates that al-Qaeda will not end if Osama bin Laden is killed."[81] Al-Qaeda's organizational structure, both a hierarchy and a decentralized network of individual cells, is particularly stable. Its leadership is structured hierarchically with a mechanism for succession, which should decrease the likelihood of organizational instability following attacks on the group's leadership.

There are other perspectives on the resilience of terrorist organizations that focus on the relationship between a group's structure and its organizational efficacy or capacity. Lindelauf, Borm, and Hamers examine the structural features of covert networks and argue that their resilience to the loss of key members can be explained by the distinction between covert and information-balanced networks.[82] As Jacob Shapiro argues, terrorist organizations experience a trade-off between efficiency and secrecy. A sparsely connected organization is necessary to maintain secrecy, but this creates communication difficulties that make it difficult to control and coordinate.[83] Lindelauf, Borm, and Hamers find that dispersed networks are more resilient to targeted attacks than other kinds of social networks:[84] "The implication for terrorist networks is obvious. Their evolution towards global, sparsely connected, leaderless networks has enabled them to survive the continuing targeted attack on their nodes."[85]

Consequences of Decapitation

While decapitation can impact a group's ability to carry out attacks, it can also result in counterproductive outcomes, such as the creation of a martyrdom effect, a surge in recruitment, retaliatory attacks, an increase in group resolve and strength, and an increase in the frequency and intensity of attacks.[86] According to Bergen, while al-Qaeda does not pose a significant threat to national security, the group is likely to withstand the capture or death of key leaders.[87] Its resilience stems from the fact that group members believe they are carrying out a holy mission.[88] While al-Qaeda operatives swore *bayat,* an oath of allegiance, to bin Laden himself, Bergen highlights the growth in popularity of Sayid Qutb's writings after Qutb's execution by the Egyptian government in 1966 as an enduring force driving al-Qaeda's religious ideals.[89] Bin Laden's death appealed to the US audience's desire for justice, yet Bergen claimed that this "will not end the war of the terrorists. Bin Laden's ideas have circulated widely and will continue to attract adherents for years to come."[90] In fact, Bergen claimed that the assassination could lead to anti-American attacks around the globe and bolster the power of bin Laden's ideas, ultimately strengthening the organization.

Decapitation can appeal to a public's sense of revenge, but it can also bring about a desire for revenge on the part of the terrorist group, resulting in retaliatory attacks. Stephen David, who ultimately recommends continuation of Israel's targeting policy, argues that while it has prevented some attacks, it can create negative ramifications.[91] In a qualitative analysis of leadership targeting, Dear argues that targeting can temporarily hinder an insurgent's capabilities and disrupt networks and leadership structure.[92] However, he concludes, repeated attacks will not cause more disruption to militant capability, as groups adapt to such countermeasures. Further, Dear finds evidence that repeated targeting efforts can result in more radicalization and the desire for revenge, eventually destabilizing government and security structures. Ultimately, Dear claims, targeted killings are often an "actively counterproductive tactic in COIN," meaning that in counterinsurgency operations, targeting leaders can be ineffective and counterproductive.[93]

Targeting can also have an effect on the tactical choices terrorist groups make. Max Abrahms and Jochen Mierau look at the impact of targeted killing on militant group tactical decision making in the Afghanistan-Pakistan and West Bank–Gaza Strip theaters.[94] Overall, they conclude that after leadership strikes, groups become less discriminate in their target selection by attacking more civilians and fewer military targets. Looking at drone strikes against leaders in Afghanistan and Pakistan and leadership strikes more generally in Israel and the West Bank, they present four theoretical mechanisms to explain these tactical changes. First, they argue that soft targets are easier to attack. Second, and consistent with the arguments presented above, they note that a rise in indiscriminate targeting may be caused by a group's desire to get revenge. Third, they identify a substitution mechanism whereby groups shift tactics when certain targets become harder to strike. Finally, they argue that leaders may possess superior cognitive abilities and judgment, and when those leaders are removed, decision making falls to less reliable agents who may be more likely to strike civilians. This is one of few studies that examine changes in terrorist groups' tactical choices. However, the analysis does not provide a way to explain variation in impact.

Conclusion

Having introduced the main elements of the controversy surrounding terrorism and leadership decapitation, I turn in the following chapters to demonstrating why decapitation is not effective except under certain circumstances. Chapter 2 develops a theory of organizational resilience that accounts for when decapitation is more or less likely to result in the decline or weakening of terrorist organizations. The theory focuses on a group's organizational characteristics, its ideology, and its degree of support from the communities in which it operates. Chapter 3 develops hypotheses regarding the efficacy of targeting and the conditions under which it is likely to result in organizational weakening or other adverse consequences. Chapter 4 presents the quantitative results from statistical analysis of the data.

Chapter 5 examines Hamas, an organization that has experienced numerous leadership attacks but has remained resilient and active, ultimately gaining strength and legitimacy over time. More precisely, while the lethality of Hamas's actions has declined over time, their frequency has actually increased. I argue that Hamas's resilience can be explained largely by its bureaucratic structure and its level of communal support, both of which have given the group the ability to develop extensive infrastructure for the provision of religious, social, and educational resources. Providing these important services influences the ideological beliefs of the community and enhances the group's legitimacy. To evaluate communal support, I examine data on Palestinian support for Hamas from 1994 to 2012. This data suggests that leadership decapitation can have adverse consequences—Hamas's subsequent retaliatory attacks on Israel led to more public support and increased its political legitimacy.

Chapter 6 explores the case of the Shining Path, whose leaders were arrested in 1999, ultimately bringing about a significant decline in organizational activity. The Shining Path was a large and relatively old organization, which runs counter to the statistical findings in Chapter 4. However, I note that earlier instances of targeting Shining Path leaders, most notably the 1992 arrest of Abimael Guzmán, was not effective, indicating that something had changed. I argue that the susceptibility of the Shining Path to organizational destabilization came about because of a decline in communal support, which occurred mainly because the group was driven by ideology, a condition inherently not as durable as religious or territorial identification.

Chapter 7 looks at al-Qaeda and its affiliates in an attempt to understand the impact decapitation attacks have had upon its operational capacity and organizational strength. This chapter focuses on understanding the differences between al-Qaeda as a larger movement and its affiliated organizations. It then focuses on the repeated targeting efforts against al-Qaeda Central and al-Qaeda in Iraq in order to explain why and when these efforts have made the groups more or less resilient. The book concludes with a discussion of the overall findings and theoretical arguments regarding the efficacy of leadership targeting. It then focuses on the case of the Islamic State of Iraq and Syria and examines its likelihood of withstanding or succumbing to repeated attacks on its leadership. It also addresses the current debate about whether there is something unique about ISIS that requires a different sort of analysis. The chapter will then conclude with policy recommendations regarding the use and impact of leadership decapitation as a counterterrorism policy.

2

A Theory of Organizational Resilience

Leadership targeting is not always an effective counterterrorism strategy, and the current literature on it lacks an overarching theory to explain why it works in some cases and not in others. Organizations can respond to the arrest or capture of their leaders in many different ways. They can fall apart, become temporarily weakened, factionalize, or experience a decline in operational efficacy. Alternatively, decapitation can embolden organizations to carry out more frequent or more lethal attacks. Groups can adapt to countermeasures, becoming stronger, more resilient, and more active in the process. This chapter will develop a theoretical explanation to account for variation in the efficacy of leadership targeting and will develop hypotheses to answer three main questions: (1) Under what conditions does leadership decapitation result in the decline of a terrorist organization? (2) Does leadership decapitation lengthen or shorten a group's life span? (3) In cases where decapitation does not result in a group's collapse, to what extent does it weaken a group and hinder its capacity to carry out attacks?

I argue that the efficacy of capturing or killing a group's leader or leadership is a function of three primary variables: the group's (1) bureaucracy, (2) communal support, and (3) ideology. Groups that are bureaucratized, have high levels of popular support from the communities in which they operate, and/or have religious or separatist ideologies are more likely to withstand the destabilizing effects of leadership targeting. Bureaucratized organizations will have an easier time reorganizing after the loss of their leaders. Groups with significant levels of communal support should have access to resources that allow them to withstand attacks and continue carrying out their activities. Finally, religious and separatist groups are more likely to be based upon an ideological belief and doctrine that emerge from local communities and are not dependent upon the leadership for their rearticulation and continuation. Would-be and existing militants from such groups are motivated by the group's ideology rather than the specific teachings of one leader.

A theory of group resilience should be able to explain why and when decapitation works. Studies have identified multiple pathways by which organizations end, but much of the evidence is anecdotal and cannot be easily generalized across multiple cases. This literature has largely overlooked specific factors that increase or decrease a group's likelihood of decline after external shocks, such as the removal of a leader. Furthermore, there has been very little discussion of the ability of organizations to regroup and reorganize after experiencing exogenous shocks.

To develop a theoretical explanation that accounts for variation in the efficacy of leadership targeting, it is essential to examine sources of organizational decline. Much of the terrorism literature has focused on causes of organizational decline, while remaining largely silent on broad trends.[1] Audrey Kurth Cronin argues that to understand how terrorism ends, it is important to examine patterns in the decline and end of terrorist campaigns. She identifies six broad explanations for such declines: (1) the killing or capturing of a group's leader (decapitation), (2) entry of the group into a legitimate political process (negotiation), (3) achievement of the group's aims (success), (4) implosion or loss of the group's public support (failure), (5) defeat and elimination by brute force (repression), and (6) transition from terrorism to other forms of violence (reorientation).[2] Cronin's work was one of the first to highlight the importance of understanding the dynamics of organizational decline in formulating counterterrorism policies.[3] While Cronin identifies important examples and overall trends in organizational demise, her study does not identify the conditions under which groups are vulnerable to destabilization. Without understanding when and why groups are more or less resilient to weakening or demise, it is difficult to comprehensively evaluate the conditions under which groups end and the efficacy of alternative pathways. This project thus seeks to understand sources of decline within the context of leadership targeting.

The remainder of this chapter will proceed as follows. First, I will examine extant theories of leadership and organizational susceptibility to leadership decapitation. The chapter will then offer an alternative theory of organizational resilience in the face of leadership targeting, focusing on how bureaucracy, ideology, and communal support explain the ability of terrorist groups to resist destabilization after the removal of their leadership. Chapter 3 will develop hypotheses based on this theory of organizational resilience in order to make predictions about the efficacy of leadership decapitation as a counterterrorism policy.

Existing Theories of Organizational Leadership

Much of the optimism regarding the efficacy of decapitation as a counterterrorism strategy stems from two theories: theories of charismatic leadership and organizational theories of leadership. Theories of charismatic leadership, which argue that terrorist groups depend upon the charisma of leaders for their cohesion, are insufficient explanations for understanding the susceptibility of an organization to decapitation. Organizational theory has also been utilized to argue that leaders play a critical role in groups' formation, recruitment, fundraising, ideological coherence, and operations. Both of these perspectives have been used as the foundation for the argument that terrorist organizations are dependent upon their leaders in order to function. As a result, their removal should destabilize and weaken a terrorist organization.

Charisma

The concept of charismatic leadership holds that terrorist organizations are led by charismatic leaders who are essential to their operational capacity. According to this perspective, charisma is a unique quality that only certain individuals possess. Weber defines charisma as a "quality of an individual personality, by virtue of which he is set apart from ordinary men and treated as endowed with supernatural, superhuman or at least specifically exceptional powers or qualities."[4] Leadership, he claims, depends on these exceptional qualities. Charisma allows leaders to attract new recruits, set a group's ideological agenda, spread its message, and overcome collective action problems.

Charismatic leadership depends upon recognition. Weber argues that a charismatic claim to authority breaks down if the leader's "mission is not recognized by those to whom he feels he has been sent."[5] The legitimacy of a leader's authority is a product of recognition and "springs from faithful devotion."[6] Because charismatic leadership is dependent upon the recognition of its exceptionality, it is unstable and a fragile basis for authority.[7] Organizations whose cohesion is dependent upon charisma tend to be more volatile than other types of organizations.[8] As a result, terrorist organizations are frequently viewed as inherently more fragile than other types of organizations because they depend upon the specific attributes of these leaders.

This belief in the fragility of charismatic leadership formed the basis of the CIA's justification of "'lethal covert operations' to remove Osama bin Laden and his high command."[9] Similarly, Abdullah Öcalan of the Kurdistan Workers' Party (PKK), Shoko Asahara of Aum Shinrikyo, and Abimael Guzmán of the Shining Path were seen as highly charismatic leaders with special qualities, making them indispensable to their groups' ideological coherence and operational activities. Their capture is often treated as the primary factor in their groups' decline. Nevertheless, the Shining Path continued carrying out terrorist activity after Guzmán's arrest under the leadership of a faction led by Óscar Ramírez Durand. Similarly, the PKK, while weakened, continued to carry out acts of violence in spite of Öcalan's repeated calls for a cessation of violence.[10]

The empirical record aside, though, charismatic leadership does not hold up as a theoretical explanation for when decapitation is likely to result in organizational disintegration.[11] Weber argues that after the death of a leader, his/her authority could be transferred to another individual, increasing the likelihood of group survival. He refers to this process as the "institutionalization of charisma."[12] Like bureaucratic authority, charismatic authority can also become routinized. Weber writes, "Perhaps it is even more important that when the organization of authority becomes permanent, the staff supporting the charismatic ruler becomes routinized."[13] According to Geoffrey Nelson, charismatic authority can be transferred from one leader to the next through a routinized mechanism of succession. This transference of authority makes a group less susceptible to collapse.

Michael Freeman argues that the collective action problems faced by revolutionary organizations can be overcome by charisma.[14] However, he also finds that while organizations with charismatic leaders tend to be more susceptible to leadership attacks, over time, charismatic leadership can become more institutionalized and thus more resilient to such attacks. According to Freeman, organizations in which the leader provides both key operational and inspirational roles are most likely to fall apart after decapitation.

Proponents of the theory of charismatic leadership often see religious organizations as more likely to be led by charismatic leaders who are essential to setting and maintaining organizational goals. Accordingly, they argue, these groups should be more susceptible to weakening after losing that leader. Given the recent increase in the number of terrorist groups driven by religion, this view continues to hold a prominent place within the literature on terrorism.[15] However, there are a number of problems with it. First, as this book will demonstrate, religious organizations are often resistant to the destabilizing effects of leadership decapitation.[16] Second, many studies on the fragility of charismatic leadership have focused primarily on cults and religious groups.[17] While some terrorist groups can also be classified as cults, this designation does not apply to all forms of religious terrorism, so the logic of charismatic leadership may not apply.[18] In many cases, these groups can more accurately be considered millenarian.

Third, the death of a group's charismatic leader can actually bring about a process of group factionalization instead of simple decline. Splintering can have a number of different effects:[19] new factions can be weaker or stronger and more or less radical; they can enter into legitimate political processes; or they can compete with one another in a process of outbidding, ultimately increasing violence.[20] As an example, the split in Jemaah Islamiyah (JI) after the death of the group's founder and leader, Abdullah Sungkar, exemplifies the incompatibility of religious movements and a leader's cult of personality. JI was co-founded by Sungkar and Abu Bakar Ba'ashir in Malaysia in 1995. Sungkar died in November 1999. While Ba'ashir was named as Sungkar's successor and head of JI, there was a group of young JI activists opposed to his succession. This opposition resulted in the group's factionalization. The split was exacerbated when Ba'ashir formed a new organization, Majelis Mujahidin Indonesia (MMI). The radicals in JI were opposed to MMI's inclusion of representatives of Muslim political parties. Thus, the death of charismatic leader Sungkar resulted in group splintering, not group collapse.

Finally, terrorist organizations have undergone learning processes and adapted in order to diminish their susceptibility to leadership attacks. For example, hierarchical organizations, in which the leader is more directly responsible for planning and recruitment, are more easily weakened with the removal of a leader. Organizations have become increasingly decentralized in response.[21] Moreover, as the institutional school of organizational theory suggests, organizations tend to develop "a life of their own, irrespective of the desires of those in control."[22] They can pursue their goals without an operational or spiritual leader, thus highlighting the need to reformulate both the charismatic model and its predictions.

Organizational Theory

Organizational theory offers a broad foundation upon which to understand the resilience of terrorist organizations and the ability of counterterrorism policies, such as targeting, to weaken those groups. The belief that decapitation is an effective counterterrorism policy is based in large part on the notion that the effective operation and survival of clandestine organizations depends upon leadership. Literature on the role of leaders within clandestine organizations has primarily focused on the role they play in a group's formation, recruitment, fundraising, ideological coherence, and operations. This research often views leaders as essential to the group's ability to attract and recruit members, the two building blocks upon which organizations are formed. Kent Layne Oots argues that leadership is essential to the formation of terrorist organizations.[23] He writes, "The formation of a terrorist organization, like the formation of any other political organization, depends on the leadership's ability to recruit and retain a committed membership."[24]

The ability to recruit is particularly important for terrorist organizations, because they face a unique challenge: their members must be committed to carry out acts of violence. By definition, terrorism involves violence against civilians, and it is difficult for individuals to overcome barriers to killing noncombatants. In most societies, individuals are socialized against such behavior, and as a result, potential militants must undergo a process of moral disengagement.[25] Organizations must convince would-be militants that the group's morals and values are legitimate and should be placed above those social norms that prohibit murdering other civilians. This creates a collective action problem; participation is costly and defies social mores. There is a strong tendency to free-ride if militants lack sufficient incentives to carry out illegal and violent activity. Furthermore, once an individual engages in illegal activity, it becomes harder to reintegrate into society. The illegality of participating in a clandestine organization and committing crimes can create high barriers to exit, making it hard to leave the organization and eliminating alternatives. Thus, participating in terrorist activity can further increase levels of violence.[26] As a result, organizations face considerable challenges in convincing individuals to incur the costs of participating in violence.

All organizations, not only violent ones, face a free-rider problem. Mancur Olson presents a rationalist framework for understanding the challenge of collective action. He argues that a lack of participation on the part of one person affects neither an organization's ability to provide goods nor the individual's enjoyment of those goods. In reference to large groups, for example, Olson writes:

> [I]f one member does or does not help provide the collective good, no other member will be significantly affected and therefore none has any reason to react. Thus an individual in a "latent" group, by definition, cannot make a noticeable contribution to any group effort, and since no one in the group will react if he makes no contribution, he has no incentive to contribute.[27]

In other words, there is no motivation on the part of an individual to obtain a collective good if the organization does not offer some kind of incentive to overcome the costs of action. Individuals are unlikely to participate unless they receive a side payment, and this is particularly acute when the group is carrying out illicit and violent activity. While it is easier to provide incentives and to motivate individuals to action in small groups,[28] this problem can still impact small groups and is particularly applicable to terrorist organizations, where the legal and moral costs of committing acts of violence provide a disincentive to act. In fact, this logic can apply to all violent social movement organizations.[29]

Olson proposes the idea of *selective incentives* as a solution to the free-rider problem:[30]

> Only a separate and "selective" incentive will stimulate a rational individual in a latent group to act in a group-oriented way. In such circumstances group action can be obtained only through an incentive that operates, not indiscriminately, like the collective good, upon the group as a whole, but rather selectively toward the individuals in the group. . . . These "selective incentives" can be either negative or positive, in that they can either coerce by punishing those who fail to bear an allocated share of the costs of the group action, or they can be positive inducements offered to those who act in the group interest.[31]

Selective incentives can take many different forms. They can be negative or positive, material or social, but the point is that individuals must receive something from the organization if they are to act in a group-oriented way. Critics of Olson's theory have argued that individuals are rational and know that a lack of participation would mean the failure of the organization. Olson argues that even patriotism is insufficient to guarantee participation on the part of group members. He finds that "patriotism is probably the strongest noneconomic motive for organizational allegiance in modern times," but that no state can support itself through the power of national ideology or a common culture alone. According to this logic, ideology alone is not enough to ensure individual participation in terrorist groups. Leaders must therefore provide selective incentives—to attract new recruits, maintain membership, and induce individuals to commit acts of violence.[32] In theory, if leaders provide incentives that are lower than the cost of membership, they can generate a surplus that can be used to lead the organization and supply goods to its members.

This belief that leaders are needed to provide the selective incentives necessary to motivate individual participation in terrorist activity has driven much of the optimism regarding the ability of leadership targeting to weaken terrorist organizations. However, the removal of leaders does not always result in a decline in individual participation.[33] According to Oots, while a group can lose the political focus necessary to direct its behavior toward specific goals, it can still carry out terrorist activity, even if it no longer operates as a unified political movement. Group activity does not always depend upon leadership, as individuals can obtain inducements from their communities, from ideology, or from other aspects of a group hierarchy.

A Theory of Leadership Decapitation and Organizational Resilience

Counterterrorism policies, such as leadership targeting, are largely intended to destabilize and eliminate the threat posed by specific organizations and the larger movements. Most policies are designed to eliminate or weaken organizations, while preventing individual "lone wolf" attacks (which have occurred globally). Terrorist groups are motivated by many of the same desires as legitimate political organizations: realizing their goals, enhancing their strengths, and ensuring their survival. While terrorists are often viewed as irrational, fanatical individuals willing to die for their cause, a strategic approach to understanding terrorism assumes that terrorist organizations, like other political groups, are rational actors trying to maximize their utility. They are motivated by the desire to achieve a specific goal, and the decision to engage in terrorism—the killing of civilians—is a strategic choice, to bring about their political goals.[34]

An organizational approach to explaining the behavior of terrorist groups focuses on the drive for survival as a motivating factor. Martha Crenshaw was one of the first scholars to think broadly about the internal politics of terrorist organizations.[35] She argues that "terrorist behavior represents the outcome of the internal dynamic of the organizational rather than strategic action."[36] Organizations want to survive, and understanding their internal dynamics has implications for the kind of policies that are likely to be effective in weakening them. This organizational approach to understanding the behavior of terrorist groups has become widely used. Eli Berman, for example, looks at the organizational advantages of religious organizations,[37] and Jacob Shapiro discusses the managerial challenges facing terrorist organizations and the impact these have upon organizational structure.[38] Examining internal organizational dynamics can provide insight into how terrorist organizations respond to countermeasures. This book will utilize both strategic and organizational perspectives in understanding group behavior in response to leadership targeting.[39]

Given the three key variables in understanding group resilience to leadership targeting—a group's bureaucracy, ideology, and communal support—leadership decapitation should be unlikely to result in the demise of groups that are highly bureaucratized. Bureaucratization is an internal mechanism that increases group stability and facilitates a clear succession process. Bureaucratized terrorist groups are diversified, have a clear division of administrative responsibilities and functions, and are more likely to withstand the sudden removal of a leader or leaders. A bureaucratic structure can also provide groups with the organizational redundancy necessary to withstand attacks. They have standard operating procedures and succession mechanisms that minimize organizational disruption. Finally, bureaucracies tend to be efficient and seen as more legitimate in the eyes of local communities.

Ideology can also impact a group's resilience in the face of leadership decapitation, and groups can be classified as advancing religious, Islamist, separatist, right-wing, or left-wing ideologies. I argue that religious, particularly Islamist, and separatist groups should be more resilient to targeting efforts as the ideology upon which they are based does not depend upon the leader for its articulation. In these cases, the ideology is often representative of a significant portion of the local communities from which the group emerges, and is thus not dependent upon a leader but is pervasive within the communities. These groups often have significant popular support, which is essential to maintaining organizational strength and capacity following an attack on their leadership.

Finally, communal support provides the resources necessary for a terrorist group to function. Groups with lower levels of local support should have fewer resources, increasing their vulnerability to destabilization, while groups with significant levels of support are more frequently seen as more legitimate to the community in which they operate, increasing their chances of survival in the face of external shocks. In these cases, leadership should matter less for perpetuating a group's doctrine or beliefs.

Bureaucracy

Bureaucracy is an organizational form that strengthens a group's ability to withstand attacks on its leadership. Max Weber offers a theoretical model for understanding authority and bureaucracy. According to Weber, there are three types of authority: (1) traditional, (2) charismatic, and (3) rational-legal.[40] Traditional authority is based on custom, in which rules are traditionally received, and is legitimized on the basis of tradition and personal loyalty.

> The person or persons exercising authority are designated according to traditionally transmitted rules. The object of obedience is the personal authority of the individual which he enjoys by virtue of his traditional status. The organized group exercising authority is, in the simplest case, primarily based on relations of personal loyalty, cultivated through a common process of education. The person exercising authority is not a "superior," but a personal "chief."[41]

In a traditional authority, obedience does not come from rules, but rather from a person who, by tradition, occupies a position of authority.

Charismatic authority, in contrast, is dependent upon a specific person believed to have extraordinary qualities.[42] It derives its legitimacy from an individual's inspirational qualities and is thus seen as an "irrational" basis for authority,[43] unlike rational-legal authority, which is based on a body of generalized universalistic rules and employs a bureaucratic administrative staff. In order to further understand bureaucracy as it relates to the stability of terrorist organizations, the remainder of this section will focus on rational-legal authority.

Weber argues that rational-legal authority takes the form of a bureaucratic structure where each member of the staff occupies an office with a clear delineation of powers.[44] Offices are organized according to levels of authority, with individuals who occupy higher levels supervising and controlling those below. The ideal form of rational-legal authority rests upon the presence of five key characteristics.[45] First, members of the group may establish legal norms through agreements. Second, the body of laws exists in a "consistent system of abstract rules."[46] Third, the person in authority occupies an "office" from which commands are issued to others. Fourth, those who obey authority do so as a "member" of the group. Finally, while members of the group may obey an individual, this obedience is a function of an impersonal order.

Bureaucratic authority consists of three primary elements: (1) fixed and official jurisdictional areas, (2) regular activities that are distributed as official duties, and (3) a stable authority delimited by rules.[47] It is important to note that these indicators are ideal types.[48] They can serve as an analytical tool in understanding how bureaucracies function and can provide a basis for comparison with other social structures. I use the term *bureaucracy* to refer to terrorist groups with an organized administrative staff, a division of labor, a hierarchy of authority, and a stable structure of rules, policies, and procedures.

Organizations with these characteristics have staying power.[49] Talcott Parsons describes Weber's notion of bureaucracy as follows:

> Where rational-legal authority involves an organized administrative staff, according to Weber it takes the form of a "bureaucratic" structure. Here each member of the staff occupies an office with a specific delimitation of powers and a sharp segregation of the sphere of office from his private affairs. . . . The different offices are organized in terms of a stringent hierarchy of higher and lower levels of authority in such a way that each lower level is subject to control and supervision by the one immediately above it. This control and supervision above all includes the power of appointment, promotion, demotion, and dismissal over the incumbents of lower offices. . . . Bureaucracy in this sense, Weber says, is by far the most efficient instrument of large-scale administration which has ever been developed and the modern social order in many different spheres has become overwhelmingly dependent upon it.[50]

This passage highlights key features of a Weberian bureaucracy. Parsons underscores the importance of hierarchically ordered offices with a clear delineation of authority, which create a smooth process of transition and allow an organization to easily replace a leader. If a hierarchy is in place at the upper levels of the administration, there should be clear succession guidelines when the leader is removed.[51] Succession is one of the major issues confronting terrorist organizations that have lost a leader. Bureaucratized terrorist organizations are likely to have a clear hierarchy of authority with a new leader ready to step in and a large supply of recruits, reducing succession problems. Audrey Kurth Cronin argues that "bin Laden has often spoken openly of a succession plan, and that plan has to a large degree already taken effect. Furthermore, his capture or killing would produce its own countervailing negative consequences, including (most likely) the creation of a powerful martyr."[52] Unlike with firms, targeting the leadership of terrorist group runs the risk of creating a martyrdom effect. Moreover, while firms tend to be hierarchically structured from the top down, terrorist organizations can be highly decentralized and still have a highly bureaucratic authority structure.[53]

Parsons also references the importance of universalistic rules, which apply to all people within the jurisdiction (or organization).[54] This system of rules reflects the impersonal nature of a bureaucratic authority. Crozier emphasizes the importance of rules for the division of responsibilities within an organization.[55] He argues that bureaucracy has a self-enforcing equilibrium that is stable, in part, through the development of impersonal rules:[56] "Impersonal rules delimit, in great detail, all the functions of every individual within the organization. They prescribe the behavior to be followed in all possible events."[57] These impersonal rules are critical for the differentiation of responsibilities and roles within the organization, a primary feature of bureaucratization. According to Weber, this clear delineation of authority, rules, and functions is what makes bureaucracy the most efficient form of large-scale administration.

There is an important distinction between charismatic authority and bureaucratic authority.[58] It is often assumed that because terrorist organizations are headed by charismatic leaders whose authority is seen as a function of their exceptional qualities, they are inherently more fragile and susceptible to destabilization through leadership decapitation. In contrast, bureaucratic authority is dependent upon individual competence, not charisma. It is sustained by rules and procedures. Bureaucratic authority "extends to individuals only in so far as they occupy a specifically legitimized status under the rules, an 'office,' and even then their powers are limited to a 'sphere of competence.'"[59] Charismatic claims to authority are at odds with the legitimation of authority in an established institutionalized order. A charismatic structure is not subject to the same succession processes that facilitate a group's staying power.[60]

Charisma and bureaucracy are not mutually incompatible, however. Weber argues that while charismatic authority is vulnerable to succession problems, there are possible solutions. A charismatic claim to authority can become institutionalized and ultimately bureaucratic through a process of routinization. As argued by Gerth and Mills:

> Weber sees the genuine charismatic situation quickly give way to incipient institutions, which emerge from the cooling off of extraordinary states of devotion and fervor. As the original doctrines are democratized, they are intellectually adjusted to the needs of that stratum which becomes the primary carrier of the leader's message."[61]

Personal charisma can drive terrorist group recruitment, and routinization can prevent succession problems by setting up norms and rules for recruitment, creating a rational-legal legitimation of authority.

For charisma to become a routine, it is necessary to change the antieconomic character of the group. A routinized organization can provide for a group's needs by developing economic conditions necessary to raise taxes and contributions. This point is fundamental. Terrorist organizations are dependent upon their ability to garner the resources necessary to function, particularly as a covert organization. Not only is routinization possible, it is essential for a terrorist group to function and remain stable.[62]

Bureaucratic Stability. As organizations grow in size and/or age, they often require a more complex administration to function effectively, increasing their stability, effectiveness, staying power, and ability to survive an attack on their leadership.[63] There are several important indicators to look for when identifying whether a terrorist organization has bureaucratic characteristics. Older and larger groups should be more likely to have an administrative staff, a hierarchy of authority, and a universalistic system of rules and regulations. These three elements are critical to identifying a bureaucratic authority and allow a terrorist group to operate efficiently and, most importantly, increase its stability.

Bureaucracies are characterized, in part, by the development of stable rules and routines, which are key sources of organizational efficiency and stability.[64] Routines are "the primary means by which organizations accomplish much of what they do."[65] Organizations will struggle until they are perceived as reliable and accountable, which can be accomplished through the establishment of routines.[66] Routines can also insulate organizations from disruption during the course of leadership turnovers by increasing the capacity for organizational learning.[67] Rules and routines are sometimes seen as a source of inertia, inflexibility, mindlessness, and stagnation,[68] but they can also be an important source of flexibility and change.[69] Cyert and March referred to this process of change as *adaptation*.[70] Organizational routines that enable adaptation are especially important during times of crisis.[71] In fact, routines enable organizational change. While they may be repetitive patterns of action, they are neither static nor unchanging.[72] Terrorist groups with a system of routines and rules in place that have experienced an external shock such as leadership decapitation should be able to adapt in a way that ensures organizational stability and efficiency.

There are, however, significant differences between clandestine organizations, such as terrorist groups, and firms, for example. The need to remain covert poses a challenge for terrorist groups. While bureaucratic forms of organizations increase a group's efficiency and capacity to withstand the loss of leadership, they can also undermine a group's ability to remain clandestine. Jacob Shapiro addresses the trade-off terrorist groups face between maintaining secrecy and security and exercising organizational control.[73] He observes that leaders have to delegate duties, which can result in preference divergence between principles and agents. To deal with these organizational dilemmas, leaders must monitor their agents. Shapiro finds that "leaders typically exercise control over their agents through a standard set of bureaucratic tools including policy memoranda, reporting requirements, and tracking spreadsheets."[74] The adoption of bureaucratic characteristics can impose risks and vulnerabilities to a group's security by making them more visible and easier to target. Looking at documents from al-Qaeda in Iraq's successor organization, ISI (Islamic State of Iraq), Shapiro shows that the organization exhibited a "nontrivial" level of bureaucracy despite risks to its security.

There are limitations to the Weberian model of bureaucratic stability. It overlooks organizational transformations such as disappearances or factional splits, a phenomenon to which terrorist organizations are especially subject.[75] In the 1990s, the IRA (Irish Republican Army) splintered into multiple groups: the Real IRA, the Irish National Liberation Army, and the Continuity Irish Republican Army. In another example, the arrest, and subsequent deaths, of Baader-Meinhoff leaders is often seen as the main factor contributing to the demise of the group, yet the Red Army Faction, which advanced the same political agenda, emerged from the remnants of the original group. Splinter groups can also be more violent and extreme than the original organization. Ethan Bueno de Mesquita finds that factions, such as the Real IRA, can actually increase the level of militancy.[76] This can occur when the splinter groups are "responding to the imperative to demonstrate their existence and signal their dissent."[77] While larger and older organizations are at risk of splintering, as seen in the case of the IRA, this process becomes less likely the more bureaucratized the organization becomes.

Bureaucracy and Decentralization. Terrorist organizations have adapted to counterterrorism policies by becoming increasingly decentralized. Operating through independent cells and decentralized units makes it harder for authorities to identify individuals and track the flow of information between individuals within an organization. The cellular structure is an intentional design that increases secrecy and makes detection harder. While older and larger terrorist organizations are likely to be more bureaucratized, these organizations also tend to be more decentralized. This may sound like a contradiction; bureaucracy and decentralization are often portrayed as opposites, particularly in the literature on terrorism. However, groups can be bureaucratized and hierarchal at their upper levels, and decentralized at lower, more operational levels. While Weber argues that a hierarchical system of authority is a critical feature of a bureaucratic system of administration, Mansfield notes, "At no point did he suggest, however, that centralization of decision making in such a hierarchy was a characteristic of bureaucracy nor did he even make explicit the relationship between bureaucracy and centralization."[78] Mansfield confirms "the absence of any positive relationship between centralization and bureaucratization. In general, there is some evidence of negative association between these variables."[79] Managers of larger organizations are increasingly forced to delegate decision-making responsibilities. This decentralization does not weaken the power of the individuals at the highest organizational levels. This hybrid structure characterizes the quasi-bureaucratic form of many terrorist organizations.

In discussing this organizational structure, Michael Kenney claims that the decentralized nature of networks "does not preclude the existence of vertical decision-making hierarchies within nodes that carry out the network's most dangerous activities."[80] For example, Kenney classifies Hezbollah as a "bureaucratic network hybrid" that coordinates different groups of Shi'ite extremists. Hamas is decentralized as well. It is made up of a network of mosques, schools, health-care centers, and paramilitary cells, yet it has a hierarchical administrative body that funds and guides cells in carrying out activities.

These quasi-bureaucratic groups are even more resilient than organizations that maintain a hierarchy over the entire organization. They have clear succession mechanisms in place, with rules and division of responsibilities, but also cells operating independently of the structure at the upper organizational levels, which are largely unaffected by leadership attacks.[81] Drawing on complexity leadership theory, Uhl-Bien and Marion argue that while the majority of groups today are organized around bureaucratic principles, the most effective organizations have both formal and informal functions.[82] Informal leadership processes can produce innovative solutions to complex problems. Organizations that display both bureaucratic and adaptive leadership functions are most likely to develop innovative responses to problems and resistance to counterterrorism policies. Lower organizational levels are also more open-ended and fluid. They are made up of entry-level volunteers and recruits, who tend to show a high level of passion and commitment. Those militants who demonstrate competence may ultimately move up the organizational ranks. As I will discuss in the next section, popular support is critical to the regeneration of these lower organizational levels, which ultimately supply candidates for higher-ranking positions. Support bolsters the bureaucracy and allows for the steady stream of volunteers and recruits necessary for a well-functioning bureaucracy.

In evaluating the effect of bureaucracy, a group's age and size will act as proxy variables for bureaucracy. If larger and older organizations are more likely to be bureaucratized, then those terrorist groups should be capable of resisting leadership decapitation efforts. The following chapter will develop hypotheses on the relationship between bureaucratization and organizational resilience following leadership decapitation.

Communal Support

Communal support is essential for explaining organizational resilience to leadership decapitation. Terrorist organizations generally depend upon resources acquired from local communities to operate and survive. Local support allows a group to replenish its membership, raise money, provide resources, and ensure its ability to operate as a covert organization.[83] Robert Pape, for example, examines the importance of popular support to suicide terrorism. He argues that suicide campaigns require significant communal support for three key reasons.[84] First, support can "enable a suicide terrorist group to replenish its membership," which groups need to maintain a supply of potential bombers.[85] Groups that are strongly grounded in their communities should have an easier time with recruitment. Second, communal support can help a group to avoid "detection, surveillance, and elimination by the security forces of the target society."[86] Finally, terrorist organizations are dependent upon their community to accept suicide terrorists as martyrs.[87]

Support and the preferences of local communities can influence the behavior and tactical choices terrorist organizations make. Mia Bloom examines the effect that local communities have upon the behavior of terrorist groups and specifically their decision to use suicide terrorism as a tactic. She argues that suicide terrorism provides radical groups with an opportunity to increase their share of the political market. It is a function of militant group competition. Social preferences towards violence have an effect upon the willingness of terrorist groups to use suicide terrorism.[88] When societies support killing civilians, terrorist groups have an incentive to adopt such measures. Terrorist organizations care about social approval and want to be seen as legitimate in order to increase their status relative to other groups.

A loss of support can contribute to a group's decline. Cronin examines the importance of social support to the functional capacity of terrorist groups and argues that the loss of social support can undermine a group's goal and is one important cause of their decline. She writes:

> They generally cannot survive without either active or passive support from a surrounding population. Active support includes hiding members, raising money, providing other sustenance, and, especially, joining the organizations. Passive support, as the phrase implies, is more diffuse and includes ignoring obvious signs of terrorist group activity, declining to cooperate with police investigations, sending money to organizations that act as fronts for the groups and expressing support for the group's objectives.[89]

The public may fear government reprisals, causing the community to limit its active and passive support. The government may offer the terrorist supporters alternatives such as reforms, increased spending, and job opportunities. Finally, it is possible for the community to lose interest in the ideology or aims of the group. This last phenomenon explains the decline of many Marxist groups,[90] whose ideology became politically irrelevant after the fall of the Soviet Union. This final pathway can account for the susceptibility of ideological groups to decapitation.

Local communities play an important part in the use of violence by militant groups. Risa Brooks attributes variation in violent militant campaigns to the "availability of social support from the militant's home constituency," which she calls the "referent society."[91] The referent society forces militants to adhere to societal norms about how violence is used. Society's tolerance for violence can influence the provision of key resources necessary for building local organizational infrastructure. Three resources are critical in developing the local structures necessary to carry out attacks: (1) physical security, (2) intelligence, and (3) defensive resources that can help to conceal militants.[92] The analysis in this book will focus on how the provision of resources by the local community influences a terrorist group's ability to build organizational infrastructure and operate a successful campaign.

Terrorist organizations also depend upon their local communities to acquire the resources necessary to carry out rebellion. Roger Petersen argues that the provision of resources, information, and recruits by the local community is key to understanding the success of rebellion. While Petersen does not directly discuss terrorist organizations, his logic of rebellion can be applied to terrorist groups, and particularly to insurgencies. He argues that sustained rebellion depends upon a significant number of individuals that can link armed resistance to fixed populations.[93] Specifically, strong communities "promote rebellion by producing accessible information, reducing communication costs, and facilitating recruitment."[94] Such communities create the conditions necessary for an effective rebellion.

Finally, and perhaps most importantly, terrorist organizations often provide social services to the communities in which they are based. This is an important means by which they acquire local support. All of the organizations examined in this book increased their support by providing a variety of resources. In many cases terrorist organizations deliver social services—such as basic necessities, food, education, and religious education—to communities where the state is weak and lacks the capacity to do so or is intentionally excluding or discriminating against a group of people. This can provide the group with a sense of legitimacy, further strengthening it and perhaps even increasing its access to the resources necessary to strengthen its hold over territory, ideology, or whatever goal it is fighting for.

Organizations with communal support should be able to exploit local infrastructure to provide social services to their communities. Alternatively, organizations that are bureaucratized can build infrastructure in order to effectively and efficiently deliver resources across a community. Bureaucracy becomes necessary to manage and distribute services. This highlights an important relationship between bureaucracy and communal support; one can strengthen the other. Hamas, for example, has developed an extensive structure of local networks by providing social services and education to the Palestinian people. These local institutions are important in providing the resources necessary for Hamas to function.[95]

Social Movement Organizations. The literature on social movements can offer additional insight into the importance of communal support. Terrorist organizations are often part of broader movements,[96] and their development can be compared to the emergence and growth of social movement organizations (SMOs).[97] Resource mobilization theory and political process theory both examine social movements and offer a theoretical framework for understanding how and why support matters to a terrorist organization. According to resource mobilization theory, support from the community in which a group operates is fundamental to the mobilization of resources necessary to that group's operational capability. It contends that grievance-based explanations cannot account for the growth or decline of social movements.[98] Instead, the success of an SMO is based upon its ability to garner resources. According to this theory, groups need access to resources to

> sustain their activities and (perhaps) motivate people to contribute to their cause. In other words, even tightly knit groups that would seem to have the opportunity as

well as an interest in acting collectively may not be able to do so effectively without substantial material resources. So again, collective action (whether revolutionary or not) may depend on much more than the extant political context.[99]

However, the concept of resources is not well defined and can refer to wide variety of capabilities.[100] McCarthy and Zald claim that resources "can include legitimacy, money, facilities, and labor."[101] Despite this lack of clarity, resource mobilization theory offers a theoretical framework for understanding how resources are critical for sustaining activity, and also for understanding the mobilization of collective behavior.

The environment in which the group operates is critical. While concrete material resources are necessary for group success, resource mobilization can also refer to constituent involvement. Zald and Ash argue that an SMO's environment comprises two elements: (1) the broader social movement and the people who identity with it, and (2) the society in which the movement operates. Members and potential supporters determine the "ebb and flow of sentiments toward an organization" and are crucial for organizational success.[102] The size of a group's resource pool, controlled by its constituents, is an important factor in organizational stability. McCarthy and Zald examine how the size of resource flows impact organizational fate. They argue that as resource flows increase, organizations develop and maintain a professionalized staff and cadre, increasing organizational complexity and stability.[103] Larger groups are also better suited to reach isolated adherents, providing them with a larger base of support and access to more resources.[104]

Political process theory also underscores the importance of support to the conduct of successful insurgencies. While this book focuses on terrorist organizations and not only insurgent organizations, analysis on insurgencies can provide useful theories for advancing an understanding of the dynamics of clandestine organizations such as terrorist groups. Doug McAdam's model identifies three factors critical to insurgencies: (1) expanding political opportunities, (2) indigenous organizational strength, and (3) the presence of shared cognitions within the minority community.[105] According to political process theory, resource mobilization theory places too much importance on elite institutions and overlooks aggrieved populations, and in doing so fails to acknowledge "the political capabilities of the movement's mass base."[106] According to McAdam it further overlooks the difference between objective social conditions and the subjective perception of grievances that can motivate political conflict. Grievances are ubiquitous and cannot account for variation in social movements, but according to McAdam, the interpretation of grievances is subjective, varies over time, and can account for the occurrence of insurgent activity.[107] This subjective perception provides the basis for a terrorist group's local support.

Political process theory evaluates how shifts in political opportunities can promote increased political activism by aggrieved populations. The ability of the minority group to convert favorable political opportunities into organized social protest depends upon "indigenous structures" within the minority communities, which "frequently provide the organizational base out of which social movements emerge."[108] These indigenous structures provide four resources that are critical to a group's ability to resist counterinsurgent activity: (1) members, (2) solidary incentives, (3) communication networks, and (4) leaders. While neither political process theory nor resource mobilization theory are specific to terrorist organizations, they offer a compelling theoretical model for understanding how resources play an important part in the mobilization and operation of militant groups.

Communal support confers groups with access to the resources, networks, and recruits necessary to withstand the loss of a leader or multiple leaders. There is also an important relationship between community and group ideology. Certain types of organizations are more likely to garner support from their local communities, further enhancing their resilience to leadership attacks. Ideology thus provides another avenue by which to understand the importance of support. This will be discussed in the following section.

Group Ideology

Ideology is the final variable that contributes to a group's ability to withstand attacks on its leadership. For this project, groups are classified as being either religious, Islamist, separatist, right wing, left wing, or a combination of these categories.[109] The susceptibility of organizations to decapitation should vary based on these organizational types. Separatist groups should be the most difficult to destabilize through leadership targeting, followed by religious organizations, with Islamist groups being more difficult than other religious organizations. Organizations that are both religious and separatist should be even harder to weaken. Islamist terrorist groups should also be difficult to weaken. Finally, I hypothesize that left- and right-wing organizations should be more likely to experience a decline in activity or fall apart in the case of decapitation. The remainder of this section will offer three arguments to explain variation in the resilience of different types of terrorist organizations: (1) social network analysis, (2) communal support, and (3) organizational doctrine.

Social Network Analysis. Research on social network analysis can provide one framework through which to explore variation in the ability of different types of groups to withstand attacks. As an analytical tool, social network analysis, which analyzes the relationships between actors, would predict more variability in the ability of decapitation to weaken a terrorist group. A network perspective focuses on structural relationships between actors. Within the context of terrorist organizations, actors can be individual terrorists, the organizations themselves, or the states with which they interact. These relationship patterns constitute a structure that can constrain or facilitate action.[110] Knoke and Yang explain that "[t]he central objectives of network analysis are to measure and represent these structural relations accurately, and to explain both why they occur and what are their consequences."[111] Analysis of structure can provide important information about the pathways through which information, knowledge, and materials flow. As a result, social network analysis provides a mechanism by which to evaluate the resilience and strength of terrorist networks that have undergone the loss of critical nodes, including leaders.

The role of the leader and other key actors within a terrorist organization is essential to understanding a group's susceptibility to decapitation. Social network analysis can identify the most prominent or central actor within a social network. Actors with a high degree of prominence are involved in a higher number of relationships with other actors, making them more visible.[112] Occupying a prominent position within a network allows an actor the ability to transfer or access information and resources.[113] Prominence can be determined by looking at measures of structural relationships, such as centrality. From a network centrality perspective, key actors with the most social ties within a network are referred to as "hubs."[114] They are the critical communicative elements of a network and are responsible for ensuring the distribution of information and logistical support. While there are a multitude of mechanisms for measuring an actor's position and role within a network, centrality is often used as a measure of prestige within a social system.[115]

While leaders may or may not be the actors with the most social ties, the notion that hubs are critical to the operational success of a terrorist organization can provide a theoretical basis for optimism about decapitation.[116] Most of the communication within and between social networks goes through hubs, and their removal should make the organization more vulnerable. Ami Pedahzur argues that hubs are "the glue that binds all of its components: logistics, intelligence, recruitment and dispatching."[117] As a result, "damage to one of the hubs will indeed lead to the speedy disintegration of the network so that the more hubs there are, the greater the resilience of the network against direct attacks."[118] Similarly, Marc Sageman writes that "if enough hubs are destroyed, the network breaks down into isolated, non-communicating islands of nodes."[119] In an analysis of al-Qaeda, Deibert and Stein likewise argue that destroying the center and removing the leader will weaken the organization.[120] The key point here is that the leader of an organization is not always the hub, and thus their removal would not always weaken the group.

Social network analysis can offer a framework through which to explore variation in the resilience of different types of organizations. Cynthia Stohl and Michael Stohl, who use communication networks perspective to understand terrorism, look beyond organizational structure and focus on the social ties between members in the organization in order to understand recruitment techniques. Their research suggests that separatist groups, and other organizations, based on ethnic ties should be more difficult to target. They argue, "Strong ties . . . were frequently formed years ago in school and training camps and keep the cell interconnected."[121] Ties between actors in an ethnically based organization tend to be more insular as they recruit from a known and closed group of potential participants.[122] These organizations are referred to as scale-free and random networks with strong ties and powerful hubs. Once the local network is identified, it may be easily destroyed, but the overall organization is especially resistant to the removal of certain nodes. The narrow distance between actors allows for efficient transmission of information and fosters robustness. Stohl and Stohl argue that within these ethnically based organizations, smaller networks have strong hubs that can be identified and removed, potentially weakening the local network, while the larger overarching organization remains intact. Identity-based organizations, which can include both religious and separatist organizations, are hard to penetrate.

Organizational structure plays an important role in understanding why certain types of organizations are more resilient than others. Separatist groups should be more likely to have bureaucratic structures in place, which would also increase their resilience to targeting efforts. In order to achieve their goals of independence or autonomy, separatist groups often develop state-like institutions and structures to ensure efficiency and strong state-building capabilities. These bureaucratic traits would make separatist groups better able to recover and survive attacks on their leadership. Separatist organizations are thus likely to have succession mechanisms and standard operating procedures that increase redundancy and, thus, organizational strength.

Sageman's work can provide insight into the role that organizational structure can have upon group resilience. He argues that social networks encourage isolated and alienated individuals to join a community.[123] These decentralized organizations are composed of dense social networks, made up of smaller cliques that are harder to destabilize through the removal of their leadership.[124] According to Sageman, this structure characterizes much of the global Salafi jihad. I would argue that many religious organizations, more broadly, tend to be decentralized, enhancing their ability to withstand leadership attacks.[125] Moreover, many currently active religious (and Islamist) organizations, such as ISIS, Hamas, and al-Qaeda, have adopted both decentralized and bureaucratic structures; these hybrid structures are exceedingly resilient.

Communal Support. Second, certain types of terrorist groups should also have more communal support than others. I hypothesize that religious, Islamist, and separatist groups should have more support than left- or right-wing political organizations, as their goals often reflect the views or struggle of the majority of the population within their local communities.[126] These arguments overlap with the discussion of social networks and the prior analysis of communal support, but this section will focus on why certain organizations are more likely to have more support and what this means for resilience after leadership targeting. Organizations that are both religious and separatist should be the most resilient. Cronin argues that "broader popular support is usually the key to the greater average longevity of ethnonationalist/separatist groups in the modern era."[127] Both separatist and religious groups fight for a cause that often resonates with local communities. For example, separatist groups often advocate for a community's independence, autonomy, basic rights, or representation. Research has found that ideological motivation, whether or not groups are nationalist or religious, is an important condition in civilian support for terrorist groups.[128] While there may be preference divergence between the terrorist group and the community in terms of toleration for violence, there should be fewer barriers to joining a violent movement in pursuit of these goals.

A number of factors can account for why some terrorist groups are more likely to be supported by their communities. Groups often seek territorial control, in part to acquire or increase their communal support. Bhattacharya has found that territorial control is a key factor in civilian support and argues that "territorial access by terrorist groups, in addition to organizational strength, ideology, financial support, competition, or partnership with other groups, is an important element in determining how frequently terrorists interact with civilians."[129] Control over territory allows groups to interact with the population more, increasing their authority. In addition, groups seeking territorial control often provide social services, in some cases operating as states. This also increases communal support. Religion and nationalism can interact in important ways here. Groups that are religious and also seeking territory should have even more support. There are a number of organizations that can be coded as both religious and separatist.[130]

Within the context of transnational terrorism, the local community is a more fluid concept. Religious organizations may not represent the views of an entire community, but are likely to represent a considerable portion of it. This support should provide the organization with access to resources that would increase its organizational capacity and ability to resist counterterrorism measures. In a study of support for terrorist organizations, C. Christine Fair and Bryan Shepherd examined a PEW study that looked at 7,849 adults from fourteen Muslim countries. The authors found that individuals who believed "that religious leaders should play a larger role in politics are *more* likely to support terrorism than those who do not hold this view, all other attributes invariant."[131] There was, however, variation between the fourteen countries. Bhattacharya also found evidence for a relationship between religious motivation and support and more specifically found that groups that are both religious and nationalist have the most support.[132] There are certainly situations in which religious groups do not have the support of their local communities or have coerced compliance (as in the case of ISIS), yet religious beliefs, especially Islamic ones, are often present to some degree within the larger society.

Religion can also have a legitimizing effect on the organization and its message. Bruce Hoffman has argued that religion can "function as a legitimizing force, specifically sanctioning wide-scale violence against an almost open-ended category of opponents."[133] While this argument does not necessarily imply that religious groups will have communal support, their ideology sets a kind of "moral framework"[134] that can motivate individuals to either passively support the organizations or act on its behalf.

Doctrine. Finally, both separatist and religious organizations should also be resistant to counterterrorism efforts because they are often not dependent upon their leadership for ideological coherence. This ideology is not dependent upon a particular leader for its articulation and re-creation but has a broad appeal because it is prevalent within the communities in which they operate. Even if an organization has a specific interpretation of the religion, its leaders can broaden the group's appeal so that their beliefs are no longer dependent upon any specific leadership.

Many religious organizations and Islamist groups such as ISIS or al-Qaeda are not dependent upon leadership for their ideology. Osama bin Laden broadened the appeal of al-Qaeda. In fact, al-Qaeda's ideological goals and messaging efforts underwent many iterations, culminating in a belief system with a wide-ranging, global appeal that has survived and become more coherent since his death. In another example, Abu Muhammad al-Adnani stated that, even if counterterrorism forces continued killing leaders and stripping ISIS of its control over territory, their ideology would remain. Further, al-Qaeda and later ISIS were able to broaden their support to a large group of foreign fighters.[135] This important point shows that leadership is less important once an ideology has a broad appeal.

In contrast to separatist and religious groups, left- and right-wing organizations are more likely to be dominated by an influential figure from whom their ideological doctrine originates and on whom they depend for its reproduction. For example, many of the smaller left-wing Marxist–Leninist organizations active in Western Europe in the 1960s and 1970s, such as the Baader-Meinhoff gang, had much less support than separatist groups such as the ETA or the PKK. These groups can have a specific interpretation of a larger movement, such as Marxism. Cronin argues that right- and left-wing groups often have a difficult time persisting over generations, because they "were notorious for their inability to articulate a clear vision of their goals that could be handed down to successors after the first generation of radical leaders departed or were eliminated."[136] The doctrinal resonance of these groups is often rooted in the communities and not in the specific philosophical interpretation of the leaders. The Shining Path, for instance, was dependent upon Abimael Guzmán's specific interpretation of Marxism, unlike groups like the PKK or Hamas, who both represented the ideals and struggles of their communities. For these reasons, separatist and religious groups often have an easier time persisting, particularly when faced with counterterrorism measures designed to undermine their message, beliefs, and organization.

While separatist and religious groups can have a similar appeal to group identity and communal support, I would argue that decapitation should be marginally less effective against separatist groups than religious ones, for two reasons. First, while separatist groups tend to reflect the views of the communities from which they emerge, there is likely to be a diversity of views regarding religion. In certain cases, it is easier for an organization to receive support for its separatist views than its religious views. Hamas and Islamic Jihad, for example, originally emphasized their religious goals, and then advocated a separatist agenda when they realized that this could have wider appeal among their supporters. Second, separatist groups are more likely to emulate military organizations and develop bureaucratic structures. Religious organizations have also adopted this model over the past twenty years, and have thus become harder to destabilize.

In addition to the hypothesis that decapitation should not work in these cases, support for a group would seem to increase the likelihood of counterproductive outcomes and backlash, further increasing support and even conferring legitimacy upon the group and the larger cause. I would thus expect that targeting efforts against religious and separatist organizations, which should have more support, are more likely to result in an increase in activity. For example, the assassinations of Hamas leaders Sheikh Yassin and Abdel Aziz al-Rantisi in March and April

2004 triggered both local and international condemnation and outrage. Yassin's death produced a substantial amount of sympathy throughout Palestinian society. Khaled Hroub notes that, "a poll carried out in the West Bank and Gaza Strip two weeks after Yassin's killing found Hamas, for the first time, the most popular movement in Palestine."[137] While Rantisi's death spurred less international condemnation than Yassin's, his was a more serious loss for the organization. Yassin was a quadriplegic and quite frail and was not involved in the day-to-day operations of Hamas. Rantisi on the other hand was a skilled organizer and leader, and, according to Hroub, "he enjoyed both great popular and unquestioned legitimacy as one of the original founders."[138] The death of these top leaders generated public sympathy for the movement, which ultimately increased the desire for revenge. In another example, the assassination of Yahya Ayyash, Hamas's chief bomb maker, on January 5, 1996, resulted in four retaliatory bus bombings in which more than fifty people were killed.[139] This increase in communal support can make a movement stronger, more effective, and thus more resilient in the face of further leadership attacks.

Finally, religion has a sacred element that inspires a level of dedication not seen in other movements, resulting in greater resilience and longer life span.[140] Given the strength and support for religious and separatist claims, decapitation against these organizations should be more likely to generate public outrage, increasing support for the movement. Despite the potential for such backlash, states continue to target leaders in order to fulfill public desire for revenge or to signal that they are strong and resolved in fighting terrorist organizations.

This chapter has developed a theory to account for variation in the ability of leadership decapitation to weaken a terrorist organization. Organizational resilience within this context can be explained by the three main variables of bureaucracy, communal support, and ideology. Bureaucratic organizations have standard operating procedures, division of labor and responsibilities, organizational diversification and mechanisms that ensure a smooth and easy process of succession if leaders are removed. Communal support provides groups with access to resources, recruits, and cohesion that can make groups stronger and better able to resist countermeasures such as targeting. Finally, ideology can account for variation in a group's susceptibility to attacks on its leadership. Religious and separatist organizations often represent the views of the larger communities from which they emerge. Together, these three variables make groups even harder to weaken. The following chapter will operationalize these theories and develop testable hypotheses regarding whether and when decapitation is effective, across a range of measures.

3

Hypotheses on Leadership Decapitation

Leadership decapitation, and counterterrorism measures more broadly, can have a number of different effects. Organizations can end or collapse, experience a decline in activity, or have their life spans shortened. Alternatively, decapitation may increase an organization's resolve, number or frequency of attacks, or survival rate. There is no one clear measure of "success" for decapitation efforts, and considerable lack of agreement over how to evaluate counterterrorism policies, resulting in disagreements over the best way to degrade and defeat terrorist organizations. This poses a problem for governments trying to develop strategies to counter terrorist groups, and for academics trying to understand whether targeting leaders actually "works." This uncertainty has made kinetic responses to terrorism the default solution.[1] To develop effective counterterrorism strategies, it is critical that analysts and policy makers agree on counterterrorism goals.

The success and failure of counterterrorism strategies can be evaluated in a number of different ways, and this study will answer three questions related to the efficacy of decapitation: Does decapitation result in organizational collapse? Does decapitation have an effect upon the occurrence and frequency of terrorist attacks? And does decapitation increase or shorten a group's life span? To answer these questions, four original databases were generated. The first includes 905 instances of leadership decapitation against 179 organizations globally from 1970 to 2012.[2] The cases were drawn from searches of newspaper articles on the arrest or killing of terrorist leaders using LexisNexis.[3] The database includes the name of the leader targeted and their nationality; the type of attack; the rank and role of the leader; the date and location of the decapitation; the size, type, age, and location of the organization; GDP, regime type, and population of the home country; the group's average number of attacks; and whether they carried out activity in a one- and two-year period after the attack. This data was used in the multivariate analyses.

The second database includes organizational data for 290 terrorist organizations from the Global Terrorism Database (GTD) that both have and have not been targeted. The GTD contains nearly three thousand organizations, many of which are very small and not active, and are thus are unlikely to be or have been targeted by counterterrorism forces. To select a sample of organizations for inclusion, both targeted and untargeted, I included only groups that carried out at least three attacks that were both claimed and successful.

The third database includes time series data for each year of an organization's "life" as well as data on the number of decapitations, attacks, and fatalities for each year that a group was active, resulting in 5,267 observations. This data is examined in Chapter 4, to identify the impact that decapitation has had on group activity. Finally, an additional 350 instances of targeting from 2013 to 2016 is examined in Chapters 5–7. This newer data is not included in the statistical analyses on efficacy.

Success and Failure of Counterterrorism Policies

The efficacy of counterterrorism policies can be evaluated by assessing measures such as a group's life span, the frequency of its attacks, the target of its attacks, and its organizational cohesion, support, propaganda output, and territorial control. There is no consensus on which measures are most reliable. Further complicating this is that extant analyses on leadership decapitation have used different criteria for inclusion, resulting in dramatically different datasets and a large variation in the conclusions about whether and when decapitation works.[4] This project is an attempt to evaluate a larger sample of cases according to three quantitative measures of efficacy: (1) organizational activity, (2) organizational existence, and (3) organizational life span (mortality rate). There are other more nuanced ways to understand the effects of counterterrorism policy that cannot be captured by the dataset created for this project, including internal changes, such as organizational weakening, restructuring, ideological shifts, or tactical modifications. While the datasets created for this project cannot capture these kinds of internal effects, the case studies provide a means by which to evaluate some of the internal dynamics that can result from the loss of leadership.

Much of the literature on leadership targeting is concerned with the question of whether it can result in the defeat, decline, or degradation of terrorist organizations, yet there is little agreement on how to evaluate organizational weakening and the success of counterterrorism policies. Some analysts view success as a decline in activity, while others see it as the complete demise of an organization. There is also disagreement in both academic and policy circles about what organizational degradation and defeat looks like. In fact, there are few clear, measurable indicators to evaluate the success of counterterrorism policies.[5]

For example, the 2006 National Strategy for Combatting Terrorism argued that targeting terrorist leaders would result in organizational degradation, but failed to offer a metric by which to measure such degradation. The 2011 National Strategy for Counterterrorism similarly lacked any quantifiable metric for success. The fight against ISIS has highlighted this lack of clear metrics by which to measure Iraqi and US counterterrorism efforts. For example, the chairman of the Joint Chiefs of Staff, US Marine Corps General Joseph Dunford, stated that the success of US campaigns against ISIS can be measured by the group's hold over territory, access to resources, and recruitment of foreign fighters,[6] metrics that are difficult to measure. Much of this problem stems from imprecise language and a lack of clear objectives for evaluating success.[7] The Obama administration's objectives were clear: to degrade and ultimately destroy ISIS through air strikes, support for forces fighting ISIS, attack prevention, and humanitarian assistance.[8] However, neither the Obama administration nor the Bush administration before them clearly described what degradation or defeat looks like. The current Trump administration is equally unclear on articulating counterterrorism success. While ISIS has lost a considerable amount of territorial control, the organization is still functional and effective in other areas of activity. Some analysts have argued that defeating al-Qaeda and ISIS is impossible and that the most we can hope for is containment.[9]

Others have argued that a decline in activity is a signal of organizational degradation. But despite repeated calls for the defeat or degradation of terrorist groups, neither the strategy for attaining that objective nor the end goal are ever articulated. In the absence of clear metrics for success, the government has relied on kinetic options such as leadership targeting, which have the potential to result in more attacks, embolden terrorist organizations, and increase radicalization.

Dependent Variable

To capture the multidimensional nature of counterterrorism efficacy, this book uses four measures of the effectiveness of leadership targeting: (1) frequency of terrorist attacks, (2) organizational survival, (3) life span, and (4) counterproductive behavior or outcomes. First, it is essential to determine the extent to which decapitation has impacted a group's ability to carry out terrorist attacks by looking at whether it is active or inactive after an instance of leadership decapitation. This is one of the most commonly used metrics for evaluating the efficacy of counterterrorism measures. In the analysis conducted for this book, group activity was determined by whether a group had carried out attacks in a one- and two-year period after experiencing a loss of its leadership. This data was collected from the Global Terrorism Database and was integrated into the dataset on leadership decapitation generated for this project.[10] If an organization was inactive for one or two years following the incident of decapitation, it was coded as "inactive" and the instance of decapitation was considered successful. Alternatively, if activity declined but resumed within that time period, the decapitation was coded as a failure.

This metric was informed by the US Department of State's designation of foreign terrorist organizations (FTO). According to the 2001 Report on Foreign Terrorism Organizations, "Designations are valid for two years, after which they must be redesignated or they automatically expire. Redesignation after two years is a positive act and represents a determination by the Secretary of State that the organization has continued to engage in terrorist activity and still meets the criteria specified in law."[11] If an organization no longer engages in terrorist activity, it is removed from the list.[12] In order to make policy-relevant conclusions, a two-year of period of inactivity is a reasonable measure of success. However, two years of no attacks is a fairly restrictive criterion for success, so a one-year period of inactivity is also considered.

It should be noted that a period of complete inactivity is a high bar by which to evaluate the efficacy of a counterterrorism policy; even a decline in the frequency or lethality of attacks can be considered a success. To address this more restrictive measure of organizational activity, I also consider a second measure of the dependent variable: changes in the frequency of attacks over time. This offers a more nuanced understanding of efficacy by evaluating whether targeting has an impact on a group's overall activity. Time series data on the number of attacks and fatalities that a group carries out for each year of its "life" is used to determine whether decapitation has an effect on the frequency of those attacks.

An alternative way to conceptualize organizational defeat is to ask the following question: does an organization still "exist"? Groups can still survive while not actively carrying out attacks; there are a number of cases in which a group didn't carry out attacks in a one-year time frame, but could still be coded as "existing." For example, a senior leader of Hezbollah, Imad Mughniyeh, was killed in Syria in 2008 by a car bomb. The organization did not carry out attacks in the year following his death, but Hezbollah clearly still existed and was in fact growing in strength (both organizationally and in legitimacy), and eventually experienced a large increase in its level of activity. In these cases, the group could be reorganizing, restructuring, changing its tactics or strategy, or waiting for an opportunity to carry out even more deadly attacks. Group "existence" is thus determined by looking at the internal and organizational dynamics of each organization individually.[13] In order to capture this phenomenon, the dataset also codes whether a group "exists" in one-, two-, and five-year periods after experiencing a leadership attack.

Finally, it is important to consider whether decapitation has an impact on a group's life span or mortality rate. If organizations that have been targeted have a longer life span than groups that have not undergone targeting, then decapitation is not an effective strategy and could in fact be counterproductive. This variable is determined by looking at changes in the survival rate of an organization compared to organizations that have not experienced decapitation. Moreover, it is essential to identify the conditions under which decapitation lengthens or shortens this survival rate. A hazard model is used in order to determine variation in the life span (or survival) of groups that have and have not been targeted.

The concept of counterproductivity is an important one when evaluating the success and failures of counterterrorism policies. Attacks on a group's leadership also have the potential to result in unintended and counterproductive consequences. This is an important and often overlooked measure of efficacy. For example, it is often argued that drone strikes do more harm than good.[14] Studies have found that they can increase the number of attacks carried out by terrorist organizations, aid in recruitment, increase radicalization, and generate both public and international outcry; for example, a report of the Task Force on US Drone Policy released by the Stimson Center claims that the use of unmanned strikes creates a large amount of resentment. Retired Army general Stanley McChrystal has argued that part of this backlash is due to the perception that drone strikes result in a high number of civilian casualties, and suggests that they can undermine sovereignty, transparency, accountability, and other human rights and legal issues. The task force concludes that "civilian casualties, even if relatively few, can anger whole communities, increase anti-US sentiment and become a potent recruiting tool for terrorist organizations. Even strikes that kill only terrorist operatives can cause great resentment, particularly in contexts in which terrorist recruiting efforts rely on tribal loyalties or on an economically desperate population."[15] Robert Grenier, head of the CIA's Counter-Terrorism Center in 2004–6, argued that drone strikes leading to civilian deaths in Yemen create the possibility for radicalization and have the potential to create a terrorist haven in Yemen.[16] A study conducted by NYU and Stanford concluded that drones create anti-American sentiment and reports, "it is clear that US strikes in Pakistan foster anti-American sentiment and undermine US credibility not only in Pakistan but throughout the region. There is strong evidence to suggest that US drone strikes have facilitated recruitment to violent non-state armed groups, and motivate attacks against both US military and civilian targets."[17] While drone strikes are not always carried out against leaders and target militants across a range of operational roles within an organization, these reports underscore the argument that targeting, drone strikes, and civilian casualties can produce adverse outcomes by encouraging radicalization.

It is important to note that these criticisms do not go uncontested; there is a debate over the effect of drone strikes, particularly with respect to radicalization. Christine Fair argues that some individuals in South Waziristan and other Federally Administrated Tribal Areas agencies are proponents of drone strikes. She has stated that "they report that the drones are so precise that the local non-militants do not fear them when they hear the drones above as they are confident that they will hit their target."[18] Another report by the International Crisis Group has examined the consequences of drone strikes, such as civilian casualties, and concludes that they have minimal impact in terms of recruitment. In fact, they find that drone strikes have become more precise over time and the number of civilian casualties has declined. Brian Glyn Williams argues that drones do not indiscriminately target civilians.[19] Recent quantitative studies on the effect of drones on the frequency of violence have argued that drone strikes decrease the number of terrorist attacks and that local populations welcome these strikes in an attempt to rid their communities of terrorist violence.[20] Walsh and Schulzke have examined how the development of combat drones influences attitudes toward the use of force by the United States. Using experimental methods, their research found that because the use of drones can reduce civilian casualties, the public is moderately more willing to support the use of combat drones. This support for the use of drones can encourage leaders to use drones to achieve low-cost military successes.[21]

These debates on the effect of drone strikes and their potential for radicalizing militants and generating sympathy for a group's cause highlight the necessity of factual assessment of counterterrorism policies and whether they actually do what we want them to do, which is reduce militant activity and community support. If decapitation increases the activity and life span of terrorist organizations, then it is clearly counterproductive. Data on public support was not included in the large datasets, so case studies offer a way to evaluate the counterproductive effects of leadership attacks, by examining whether they had an impact on support for groups, changes in recruitment, and organizational changes over time.

Finally, the loss of a leader can have other outcomes for a group, such as splintering or factionalization.[22] Once an organization splinters, it may cease to exist in its original incarnation, making it appear as if the organization has collapsed. However, a splinter group can remain capable of carrying out terrorist activity and, in certain cases, can be even more radical or violent than the original group. There are instances in which an organization was essentially defeated after decapitation, yet its members continued to carry out terrorist activity under a different group name, but in pursuit of the same goals. These cases are coded as decapitation failures in the dataset for this book. As an example, after the arrest and suicide of its founders, the Baader-Meinhof Group ceased to exist, but the Red Army Faction, which was formed from the remnants of the Baader-Meinhof, fought for the same cause and carried out terrorist activity with the same political purpose.[23]

The remainder of this chapter will develop hypotheses regarding the consequences of leadership targeting. First, it will discuss whether leadership targeting is likely to result in organizational defeat or collapse, impact the frequency of lethality of terrorist attacks over time, or have an effect upon a group's life span. Second, the chapter will identify the conditions under which decapitation is more likely to result in a group's decline or an increase in activity. These analyses provide a means by which to assess the explanatory power of the theory advanced in the previous chapter.

When Does Decapitation Work?

The effect of leadership targeting is variable. Sometimes it works and sometimes it doesn't, and this book is largely an attempt to identify the conditions under which it does and does not work. To develop good counterterrorism policies, it is critical to know whether certain tactics are better than others. As noted in Chapter 1, in some cases decapitation results in a reduction in terrorist group activity, and in other cases, it leads to an increase. The following section will advance hypotheses regarding the impact that targeting has upon a group's activity, existence, and organizational life span, while examining the impact of the following variables: type of decapitation, leader's position, organizational type, organizational age, organizational size, GDP per capita, and regime type.

Type of Decapitation

Leaders can be targeted in different ways. Generally, the term *leadership targeting* refers to the killing of a terrorist leader, but leaders can also be killed or captured.

It is often assumed that killing a leader is more damaging to a group. The intuition is that the death of a leader can damage morale and cause organizational disarray, ultimately weakening the organization. However, because it is possible to obtain intelligence about the group from a captured leader, arresting leaders could more effective. Cronin argues, "There is some reason to believe that arresting a leader is more effective in damaging a group than is killing or assassinating him."[24] She claims that killing a terrorist leader may increase publicity for the cause and create a martyr that could attract new members to the organization. Cronin's argument provides a more theoretical basis for the finding that decapitation is rarely effective. An increase in publicity and sympathy can sometimes have adverse reactions.

I predict that the death of a leader should result in the degradation of a terrorist organization more often than the arrest of a leader. Terrorist activity can continue and even increase following the arrest of a leader. A leader may be able to maintain influence while in prison, and members can engage in further activity to facilitate the release of their leaders.[25] For example, after the arrest of Baader-Meinhof leaders, the remaining members of the organization continued to carry out terrorist activity in order to free their leaders from prison.[26] The Black September Organization took nine Israeli hostages at the 1972 Munich Olympics and demanded the release of 236 imprisoned Palestinians and five terrorists being held in Germany, including Andreas Baader and Ulrike Meinhof.[27] While the arrests of Baader and Meinhof did not cause the Munich kidnappings, they were related. Assassinating leaders can also result in power vacuums and then struggles for succession, which can temporarily weaken an organization. Killing leaders should thus result in the decline of terrorist organizations more than arresting leaders.

Leader's Position

For this study, leadership is defined broadly, as the top leader of an organization or a member of the upper echelon who holds a position of authority within the organization. An *incident of decapitation* refers to the arrest or killing of a leader carried out by a government. I exclude cases where the leader is killed or removed by other members within the organization. To identify whether the individual targeted was a top leader or a member of the upper echelon, each instance of targeting was evaluated according to reporting in the sources used to create the dataset. If an individual was identified as a top leader, leader, or a member of the upper echelon, then that individual was coded as such in the dataset. The dataset includes two separate variables in order to evaluate whether and how leadership type interacts with organizational activity and life span. The first variable accounts for whether the individual targeted was a top leader or anyone else with a position of leadership within the organization. The second variable makes further distinctions and codes whether the individual targeted was the top leader, part of the upper echelon, or in a category that includes all other commanders, leaders, expert bomb makers, or senior operatives.

The removal of a top leader should be more effective than the removal of members of the upper echelon. In many terrorist organizations, the leader has little direct contact with the active members of the organization.[28] The leader may be necessary to authorize a specific activity, but the upper echelon often ensures operational success. While members of the upper echelon may be crucial for carrying out terrorist acts, the upper echelon can also be replaced more easily than a top leader. However, removing both the upper echelon and the leader should be most effective, severely hindering the ability of an organization to coordinate and carry out an activity.

Organizational Type

It is also possible to code organizations according to the means by which they try to achieve their goals.[29] In analyzing the psychology of political leaders, Gerald Post, Keven Ruby, and Eric Shaw look at variation in the psychology of members and leaders in organizations with different goals.[30] Post et al. identify seven indicators of group goals: The group (1) believes that radical change is necessary, (2) believes that violence is necessary, (3) specifies its targets, (4) expands the spread of targets from specific to general, (5) emphasizes the historical sins of a designated group, (6) characterizes group members as righteous, and (7) idealizes the goals of a terrorist group or revolutionary nation. It is important to understand the means by which a group wishes to change society, target certain groups, or work within the confines of an existing system, and organizational type can capture these indicators.

Some groups seek radical social change. These organizations aim to transform society according to a political ideology. They include Marxist, Leninist, social revolutionary, fascist, and white-supremacist organizations, and both left- and right-wing organizations, which were coded accordingly. Separatist groups aim to establish an independent state, achieve autonomy, or change their political status within a particular country. Religious groups can also advocate radical social change, but they seek to achieve political change based on a specific religious ideology. Much of the literature examines whether there is something distinct about Islamist terrorist organizations, whether they are more violent, stronger, and harder to weaken.[31] In this study, groups are also coded according to whether they have an Islamist agenda in order to understand whether Islamist terrorist groups are differentially impacted by leadership targeting.

The susceptibility of organizations to decapitation should vary based on these organizational types. This argument was developed in Chapter 2 in the discussion on group ideology. Separatist groups should be the most difficult to destabilize through leadership targeting, followed by religious organizations, with Islamist groups being more difficult than other religious organizations. Organizations that are both religious and separatist should be even harder to weaken. Finally, I hypothesize that left- and right-wing organizations should be more likely to experience a decline in activity or fall apart in the case of decapitation.

Organizational Age

Organizational age should also have an effect on the efficacy of leadership targeting. The first year of an organization's life was coded according to the year in which it began conducting terrorist activity. Organizations were coded according to the number of years they had been active at the time of decapitation and were also coded in five-year increments. In addition to decapitated organizations, I also examine the life span of organizations that have not experienced decapitation. If younger organizations tend to be more likely to collapse absent decapitation, then those organizations should also be more susceptible to decapitation.

Extant research has found that younger organizations are more fragile and susceptible to counterterrorism measures. In reference to the life cycle of terrorist organizations, Martha Crenshaw argues, "Possibly, there is a threshold point, beyond which the extremist organization becomes self-sustaining. The younger the organization, the greater the likelihood of its ending."[32] Older organizations have had more time to develop complex structures, which are harder to combat, as there may be overlap between operational units. As groups age, they tend to develop organizational complexity and bureaucratic structures that make them harder to defeat or even weaken.[33] This organizational complexity should increase a group's resilience to leadership decapitation; conversely, a younger organization should be more likely to experience a decline in activity, have a shorter life span, or even cease to exist after having experienced leadership attacks. I predict that older organizations should be highly resilient to leadership attacks and even experience counterproductive effects, such as an increase in activity, after decapitation.

Organizational Size

Organizational size should also have an effect upon the success of decapitation. This variable is coded according to the number of active members. The coding for this variable was drawn primarily from data on group size in the Big Allied and Dangerous (BAAD) database as well as from the GTD dataset, both maintained at the National Consortium for the Study of Terrorism and Responses to Terrorism (START). The BAAD and GTD databases occasionally had conflicting numbers for organizational size, and in these cases, I utilized BAAD's coding. For organizations that were in neither dataset, I utilized other sources to verify a group's size. Organizations were divided into the following categories for size: 1–100, 100–500, 500–1,000, 1,000–5,000, 5,000–10,000, and 10,000 and above.

There are a number of reasons to expect that larger organizations would be more resilient in the face of leadership decapitation. Larger organizations should have more time to develop complex structures that would make them more resilient to leadership decapitation. As a group grows in size, it is also more likely to become specialized, creating redundancy, another mechanism that contributes to a group's resilience to targeting. Larger organizations can rely upon the planning and operation of localized networks, which are stronger and more resistant to attacks. James March and Mancur Olson argue that there is less interaction between the group and the individual in larger communities.[34] Limits to exposure would suggest that individuals operate more independently in larger organizations, which should make it harder for states to effectively decapitate an organization.

These predictions are consistent with the theory of organizational resilience. As organizations become larger, they often need to adopt more bureaucratic and centralized administrative structures and institutions to manage their affairs and operate efficiently. At the same time, larger organizations are also able to take advantage of their size to operate in a decentralized manner. Delegating operational capacity to smaller cells can increase group activity and create a structure in which a group is more immune to destabilization from targeting the group's upper echelon.

Organizational size can interact with other variables in important ways. For example, while young organizations may have higher rates of failure than old organizations, these findings may be due to heterogeneity in the population. The liability of newness may in fact be a liability of smallness, and it is thus necessary to control for size. James Ranger-Moore finds that large groups almost always have lower failure rates, and Freeman, Carroll, and Hannan argue that there is both a "liability of newness" and a "liability of smallness" with respect to the rate of organizational dissolution.[35] As a result, it is necessary to look at how size and age interact. Finally, there should be an important relationship between group size and structure. If larger organizations are more likely to develop decentralized structures, then religious organizations should be larger. I also expect separatist organizations to be larger given that they often have a large base of communal support.

GDP

The GDP of the country in which the group is based is included in the statistical analysis. After 9/11 several policy makers called for foreign aid and education in the fight against terrorism. In 2002, President George W. Bush stated, "We fight against poverty because hope is an answer to terror."[36] The idea that poverty and lack of opportunity breed terrorism has been pervasive in the public debate surrounding counterterrorism policies. This echoes findings in the economics literature that there is a relationship between poverty and intrastate violence.[37] However, much of the research on the relationship between economic growth and terrorism has been inconclusive. While some studies have found a positive correlation between economic growth and the occurrence of terrorism, others have found a heterogeneous or even negative correlation.[38] Examining data on Palestinian groups and Hezbollah, Krueger and Maleckova found no relationship between poverty and terrorism.[39] James Piazza similarly finds that poverty, as measured through the Human Development Index, GDP, or the United Nations Development Programme, is not a driver of terrorism.[40] He concludes that "the socio-economic status of marginalized (though not necessarily impoverished people) within society might be."[41] Moreover, the argument that grievances are a root cause of terrorism is problematic. Poverty, lack of education, and lack of access to political participation are all ubiquitous, and only a small minority within any population engage in political violence, be it on behalf of a terrorist organization or as "lone wolves."

Studies on the relationship between poverty and terrorism also tend to overlook the role economic variables can play in counterterrorism policies. The literature on failed states and terrorism can provide a basis upon which to develop predictions regarding the relationship between GDP and targeting effects. There is considerable agreement that weak and failed states are more likely to breed terrorism and provide a home base for terrorist groups.[42] Stohl and Stohl argue that terrorist groups can more easily develop in failed states for a number of reasons.[43] A lack of control by the government allows for the development of infrastructure for illicit activity and for control over land by militant groups. Failed states also provide a larger pool of potential recruits as "civil society collapses."[44] Finally, interference by outside states is discouraged in order to respect norms of sovereignty. The inability of governments to govern and provide basic needs and services for individuals also provides an opportunity for terrorist groups to act as social service providers.[45]

The provision of services and goods can make groups stronger and more lethal.[46] Eli Berman seeks to understand why religious radicals, when they choose to engage in violence, are so effective at it. Berman argues that it is important to look at the organizational dynamics of terrorist groups, not at their individual motivations.[47] He argues that one of the main reasons for the lethality of religious organizations is their ability to inspire commitment through the provision of public goods. In doing so, he finds that successful militant groups can control defection through mutual aid, which refers to the provision of goods and services by individual members within a community through acts of charity. This aid is dependent upon members' participation, and not free-riding. This can, in part, be accomplished through accepting those who participate as full members of the community and expelling or marginalizing those who do not.[48] Militant groups have already weeded out the shirkers. Their members are committed, and this commitment is maintained through providing tangible services to them. Berman concludes that "radical religious communities with strong mutual aid provision have the potential to be potent providers of coordinated violence."[49] If failed states create an environment in which militant groups can deliver important and necessary services to those in need, these groups can broaden their base of support and create conditions under which the beneficiaries develop a commitment to the organization and to participating in acts of violence. As an example, Flanigan, Asal, and Brown argue that the provision of community services is part of a political strategy for groups in the Middle East and North Africa.[50] Not all individuals will actively participate in violence, but local support matters and enhances a group's resilience. Finally, in order to effectively provide services, organizations often develop institutions and infrastructure that further increase their strength and ability to resist countereforts.

Failed states also tend to have lower economic growth and a lower GDP. As a result, groups from countries with a lower GDP should be more resilient in the face of leadership targeting. States with lower economic capacity often compete with militant groups in the provision of services. As a result, organizations in these countries have more opportunity for expansion, control of territory, recruits, and more control over areas that are not within the government's reach, making them harder to weaken through counterterrorism measures such as targeting. Countries with a higher GDP should have a greater capacity to engage in more sustained targeting campaigns and the ability to employ alternative counterterrorism measures, increasing their ability to degrade terrorist organizations.

In order to evaluate the effect of these economic variables, the dataset examines GDP per capita, in 2005 US dollars, for a group's home country for the year of each decapitation. Some organizations have home bases in more than one country, in which case the primary country in which the group operates is analyzed. I predict that terrorist groups based in countries with a lower GDP should be more resilient to targeting efforts.

Regime Type

Finally, the statistical analysis includes a measure of regime type for the countries in which each group is based and/or emerged. This data is taken from the Polity IV dataset, which codes whether a country is a democracy or an autocracy on a scale from -10 to +10, with a lower score indicating a more authoritarian regime, and a higher score a democratic regime.[51] This variable was derived from three composite indicators: (1) the competitiveness of political participation, (2) the openness and competitiveness of executive recruitment, and (3) constraints on the chief executive. The Polity IV score for the year in which the decapitation occurred is utilized.

The democratization of illiberal societies is often seen as an effective and important goal in the war on terrorism. While the promotion of democracy has been an important aspect of US foreign policy, there are two divergent views on the relationship between regime type and the occurrence of terrorism, and little consensus. It is important to examine these debates in order to develop hypotheses regarding the regime type of the country in which terrorist groups are operating. Some studies have argued that democracies reduce terrorism as there are legitimate political channels through which groups and individuals can express and peacefully resolve their grievances.[52] Nondemocratic regimes are seen as repressive and humiliating toward certain groups, which can encourage political violence.[53]

The relationship between terrorism and democracy can be seen as a function of other variables associated with democratic participation. Risa Brooks unpacks the causal mechanisms underlying the relationship between regime type and terrorist attacks and argues that rather than focusing on democracy, it is critical to examine the effect that political access has upon the occurrence of terrorism and the ability of governments to fight it. She finds that there are multiple causal pathways between democracy and terrorism, and it is essential to consider *when* democracy or others forms of political access may reduce violence.[54]

Others have argued that terrorism is more likely in democracies because there are institutional constraints on the kind of counterterrorism measures they can employ, while authoritarian regimes can utilize more repressive and stronger countermeasures.[55] For example, in a quantitative analysis of transnational terrorist attacks, Quan Li argues that democratic participation was associated with fewer attacks through "improving citizen satisfaction, electoral participation, and political efficacy."[56] However, Li also finds that countries with institutional constraints experience more attacks because those constraints can weaken a country's ability to fight terrorism.[57] First, institutional constraints hold the government accountable to a broad range of societal interests, which makes it more difficult for democracies to enact the kind of heavy-handed measures that would be possible under a nondemocratic system. Second, repression can be costly to leaders and governments who are accountable in a competitive political system where they could lose political support. Finally, Li argues, institutional constraints actually strengthen the strategic environment in which groups operate.[58] The restriction of civil liberties, however, does not lead to a decline in attacks.

Taking these studies into consideration, I predict that targeting the leaders of terrorist organizations based in democratic countries should be less effective in degrading or destroying these groups, while nondemocratic governments should exhibit greater success through their targeting efforts.

This chapter developed hypotheses to answer the following questions: Does decapitation result in organizational collapse? Does decapitation have an effect upon the occurrence and frequency of terrorist attacks? Does decapitation increase or shorten a group's life span? The hypotheses which will be tested in the following chapter can be summarized as follows:

> H1: Decapitation should be more effective when the leader is killed than arrested.
> H2: The removal of a top leader should be more effective than the removal of members of the upper echelon.
> H3: Separatist groups should be the most difficult to destabilize through leadership targeting, followed by religious organizations, with Islamist groups being more difficult than other religious organizations. Left- and right-wing organizations should be more likely to experience a decline in activity or fall apart in the case of decapitation.
> H4: Decapitation should be less effective against older terrorist organizations.
> H5: Decapitation should be less effective against larger terrorist organizations.
> H6: Decapitation should be less effective against terrorist organizations based in countries with a lower GDP.
> H7: Decapitation should be less effective against terrorist organizations based in democratic countries.

The following chapter will discuss the results of statistical tests to determine whether metrics—such as the position of a leader within the organization, the type of decapitation, organizational variables (size, age, or type), GDP, or regime type—will have an effect upon the efficacy of decapitation. It will also examine data on the survival rate of targeted and nontargeted groups to determine whether decapitation is an effective means by which to reduce organization's life span.

4

Is Leadership Targeting Effective?

There are a number of different ways to determine whether leadership targeting actually "works." A terrorist organization can experience a decline in activity or the lethality of its attacks, an increase in its mortality rate, or a period of organizational weakening. Alternatively, the group can adapt, emerging stronger and more emboldened or carrying out attacks as retaliation or to signal its continuing strength. This chapter will utilize a number of different metrics and statistical tests to evaluate whether and when decapitation has been effective. Specifically, it will examine whether decapitation of terrorist organization brings about a decline in its activity, reduces the frequency of its attacks, impacts its life span, or results in its collapse.

The chapter begins by looking at trends in leadership targeting. It then examines the impact of decapitation on organizational activity, organizational existence, attack frequency, and organizational survival. The chapter concludes with an overall assessment of the theoretical implications and policy recommendations regarding the efficacy of leadership targeting. In brief, the data shows that organizational size, type, and leadership rank all have an impact on the probability that a group will experience a cessation of terrorist activity after leadership decapitation. While there is some variation, generally large groups are better able to withstand leadership attacks. Religious, separatist, and Islamist groups are also resilient and likely to continue carrying out activity. Targeting the top leader as opposed to members of the upper echelon is more likely to result in a cessation of activity, and groups in countries with a larger population are more likely to withstand leadership attacks. The results were similar when examining one- or two-year periods of activity and when determining whether a group continues to exist as an organizational entity or collapses.

The results on attack frequency indicate that while in certain situations decapitation reduces the probability that groups will experience an increase in attacks, the picture is more nuanced. First, it is critical to look at changes in attack frequency for both decapitated and nondecapitated groups. Second, the change in the probability of a group increasing or decreasing the number of attacks after decapitation depends on its prior level of activity. Finally, the effect of decapitation can also depend upon the characteristics of the group itself. While the data as a whole might show a reduction in the frequency of attacks, in some cases decapitation results in a significant increase, especially in the nine largest, most active organizations in the dataset, which are analyzed separately. Overall, data from transition matrix analyses indicates that decapitation does not significantly hinder a terrorist group's operational capacity, and, in certain cases, may increase the frequency of attacks. It is thus essential to identify when decapitation can reduce a group's activity and when it can result in more activity.

Finally, the data on organizational survival reveals that decapitation does not reduce an organization's mortality rate. Separatist groups, religious groups, Islamist groups, and organizations in countries with a higher GDP have a lower hazard rate, while groups in countries with a higher population and groups that carry out a higher number of attacks have a higher hazard rate. Overall, the data suggests that decapitation does not impact organizational life span and that the organizations against whom decapitation is not likely to be effective tend to have a higher survival rate overall.

Trends in Leadership Targeting

In order to evaluate the impact of leadership decapitation, I created a dataset of nearly 1,000 leadership attacks against 180 terrorist organizations from 1954 to 2012.[1] This dataset does not include all known leadership attacks, but is a large enough sample to identify trends about the efficacy of targeting and to make predictions about its utility as a counterterrorism policy. I also looked at the activity of terrorist organizations that have not been targeted in order to determine whether decapitation is an effective counterterrorism strategy. I examined a separate database of 350 cases from 2013 to 2016, focusing on ISIS and al-Qaeda. LexisNexis was used to identify and collect information reported in the media about incidents of leadership targeting. Additional data was drawn from the following datasets: the Global Terrorism Database, the Big Allied and Dangerous database (BAAD), Polity, and the World Bank.[2]

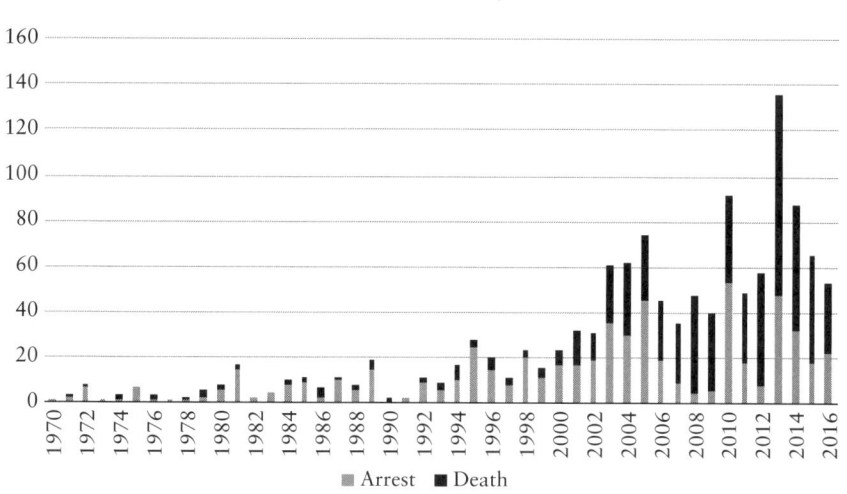

FIGURE 4.1 Decapitation of terrorist leaders, 1970–2016

Figure 4.1 displays the frequency with which terrorist leaders have been both arrested and killed by governments since 1970. The graph demonstrates a dramatic increase in the number of attacks since 2011, and that, despite a few periods of decline, targeting has steadily increased over time. However, it is essential to determine trends in the targeted groups.

Ideally, the database would include information on whether countries were only targeting the "strongest" terrorist organizations. If so, it would be unsurprising that decapitation is unsuccessful in a great many cases, biasing the findings. However, determining the organizational strength of terrorist groups is not an easy task. While extant datasets such as BAAD utilize age, type, and size as proxies for organizational strength. These are explanatory variables in the statistical models for this book, and thus cannot be used to determine a group's strength or capacity. There are other measures of group strength—such as territorial control, access to resources, natural resources, recruitment, or finances—that can help analysts to understand a group's strength, but given the clandestine nature of terrorist groups, they too are difficult to determine. Ideally, one would utilize the same measure of strength across all organizations in space and time. Such data challenges are endemic to the field of terrorism studies.

The organizations targeted span a wide range of sizes, ages, and types. Figure 4.2 demonstrates that there is a fairly even distribution of sizes, with smaller groups (those with between 101 and 500 members) targeted more often. However, Figure 4.3 shows that when looking at all instances of decapitation, groups with between 5,001 and 10,000 members are targeted most frequently, with

Is Leadership Targeting Effective? 65

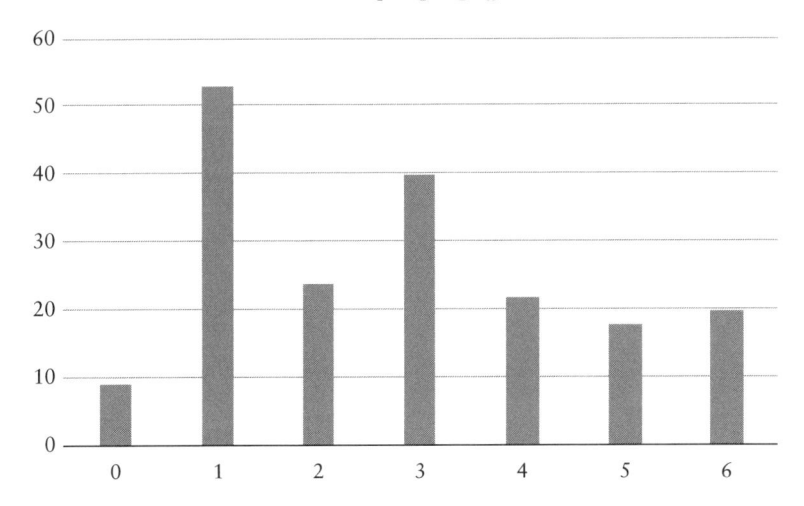

FIGURE 4.2 Distribution of targeted groups by size, 1970–2016
Size is coded as follows: 0 = 1–100 members; 1 = 101–500; 3 = 501–1,000; 4 = 1,001–5,000; 5 = 5001–10,000; and 6 = 10,001+

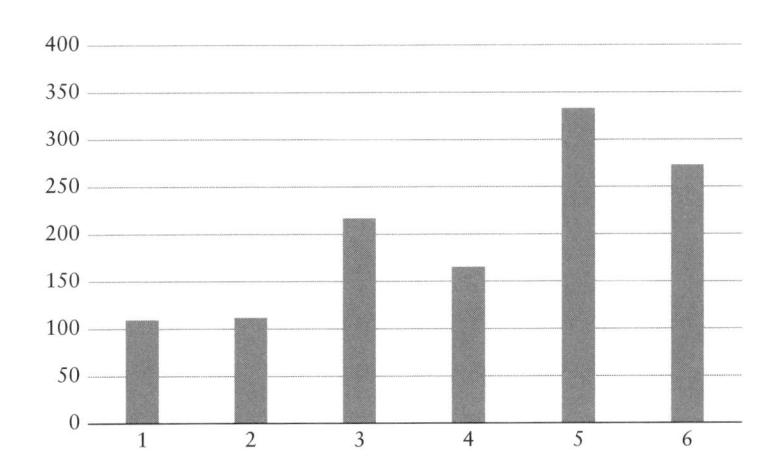

FIGURE 4.3 Decapitation incidents coded by group size, 1970–2016
Size is coded as follows: 0 = 1–100 members; 1 = 101–500; 3 = 501–1,000; 4 = 1,001–5,000; 5 = 5,001–10,000; and 6 = 10,001+

some organizations having experienced many more attacks on their leadership than others. The oldest groups are also targeted more frequently, as evidenced by Figure 4.4. Finally, Figure 4.5 displays the distribution of targeted groups by organizational type, which is fairly even, with right-wing groups targeted the least. These graphs provide one way to evaluate whether counterterrorism measures such as decapitation are directed primarily against the strongest or the

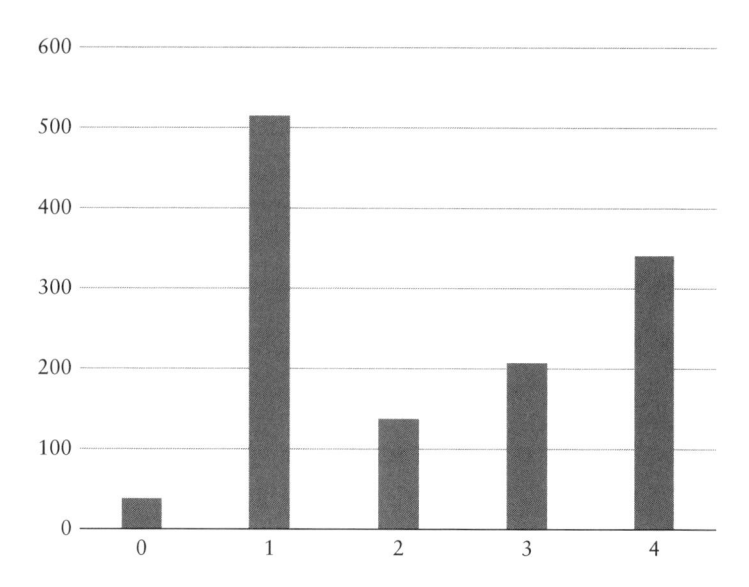

FIGURE 4.4 Distribution of targeted groups by age, 1970–2016
Age is coded as follows: 0 = 1–5; 1 = 6–10; 2 = 11–15; 3 = 16–20; 4 = 21+

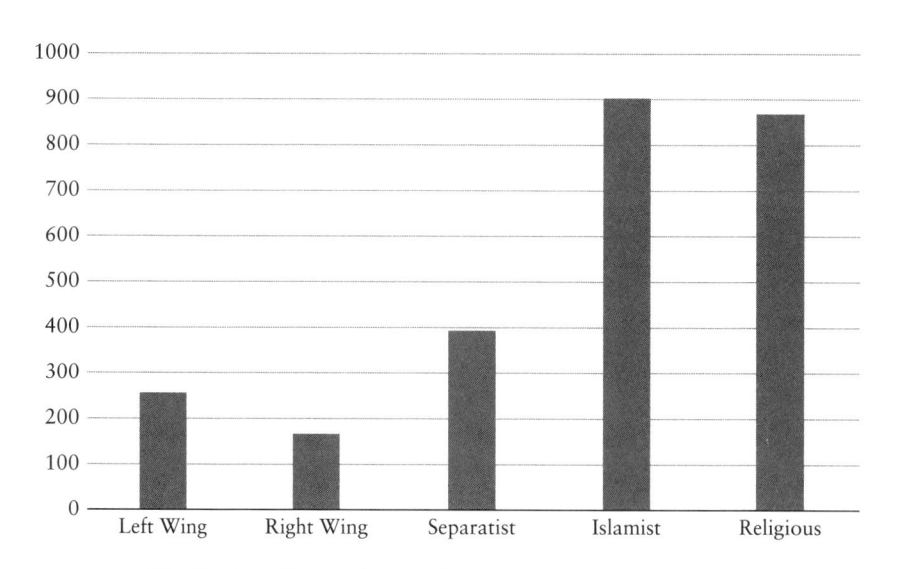

FIGURE 4.5 Distribution of targeted groups by type

weakest groups. They illustrate that the largest and oldest groups are not disproportionately targeted. In order to avoid biasing the statistical results, the nine most active organizations were analyzed separately. This will be discussed further later in the chapter. The remainder of this chapter examines quantitative trends in the efficacy of leadership targeting.

Impact of Decapitation on Activity and Existence

There are a number of different ways to evaluate the efficacy of counterterrorism measures. This section will present statistical analyses that examine whether a group carried out activity in a one- and two-year period after an instance of decapitation. This measure was informed by the US Department of State's list of Foreign Terrorist Organizations, which is redesignated every two years. To make policy prescriptions regarding the efficacy of counterterrorism policy, this study also utilizes a one- and two-year period of inactivity as one measure of efficacy. However, groups can be inactive yet still exist as an organizational entity, and in order to capture this, the analyses in this chapter examine both organizational activity and organizational existence. In order to determine whether decapitation is effective, three logistic regression analyses were conducted on three separate binary dependent variables: whether a group carries out attacks within a one-year period or a two-year period, and whether it ceased to exist as an organizational entity, essentially collapsing. The following variables are included in the analyses: an organization's size, age, and type (left-wing, right-wing, religious, separatist, Islamist); GDP, Polity score, and population of the country in which the group is primarily based; whether the decapitation was a death or an arrest; and finally, the rank of the targeted leader (top leader or member of the upper echelon).

The analyses include 180 organizations targeted between 1970 and 2012. To avoid bias in the statistical results, nine organizations were removed from the regression analysis because they carried out far more activity than other groups in the dataset: al-Qaeda in the Arabian Peninsula (AQAP), al-Shabaab, Basque Fatherland and Freedom (ETA), Boko Haram, Kurdistan Workers' Party (PKK), Liberation Tigers of Tamil Eelam (LTTE), New People's Army (NPA), Taliban, and Tehrik-i-Taliban Pakistan (TTP). All of these organizations continued to carry out attacks after experiencing decapitation, in many cases becoming more active. These groups are all large, and except for NPA, which is a communist organization, they are either religious or separatist. Their exclusion from the dataset provides a harder test of the hypotheses, which are based in part on the assumption that large, religious, and separatist groups are harder to weaken. These groups will be further analyzed later in the chapter. After removing these nine organizations, there are 339 instances of decapitation in the multivariate statistical analyses.

Bivariate Analyses

Before examining multivariate analyses on the efficacy of targeting, this section will discuss results of bivariate analyses of the relationship between the independent variables and two measures of efficacy. Table 4.1 looks at the relationship between organizational size and the outcome of decapitation. It reports the percentage of organizations, by size, that experienced a cessation of activity one and two years after an instance of decapitation. It also reports the percentage of organizations that fell apart or collapsed. Essentially, it shows how often decapitation "worked." Organizational size is coded according to the number of active members: 1 (1–100 members), 2 (101–500 members), 3 (501–1,000 members), 4 (1,001–5,000 members), 5 (5,001–10,000 members), and 6 (10,001 or more members). The table evaluates the relationship between size and different measures of efficacy or organizational resilience. The first two rows measure whether a group carried out any attacks one and two years following an instance of decapitation. The following two rows measure whether a group was still in existence.

The data shows that 61 percent of the smallest groups, those with fewer than 100 active members, stopped carrying out terrorist attacks in a one-year period following an instance of leadership targeting, and 67 percent stop carrying out attacks within a two-year period. For all values of the dependent variables, decapitation has a much stronger effect on the smallest organizations. However, contrary to hypotheses in Chapter 3, there was variability in the impact of group size. A higher percentage of groups with over 10,000 members stopped carrying out attacks than all groups other than the smallest. In approximately 25 percent of cases, groups with between 1,000 and 10,000 members carried out no activity in the year following an incident of decapitation. However, while the largest groups

TABLE 4.1
Organizational size and activity after decapitation

Size	1	2	3	4	5	6
No attacks—1 year	0.61	0.28	0.32	0.26	0.24	0.43
No attacks—2 years	0.67	0.38	0.41	0.33	0.29	0.50
Collapse—1 year	0.26	0.10	0.03	0.05	0.05	0.00
Collapse—2 years	0.33	0.16	0.05	0.10	0.08	0.07

experienced a disruption in activity, in almost no cases were they defeated. As expected, the smallest groups were more susceptible to decline. Furthermore, for all groups, regardless of size, a higher percentage were adversely impacted by decapitation two years after an instance of decapitation. The longer-term rate of decline and variation in these trends could be due to a number of factors that are not captured by the bivariate analysis and that will be examined in the multivariate analyses.

Second, Table 4.2 shows the percentage of organizations, by ideology, that cease to carry out attacks or exist following decapitation. To account for overlap in certain groups, organizations are coded as 0 or 1 for each category of analysis. The data demonstrates that right-wing groups have a much higher probability of not carrying out attacks after decapitation (61 percent of all right-wing groups stopped carrying out attacks after two years), while left-wing groups were more likely than all other types of organizations to fall apart after two years. This latter finding could be due to the fact that many left-wing groups have shorter life spans in general, a trend that will be discussed later in the chapter. Religious, Islamist, and separatist groups are less likely to stop attacks after decapitation than other types of organizations, and have an even lower probability of falling apart entirely. Again, this particular trend of existence could be explained by overall life span. However, the main finding here is that religious and separatist groups have the lowest probability of not carrying out attacks, followed by left-wing and then right-wing organizations.

Third, Table 4.3 examines the relationship between leadership rank and organizational activity and existence. The variables were coded as 1 if the organization's singular top leader was targeted; 2 if the leader was a member of the upper echelon, including if several top leaders were targeted simultaneously; and 3 if the leader was a commander, leader, expert bomb maker, or senior operative. When the group's top leaders were targeted, 42 percent of organizations stopped carrying out attacks in a one-year period and 52 percent in a two-year period. The percentage of groups that collapsed after one or two years is much smaller, indicating that while the rank of the leader killed might affect a group's activity, it is much less likely to lead to its total demise.

Fourth, Table 4.4 examines the relationship between age and organizational activity and indicates that in a vast majority of cases, the youngest organizations were more likely to stop carrying out attacks after decapitation. However, contrary to the original hypotheses, none of the youngest organizations experienced a complete demise after decapitation: 40 percent of groups over twenty years of age stopped carrying out attacks one year after an instance of decapitation, and 51 percent stopped in the year following. Surprisingly, a higher percentage of

TABLE 4.2
Organizational type and activity after decapitation

	Not Left Wing	Left Wing	Not Right Wing	Right Wing	Not Separatist	Separatist	Not Religious	Religious	Not Islamic	Islamic
No attacks—1 year	0.36	0.37	0.32	0.61	0.40	0.31	0.42	0.31	0.42	0.28
No attacks—2 years	0.41	0.48	0.41	0.61	0.48	0.37	0.51	0.37	0.51	0.34
Collapse—1 year	0.08	0.13	0.09	0.13	0.12	0.06	0.14	0.05	0.14	0.04
Collapse—2 years	0.10	0.21	0.13	0.17	0.17	0.09	0.20	0.08	0.20	0.06

TABLE 4.3
Leadership rank and activity after decapitation

Rank	1	2	3
No attacks—1 year	0.42	0.28	0.34
No attacks—2 years	0.52	0.32	0.41
Collapse—1 year	0.10	0.05	0.12
Collapse—2 years	0.15	0.10	0.17

TABLE 4.4
Organizational age and activity after decapitation

Age	0	1	2	3	4
No attacks—1 year	1.00	0.45	0.26	0.15	0.40
No attacks—2 years	0.75	0.42	0.32	0.23	0.51
Collapse—1 year	0.00	0.03	0.11	0.03	0.12
Collapse—2 years	0.00	0.05	0.18	0.05	0.16

TABLE 4.5
GDP and activity after decapitation

GDP	0	1	2	3
No attacks—1 year	0.34	0.35	0.50	0.36
No attacks—2 years	0.40	0.44	0.58	0.45
Collapse—1 year	0.01	0.08	0.23	0.18
Collapse—2 years	0.05	0.14	0.29	0.18

groups twenty years or older stopped carrying out attacks both one and two years after decapitation than groups between ten and twenty years old. Furthermore, a higher percentage of the oldest groups also collapsed, though this could be due to the fact that as groups age, they tend to decline. The most active groups were left out of this analysis so as not to bias the results. These groups have all been resilient and are also in the oldest age category, and their inclusion would result in a much lower percentage for category 4. However, age was insignificant in most of the multivariate analyses on group activity.

Fifth, Table 4.5 looks at the relationship between the GDP of the countries in which each group is based and its organizational activity. The data shows that decapitation has not been as effective against groups in countries with the highest or lowest GDP. It is more effective for groups based in countries with a per capita GDP between US$7,000 and 30,000, that is, based in richer (but not the richest) countries.

TABLE 4.6
Regime type and activity after decapitation

Polity		0	1	2	3
No attacks—1 year	None	0.38	0.25	0.42	0.41
No attacks—2 years	None	0.52	0.39	0.54	0.45
Collapse—1 year	None	0.08	0.14	0.08	0.12
Collapse—2 years	None	0.13	0.18	0.15	0.17

Finally, Table 4.6 looks at how regime type in the country in which a group is based has impacted activity. The variable is divided into four categories, based on Polity scores. The most autocratic countries with a Polity score between -10 and -5 are coded as 0; between -4 and 0 as 1; between 1 and 5 as 2; and between 6 and 10 (most democratic) as 3. There was an insignificant difference between the impact of regime type on organizational activity and continued group existence. Groups in autocratic countries, with a Polity score between -4 and 0, were less likely to experience a decline in activity than other organizations, including groups in more autocratic and more democratic countries. However, the differences between all of the categories were quite small.

Multivariate Analyses

In order to understand the interaction between the variables discussed in the bivariate analyses above, this section identifies the conditions under which decapitation impacts group activity and examines regression analyses for both one- and two-year periods of organizational activity and organizational existence following an incident of decapitation. The model is defined as follows:

$$(1) \quad \log \frac{p(x_1,...,x_n)}{1-p(x_1,...,x_n)} = \beta_0 + \beta_1 x_1 + ... + \beta_n x_n$$

Solving for p gives

$$(2) \quad p(x_1,...,x_n) \frac{\varepsilon^{\beta_0+\beta_1 x_1+...+\beta_n x_n}}{1+\varepsilon^{\beta_0+\beta_1 x_1+...+\beta_n x_n}} = \frac{1}{1+\varepsilon^{-(\beta_0+\beta_1 x_1+...+\beta_n x_n)}}$$

Here $p(x_1,...,x_n)$ is the probability that the binary response variable equals 1.

Terrorist activity: One year after decapitation. The data first identifies which variables have an impact on the likelihood that a group will carry out activity within a one-year period after an instance of decapitation. Model 1 (Table 4.7) documents that the following coefficients are statistically significant for a group activity in a one-year period following decapitation: size, whether the leader was arrested or killed, and whether a group was separatist or right wing. Groups with between

TABLE 4.7
Impact on group activity one year postdecapitation

	Model 1	Model 2	Model 3
(Intercept)	-0.763733	0.58998	4.3816*
	(0.525837)	(0.59288)	(2.1549)
Size: 101–500	1.298962**	0.89662	1.1294*
	(0.423643)	(0.56744)	(0.4765)
Size: 501–1,000	0.962324**	2.06133**	0.9016*
	(0.355216)	(0.65974)	(0.4192)
Size: 1,001–5,000	1.389327**	1.60947*	2.279***
	(0.483611)	(0.7974)	(0.616)
Size: 5,001–10,000	1.189065**	1.29013.	0.326
	(0.440734)	(0.71754)	(0.5348)
Size: 10,000+	1.000829*	17.79169	1.0424.
	(0.503968)	(1194.92947)	(0.5888)
Islamist	0.63565	1.63376**	1.0548**
	(0.479144)	(0.60851)	(0.3807)
Left wing	0.480939	0.77805	.
	(0.439979)	(0.53207)	.
Separatist	0.818818**	1.07315*	.
	(0.296182)	(0.52174)	.
Age	-0.003312	-0.01723	.
	(0.007194)	(0.01134)	.
Right wing	-1.03859*	.	-1.3369**
	(0.413382)	.	(0.4329)
Decapitation type	-0.617823*	.	-0.8238*
	(0.290906)	.	(0.3565)
Religious	0.109262	.	.
	(0.530344)	.	.
Decapitation frequency	0.04448	.	.
	(0.061604)	.	.
Upper leadership	0.278105	.	.
	(0.316816)	.	.
Lower leadership	-0.00695	.	.
	(0.316278)	.	.
log(pop)	.	.	-0.2568*
	.	.	(0.1223)
N	339	339	249
AIC	426.01	410.78	298.39

SOURCE: National Consortium for the Study of Terrorism and Responses to Terrorism (START), University of Maryland. (2018). The Global Terrorism Database (GTD) [Data file]. Retrieved from https://www.start.umd.edu/gtd.
SIGNIF. CODES: 0 '***' 0.001 '**' 0.01 '*' 0.05 '.'

1,000 and 5,000 members were the most resilient, or least likely to cease activity in a one-year period after having their leaders removed. Killing a leader was also correlated with a cessation of activity. The regression shows that right-wing groups are more likely to fall apart after an instance of decapitation, while separatist groups were more resilient. Surprisingly, age was not significant in this analysis.

Model 2 includes all statistically significant variables from Model 1, but also includes a variable for whether a group is Islamist. Within a one-year period, groups with between 500 and 1,000 members have a lower probability of ceasing terrorist attacks, and are thus more resilient than groups with between 1,000 and 10,000 members. This is an interesting and unexpected finding. Some of the organizations in this category are older, established organizations with a bureaucratic structure and are highly grounded in their communities, which could account for their resilience. Furthermore, groups with between 5,000 and 10,000 members are targeted quite frequently and are subject to other military measures. The main point, however, is that once a group crosses a threshold of 500 members, it becomes quite strong. The largest groups, those with over 10,000 members, are by far the most resilient, which is why the nine most targeted groups, also among the largest, are excluded.

Given that terrorist groups can be classified in multiple categories, the variables are not independent. As a result, holding other variables in the model at a fixed value, Islamist groups are more likely to continue carrying out attacks than non-Islamist groups, and separatist groups are more likely to continue carrying out attacks than nonseparatist groups. The results indicate that an "Islamist, nonseparatist" group has a 0.56 lower probability of continuing terrorist attacks than a "non-Islamist, separatist" group. These findings are consistent with the predictions in Chapter 3 about the resilience of both Islamist and separatist groups. Islamist, nonseparatist groups have a 1.07 higher probability of conducting attacks one year after decapitation than the default group, while non-Islamist, separatist groups have a 1.63 higher probability of carrying out attacks. Finally, groups that are both separatist and Islamist have a 1.7 higher probability than the default group of continuing their activity after an instance of decapitation.

Model 3 includes GDP, population, and regime type. In order to account for missing observations in GDP, population, and Polity scores, ninety observations were removed. After adding these three variables, GDP and Polity are insignificant while "log of population" is significant, indicating that decapitation is more effective in countries with larger populations. According to this model, decapitation is less likely to result in a decline in activity in a one-year period for Islamist groups over non-Islamist groups, non-right-wing groups over right-wing groups, or when the organization is based in a country with a larger population. Killing a leader is more likely to result in a cessation of activity than arresting a leader. Size is also significant; however, the relationship is more complicated. The most resilient organizations have between 1,000 and 5,000 members, and this is also the most statistically significant finding. There is some variation from previous models in terms of how resilient the largest groups are, but generally

TABLE 4.8
Odds ratio for cessation of activity one year postdecapitation

	Ratio (p/(1-p))
(Intercept)	79.97
101–500 members	3.09
501–1,000 members	2.46
1,001–5,000 members	9.77
5,001–10,000 members	1.39
10,000+ members	2.84
Right wing	0.26
Decap type	0.44
Islamist	2.87
Log (pop)	0.77

SOURCE: National Consortium for the Study of Terrorism and Responses to Terrorism (START), University of Maryland. (2018). The Global Terrorism Database (GTD) [Data file]. Retrieved from https://www.start.umd.edu/gtd.

the data indicates that the largest groups will likely continue carrying out attacks after decapitation.

Table 4.8 transforms the coefficients from Model 3 into odds ratios, which can be interpreted as the odds of ceasing terrorist attacks in a one-year time period following an instance of decapitation for specific variables, while holding all other independent variables constant. According to the model, the odds of an Islamist group carrying out attacks in the year following an instance of decapitation were 2.87 times higher than those of a non-Islamist group. The odds that a group with between 100 and 500 members will cease activity in a one-year period after an instance of decapitation are 3.09 times greater than those for groups with fewer than 100 members. The odds that the largest groups, those with over 10,000 members, will cease activity are 2.84 times greater than those for groups with between 5,000 and 10,000. Finally, the odds that killing a leader will result in the cessation of activity are 0.44 times greater than those for arresting a leader. In sum, the data indicates that decapitation has the lowest probability of bringing about the cessation of terrorist activity under the following conditions: groups with between 1,000 and 5,000 members, Islamist groups, left-wing groups, groups in which the leader was arrested (as opposed to killed), and organizations in countries with a greater population. A larger Islamist group has the highest odds of withstanding attacks on its leadership.

Terrorist activity. Two years after decapitation. A second set of logistic regression analyses (Table 4.9) is conducted to evaluate whether a group carried out activity in the second year after an instance of decapitation. The variable is coded

TABLE 4.9
Impact on group activity two years postdecapitation

	Model 1	Model 2
(Intercept)	-0.85757**	-1.730155**
	(0.29746)	(0.609582)
Size: 101–500	1.04824*	1.353004**
	(0.40786)	(0.476831)
Size: 501–1,000	0.81019*	0.843065*
	(0.35076)	(0.430101)
Size: 1,001–5,000	1.24548**	2.004598***
	(0.45327)	(0.574508)
Size: 5,001–10,000	1.22971**	0.978039
	(0.4203)	(0.528199)
Size: 10,000+	0.77835	1.283184*
	(0.48245)	(0.579544)
Islamist	0.5207	1.68469***
	(0.27239)	(0.467755)
Decapitation type	-0.58255*	-0.634979.
	(0.27525)	(0.337587)
Upper Leadership	0.59809*	.
	(0.29312)	.
Lower leadership	0.05125	.
	(0.30153)	.
Separatist	0.72123**	.
	(0.26159)	.
Right wing	-0.8002*	.
	(0.37129)	.
Left wing	.	0.876125*
	.	(0.412481)
Polity (-5,0)	.	1.191992*
	.	(0.520129)
Polity (0,5)	.	-0.212689
	.	(0.565443)
Polity (5,10)	.	0.727766.
	.	(0.385676)
Age	.	-0.013762
	.	(0.008482)
N	339	339
AIC	443.84	318.33

SOURCE: National Consortium for the Study of Terrorism and Responses to Terrorism (START), University of Maryland. (2018). The Global Terrorism Database (GTD) [Data file]. Retrieved from https://www.start.umd.edu/gtd.
SIGNIF. CODES: 0 '***' 0.001 '**' 0.01 '*' 0.05 '.'

as 0 if a group carried out no terrorist attacks in the second year after an instance of decapitation, and coded as 1 if a group carried out activity. If a group carried out activity in the first year after an instance of decapitation, but not in the second year, the observation would be coded as 0, which occurred in 46 instances for 29 groups. In these cases, while an organization might conduct an attack immediately after losing a leader to signal to the public and governments that it has not been weakened, over time it may experience a diminished organizational capacity. Decapitation could have a delayed effect in which a group may experience a temporary decline in activity while the organization regroups and reorganizes, but then continues activity. There were 39 instances of decapitation against 22 organizations, in which there were no attacks in the year following an instance of decapitation, but then the organization resumed activity. A two-year period of inactivity is a restrictive criterion as it sets a much higher bar for success. In some cases, a one-year period of inactivity could be seen as a counterterrorism success. However, there are many instances in which a group carried out no attacks in a one-year period and then resumed attacks, in some cases deadlier and more frequent.

In Model 1, the coefficients for decapitation type, organizational type, and leadership rank are statistically significant. This data shows that after two years, larger groups are more likely to carry out attacks than smaller organizations. Groups with between 500 and 1,000 members have a slightly lower probability of resuming attacks than groups with between 100 and 500 members. Separatist groups are more resilient than nonseparatist groups, Islamist groups are more resilient than non-Islamist organizations, and right-wing groups are more vulnerable to a decline in activity than non-right-wing groups. Leadership rank is also significant; targeting the leadership's upper echelon as opposed to the top leader is more likely to result in the continuation of activity. Finally, a group has a higher probability of not conducting attacks in a two-year period if the leader is killed.

Model 2 includes variables for GDP, population, and Polity scores, and the results document that left-wing and Islamist groups are more resilient to leadership targeting. Decapitation type is also significant. The death of a leader is more likely to result in a cessation of attacks than an arrest. Regime type is significant as well. Compared to the most autocratic states, organizations in states with a higher Polity score are more to resilient to decapitation; groups in autocratic states are more susceptible to leadership targeting. Age is not significant in this model.

Group existence. Finally, logistic regression analysis was also conducted using group existence as a dependent variable in order to determine when decapitation was likely to result in organizational "death"—one and two years after targeting. Group existence is by far the most restrictive metric by which to evaluate counterterrorism measures. Groups can still exist but suffer a decline in attacks, and this is often treated as counterterrorism success. In many cases, as indicated above, groups can stop carrying out attacks and then resume activity, in some cases becoming stronger. However, groups do end and fall apart, and there is a body of literature dedicated to understanding organizational death.[3] In order to capture the relationship between group existence and decapitation, analysis was done on a one- and two-year period of "group existence." Overall, the results were fairly consistent with the analyses on group activity, but age was significant in these models, with younger groups more likely to fall apart than older groups. Size was also significant; groups with between 500 and 10,000 members had a lower probability of falling apart in a one-year period. Islamist groups and separatist groups were also less likely to "die" after decapitation. The results were largely unchanged when adding GDP, Polity, and population, yet whether a group was separatist was no longer significant in this model. The results were similar for group existence two years after decapitation as well: younger groups, smaller groups, and non-Islamist groups were more likely to fall apart.

Impact of Decapitation on Attack Frequency

The previous section evaluated the conditions under which decapitated groups would terminate their activity. It is also important to determine whether decapitation itself has an impact on the frequency with which groups carry out terrorist attacks. This section will utilize time series data on terrorist attacks in determining whether decapitation resulted in a change in attack frequency. This analysis compares attack frequency for the control group (either nondecapitated or pre-decapitation) to the experiment group (after decapitation). In examining changes in the frequency of terrorist attacks, a transition matrix analysis was chosen over a traditional multivariate time series analysis for three primary reasons. First, organizations in the dataset have different start years, different end years, and varying duration, and traditional time series or panel data models require consistency in years examined. Second, some groups are targeted infrequently and data exists for only a few years. Third, a transition matrix can capture the probability of changing states of activity. For example, if the experiment group has higher p_{13} than the control group, then it is possible to assume that decapitation results in more frequent attacks.

A chi-square test for Markov chain analysis was calculated to determine whether there is a statistically significant difference between the transition matrix of the control group and the experiment group. The transition matrix provides the probability of transitions from one state to another. There are three activity states to account for the number of attacks an organization carries out each year: decreasing, flat, and increasing. Table 4.10 is a transition matrix in which p_{13} refers to the probability that a group's attacks will increase given a decrease the year

TABLE 4.10
Transition matrix on attack frequency after decapitation

Phase 0 \ Phase 1	Decreasing	Flat	Increasing
Decreasing	P_{11}	P_{12}	P_{13}
Flat	P_{21}	P_{22}	P_{23}
Increasing	P_{31}	P_{32}	P_{33}

before. In other words, the test calculates the probability that a group will transition from state 1 (decreasing) to state 3 (increasing).

Much of the extant work on leadership targeting finds that it is an effective means by which to weaken a terrorist organization. Recent quantitative studies have found that it shortens the life span and hinders the operational efficiency of terrorist groups. Individual studies of leadership targeting have found that it decreases the frequency of attacks in some cases[4] but increases them in others.[5] Price has found that it increases the mortality rate of terrorist groups, while Johnston found a decrease in the frequency of attacks after decapitation. The results from the transition matrix indicate that under certain situations decapitation reduces the likelihood that groups will experience an increase in attacks. First, it is critical to look at changes in the frequency of attacks carried out by both decapitated and nondecapitated groups. Second, the probability of attacks increasing or decreasing after a group experiences decapitation depends on a group's prior level of activity. Finally, the effect of decapitation can also depend upon the characteristics of the organization itself. While the data as a whole might show a reduction in the frequency of attacks, in some cases it results in a significant increase.

Time series data on individual organizations highlights this point. It is critical to understand when decapitation might result in an increase or a decrease in the frequency of attacks. If certain organizations are not only resilient but emboldened by decapitation, then it would not be a prudent counterterrorism strategy. As demonstrated in the regression analysis, the type of organizations currently targeted by the United States and other nations—Islamist, religious, large, or separatist—tend to be resilient and, in many cases, more active after decapitation. The transition matrix analyses provide data on specific conditions under which decapitation affects the frequency of attacks: organizational type, size, and prior amount of activity. Overall, data from the transition matrix analysis indicates that decapitation does not significantly hinder the operational capacity of organizations, and in certain cases, may increase the frequency of attacks.

TABLE 4.11
Change in attack frequency for targeted groups, before and after decapitation

A. TARGETED GROUP BEFORE DECAPITATION

	Decreasing	Flat	Increasing
Decreasing	0.2246	0.2415	0.5339
Flat	0.0261	0.8129	0.1610
Increasing	0.5786	0.0712	0.3501

B. TARGETED GROUP AFTER DECAPITATION

	Decreasing	Flat	Increasing
Decreasing	0.2862	0.3292	0.3846
Flat	0.0916	0.7125	0.1959
Increasing	0.6274	0.0837	0.2890

SOURCE: National Consortium for the Study of Terrorism and Responses to Terrorism (START), University of Maryland. (2018). The Global Terrorism Database (GTD) [Data file]. Retrieved from https://www.start.umd.edu/gtd.

I will first compare changes in the frequency of terrorist attacks for all decapitated groups before and after experiencing an instance of decapitation. Table 4.11 shows the probability that groups will experience an increase, a decrease, or no change in the number of attacks. After rescaling the percentages into frequency, the chi-square p-value in comparing the two matrices is almost 0, which means the pattern of activity before and after decapitation is significantly different. The transition matrix reveals generally that targeted groups are less likely to experience an increase in attack frequency than groups that have not yet experienced the targeting of their leadership. However, organizations in the predecapitation control group, which carried out attacks for three continuous years with fewer attacks in the second year than the first, have a 0.2246 probability of a reduction in attacks, a 0.2415 probability of carrying out the same number of attacks, and a 0.5339 probability of increasing the number of attacks. For the experiment group that had a flat rate of attacks (that is, no change) in the three years prior to an instance of targeting, decapitation results in a small probability that attack frequency will increase. Finally, for groups that had an increasing rate of attacks in the years prior, decapitation slightly reduced the probability that its attacks will increase. The probability that decapitation will result in an increase or decrease is thus impacted by the prior level of activity.

To determine whether decapitation is actually an effective counterterrorism policy, it is essential to compare changes in the frequency of attacks for groups that have experienced decapitation and those that have not. Table 4.12 compares the matrices for the control group (nondecapitated) to the experiment group (decapitated). The chi-square p-value between matrix A and B is almost 0, meaning that the null hypothesis, that the two matrices are similar, can be rejected. Further, the p-value for matrix A and matrix C is also almost 0, indicating that the pattern of activity between nondecapitated groups and decapitated groups, after their first decapitation, is significantly different. The data shows that regardless of whether groups have an increasing or decreasing rate of attacks, targeted groups, both before and after decapitation, have a higher probability than nontargeted groups of increasing their attacks. However, the difference in probabilities between the control group and the experiment group after decapitation is quite small, indicating that decapitation does not seem to have much effect on the attack frequency of a group in either direction. These findings challenge extant work arguing that decapitation results in a decline in terrorist attacks, suggesting instead that it does not result in a decrease in activity, and in some cases can actually lead to an increase in the frequency of terrorist attacks.

Extant research on decapitation has found that it results in a decline in the frequency of attacks over time, yet these studies do not compare the activity of targeted and nontargeted groups. The matrix analyses reveal that the nondecapitated experiment group has a higher probability of an increase in attacks than the

TABLE 4.12

Change in attack frequency between nontargeted and targeted groups

A. CONTROL GROUP (NOT DECAPITATED)

	Decreasing	Flat	Increasing
Decreasing	0.3139	0.3291	0.3570
Flat	0.0473	0.7461	0.2066
Increasing	0.6493	0.0640	0.2867

B. EXPERIMENT GROUP 1 (DECAPITATED, BUT BEFORE FIRST DECAPITATION):

	Decreasing	Flat	Increasing
Decreasing	0.2246	0.2415	0.5339
Flat	0.0261	0.8129	0.1610
Increasing	0.5786	0.0712	0.3501

C. EXPERIMENT GROUP 2 (DECAPITATED, AND AFTER FIRST DECAPITATION)

	Decreasing	Flat	Increasing
Decreasing	0.2862	0.3292	0.3846
Flat	0.0916	0.7125	0.1959
Increasing	0.6274	0.0837	0.2890

SOURCE: National Consortium for the Study of Terrorism and Responses to Terrorism (START), University of Maryland. (2018). The Global Terrorism Database (GTD) [Data file]. Retrieved from https://www.start.umd.edu/gtd.

control group. This is intuitive given that counterterrorism polices tend to be focused on the most active groups. The decapitated experiment group also has a higher probability of increasing attacks than the control group, indicating that overall, decapitation is actually a counterproductive strategy; if it were effective, the decapitated experiment group would have a significantly lower probability of increasing their attacks than the nondecapitated experiment groups, which is not the case. In fact, groups that had a flat rate of attacks two years prior to decapitation experienced an increase in attacks after decapitation. However, this could be due, in part, to the fact that the matrix analysis looks only at the first instance of decapitation, and group resilience could possibly strengthen over time.

These mixed results suggest that decapitation is not as successful as is commonly assumed. Looking at specific variables might provide a more precise understanding of when targeting might be more or less likely to result in an increase or a decline in activity.

Given that results from the logistic regression analysis reveal that larger, Islamist, separatist, or older groups are the most resilient to targeting, I also examine transition matrices for group type and size. Age was not included as an independent variable in this analysis because a transition matrix examines the change in status over a period of time, and "age" measures a specific point in time. (See Appendix, Table A1.) Decapitation should be unlikely to result in a significant change or increase in attacks for these groups. First, the findings on organizational size reveal that for the largest groups (those with over 1,000 members), compared to nondecapitated groups, decapitated groups have a higher probability of experiencing an increase in attack frequency. This was true for groups that had both increasing and decreasing rates of attacks, but not for groups that had a flat rate of attacks. Comparing groups before and after decapitation, there is a very slight decline in the number of attacks after decapitation. This could be due to other variables, however, particularly given that decapitated organizations often experience other counterterrorist measures simultaneously. This finding suggests that decapitation has an adverse effect and increases attack frequency for the largest groups.

Islamist groups, which were more resilient to targeting, should also be more likely to experience an increase in attack frequency. (See Appendix, Table A2.) Compared to nontargeted groups, targeted Islamist groups, both before and after decapitation, have a considerably higher probability of experiencing an increase in attacks and a lower probability of a decline in attacks. However, there was no statistical difference between the control group and the experiment group after decapitation, though there was a statistically different finding between the control group and the predecapitation group, indicating that Islamist groups selected for targeting by counterterrorism forces were more active to begin with. There was also a significant difference between the experiment groups, which suggests that depending on the prior level of activity, decapitation resulted in more attacks in some cases and fewer attacks in others. Overall, this data suggests that targeted Islamist groups are more likely to increase activity than nondecapitated groups.

A similar trend exists for separatist groups. (See Appendix, Table A3.) All of the results were statistically significant and show that the experiment group has a higher probability of increasing activity than the control groups. The difference in attacks between the two experiment groups is small enough to be negligible, except for groups that have a flat rate of attacks prior to decapitation. In those cases, decapitation results in a higher probability that attacks will increase. This is even more significant given that those same groups have a lower probability of increasing attacks than the control group, prior to decapitation. Overall, the data suggests that decapitation does not significantly increase the probability that separatist groups will experience a decline in attacks, and the opposite is true in certain instances.

Overall, the time series data on leadership decapitation and attack frequency suggests that in some cases, groups can experience a slight reduction in activity following decapitation. These trends are due to multiple factors. First, the level of prior activity—whether a group's attacks prior to decapitation were increasing, decreasing, or flat—matters. Second, the group's size and type also influence attack frequency over time. These findings suggest that the results regarding the efficacy of decapitation are much more nuanced than assumed in the extant literature on targeting and provide some evidence for the fact that targeting can result in even more active organizations. The following section will look at attack frequency for the largest nine groups in the dataset.

The Largest Terrorist Groups

There are a number of terrorist organizations that conduct far more terrorist attacks than others. These include AQAP, al-Shabaab, ETA, Boko Haram, the PKK, the LTTE, the NPA, the Taliban, and the TTP. In analyzing the data on organizational activity and existence, the nine most active groups were removed from the dataset so as not to bias the statistical results. Although not in all cases, these groups also tend to be targeted more frequently. They are the largest, carry out more attacks than other organizations, and are all still currently active. As a result, their inclusion in the logistic regression could result in less robust findings. For example, al-Qaeda and all of its affiliates was targeted 287 times between 1995 and 2016 and carried out an average of 1,664 attacks from 1998 to 2014. The Taliban is even more active, with a total of 5,502 attacks between 1995 and 2015 and 24 cases of leadership targeting. Al-Shabaab has not been targeted as frequently as other organizations (only twice), but carried out 1,730 attacks between 2008 and 2014.

In this section, time series data is used to assess the frequency of attacks over time with a focus on the time period just following an instance of decapitation. The following graphs plot the number of attacks over time, with the vertical lines representing years in which a group was targeted. (See Appendix, Figure A1, for graphs that plot time series analyses on decapitation and organizational activity for each of the nine organizations.) I will look at each organization in turn.

Five organizations generally saw an escalation in activity after decapitation. These findings are consistent with the regression analysis presented above, particularly since most of these organizations are larger, Islamist and/or separatist, and older. The data shows that despite a slight decline in 2012, AQAP experienced an increase in attacks after decapitation. Al-Shabaab saw an abrupt increase in attacks two years after it experienced two decapitations in 2012. Boko Haram experienced an immediate decline following decapitation but an even larger increase in the year following. The NPA saw a large decline in attacks after its first decapitation in 1990, but then in 2010, after the majority of its leaders were targeted, its attacks increased from about 50 to over 250 in a two-year time period. The Taliban's trends are the most consistent; the group has seen a steady increase in activity since 2000, when targeting efforts began. In 2010 it suffered 21 instances of decapitation, and while there was an initial decline in activity, from 306 attacks in 2010 to 215 in 2011, the group carried out 796 attacks in 2012 after losing seven more leaders. Of all the organizations studied, the Taliban seems most unaffected, and in fact, more emboldened after sustained attacks on its leadership.

The results were more variable for the remainder of the organizations. TTP saw very little change in the frequency of its attacks after experiencing the loss of its leaders. The arrest of Abdullah Öcalan, leader of the PKK, in 1994 is often treated as a classic example of a successful decapitation effort. There was a considerable drop in activity after the arrest, and while the group's activity never returned to its peak level of the early 1990s, it was still active. The PKK conducted 36 attacks in 1999 and then fewer than five attacks per year over the next four years. But beginning in 2004, it started carrying out more attacks, provoking another round of targeting efforts that resumed in 2007. Despite a ceasefire in March 2013, attacks continued to increase through 2014.[6] While the organization then underwent a drop in its activity, the ceasefire officially ended in July 2015 and activity has again increased with the PKK now targeted as part of a government crackdown.[7]

The LTTE underwent two periods of decapitation, in the 1990s and after 2005. Between 1995 and 1997, it lost five leaders and experienced an increase in attacks, followed by a general decline, with a few smaller increases until 2001. After 2001, the group underwent the largest increase in attacks in its history, from nearly 0 to almost 150. After this point, the Sri Lankan government began a steady campaign of leadership targeting, leading to a consistent and significant decline in attacks and culminating in the death of the LTTE's founder and top leader, Velupillai Prabhakaran, in May 2009.

The demise of the LTTE has often been attributed to the killing of Prabhakaran by Sri Lankan military forces.[8] However, decapitation was not the key factor. Its defeat can be attributed to major military offensives carried out by the Sri Lankan Army, the arrests of thousands of suspected LTTE soldiers, and the displacement of large numbers of the Sri Lankan Tamil population.[9] The Sri Lankan government's success in defeating the LTTE can be traced to capturing territory in the Northern and Eastern Provinces and denying the group a local base of support through large-scale displacement. This case would seem to be an outlier to the findings presented thus far. The LTTE was a large organization, over twenty years old, and separatist—all indicators that it would be resilient to leadership decapitation. However, had the Sri Lankan government relied exclusively on decapitation, it would have failed in defeating the LTTE. Territorial defeat and attacks on the local community seriously destabilized the organization.

Finally, ETA has experienced a large number of leadership attacks: 57 between 1989 and 2014. After losing two leaders in 1989, the group underwent a decline in attacks, from a high of about 120 attacks a year to almost 0. There were periods in which ETA experienced an increase in attacks after decapitation, but the decline was more frequent and more dramatic. These findings were surprising given that ETA is an old, large, separatist group, which according to the data should be more resilient. While there is variance in the time series of these nine organizations, all of them remained active after decapitation, which in many cases emboldened them and increased their activity.

Impact of Decapitation on Organizational Survival

Decapitation can also affect a group's life span or its mortality/survival rate. While the above statistical tests focus on an organization's activity, this final section will examine organizational life span using a hazard analysis. The survival model is defined as

$$(1) \quad S(t) = P(T > t)$$

The survival function is the probability that the time of death (T) is greater than some specified time t. It is composed of (1) the hazard function (how the risk of death per unit of time changes over time at baseline covariates) and (2) the effect parameters (how the hazard varies in response to the covariates). The Cox-proportional hazard function is defined as:

$$(2) \quad h_i(t) = h_0(t) exp\{\beta_1 x_{i1} + ... + \beta_n x_{in}\} f$$

The model estimates the parameter β to show how explanatory variables influence the hazard rate. The point at which an organization begins, the end or censored time point, and binary event variables are used to determine the life span of each group. Two types of survival analyses were conducted. Type 1 uses the year the organization formed as the starting point, and the year it ended as the end point. Type 2 uses the year the organization carried out its first attack as the starting point, and the year it carried out its last recorded attack as the end point. If the organization is still active in 2012 (when the dataset ends), it is treated as a censored observation. For example, if an active group started carrying out attacks in 1990, and its last reported attack was in 2012, then its life span is [1990, 2012+]. If an inactive group started in 2000, and its last reported attack was in 2010, then its life span is [2000, 2010].

I first examine whether decapitation has an overall effect on a group's survival rate. Figure 4.6 shows the comparison of a survival rate curve between decapitated groups and a nondecapitated group. The graph indicates that earlier in a group's life span, a decapitated group has a higher survival rate than a nondecapitated one. However, this difference becomes smaller over time, up to a point at which there is very little difference in the survival rate of decapitated and nondecapitated organizations. In fact, whether the organization is decapitated does not have a statistically significant influence on the overall hazard rate. This finding was true for both Type 1 and Type 2 survival analysis. Advocates for targeting as a counterterrorism strategy frequently argue that decapitation shortens a group's life span, yet the data is inconclusive. For example, Bryan Price finds that decapitation increases a group's mortality rate, effectively reducing its survival rate. He writes, "Regardless of how I conceptualized the effect of decapitation, terrorist groups that experienced the loss of a leader had higher mortality rates than those that did not. Depending on how I modeled the effect of decapitation, terrorist groups were 3.6 to 6.7 times more likely to end than those that did not experience decapitation."[10] It is important to explore why these analyses resulted in such different results.

These divergent findings are largely a function of the differences in data. All of the extant quantitative analyses of leadership targeting analyze a different set of cases with different criteria for inclusion. First, some datasets look only at the top leaders; others (including my own) also incorporate members of the upper

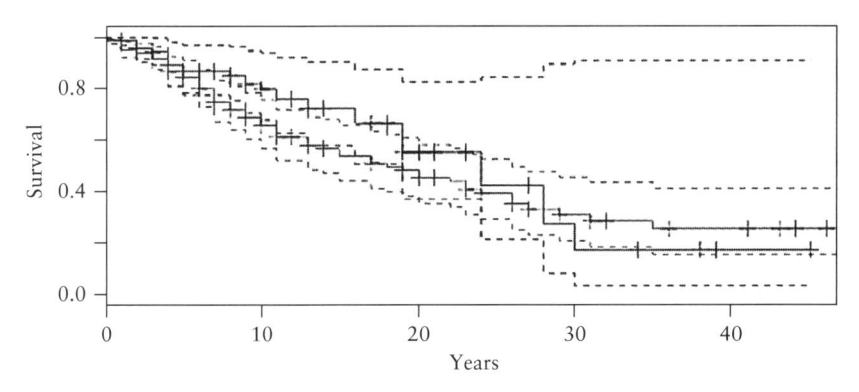

FIGURE 4.6 Survival rate of decapitated and nondecapitated organizations

echelon. Second, some datasets use a different threshold of group activity as a benchmark for inclusion and exclude the weakest and smallest organizations, while others have no threshold. Third, datasets such as Johnston's focus specifically on insurgent organizations in specific geographic areas. Fourth, the time period under examination is different. For example, much of the data only codes cases of targeting through 2008, while the data for this project ends in 2016. This is a significant year in that the election of President Obama resulted in a large increase in the use of special operation forces and drones in the targeting of a terrorist group's leadership, creating a considerable number of cases that would not be included in this data. Finally, and perhaps most significantly, targeting itself is a category that is open to much interpretation. In the dataset for this study, I included only instances in which a leader was arrested or killed by a state's forces. Price includes three other means by which groups lost a leader: they were expelled from their group or died of natural causes or accidents, they resigned from their leadership position; or they accepted a ceasefire agreement with the government and formally entered the political process.[11] The nature of the data collection process can thus result in a significantly different set of cases and accordingly different results.

The data in Table 4.13 evaluates the survival rate for the period between a group's formation and its end. The numeric variables for the data in this model were normalized by logarithmic transformation. The data indicates that a group's survival rate was impacted by its size, type, the GDP of its host country, and the average number of attacks and injuries it carried out. It also suggests that the largest organizations have a 30 percent lower hazard (and thus higher survival rate) than smaller organizations. Separatist groups, religious groups, and left-wing groups also have a lower hazard rate. Decapitation was not significant in the sur-

TABLE 4.13
Impact of decapitation on group survival

	Model 1	Model 2
Decap	0.006	0.041
	(0.204)	(0.210)
Number attacks	0.186★	0.153★
	(0.072)	(0.066)
Injuries	0.130★★★	-0.198★★★
	(0.040)	(0.042)
Separatist	0.897★★★	-0.851★★★
	(0.227)	(0.231)
Size: 101–500	-0.222	.
	(0.311)	
Size: 501–1,000	0.994★★★	.
	(0.291)	
Size: 1,001–5,000	-0.662★	.
	(0.309)	
Size: 5,0001–10,000	-0.673★	.
	(0.320)	
Size: 10,000+	-1.091★★	.
	(0.396)	
Religious	-0.805★★	.
	(0.301)	
Left-wing	-0.388	.
	(0.245)	
Population	.	-0.192★★
		(0.071)
GDP	.	0.128.
		(0.076)

SOURCE: National Consortium for the Study of Terrorism and Responses to Terrorism (START), University of Maryland. (2018). The Global Terrorism Database (GTD) [Data file]. Retrieved from https://www.start.umd.edu/gtd.
SIGNIF. CODES: 0 '★★★' 0.001 '★★' 0.01 '★' 0.05 '.'

vival analysis, and as a result, the dataset was split into decapitated and nondecapitated subsets, with separate models for each in order to provide a more granular analysis. The data reveals that the survival of decapitated organizations is influenced by a group's average number of injuries, a measure of their ability to inflict damage. The higher the average number of injuries, the higher the survival rate. The survival rate of nondecapitated organizations is influenced by the average number of attacks and fatalities. The higher the average number of attacks, the higher the hazard rate.

Introducing GDP and population into Model 2 reveals that organizations in countries with a higher GDP have a higher hazard rate, while those in a country with a higher population have a lower hazard rate. The survival rate of a decapitated organization is also influenced by the average number of injuries.

The higher the average number of injuries, the lower the hazard rate, and the higher the average number of attacks, the higher the hazard rate. However, whether the organization is decapitated does not have significant influence on hazard rate. Looking at the prior level of activity for decapitated and nondecapitated groups in more detail provides a different story of life span and a statistically significant result.

The above data evaluates the life span of an organization as a function of group existence, with its start date as the date that the group was first formed. I also look at the mortality rate of groups between their first and last recorded attacks. These findings are nearly identical. Whether a group was decapitated was not significant; the variables that affect survival were nearly the same as the model that evaluated organizational existence. Separatist groups, religious groups, and organizations in countries with a higher GDP have a lower hazard rate, while those in a country with a higher population have a higher hazard rate. Finally, groups with a higher number of average attacks have a higher hazard rate.

If targeting the leadership of terrorist organizations shortens a group's life span, then it would seem to be an effective way of weakening organizations. However, the data in this study shows that decapitation does not have a statistically significant influence on the survival rate or life span of terrorist organizations. Even when evaluating separate models for decapitated and nondecapitated organizations, the survival rates of the two groups are so similar as to not be significant. Examining specific variables provides a more detailed story—a group's size, type, prior level of activity, GDP, and population all impacted its overall hazard rate. Separatist groups, Islamist groups, and larger groups all have a higher survival rate and should be harder to weaken through targeting efforts. In addition, organizations in countries with higher GDP and more autocratic governments had a higher hazard rate, suggesting that perhaps democracies are constrained in their counterterrorism efforts, or that countries with more resources were better able to weaken terrorist organizations.

Finally, groups that carry out more attacks have a higher hazard rate while groups that cause a higher number of deaths have a lower hazard rate. These findings could suggest that counterterrorism forces believe that more active groups require stronger countereffort, resulting in a higher hazard rate. Alternatively, the most active groups may not be carrying out the most lethal or damaging attacks, and could be weaker and easier to destabilize. This finding is consistent with the result that organizations conducting very deadly attacks could be stronger and thus harder to weaken in the long run. Overall, the data suggests that the organizations against which decapitation is not likely to be effective tend to have a higher survival rate overall, and that decapitation does not impact organizational life span.

Conclusion

The data collected for this book suggests that overall, decapitation is not an effective counterterrorism strategy. It does not reduce a group's life span, likelihood of collapse, or frequency of attacks, and in certain cases actually increases a group's activity. It is important to acknowledge that in some cases decapitation does work. However, it is unlikely to have much effect, and has the potential for adverse consequences when used against organizations such as ISIS, al-Qaeda, and Hamas—groups that the United States and other nations are currently targeting. More specifically, targeting is unlikely to result in the significant weakening of larger groups, religious groups, separatist groups, and specifically Islamist groups. In some cases, right-wing groups were also more resistant to targeting efforts. Furthermore, while age did not have an effect on group activity in the multivariate analyses, when looking at bivariate analyses, decapitation resulted in a decline in activity in nearly all of the youngest groups. The overall takeaway is that targeting is not likely to result in a significant decline and may increase the activity of a great number of organizations.

This chapter first examined whether groups failed to carry out terrorist attacks or collapsed after decapitation. The analyses on organizational activity and group existence reveal that larger organizations (with the largest being the most resilient) are more likely to continue carrying out activity and less likely to fall apart after targeting. In some cases, the longer-term effect of size on decapitation is stronger. Islamist and separatist groups are also less likely to experience a cessation of activity in both one- and two-year periods after decapitation. Right-wing groups are more susceptible to targeting, and left-wing groups are more resilient. Finally, organizations in countries with a larger population are also less likely to be negatively impacted by targeted attacks.

The data was also analyzed in order to determine whether decapitation had an impact on the frequency of attacks. A transition matrix analysis revealed that decapitated groups have a higher probability of increasing activity than nondecapitated groups, indicating that, overall, decapitation can be a counterproductive strategy. The probability of an increase or decline in activity after decapitation depends on a group's prior level of activity. Finally, the data as a whole might show a reduction in the frequency of attacks, but in some cases it shows a significant increase in the number of attacks, and that the characteristics of the group targeted matter. Islamist, large, or separatist groups tend to be more active after decapitation.

Finally, a survival analysis shows that decapitation does not negatively impact a group's life span. This is an important finding that challenges much of the current literature on targeting and its ability to hasten a group's demise.[12] The data indicates that a group's overall survival rate was impacted by its size and type, the GDP and regime type of the host country, and the average number of attacks and injuries it carried out. For example, the largest organizations have a 30 percent lower hazard rate than smaller organizations. Separatist groups, religious groups, and left-wing groups also have a lower hazard rate. In addition, organizations in countries with higher GDP and more autocratic systems of government had a higher hazard rate. However, decapitation was not significant in the model. Looking at decapitated and nondecapitated organizations reveals that the life span of decapitated organizations was influenced by the average number of injuries carried out by each group. In other words, their ability to inflict damage has an effect on their resilience. The higher the average number of injuries, the higher the survival rate. Essentially, the data suggests that the organizations against which decapitation is not likely to be effective tend to have a higher survival rate overall, and that decapitation does not impact that organizational life span.

The findings in this chapter are consistent with the theoretical explanations developed in Chapters 2 and 3. First, as an organization becomes larger, and in some cases, older, it is much more likely to withstand attacks on its leadership. All organizations need to replenish both members and leaders, and larger organizations should have developed the networks and support systems necessary for this. This argument is consistent with the organizational literature on bureaucratic organizations.[13] As an organization ages and grows in size, it is also more likely to become bureaucratized and develop a division of labor based on specialization.[14] It should be easier for organizations with a higher degree of specialization to replace leadership. This dynamic can be seen in the cases of Hamas, al-Qaeda, and ISIS. The model of the firm may also be useful in understanding the strength of terrorist organizations. Early in its creation, a firm should have a higher likelihood of falling apart. These variables suggest that the dynamic nature of organizations is essential to understanding the impact of decapitation and can provide a richer basis for social network models of organizational strength and weakness.

Second, organizational typology is an important predictor across all measures of efficacy for leadership targeting. Islamist and separatist groups are highly resilient, as are left-wing organizations to a slightly lesser degree. The susceptibility of right-wing organizations was more variable, resilient in some models and not in others. These results are consistent with the theory of resilience and the hypotheses developed in the two previous chapters. If communal support is an important explanatory factor in the resilience of groups to targeting efforts, then it is understandable that separatist groups would be resilient. These organizations are highly grounded in their local communities, more so than other types of organizations, an intuition supported by public opinion polls examined in later chapters. Many Islamist groups also represent the religious beliefs of local communities. There is much variation in the interpretation of religious beliefs and wide variation in support of a group's tactics, but for many of these groups, articulation of the group's beliefs does not depend upon leadership. This is apparent in the case of Hamas and al-Qaeda and is discussed in the next three chapters.

Three implications can be derived from these findings on organizational typology. First, the charismatic theory of leadership is insufficient to account for these findings. If religious and separatist organizations are more likely to have a charismatic leader, which is commonly predicted, they should be more likely to fall apart when the charismatic leader is removed. Islamist groups and separatist groups were the most resilient, given all measures of efficacy. Second, the significance of organizational typology also signals an important relationship between organizational structure and a group's susceptibility to decapitation. I argue that the resilience of religious and separatist organizations can be attributed in part to the fact that many of these groups are larger. Third, it is frequently assumed that religious and separatist organizations are more decentralized in structure, while ideological organizations are more hierarchical.[15] The literature on social network analysis suggests that decentralized organizations are less likely to suffer setbacks than hierarchically structured organizations. Initial findings support this claim. I argue that the weight of key organizational variables provides a more detailed understanding of organizational structure and can account for more variability in the success of decapitation.

The results of this chapter suggest that while decapitation is effective in some cases, it does not result in a decline in activity by many of the most dangerous and lethal organizations. Decapitation is also likely to result in an increase in attacks in many of the largest organizations, and in Islamist and separatist groups as well. Further, it does not hasten a group's demise by increasing their mortality rate. In fact, for organizations carrying out the most attacks, it can actually reduce the group's hazard rate.

The next three chapters will examine the impact of decapitation on Hamas, al-Qaeda, and the Shining Path. The conclusion will examine the recent targeting campaign waged against ISIS.

5

Hamas

Bureaucracy, Social Services, and Local Support

Hamas has been subject to nearly thirty years of leadership targeting. Both scholars and policy analysts have argued that the capture and killing of terrorist leaders have weakened Palestinian terrorist organizations and curtailed violence.[1] While repeated strikes against Hamas's leadership have affected its ability to carry out attacks, leadership decapitation has led neither to the collapse nor to a substantial weakening of the organization. While the lethality of attacks has declined over time, the number of attacks has increased. In some cases this had adverse consequences, increasing the organization's legitimacy within its local community, making Hamas more effective and even more likely to resist a policy of leadership targeting. Given the finding that larger, Islamist, and separatist groups tend to be more resilient to leadership targeting efforts, decapitation should not result in the destabilization of Hamas.[2]

This chapter examines Israeli attempts to capture or kill Hamas leaders from 1988 to 2014. It begins by looking at changes in the frequency and lethality of both conventional and suicide attacks in order to determine whether leadership targeting has affected Hamas's operational capacity. It then examines why decapitation has not resulted in Hamas's decline. First, Hamas's bureaucratic hierarchy has increased the group's organizational stability and its ability to withstand leadership attacks. Second, the high degree of Palestinian support for Hamas has increased not only its strength and resilience to decapitation, but also its legitimacy. The data shows that Palestinian support has increased over time, making Hamas even more resilient to leadership attacks. Finally, ideology is a critical factor; Hamas is both a separatist and a religious organization, which also plays a role in its ability to withstand repeated attacks on its leadership.

This case is a good test of the theory for three reasons. First, while Hamas is an example of an unsuccessful attempt at group decline through decapitation, the case can be disaggregated in multiple ways, allowing for more variation on the dependent variable. In some instances of decapitation, the organization was temporarily weakened, yet in others the organization became stronger, more active, and gained a great deal of public sympathy and support. Through a qualitative analysis, it is possible to evaluate the ebb and flow of shifts in activity. As a result, this chapter provides a way to understand why Hamas was resistant to overall efforts at decapitation, but also to understand how it adapted to and changed in response to leadership targeting. Second, the case occurs over a long period of time. This allows for variation in the independent variables over time. As Hamas experienced the targeting of its leadership, it adjusted in important ways that increased and decreased its resilience to decapitation. Finally, this is a case where the government had good intelligence and long-standing surveillance deep within the opponent's territory. This counterterrorism intelligence should make decapitation even more likely to result in organizational weakening, and is thus a hard test for the book.

This chapter proceeds in five parts. First, I analyze the literature on leadership targeting against Hamas. Second, I present a history of Hamas and discuss some key decapitation efforts against it. Third, I discuss the data used in this study and evaluate changes in the frequency and lethality of Hamas's attacks over time. Fourth, I look at how Hamas has adapted in response to key cases of leadership targeting. Finally, I examine how bureaucratization, communal support, and ideology can explain Hamas's resilience to leadership targeting.

Existing Explanations

There is a considerable amount of literature on the effectiveness of the Israeli targeting policies.[3] While the debate over the efficacy of targeting as an Israeli counterterrorism measure is ongoing, there is support for the view that even if targeting does not considerably weaken a terrorist organization, it should remain an important tool in Israeli counterterrorism policy as it demonstrates resolve and strength and can reassure a nervous public. Stephen David argues that Israeli targeting policies have been effective in reducing the frequency and severity of Palestinian attacks and are important "in providing retribution and revenge for a population under siege and may, over the long term, help create conditions for a more secure Israel."[4] He finds that Israel's policy has prevented some attacks, keeps potential bomb makers on the run, has a deterrent function, and has generated a large amount of Israeli support. However, David claims that "targeted killing has not appreciably diminished the costs of terrorist attacks and may have even increased them."[5] In fact, he explicitly argues that it has "provoked far more killings of Israeli civilians than it has saved lives."[6] Nevertheless, he supports a policy of targeted killings concurrent with other counterterrorism measures, including checkpoints, blockades, and incursions.[7]

Daniel Byman also assesses the efficacy of targeting Hamas leaders. Byman suggests that the outcome of targeting is mixed. He argues that targeting killing does not affect the long-term popularity of groups like Hamas. Rather, support for violence is a product of the public faith in the peace process. According to Byman, targeted killings can serve a retributive function by boosting morale and can "satisfy domestic demands for a forceful response to terrorism."[8] Examining trends in activity, Byman finds that while the number of Hamas attacks has increased, the lethality of each attack has declined, "suggesting that the attacks themselves became far less effective."[9] Further, he argues that targeting leaders puts stress on the organization as leaders must spend increased time and resources protecting themselves and changing locations, which can hinder the flow of information within the movement. Byman concludes that targeting has weakened Palestinian groups but also acknowledges that changes in the frequency and lethality of attacks can be attributed to other counterterrorism measures, such as the construction of a border fence separating Palestinian and Israeli territories. Moreover, he finds that targeting can have adverse consequences. Terrorist groups often retaliate when their leaders are killed, creating martyrs that "help a group sell itself to its own community."[10] Palestinian groups have adapted in response to targeting policies, allowing local operatives more initiative in planning attacks. Finally, Byman discusses the potential for the killing of innocent civilians and other collateral damage in the process of carrying out the targeting operation.

Many studies have examined whether targeting efforts have resulted in a rise or decline in terrorist group activity by examining data on attack frequency. Kaplan, Mintz, and Mishal find that targeted assassinations increase the number of suicide attacks.[11] In a departure from many other studies on Hamas that focus exclusively on targeted killings, their study distinguishes between capturing and killing terrorist operatives. They find that while preventive arrests lower the rate of suicide bombing attacks, the negative impact of a single targeted killing outweighs the benefit of a single preventive arrest.[12] In another study Hafez and Hatfield look at the effect of Israel's assassination policy on rates of Palestinian violence from September 2000 to June 2004.[13] They find that targeted killings do not decrease the rates of Palestinian attacks, nor do they increase rates of violence.

As these studies demonstrate, there are widely divergent findings regarding the effectiveness of decapitation as a policy.

It is possible to evaluate the efficacy of targeting through variables other than number of attacks committed by a terrorist group.[14] Zussman and Zussman evaluate two conflicting effects of targeted killings.[15] They argue that while assassination can hinder a group's capabilities, it can also create a motivation for carrying out further attacks.[16] Using reactions to the Israeli stock market as a measure of efficacy, they find the market does not react to the assassination of low-ranked members of Palestinian terrorist organizations, but it does react strongly to the assassination of senior leaders. It rises after the killing of senior political leaders and declines after the killing of senior military leaders. They conclude that these trends indicate that targeting low-level operatives is counterproductive while targeting the leaders of terrorist groups is effective.

There is also debate over the political effects of targeting terrorists. Avery Plaw refers to the work of Ward Thomas, who argues that targeted killing has made Israelis less secure.[17] Thomas argues that the "political wisdom" of targeted killing can be determined by understanding whether attacks can be deterred or prevented and the implications for Israel's long-term security.[18] Gal Luft references the critics of leadership targeting who argue that targeting terrorists is "operationally senseless because assassinating Palestinian militants only brings harsh retaliatory action, resulting in even more casualties."[19] One way to evaluate the political impact of targeting is to examine whether it contributes to a rising cycle of violence. In the months following the assassination of Hamas's Yahya Ayyash, there were four retaliatory bus bombings that resulted in more than fifty deaths.[20] While many scholars advocate a continuation of the Israeli policy, they also recognize that retribution is a recurrent motive in many terrorist attacks. Byman and David support the view that targeted killings have an important revenge function for Israelis, contributing to a continuing cycle of violence. In fact, given these political impacts, Plaw claims that arresting terrorists is always preferable to killing them.[21] However, the effectiveness of targeting and its effect on levels of violence is highly controversial and "the matter remains under legitimate dispute."[22]

While these studies have made important contributions to the study of Israeli counterterrorism policies, there are some critical limitations. First, existing work has focused on targeted killing in general. These studies have not differentiated between top leaders and lower-level operatives and thus have not analyzed the effectiveness of targeting the senior leaders of terrorist organizations. By looking specifically at *leadership* decapitation, this paper offers an empirical test of a policy that is generally seen as highly effective. Second, these studies have examined Palestinian violence as a whole. Each group has different goals, structures, and capabilities, and it is important to consider them separately. By concentrating on Hamas, this study tests the resilience of a religious/separatist organization, which should be particularly resistant to leadership decapitation. Third, extant empirical work focuses on the Second Intifada, yet there is little agreement regarding whether targeted killing has increased or decreased levels of violence since Hamas's foundation in 1987. Finally, these studies tend to focus on whether targeted killings have increased suicide bombings or conventional attacks, and do not to look at both types of attacks simultaneously.

Background

The history of targeting Hamas's leadership must be considered within the context of Palestinian violence in general. Hamas emerged from the violence of the First Intifada, which began on December 8, 1987, when several Palestinian workers were killed in a motor accident with an Israeli truck. This event triggered riots, ultimately leading to the Intifada.[23] According to Abu-Amr, the following day leaders of the Muslim Brotherhood (MB) met in Gaza to discuss the use of public demonstrations in order to "to stir up religious and nationalist sentiments."[24] The organization first released leaflets under the name "Hamas" in January 1988,[25] and its charter was issued in August 1988.[26] Despite the simultaneity of these two events, Tamimi argues that the factors that precipitated the Intifada were not the same ones that lead to the emergence of Hamas.[27] Rather, the leaders of the Ikhwan[28] utilized the frustration and anger of the people in Gaza to transform their movement into one of resistance.

The Muslim Brotherhood is an Islamic organization, and ultimately the leaders of Hamas wanted to establish an Islamic society and state. Initially, Hamas, led by Sheikh Ahmed Yassin, focused primarily on instilling Islamic values within the community's youth. However, in order to garner widespread support among the Palestinian people, it was necessary for Hamas to support the Palestinian national movement. Mishal argues, "By interpreting the political agreement involving the West Bank and Gaza Strip as merely a pause on the historic road of *jihad*, Hamas achieved political flexibility without forsaking its ideological credibility."[29] While the Palestine Liberation Organization (PLO) seemed to have given up on armed struggle and was willing to accept territorial compromise, Hamas advocated armed struggle in the liberation of Palestine and developed an Islamic version of Palestinian nationalism. The organization envisioned that, through *jihad*, Palestine would be unified under Islamic Law.

Under Yassin's leadership, Hamas's institutional and social infrastructure began to develop. Yassin had previously served as the impetus behind the rise of the Muslim Brotherhood in Gaza, "which was spearheaded by his institutionally based efforts to imbue society with *da'wa*, religious preaching and education."[30] He believed that an Islamic society was a necessary precursor to resistance and focused on promoting Islamic values and ethics in young Palestinians.[31] Yassin was successful in penetrating society through the creation of small cells in almost every neighborhood. With the founding of the Islamic Center (al-Mujamma' al-Islami) in 1979, the MB became officially institutionalized in Gaza.[32] The Islamic Center was focused on developing a civil society in Gaza through the provision of social, medical, and educational services to the community south of Gaza City. This strong community basis is the source of Hamas's strength in Palestine, and Yassin played a major role in the development of these important community organizations.

Before 1988, Hamas did not exist as a political organization and was not engaged in armed struggle. Islamic Jihad, led by Dr. Fathi Shiqaqi, had emerged as a revolutionary organization dedicated to carrying out defensive jihad. While Islamic Jihad advocated armed struggle, the MB in both Gaza and the West Bank refrained from carrying out violent activity against Israel. Instead, the Mujamma believed that society should be transformed through the Islamicization of society. Once an Islamic state was established, the external jihad against Israel could be carried out. Israel was viewed as a religious and political enemy, whose existence was the result of the abandonment of Islamic norms. The creation of an Islamic state was a necessary prerequisite to armed struggle.

Prior to the events in 1987, the PLO was becoming politically weak and gaining adversaries outside of Palestine. Furthermore, the situation in the occupied territories became increasingly deplorable. The PLO's weakness convinced the MB that they could provide an alternative. However, to serve as a legitimate successor, the MB had to undergo "conceptual and structural changes, expressed particularly in the actions of a national nature, which meant in practice, armed struggle against Israel."[33] Thus in 1983, Sheikh Yassin ordered members to gather firearms. Weapons were discovered in his home in 1984, and Yassin was sentenced to thirteen years in prison. He was released after less than a year as part of a prisoner exchange between Israel and the Popular Front for the Liberation of Palestine General Command (PFLP-GC). In 1986, Yassin established a security apparatus intended to combat Israeli counterintelligence efforts. This security unit would also be involved in ensuring that Islamic rules were pervasive in Palestinian society. Yassin realized that it was necessary to compartmentalize activity, whereby less-important members of the organization carried out violent activities. This new apparatus, called Majd,[34] was headed by Salah Shehada.

The eruption of the Intifada provided an opportunity for mass mobilization, and in order to compete with other groups such as Islamic Jihad, the MB adopted a more violent policy, resulting in the establishment of Hamas. This allowed the MB to remain a separate religious and community organization, escaping Israeli reprisals.[35] Essentially, Hamas became a way for the MB to adopt jihad while maintaining a focus on the provision of social services. While the MB ultimately wanted to establish an Islamic state, the creation of Hamas was an attempt to unify Palestinian nationalism and Islamism. By adopting a nationalist ideology, Hamas was able to broaden its base of support. Hamas's strength is based in its communal support and its ability to adapt in response to Israeli counterterrorism efforts. The creation of institutions designed to provide civil services was especially salient given the poor occupation services and reductions in Israeli social and economic investments in the 1970s.[36] Hamas's existence was based on its steady stream of followers, from which new activists were recruited.[37]

Data on Hamas Attacks

This chapter will examine data on 81 incidents of leadership targeting against Hamas leaders from 1988 to 2010. This is by no means the universe of cases, but I believe that it is large enough to develop arguments about the effect of targeting Hamas leaders. This chapter will also examine the frequency and lethality of Hamas attacks, both conventional and suicide. The data on Hamas terrorist attacks is from the Global Terrorism Database, and data on suicide attacks is from Robert Pape's Chicago Project on Security and Threats.[38] Overall, the data indicates that Hamas has been largely resistant to leadership attacks. On a very basic level, sustained decapitation efforts have been unable to completely wipe out Hamas, and this chapter will look at changes in the frequency of Hamas attacks over time and will attempt to explain why decapitation has failed to result in organizational decline.

To reiterate, leadership is defined as either the top leader of an organization or a member of the upper echelon who holds a position of authority within the organization.[39] Identifying the top leader is usually straightforward; for example, Yassin and Rantisi were clearly the top leaders of Hamas. However, identifying upper-echelon leaders is more difficult. Moreover, after the 2004 deaths of Yassin and Rantisi, the organization made an intentional effort to keep the identify of its leaders hidden, essentially going underground to protect them from strikes by Israeli forces. This made it difficult not only to identify leaders but also to identify characteristics of specific leaders. Between 1989 and 1993, Israel claimed to have arrested more than two hundred leaders. However, many of these individuals did

CHAPTER 5

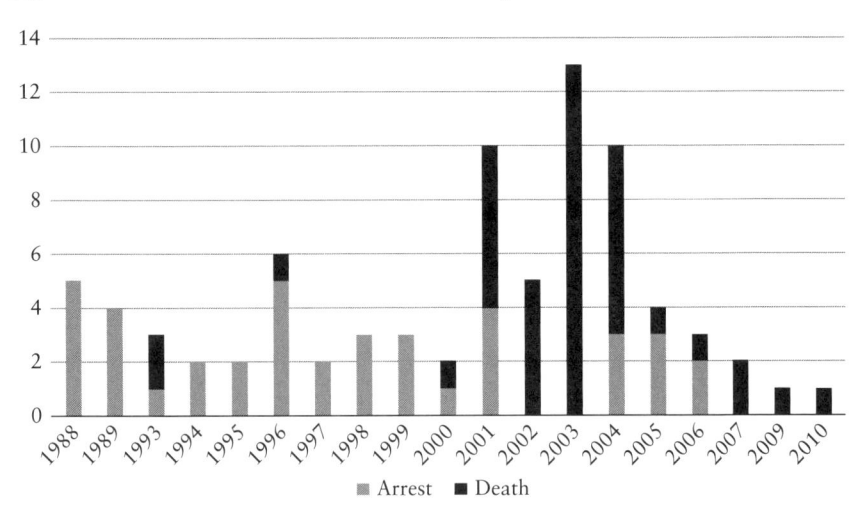

FIGURE 5.1 Decapitation of Hamas leaders, 1988–2010

TABLE 5.1
Number of Hamas leaders arrested or killed, 1987–2010

	Top Leader	Upper Echelon	Total
Arrested	7	33	40
	70%	46%	50%
Killed	3	38	41
	30%	54%	50%
Total	10	71	81
	100%	100%	100%

not hold senior positions and are not included in the data analyzed for this book. Furthermore, Israel has an incentive to overrepresent the number of leaders as opposed to lower-level foot soldiers targeted, in a bid to increase the salience of the operations. The analysis in this chapter will focus specifically on those individuals who held senior positions within the larger political or military umbrella organizations as identified in news reports on the targeting incident.

Figure 5.1 displays the frequency of leadership attacks, both arrests and deaths of leaders, over time. Israel initially focused primarily on arresting leaders. As reported in Table 5.1 a majority of decapitation cases (71) were against members of the upper echelon rather than top leaders. Overall leaders were killed and arrested with nearly the same frequency. Top leaders were arrested more frequently than they were killed, while members of the upper echelon were killed more frequently, although not by much more. In the First Intifada, Israel focused its efforts on large-scale arrests of Hamas operatives and leaders, while killing leaders became much more common in the Second Intifada, peaking in 2003 with the death of thirteen leaders. Targeting efforts have since declined. Leaders from both military and political wings were targeted with relatively equal frequency, with military leaders targeted more frequently in the Second Intifada.

The remainder of this section will examine data from the Global Terrorism Database on Hamas activity after leadership attacks.[40] While the GTD database has no Hamas attacks listed for 2009–2011, there were a significant number of rocket attacks during this period. See Figure 5.2 for numbers of attacks and fatalities per year for Hamas during this time period. In 1988 and 1989, Israel began a major campaign targeting Hamas operatives and leaders and arrested hundreds of people involved in Hamas activities, individuals that had been influential in the running of the group, and approximately nine leaders. Hamas carried out no attacks in the remainder of 1988. However, beginning in 1989, its attacks began to increase, with the group carrying out 16 attacks resulting in 16 fatalities in 1992.

However, in the early years of targeting efforts, most Israeli attacks were directed at operatives and lower-level leaders. Israel arrested hundreds of Hamas operatives and many leaders in 1988 and 1989, but did not target the group's top leadership in 1992, despite the increase in attacks.

With the conclusion of the Oslo Accords and the signing of the Declaration of Principles on September 13, 1993, Hamas found itself in a dramatically different

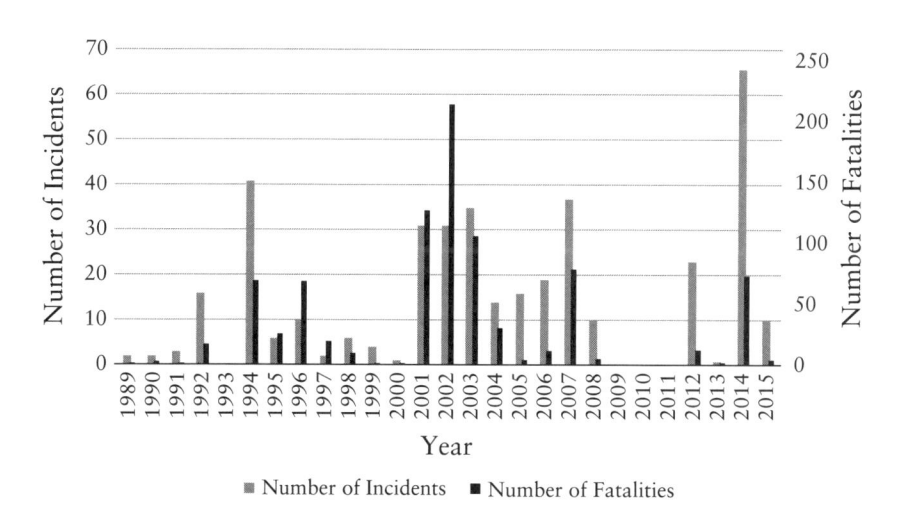

FIGURE 5.2 Hamas attacks and fatalities, 1989–2015
SOURCE: National Consortium for the Study of Terrorism and Responses to Terrorism (START), University of Maryland. (2018). The Global Terrorism Database (GTD) [Data file]. Retrieved from https://www.start.umd.edu/gtd.

strategic position. The agreement, which ended the First Intifada, "confronted Hamas with nothing less than an existential crisis."[41] Hamas believed that international and Palestinian support for the PLO-Israeli agreement was a sign of its own weakness. Hamas intensified its armed struggle in the months following the signing of the Oslo Accords, while Israel killed two leaders, and arrested Rantisi in December 1993. Hamas increased its activity, carrying out 41 attacks in 1994 that resulted in 67 fatalities. Israel arrested two more Hamas leaders in 1994. There was then a sharp decline in the group's activity in 1995, with 5 attacks, but 1996 saw 10 attacks that resulted in the death of 66 people, the bloodiest seven days of the Intifada up to this point. Consequently, acting Israeli defense minister Shimon Peres demanded that PLO leader Yasser Arafat begin arresting terrorist leaders.[42] Thus from 1996 to 1999 Israel curtailed its efforts at decapitation, and Arafat began arresting key terrorist leaders. The number and lethality of attacks continued to decrease until the start of the Second Intifada in September 2000.

With the beginning of the Second Intifada, Israel dramatically increased its efforts at targeting leaders, relying more heavily on assassination instead of arrest. Ten leaders were targeted in 2001, 5 in 2002, 13 in 2003, and 10 in 2004. The numbers steadily declined, with only one leader targeted in 2010. The first eight years of the Second Intifada through 2008 saw a steady number of attacks and fatalities ranging from 15 to 35 per year, with a peak of 195 fatalities and 726 injuries in 2002. Interestingly, a decline in targeting efforts coincided with a decline in the number of attacks carried out by Hamas. See Figure 5.2 for the number of attacks and fatalities carried out by Hamas per year.

I do not mean to suggest that there is a causal relationship between these trends, but the increase in attacks following a rise in targeting efforts would run counter to the belief that targeting works to significantly hamper a group's activity. For example, Hamas carried out 66 attacks with 71 fatalities in 2014. Figure 5.3 plots decapitation against the number of attacks carried out by Hamas and the resultant fatalities. These graphs demonstrate the expected relationship, that targeting efforts did not result in a substantial decline in Hamas attacks. It is, however, important to note out that these trends could be due to a number of factors, both internal and external to the organization.

Byman claims that after continued decapitation efforts, Hamas carried out more but less lethal attacks.[43] This increase in the quantity of attacks is due in part to a large number of Qassam rockets fired from Gaza. These attacks occurred frequently yet rarely resulted in civilian casualties. While Hamas's attacks became less dangerous over time, their increase in frequency indicates that not only was Hamas able to continue its activities in the face of repeated attacks against its leadership, it also gained strength as the Intifada continued. Pedahzur

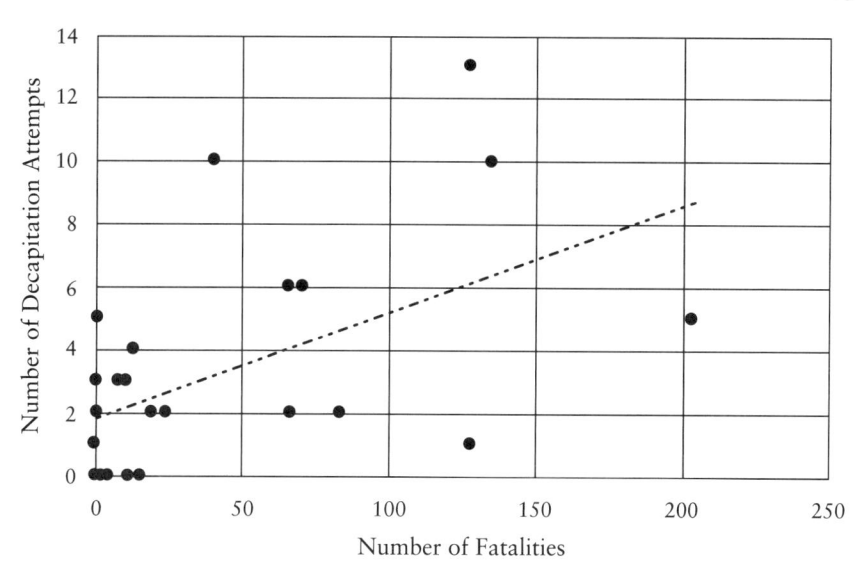

FIGURE 5.3 Hamas decapitations vs. fatalities
SOURCE: National Consortium for the Study of Terrorism and Responses to Terrorism (START), University of Maryland. (2018). The Global Terrorism Database (GTD) [Data file]. Retrieved from https://www.start.umd.edu/gtd.

explains that Hamas's structure of local networks made the organization very difficult to destabilize.[44]

It is important to note that the sustained increase in the number of Hamas attacks from 2001 to 2003 and the decline in lethality in 2004 would seem to indicate that a policy of targeted killings was not effective in hindering the group's operational capacity. It appears that the high-profile killings carried out by Israel during the Second Intifada increased Hamas's resolve and retaliatory motive in carrying out further attacks. The assassinations of Yassin and Rantisi triggered massive local and international outrage. Yassin's death was condemned by the international community and triggered sympathy throughout Palestinian society. Hroub notes that "a poll carried out in the West Bank and Gaza Strip two weeks after Yassin's killing found Hamas, for the first time, the most popular movement in Palestine."[45] While Rantisi's death spurred less international condemnation, his was a more serious loss for the organization. Yassin was a quadriplegic and quite frail, and was not involved in the day-to-day operations of Hamas. Rantisi, on the other hand, was a skilled organizer and leader and, according to Hroub, "enjoyed both great popular and unquestioned legitimacy as one of the original founders."[46] In response to his assassination, Hamas no longer publicized the names of its top leaders.

Civilian casualties, and the death of family members in particular, can increase the motive for revenge and retaliation. For example, on July 22, 2002, an Israeli F-16 dropped a one-ton bomb onto the Gaza City apartment of Hamas leader Salah Shehada. Fourteen civilians were killed, including nine children.[47] Rantisi described the August 2002 suicide attack at Hebrew University as retaliation for the killing of Shehada.[48] Avery Plaw notes that fourteen civilians, including nine children were killed in this leadership attack.[49] In another prominent case, the decision to assassinate Yassin drew criticism from inside Israeli policy circles. He was killed in March 2004 by a hellfire missile fired from an Israeli Apache helicopter, along with six bystanders. Dozens of civilians were also injured. In the aftermath, Interior Minister Avraham Poraz argued that he was "afraid of a revenge from the Palestinian side."[50] In another example, on May 18, 2001, in retaliation for a suicide bombing at a shopping mall in Netanya, Israel fired missiles at a Palestinian prison in Nablus, killing eleven Palestinian policemen. Mahmoud Abu Hanoud, leader of Hamas's West Bank military was killed in November, and Hamas credited many of its attacks as vengeance for his death.[51] Even when Arafat implemented a crackdown on militants in the Gaza Strip in 1995, there were frequent threats of retaliation.[52] This indicates that not only does decapitation not seem to significantly reduce the amount of Hamas violence, but it can actually increase the motive for violence by eliciting a desire for revenge on the part of the organization and the communities in which it is operating.

While decapitation may temporarily incapacitate a movement, it did not have a negative impact on Hamas's ability to carry out attacks, and may in fact have had counterproductive consequences. Hamas's resilience to leadership attacks can be attributed to communal support, bureaucracy, and ideology. The findings in Chapter 4 are consistent with the Hamas case, a large, older, Islamist, and separatist organization that has resisted consistent targeting efforts.

Organizational Adaptation

The prior section evaluated data on the frequency and lethality of Hamas attacks over time, suggesting that decapitation was not effective in substantially reducing the number of Hamas attacks. While attacks became less lethal over time, the organization continued to function and, as this section will show, underwent important adaptive processes that increased its resilience to Israeli counterterrorism efforts. Hamas adapted to Israeli leadership targeting campaigns in ways that not only allowed it to continue carrying out attacks, but also strengthened the organization. This section identifies a few critical instances of decapitation against Hamas from 1988 to 2012 and focuses on how Hamas responded to these prominent cases of leadership targeting.[53] It examines 81 cases of decapitation against Hamas, divided into four periods: 1988–89, 1993–2000, and 2001–5, and 2006–12. I argue that as Hamas grew in size and age, it developed a bureaucratic structure, increasing its resilience and strength over time. The growing communal support for Hamas, and its religious and separatist claims, further strengthened the movement.

1988–89

This early period was characterized by a large-scale targeting campaign against Hamas operatives. Israel arrested hundreds of militants and suspected members, along with a large number of leaders. Dr. Abdel Aziz al-Rantisi, a founding member of Hamas, was arrested on January 15, 1988, and two leaders of Hamas's security apparatus, Yahya al-Sinwar and Rawhi Mushtaha, were also detained.[54] According to Tamimi, the declaration of jihad in 1988 provided Israel with the opportunity to target Hamas's leadership, resulting in an Israeli detention campaign against Hamas leaders and activists. During this time, Hamas ensured that there would be no leadership vacuum following the mass arrests. In response to the attacks against Hamas operatives in Gaza in September 1988, the organization tightened its horizontal compartmentalization while adopting a more hierarchical structure at the top. This was the beginning of Hamas's process of bureaucratization and as explained in Chapter 3, the development of a hierarchical administrative staff is a key component of a bureaucracy.

In response to this wave of arrests, Yassin further compartmentalized the organization. The vertical structure between activists and its headquarters abroad required that the group rely upon phone, fax, written messages, and meetings outside the country. While Hamas developed a hierarchical leadership structure, it retained elements of its decentralized structure. Mishal argues that this maintained a "horizontal separation between active members, in an effort to slow the arrests of leading figures."[55] Notwithstanding this horizontal structure, the leader remained able to maintain contact with the movement and provide operational orders. This hybrid organizational structure allowed for flexibility, with a hierarchy at the upper levels of the administration and a division of labor within the organization.

Hamas has played a significant role in important social institutions and communal infrastructure since its inception. By building upon the extensive infrastructure of the Muslim Brotherhood, Hamas was able to expand its base of operations by controlling nursery schools, kindergartens, social and sports clubs, libraries, the Islamic University, and other social institutions.[56] Abu-Amr writes that these "various institutions—to say nothing of the network of mosques—are useful vehicles for spreading Hamas's ideas and influence and enlisting supporters. Following the example of the Brotherhood, Hamas also organizes trips, particularly among university students, as well as visits to the Dome of the Rock."[57] This extensive network of religious, social, and educational institutions has created a strong base of public support, which increases Hamas's resilience in the face of repeated attacks on its leadership.[58]

Israel continued to target Hamas's leaders, and from February to March 1989 Hamas kidnapped and then killed Israel Defense Forces (IDF) sergeants Avi Sasportas and Ilan Sa'adon.[59] After Israel discovered that the soldiers had been kidnapped, members of Hamas's military "Cell 101" were moved outside of Palestine, except for the cell's leader, al-Sharitha. He was arrested and revealed the name of an accomplice, who claimed that Yassin was behind the kidnapping. Yassin was arrested on May 18, 1989, and Israel began its second arrest campaign against Hamas, arresting more than 1,500 members throughout Gaza and the West Bank. According to Tamimi, these arrests effectively decapitated the organization as "all of its first and second ranking officials were detained."[60] Tamimi argues that the crackdown revealed the extent of Hamas's military capacity. The structural changes made prior to the crackdown had also strengthened the movement, as had the strong base of communal support.

In response to the arrests of 1989, control of the organization shifted outside of the territories, to Springfield, Virginia, where Abu Marzuq lived; Amman, Jordan;[61] Kuwait; and London.[62] The presence of leaders outside of Palestine protected the movement from Israeli counterleadership activity and from attacks by the PLO. In response to this campaign, Hamas formed its military apparatus, Izz al-Din al-Qassam, signaling an escalation in its military activity. The organization was further compartmentalized with functional differentiation among its units. Abu-Amr notes that "leadership wings and other committees were set up to take charge of the political matters, security, military operations, and the media."[63] This first campaign was critical to Hamas's process of bureaucratization. Hamas responded to Israeli targeting policies by solidifying its hierarchy of authority through increasing centralization at the upper levels of the organization. The creation of separate organizational "wings" also allowed for a division of labor, a critical feature for bureaucratic development. In addition, the creation of social and religious institutions provided a strong foundation for communal support.

Overall, these mass arrests were not excessively damaging to the organization, and because of the strategy designed by Abu Marzuq, reconstruction was possible. The organization had developed a resilient structure and "a seemingly inexhaustible supply of recruits."[64] Not only was Hamas able to recover quickly and easily from these mass arrests, but each attack increased popular Palestinian sympathy and support for the group, allowing Hamas to emerge as a credible alternative to the PLO.

1993–2000

The mass deportation of 415 Islamic militants to Lebanon in December 1992 was a key factor in Hamas's decision to use car bombs and suicide attacks. Mishal argues that this escalation of tactics was "an indirect result of the presence of the deportees for almost a year in south Lebanon, which provided the Palestinian Islamists an opportunity to learn about Hizballah's experience in fighting the Israelis, the effect of suicide attacks, and the construction of car bombs."[65] Despite the large number of deportations, the PLO and the Jordanian authorities felt that Hamas was a serious contender for power. A new political bureau developed under Hamas, headed by Abu Marzuq. Tamimi argues that these developments would not have occurred absent the deportations to South Lebanon, an event that dramatically increased Hamas's popularity within Palestine and across the region.[66]

Beginning in 1993 and increasing at the beginning of the Second Intifada, Israel shifted to killing Hamas leaders. During this same period, Hamas began using suicide attacks, despite the fact that public support for suicide terrorism was very low at the time. Mia Bloom shows that from 1994 to 1996, public "support for suicide operations never exceeded a third of Palestinians polled."[67] There are different arguments for the initiation of suicide attacks. Robert Pape argues that suicide terrorism occurs in order to compel modern democracies to withdraw military forces from territories considered to be homeland.[68] Alternatively, Bloom argues it is a tool that can provide radical groups with an opportunity to increase their share of the political market.[69] Mishal and Sela find that the mass deportations in 1992 were a major contributing factor.[70] I do not claim that a policy of leadership targeting contributed to the emergence of suicide attacks. Rather, I wish to show that leadership targeting has not contributed to the weakening of Hamas and may have increased the frequency of suicide and conventional attacks, generated support for the organization, and created a motivation to appear strong and resilient, further increasing radicalization. Hamas was clearly not adversely impacted by the sustained attacks against its leadership from 1988 to 1993, and in fact changed its tactics by initiating suicide attacks against Israel.

In response to this decline in public support, Hamas began to shift its emphasis to the social sector of the Islamic movement, which according to Sara Roy "had always been a critical component of that movement, providing a range of important services and doing so effectively."[71] This shift in emphasis was strategically important for Hamas as it created a "public space in which they could operate without too much harassment from the Israeli or Palestinian authorities."[72] Moreover, the provision of much-needed social services through a developed institutional infrastructure allowed Hamas to maintain and increase its base of support. This important process of organizational adaptation provided a way for the group to increase its level of public support and strengthen its bureaucratic functioning through the institutionalization necessary to distribute such services. This is an important example of how Hamas has been able to adapt to changes in counterterrorism policies and overall levels of public support.

In 1995, Israel arrested two key Hamas leaders. Hamas continued its attacks and carried out a major suicide attack the same year. Despite talks in Cairo with the Palestinian Authority (PA) in December 1995, Hamas continued its armed struggle, though it did promise not to carry out military operations against Israel from territories under PA control. However, there was still disagreement between Hamas factions in Jordan, who were opposed to any truce with Israel or the PA.

In 1996, Israel killed two prominent Palestinian leaders, Fathi Shiqaqi of Islamic Jihad and Yahya Ayyash of Hamas, which resulted in vows of retaliation by both groups and led to a series of suicide attacks in February and March 1996.[73] The Hamas attacks, in direct retaliation for the killing of Ayyash, were the deadliest suicide attacks in Israeli history and had a great societal impact. In September 1997, Israel failed in its attempt to assassinate Khaled Mishal, the chief of Hamas's Political Bureau, in Amman.[74] Mossad agents posing as Canadian tourists injected Mishal with a lethal poison but were apprehended and later confessed to the poisoning. King Hussein demanded that Israel supply an antidote, which they did. This incident provided Hamas a strong retaliatory motive and salvaged the weakened Hamas-Jordanian relationship.[75] Relations between Hamas and the PA also improved following this event. King Hussein called upon Netanyahu to rebuild trust between the two nations by releasing Sheikh Yassin. The release of their leader gave Hamas a boost "at a time when the PA and Fatah had striven for two years to marginalize it."[76] Rallies were organized to celebrate his return home, providing a focus for Hamas's struggle for liberation.

The victory of Ehud Barak on May 17, 1999, provided many with hope that the Palestinians would be able to achieve statehood. Furthermore, in coordination with the Israeli intelligence, Arafat began neutralizing Hamas's military wing. As a result, Hamas's popularity fell and the organization "began to fracture and disintegrate from within."[77] Arafat had been the unquestioned leader of the Palestinians from 1994 to 1996, but by 1999 his authority was being challenged. He appeared weak and particularly vulnerable after his rejection of Barak's peace offer in 2000, and his popularity level plummeted below 27 percent. As Mia Bloom argues, the inability of the Palestinian Authority to improve the daily lives of the Palestinians and the high levels of governmental corruption provided an incentive for Hamas and Islamic Jihad to engage in a new cycle of violence in November 2000.[78] The start of the Second Intifada saw a dramatic increase in public support for suicide bombings.

2001–2005

Ariel Sharon's visit to the al-Haram al-Sharif compound on the Temple Mount on September 28, 2000, triggered the Second Intifada. Israel resumed its policy of targeting terrorists and carried out two high-profile attacks, against two Fatah leaders.[79] These attacks left Hamas undeterred, and the organization dramatically escalated its attacks, with 31 in 2001, resulting in 135 casualties. A suicide attack on March 4, 2001, during rush hour in Netanya, killed three and injured dozens,[80] and was just one of five in March alone, with further attacks continuing every month for the remainder of the year.

Decapitation efforts against Hamas increased significantly. Prior to the Second Intifada, leaders were primarily arrested, but, starting in 2001, the policy shifted largely towards assassination. Despite a massive military effort in the West Bank, Israel was unable to quell the violence, and Ariel Sharon expanded the policy of assassinating Hamas leaders,[81] resulting in a major rise in the number of leaders killed from 2001 to 2006. As Figure 5.1 shows, Hamas attacks continued to increase in 2002 and 2003. It appears that killing leaders, as opposed to arresting them, provided a strong motive for revenge and an impetus for retaliatory attacks.

On March 27, 2002, Hamas carried out a suicide attack at a Passover seder at the Park Hotel in Netanya, resulting in 30 deaths and over 100 injuries.[82] Sharon responded with Operation Defensive Shield, conducted between March 29, 2002, and April 21, 2002,[83] which involved the reoccupation of major cities in the West Bank. Pedahzur argues that this operation "actually heightened the motivation of terrorist cells to act, and it also created fertile ground for the expansion of the ranks of these groups."[84] The number of individuals killed in Hamas attacks peaked at 204 in 2002, with an average number of nearly seven people killed per attack.

The number of attacks slowly declined as the Second Intifada wore on, as did the overall number of casualties and the average number of fatalities per attack. Fatalities decline to 102 in 2003, 30 in 2004, and 4 in 2005. See Figure 5.4 for data on the average number of fatalities per attack. This decline can be attributed in part to the erection of the separation fence in 2003.[85] Pedahzur argues that "the

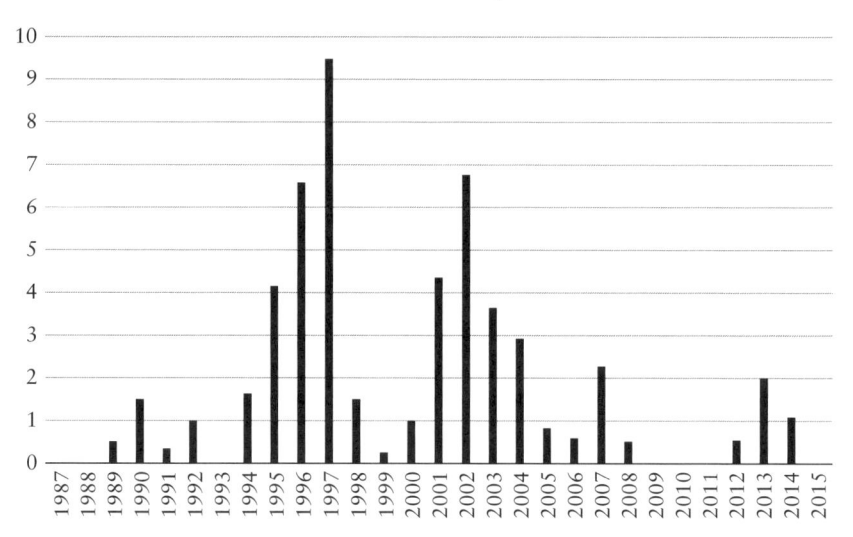

FIGURE 5.4 Average number of fatalities per Hamas attack, 1987–2015
SOURCE: National Consortium for the Study of Terrorism and Responses to Terrorism (START), University of Maryland. (2018). The Global Terrorism Database (GTD) [Data file]. Retrieved from https://www.start.umd.edu/gtd.

erection of the fence, combined with IDF blockades on areas and cities in the West Bank, proved to be an effective strategy against the Palestinian suicide attack campaigns."[86] Between June 2003 and April 2007, there were 37 suicide attacks in Israel, and three suicide bombers were able to penetrate the fence. All other attacks occurred in either the West Bank or in areas where the fence had not been built. In contrast, from 1993 to 2003, there were 30 suicide attacks, 35 percent of which occurred in northern Israel in areas that since 2003 have been protected by the fence. It is important to note that there were other defensive measures contributing to these statistics, yet I highlight the role of the separation barrier to illustrate that there are other possible explanations for the decline in terrorist activity.

The number of Hamas attacks eventually increased to a high of 37 in 2007, the largest number per year since 1994, with 76 fatalities. After 2007, the group saw a decline in attacks, but eventually carried out 66 attacks in 2014. However, even during this period of decline, the organization was quite active in carrying out rocket attacks in Southern Israel. This data is meant to highlight that while there was a decline, in the number of attacks committed by Hamas, the organization was still active despite increasing Israeli countermeasures that increased even further after the death of its two founders in 2004.

On February 2, 2004, Prime Minister Sharon gave orders that Israel would withdraw from settlements in Gaza. Disengagement occurred the following year.

On March 14, two suicide bombers from Gaza detonated themselves in Ashdod, killing 10 Israelis. Sharon responded by having Sheikh Yassin killed on March 22, 2004.[87] Yassin's targeting provoked much international condemnation. Within less than a month, on April 17, Israel killed Yassin's replacement, Abdel Aziz al-Rantisi, with a missile attack on his car.[88] Tamimi argues that Sharon had vehemently targeted Hamas to ensure that the group would not take over Gaza after the Israeli withdrawal.[89] Following the assassinations of Yassin and Rantisi, Hamas saw a decline in attacks, from 14 in 2004, resulting in 41 fatalities, to 13 in 2005. Hroub argues that the organization was seriously weakened by the assassinations and arrests of its members, "as is obvious from the decreased number of suicide attacks and Hamas's inability to retaliate immediately for the assassinations of Yassin and Rantisi." However, he argues that, structurally, "the movement has remained surprisingly intact." Hamas has an ability to quickly adjust. According to Hroub this is because its structure functions on various levels—religious, charitable work, political activities, and military activities—which can immediately fill "the gaps created by assassinations, arrests, or clampdowns."[90] The Second Intifada ended in February 2005, with a summit at Sharm al-Sheikh, but attacks continued through 2007.

2006–12

This final period is characterized by a steep decline in targeting efforts against Hamas and two major conflicts, the 2008–9 Gaza War and Operation Pillar of Defense in 2012. On January 25, 2006, Hamas received a majority of the seats in the Palestinian Legislative Council: seventy-four compared to Fatah's forty-five.[91] This political victory is clear evidence of the support and strength that Hamas was able to amass in the Second Intifada.[92] Tamimi cites four primary explanations for Hamas's victory: (1) its commitment to a Palestinian homeland, (2) provision of social services, (3) Islamic ideology, and (4) the failure of the peace process.[93] Further, he sees the victory as a direct "response of the Palestinians to Israel's unilateralism."[94] The Palestinians felt that the Israeli withdrawal from Gaza was not part of a peace deal or agreement. While Israel withdrew troops and settlers, its continued border controls made life difficult for inhabitants of Gaza, particularly farmers. Further, Israeli occupation of the West Bank continued. The outcome of the elections in Gaza shows that Hamas was not weakened by the nearly twenty years of targeting; it gained legitimacy and support.

Despite a Hamas victory in the elections, the organization carried out 19 attacks in 2006 and 37 in 2007, resulting in nearly 100 casualties. However, Israeli forces significantly reduced their targeting efforts against the Hamas leadership in this latter stage, targeting three operational leaders in 2006 and only two in 2007. Hamas attacks declined even further, with the group carrying out only 10 attacks in 2008 and no conventional or suicide attacks recorded in 2009 and 2010. However, as mentioned earlier, these figures are from the Global Terrorism Database and do not include the hundreds of rockets and mortars fired from Gaza into Southern Israel. The Israel Security Agency reports that over 2,000 rockets and mortars were fired from Gaza in 2008, followed with a steep decline of 569 in 2009 and 150 in 2010.[95]

This drop in the number of attacks took place within the context of important changes in the Hamas-Israel relationship. Hamas entered into a ceasefire agreement with Israel brokered by Egypt in June 2008. Under the terms of the agreement, Israel would stop air strikes and other attacks on Gaza, and Hamas would cease rocket fire into Southern Israel. Over time, the agreement called for an end to the Israeli blockade of Gaza. The ceasefire officially ended on December 20, 2008, and on December 27, Israel launched Operation Cast Lead, an attack on Gaza that ended in a unilateral ceasefire on January 18, 2009. Israel withdrew its forces on January 21, 2009, after which Hamas agreed to halt attacks. In spite of the ceasefire, both sides continued attacks, with Palestinian militants launching rockets and mortars and Israeli forces launching air strikes. However, there was a major decline in rockets and mortars fired from Gaza and other terrorist attacks from 2008 to 2011.

There was a resumption of violence in 2012. On November 14, Israel launched Operation Pillar of Defense, an eight-day operation carried out in Gaza, which began with the killing of Ahmed Jabari, chief of Hamas's Gaza military wing. The Israeli government stated that the operation was intended to halt rocket attacks against Israeli citizens and to degrade the capabilities of Palestinian militant groups. Hamas, however, argued that Israel had attacked citizens in Gaza in the days just prior to the operation, and that the rockets were carried out in response to the Israeli occupation of the West Bank and blockade of Gaza. There was a decline in Hamas attacks in 2013, but an even further escalation in 2014 and 2015, providing some support for the argument that every action provokes a reaction. This process is essential when considering the possibility for counterproductive outcomes, not only in response to leadership decapitation but also to other counterterrorism measures, in this case an invasion in which civilians on both sides were killed.

The following two points are important for understanding variation in the frequency and lethality of Hamas attacks. First, the decline in attacks beginning in 2008 coincided with a decline in Israeli targeting efforts. Second, both Israel and Hamas changed their tactics. Instead of carrying out large-scale attacks and suicide bombings, Hamas focused on building tunnels in the aftermath of the

Second Intifada. It is difficult to attribute a cause to these trends; however, the fact that periods of high targeting efforts coincide with a large number of attacks, while times of decline saw fewer attacks, is illustrative that targeting efforts do not seem to be the silver bullet they are often assumed to be. Rather, there is a substitution effect; groups can substitute one tactic for another. Groups also respond to countermeasures by making tactical changes. This is to say that there is a causal relationship between targeting efforts and shifts in attacks, but given that operational capacity is the primary indicator of success, it is essential to examine changes in attacks and lethality over time.

Analyzing Hamas's response to Israeli leadership targeting campaigns demonstrates how Hamas adapted its organizational infrastructure in ways that increased its resilience. These organizational changes further strengthened the movement as Israeli targeting efforts continued. Hamas not only adapted its organizational form in response to targeting efforts but also altered its strategy and tactics. Finally, it is important to point out that as Israel increased its targeting efforts, condemnation over certain attacks resulted in an increase in support and sympathy for Hamas and its cause.

The remainder of this chapter looks at whether the theory of organizational resilience, developed in Chapter 2, can provide an explanation for the effectiveness of decapitation against Hamas. In the next section, I analyze changes in public support for Hamas in much greater detail to reveal whether leadership attacks have influenced levels of Palestinian sympathy, and discuss the role of communal support in organizational strength.

Explaining Hamas's Resilience

Hamas successfully adapted to Israeli counterterrorism policies by developing and strengthening its bureaucratic characteristics and creating institutions that generated and sustained support. The quantitative analyses presented in Chapter 4 indicate that Hamas's resilience can be explained largely by organizational size, type, and, in some cases, age. Hamas is a larger, older, Islamist, and separatist organization, all indicators that it should resist collapsing in the wake of leadership targeting. This section will discuss how the theoretical argument regarding group resilience can offer an explanation these statistical findings in the case of Hamas.

Bureaucracy

The degree to which an organization is bureaucratized can account for its resilience and explain in part the statistical results regarding size (and age, but to a lesser degree given that it was insignificant in some of the multivariate analyses).

As an organization grows in age and/or size, it is more likely to have developed characteristics of a complex bureaucracy, increasing its stability, efficiency, and resilience to counterterrorism policies. I argue that Hamas's bureaucratic structure has contributed to its resilience and ability to survive repeated and sustained attacks against its leadership. Key elements of a bureaucracy include a hierarchy of authority, a division of labor, an organized administrative staff, and a stable structure of rules and procedures. Hamas is organized as a bureaucratic hierarchy, and "its inter- and intra-organizational activity is grounded in its hierarchical structure and interpersonal relations."[96] The organization is headed by a *majlis shura*, a council headed by members from Gaza, the West Bank, and outside of the Occupied Territories.[97] Its organizational infrastructure includes internal security, military, political, and religious activities, and there is a division of labor along these lines, within both the leadership and the rank and file.[98] Hamas's organizational structure is thus characteristic of a bureaucratic model with a hierarchy of authority, a division of labor, and an administrative staff. I argue that this structure is a major factor in Hamas's strength and resilience to leadership decapitation.

Hamas's bureaucratic capacity is reflected in its organizational infrastructure within the Palestinian community. As discussed in Chapter 2, Doug McAdam references the importance of indigenous organizational strength for the provision of resources necessary to function. McAdam argues that resources of the minority community enable insurgent groups to exploit opportunities for successful action.[99] In order to generate a successful social movement, the aggrieved indigenous population "must be able to 'convert' a favorable 'structure of political opportunities' into an organized campaign of social protest."[100] This capacity for conversion is dependent upon the extent to which the group is organized within the minority community. Indigenous structures provide the organizational base from which social movements emerge. In this respect, McAdam references Anthony Oberschall, who also emphasizes the importance of the degree to which a group is organized within the minority community.[101]

Hamas's structure of local networks, resources, and communal support have made the group difficult to destabilize.[102] Local networks have provided critical educational, social, and religious services to the Palestinian people in Gaza and the West Bank, and a bureaucratized organization is necessary to manage this system of local networks and efficiently distribute and manage the vast array of social services that Hamas provides. Through this infrastructure and resulting institutionalization, Hamas is able to obtain the resources necessary for political action and gain continued support for the organization.

Hamas's bureaucratic hierarchy, which developed in part out of necessity, has strengthened the organization and is fundamental to its survival.[103] Mishal argues that Hamas depends upon the ability to mobilize mass action, which necessitates "a structure based on vertical relations and a hierarchical chain of command."[104] This need for a formal structure was also a function of exogenous pressures. Hamas adapted its organizational structure in response to Israeli counterterrorism measures in ways that ultimately both increased bureaucratic infrastructure and implemented policies designed to sustain support from the local Palestinian community.

Bureaucracies have features that contribute to a group's ability to resist destabilization after undergoing counterterrorism efforts, such as leadership targeting. However, decentralized organizations have characteristics that can also contribute to a group's resilience. The literature on social network analysis has examined the stability of decentralized organizations, which are often more stable[105] and tend to withstand counterterrorism policies due to their flexibility. Siggelkow and Levinthal argue that in the short run, decentralized groups have some advantages over centralized organizations, as they can more easily change their activities.[106] Hamas adopted a structure that was both hierarchical and decentralized, a combination that resulted in a very resilient organization.

In its early years, Hamas's structure was less bureaucratic and hierarchical: "Hamas was affected less by authoritative, bureaucratic, and vertical relations and a hierarchical chain of command than by group interaction and lateral relations based primarily on solidarity among the participants, self-identification as a collective unit, a common background, and sharing of basic knowledge and values."[107] After the initial targeting campaign carried out by the Israelis against Hamas, control of the organization shifted outside of the territories. Hamas's structure underwent a process of bureaucratic consolidation and horizontal compartmentalization.[108] The "outside" leadership became paramount and was organized hierarchically, while the local leaders were organizationally decentralized around ties based on solidarity and traditional attachments.[109] Mishal finds that "Israel's repressive policy led the movement to seek more effective measures to secure its survival and continue its activities, hence its emphasis on discipline, secrecy, compartmentalization, and hierarchy."[110] As the organization continued to adapt, particularly in response to Israeli counterterrorism policies, its organizational infrastructure was increasingly based on both a vertical chain of command and horizontal compartmentalization, in which individuals are functionally differentiated according to tasks. Essentially, Hamas adapted and developed a hybrid organizational structure, one that is both hierarchal and decentralized.

This hybrid structure has contributed to its resilience in the face of sustained counterterrorism efforts. Because Hamas is decentralized at the operational level but more hierarchical at the upper level, it is more fluid, and leadership decapitation does not affect its ability to carry out terrorist attacks. For example, the effect of the mass deportations of December 1992, which removed most of the frontline leaders and a significant number of the lower-level leaders as well, was lessened by the fact that Hamas relied so extensively on the extended leadership abroad.[111] So while decapitation may result in a temporary disruption of activities, which happened after the assassinations of Yassin and Rantisi, the group is able to recover easily from attacks.

Communal Support

Communal support can also contribute to a group's resilience to leadership attacks in two primary ways. First, organizations depend upon their communities to replenish recruits, gain resources, maintain secrecy, and avoid detection. As discussed in Chapter 2, resource mobilization theory argues that the success of a social movement organization depends upon its ability to garner resources. Groups with more support should have more access to the resources needed to mobilize and sustain collective behavior.[112] Second, support can provide a basis for group legitimacy. Finally, local support allows a group to reproduce the doctrine upon which it is based. The ideology upon which religious and separatist groups are based is often well entrenched in the community in which they operate, and leaders are often not necessary to articulate and reproduce it. This is in contrast to many of the right- and left-wing ideologically driven groups that depend upon the specific doctrinal interpretation of their leaders.

Terrorist organizations that carry out suicide attacks can serve as an example of organizations that require significant support. Robert Pape offers three reasons for why communal support matters to suicide terrorist organizations.[113] First, communal support can "enable a suicide terrorist group to replenish its membership."[114] While Hamas is already deeply entrenched in social and religious institutions in both the West Bank and Gaza Strip, communal support can further strengthen it. Second, communal support can help a group to avoid "detection, surveillance, and elimination by the security forces of the target society."[115] As leadership targeting has increased in frequency, organizations have realized the necessity of hiding and operating in more secretive conditions. As decapitation generates a sense of outrage within the community, it becomes easier for the leaders to avoid detection, as the local community becomes more willing to provide safe places for leaders and key operatives to hide. Finally, Pape argues, "community support is necessary for martyrdom."[116]

Understanding whether decapitation affects communal support is essential in evaluating the effectiveness of leadership targeting as a counterterrorism policy.

While decapitation may have short-term success, the significance of communal support to a terrorist organization highlights the importance of the long-term consequences of leadership decapitation. If leadership targeting generates increased support for an organization and provides a constant pool of new recruits, then decapitation would not negatively affect the long-term stability of the organization.

Communal support can also confer legitimacy upon a group, which is important for an organization to function effectively. Legitimacy is often seen as essential to continued organizational existence and effectiveness. In a study of organizational effectiveness, Raymond Zammuto argues that legitimacy is necessary for organizational existence.[117] He claims that organizational legitimacy is based largely on public confidence and is dependent upon the satisfaction of constituent preferences for the group's performance.[118] By satisfying the evolving constituent preferences, an organization can renew the basis of its legitimacy.[119] According to Zammuto, this is the basis for organizational effectiveness. Following these studies on legitimacy, I argue that it is necessary to look at organizational support from the community in which the group is active. The remainder of this section will look first at how communal support has strengthened Hamas and its ability to withstand attacks. An analysis of changes in Palestinian support for Hamas will follow, as a means by which to empirically assess the changes in Hamas's legitimacy.

Hamas and Communal Support. Hamas has placed a great deal of importance upon the provision of social services to the Palestinian people. In doing so, the organization developed a strong infrastructure in order to effectively disseminate services to communities in need. Hroub argues that the provision of charitable social services provided Hamas influence within Palestinian communities: "Hamas's concern with social issues found expression in the extensive infrastructure of charitable social services the movement established for the poor. . . . Subsequently, these social services became one of the most important sources of influence that Hamas had with broad strata of the public."[120] The provision of religious, social, and educational resources afforded Hamas considerable support, and enabled the group to influence the ideological and religious beliefs of the community.[121] It also gave Hamas a mechanism by which to disseminate its political and religious message. The group combined "the social-instructional discourse" that emerged from providing social services with "the discourse of national resistance."[122]

Commitment to religious principles helped to further the interests of the Palestinian national struggle and vice versa.[123] Sara Roy argues that Islamic institutions created a private sector that felt safe and familiar to the Palestinian people.[124] There was an Islamist focus on working with children, which emphasized the importance of creating a religious and cultural framework for community development—helping young people to find meaning, identity, and a sense of belonging. Sara Roy argues that Islamic institutions in Gaza and the West Bank "provided islands of normality and stability in a sociopolitical context of chaos, dislocation, and pain."[125] This sense of identity that emerged from civic work and community involvement resulted in a high degree of volunteerism. Terrorist groups require committed social action, and Hamas was able to generate this momentum.

In addition to religious, educational, and medical programs to help the Palestinian people of Gaza and the West Bank, Hamas also organized political events that furthered its influence within the community in which it operated. Abu-Amr states:

> In the political realm, Hamas sponsors forums, political gatherings, and Islamic exhibitions, particularly on university campuses, that serve as vehicles for its influence. It issues statements, brochures, and pamphlets, and commemorates martyrs and Islamic events. It organized demonstrations and strikes and other expressions of protest. Its success in calling for comprehensive strikes is testimony to its influence; it is doubtful that any PLO faction, except for Fatah, could alone find a similar response to its strike calls.[126]

However, the success of its political events was largely dependent upon the strong civil society Hamas was able to create through the development of institutions and services within society.

Hamas's social infrastructure, which further enhanced its popular support, afforded the group a sense of legitimacy within society. In fact, Israeli efforts against Islamic social institutions and Hamas were motivated in part by concerns about the growing legitimacy of the organization. The International Crisis Group reports that "the mere existence of a network of social welfare organizations affiliated with an organization that deliberately targets civilians is considered unacceptable. It legitimizes an organization that reports to patently illegal acts . . . ultimately strengthens it and the ideology it practices and promotes."[127] This report highlights how Hamas's high degree of support through the establishment of social and religious institutions can enhance its legitimacy. Israel's concern about Hamas's growing legitimacy resulted in attacks on the broader Palestinian social infrastructure, a shift from tactics more focused on targeting Hamas's leadership and operatives.

Measuring Communal Support. This section looks at data on changes in Palestinian support for Hamas from 1989 to 2007. Civilian deaths, which can occur during leadership targeting and Israeli crackdowns on civilian populations, can fuel Palestinian public support for Hamas. It stands to reason that anything influencing the lives of civilians would help mobilize support for Hamas. In fact, public support for Hamas reached such a high level in 2006 that the group was able to win a majority of the seats in the Palestinian Legislative Council, strengthening it organizationally and instilling political legitimacy. This section discusses public opinion polls from the West Bank and Gaza Strip to determine whether occurrences of decapitation have coincided with an increase or decrease in levels of support for Hamas. Overall, the data shows that Palestinian support for Hamas is positively correlated with occurrences of decapitation. I argue that prominent instances of decapitation resulted in public outrage, which increased levels of support for Hamas and sympathy for the cause. This increase in support should correspond with the degree to which Hamas and its cause is seen as legitimate within the communities in which it is based.

Looking at reports and polls from the Jerusalem Media Communications Center (JMCC), I examine changes in levels of support for Hamas from 1994 to 2007. The individuals polled responded to the following question: "Which of the following factions do you support/trust most?" Analysis from a JMCC report finds that "Palestinians who trust Hamas and Islamic Jihad are most consistently supportive of military operations," indicating that trust in Hamas can be seen as support for armed violence.[128]

It is important to consider whether the ebbs and flows in support are correlated with instances of leadership targeting. Examining polls carried out by the JMCC indicated that after a decline in decapitation in 1994 and 1995, support for Hamas dipped from January to December 1995. In 1996, Israel resumed its targeting efforts and support increased through 1997. In March 1998, Israel arrested a key Hamas leader in Nablus, and support steadily increased over the next year. In 1999, Israel arrested another influential leader, Ibrahim Ghousheh. Surprisingly, support for Hamas declined in the following month, and continued to do so, until the start of the Second Intifada, after which the percentage of respondents that expressed trust in Hamas increased.

After the start of the Second Intifada, Hamas emerged as a viable political alternative to Fatah, public support for Hamas increased significantly, and support for suicide attacks and armed violence reached an all-time high. The highest point of public support for military operations was in September 2001, at 84.6 percent, and its lowest point was in November 2011, at 29.3 percent.[129] The period from 2000 to 2007 is analyzed in Figure 5.5 using an aggregation of information taken from a number of different polls carried out by the Center for Development Studies at Birzeit University.[130] In the polls carried out by Birzeit, respondents were asked some variation of the question "Which of the following

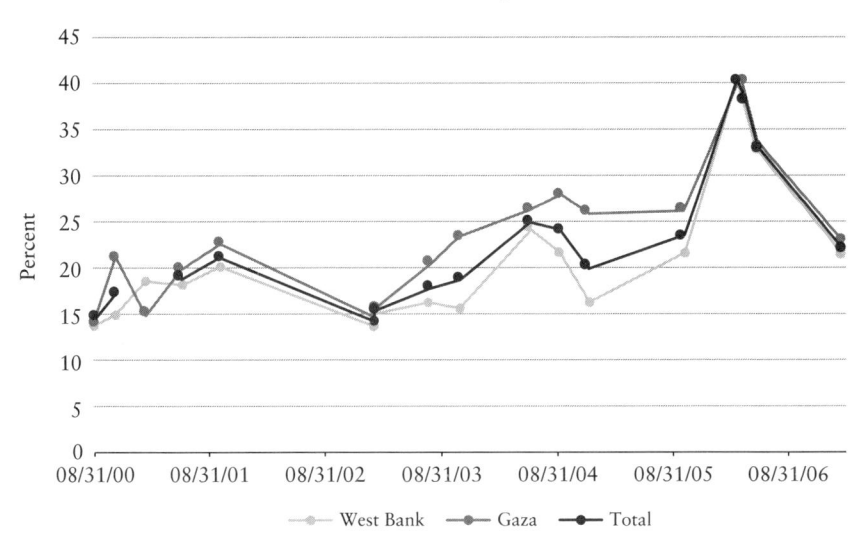

FIGURE 5.5 Palestinian trust in Hamas, 2000–2007
SOURCE: Jerusalem Media and Communications Centre

political groups do you support?" and given the following choices: Hamas, Fatah, Islamic Jihad, PFLP, DFLP, PPP, Nationalist Independents, Others, and No one. This question was extracted from each poll, which was used to create a timeline of the percentage of people who answered that they supported Hamas more than other Palestinian factions.

Following the start of the Second Intifada, leadership decapitation efforts increased, as did support. It is important to underscore that I am not suggesting that there exists a direct relationship between the occurrence of targeting and changes in support for Hamas. For example, a spike in support in the months directly following a leadership attack on the organization could be due to changes in larger Israeli counterterrorism measures. Support increased at the beginning of the Second Intifada and during Operation Cast Lead in 2009. The JMCC finds that "public support for military operations roughly correlates with the number of Palestinian fatalities at the hands of the Israeli military and settlers. The relatively few Palestinian fatalities in 2011 may be one reason why current support for military operations remains low, despite the current collapse in the peace process between Israel and Palestinians."[131] While the JMCC argues that these shifts in support are correlated with Palestinian fatalities, it also mirrors the targeting of Hamas leaders, which is likely correlated with overall fatalities and surges in Israeli countermeasures. Overall, the JMCC concludes that support for military operations is related to violence between Palestinians and Israelis. The findings in this book supports that claim and provides an analysis of a specific form of violence.

Beginning in late 2000 with the outbreak of the Second Intifada, Figure 5.6 indicates a shift in Palestinian support for military operations and suicide attacks. Polls carried out by JMCC show that by "September 2001, Palestinian support for military operations was at the highest level it would reach over the coming decade, at 84.6 percent."[132] However, after three attacks in September and October 2004, support for Hamas declined, and between June and December 2004, public support for military operations dropped from 65.4 to 41.1 percent.[133] In the beginning of 2006, support for Hamas and for military action skyrocketed, culminating with Hamas's victory in the elections.

Overall, the data indicates that while decapitation does not seem to have a huge effect on the levels of support for Hamas, there does seem to be a correlation between instances of leadership targeting and some increases in support. This data is intended to show that targeting efforts can result in an increase in trust in Hamas, support for military action, and support for suicide attacks. As a result, decapitation does not seem to be an effective policy. Since communal support is essential in generating group legitimacy, targeting leaders could increase Hamas's

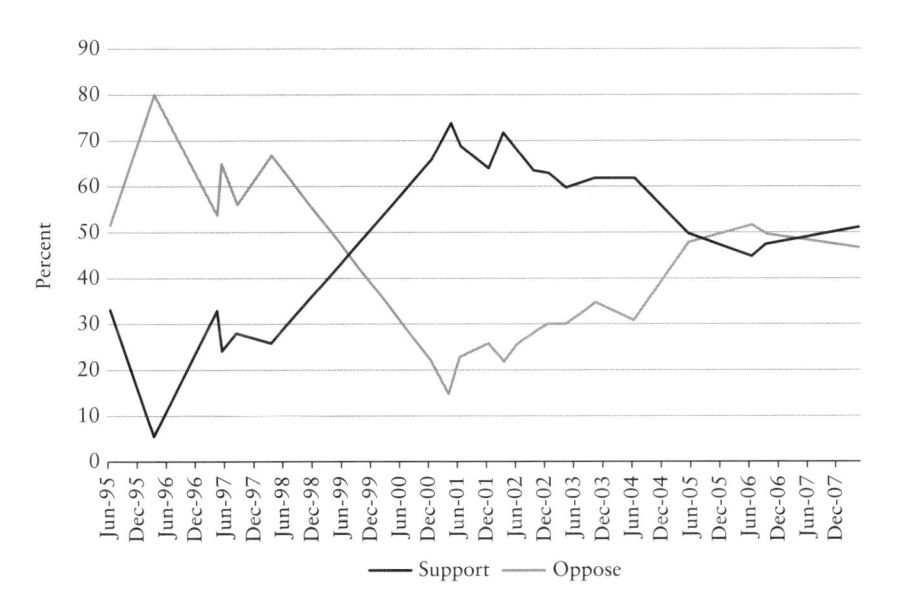

FIGURE 5.6 Palestinian opinions of suicide attacks, 1995–2008
SOURCE: Jerusalem Media and Communications Centre

legitimacy in both the West Bank and Gaza. As Hamas becomes more legitimate, efforts at destabilization through decapitation are likely to fail.

Ideology

Finally, organizational ideology overlaps with communal support in important ways. Chapter 2 makes the case that ideology is an important factor in a group's ability to withstand attacks on its leadership. There are good theoretical reasons to expect that separatist groups, religious groups, and specifically Islamist groups are harder to weaken through the removal of their leadership. Separatist groups often represent the views of a sizeable portion of the communities from which they emerge, and, as argued earlier, support contributes to resilience in important ways. This is true for some religious groups, and as the data indicates, even more true for Islamist organizations, but there are certainly notable exceptions. More directly, the ideology upon which religious (and specifically Islamist) groups are based does not depend upon the leadership for its articulation; for separatist and religious groups, it becomes institutionalized. Being both religious and nationalist, Hamas succeeded in legitimizing its ideologies, and its strategic reorganization succeeded in shifting the emphasis of the movement between its religious and nationalist doctrines to appeal to a wider audience or legitimize its message to different audiences. This flexibility and ability to adapt to political and social changes is emblematic of a strong and resilient organization.

When Hamas emerged from the Muslim Brotherhood in 1987, its goals included both the liberation of Palestine and the eventual creation of an Islamic state there. In its 1988 Charter, the organization stated that the Palestinian question could only be addressed though jihad and that Hamas would bring about a return to true Islam.[134] Further, the Charter contrasted Hamas's religious orientation to the PLO's secular ideology. However, Hamas's leadership recognized early on that to garner even more support from their local communities, it would be important to also emphasize its nationalist goals. More recently, both before and after Hamas's victory in the 2006 elections, the organization shifted its discourse from a focus on religion to nationalism, with an emphasis on national rights. Hamas has increasingly justified its violence through the lens of a nationalist discourse. Neven Bondokj finds that this shift can be seen in its use of the term *resistance* over *jihad*, a focus on Israel rather than Judaism, and reference to a national community as opposed to a Muslim community.[135] Resilient organizations such as Hamas recognize the importance of flexibility in their ideological focus and political discourse.

Both separatist and religious ideologies have the ability to transcend leadership; they are not dependent upon the leadership for their rearticulation. That

Hamas is both an Islamist and a separatist organization gives it an even stronger base within the local community. Separatist groups usually have a high degree of communal support, and decapitation can generate more sympathy for the Palestinian struggle for statehood. Communal support is also important for religious organizations. Hamas has spent a great deal of resources on developing religious institutions that provide education and social services, so its base of communal support should be even stronger.

Conclusion

This chapter argues that decapitation has not been effective against Hamas. The data on Hamas shows that leadership decapitation does not adversely affect a group's ability to carry out terrorist attacks. In fact, the organization has gained strength since its formation in 1987. Further, the number of attacks frequently increased following targeted assassinations. While the lethality of attacks has declined since 2003, this trend can be attributed in part to the erection of the separation barrier. Most importantly, repeated campaigns of leadership targeting have not dramatically hindered the ability of Hamas to carry out attacks. This resilience to decapitation can be explained by three variables. First, Hamas has become increasingly bureaucratized at the upper levels of the organization. This has facilitated a clear succession process and has increased organizational stability and efficiency. Second, Palestinian support for Hamas has generally increased over time, which has further solidified Hamas's legitimacy, making the organization stronger and more likely to withstand leadership attacks. I suggest that decapitation can increase Palestinian public support for Hamas by generating an increase in sympathy for the struggle for statehood. Finally, Hamas's ideology is drawn from the beliefs of both a separatist and religious, specifically Islamist, movement. This ideological grounding not only underscores the ability of the group to garner significant amounts of communal support, but is also not dependent upon the leadership.

The fact that decapitation has not been successful in weakening Hamas suggests the need for Israel to rethink its targeting policies. Going after lower-level and upper-level leaders may have a short-term effect upon the ability to carry out retaliatory attacks, but the long-term consequences seem to be particularly adverse. Decapitation can result in more, not fewer, attacks. Furthermore, killing leaders can increase communal support for the organization, instilling a sense of political legitimacy, as happened in 2006 in Gaza. Public support can also increase the desire for a group to exact revenge on the state carrying out targeted killings. It is essential to consider these long-term consequences when assessing the effectiveness of leadership targeting as a counterterrorism policy.

6

The Shining Path
The Organization and Support of a Left-Wing Group

The arrest of Abimael Guzmán, leader of the Communist Party of Peru (also known as the Shining Path, el Sendero Luminoso, Sendero, or SL) on September 12, 1992, is often seen as a quintessential case of successful leadership decapitation.[1] Photos of Guzmán in striped prison attire, held in a tiger cage, were widely broadcasted. This was intended to be a demoralizing blow for both Guzmán and the organization he led. Guzmán was sentenced to life in prison and called upon his followers to renounce violence. The Peruvian government arrested thousands of militants and cadres, along with nearly half of the leadership. Thousands of members accepted government amnesty, and the organization experienced a significant decline in activity.

At its height, the Shining Path had roughly one thousand militants responsible for nearly 508 attacks in 1989 alone. However, in spite of the loss of its charismatic leader and the capture of a significant number of its cadres and leaders, the organization remained active. After Guzmán's arrest, a group of activists worked to rebuild the organization, which remained active, although less so, until 1998 when its activity declined considerably. In 1999, new leader Óscar Ramírez Durand was arrested and the organization was nearly incapacitated, yet a few hardcore factions remained. By 2001, the organization was resurfacing, although it is unclear whether it was pursuing its political goals or, similar to FARC in Colombia, focusing primarily on the drug trade.[2] The organization was largely inactive. It carried out only two attacks in 2001 and one in 2002. By 2003, the organization had split again into three different factions, each with different priorities and immediate goals, but only carried out one attack. By 2009, it had changed tactics, focusing less on terrorist activity and more on drug production. In 2012, Peruvian security forces captured Florindo Eleuterio Flores Hala, known as Comrade Artemio, along with Comrade Feliciano, the organization's number two. At that time, Artemio was the highest-ranking member of the Shining Path, and aside from Guzmán and Durand, the highest-ranking member to have been arrested. Several of the group's top lieutenants were also arrested and killed in 2012 and 2013. Just before his arrest, Artemio essentially conceded that the group had been organizationally defeated. While it still carries out a limited number of attacks, these appear to be primarily drug related, and the group has acted less as a terrorist organization.

This chapter will seek to understand variation in the decapitation efforts against the Shining Path by answering the following questions: Why did the organization continue carrying out terrorist activity after Guzmán's arrest (along with the arrest of thousands of militants) in 1992, while Durand's 1999 arrest resulted in a considerable organizational weakening and a significant decline in activity? What accounted for the group's eventual demise?[3]

The decline (albeit temporary) in activity after Durand's arrest in 1999 and following the arrest and killing of the group's leadership in 2013 seems to run counter to the statistical predictions and theory of organizational resilience as presented in Chapter 4. At the time of Sendero's decline, it was a very large organization and over ten years of age, both factors that should have increased its resilience to leadership targeting, yet it ultimately succumbed to the removal of its leadership. This variation in the ability of decapitation to weaken Sendero Luminoso provides a hard test for the theory and is thus an important case to consider. However, I would expect that, as a left-wing organization, it might be more likely to experience some weakening after decapitation.

The ideology upon which the group relied was based on Guzmán's interpretation of Marxist thought. But given the group's high degree of institutionalization, its ideology became entrenched and was ultimately not dependent upon Guzmán for its articulation and spread. The movement continued for a time after his arrest. I argue that this variation in the effectiveness of decapitation against the Shining Path can be explained by two key variables: (1) bureaucratic organization and (2) communal support. As Sendero became less bureaucratic and experienced a loss in communal support, it became more susceptible to destabilization in the wake of leadership attacks. When Guzmán was arrested in 1992, the organization had a strong bureaucratic structure in place. It held a considerable amount of territory and provided both resources and services for people in the area it controlled. A strong bureaucracy was necessary to manage these functions. The group also had a considerable amount of communal support, which allowed for its initial consolidation of power. As a result, the organization was able to withstand the capture of Guzmán and other leaders. However, at the time of Durand's arrest, the organization was already in a state of decline. It had lost a considerable number of members and much of its territory, and its bureaucratic structure had been severely weakened. The group also had lower levels of support in both urban and rural communities at the time of Guzmán's arrest. This can offer an explanation for Sendero's inability to survive the capture of its top leader in 1992 and its decline in 1999. The organization was still active, carrying out a limited number of attacks, but had completely shifted in both goals and tactics, focusing more on its role in the Peruvian drug trade.

This chapter will proceed in four parts. I will first look at a brief history of Sendero Luminoso. Second, I will examine Peruvian counterterrorism policies, discussing key instances of leadership targeting and Sendero's response. Third, I will examine how the organization adapted and changed in the aftermath of Guzmán's arrest. Fourth, the chapter will discuss how the theory of organizational resilience can account for variation in the group's responses to targeting efforts. Finally, I will discuss how Sendero's case as an outlier is an important means by which to understand the theory of organizational resilience.

History of the Shining Path

The Shining Path, a Maoist terrorist organization, originated in Ayacucho, the capital city of the south-central highland province of Huamanga. The organization emerged from the Peruvian Communist Movement (PCP), formed in 1928 by José Carlos Mariátegui.[4] In the early 1960s, the PCP split into pro-Sino and pro-Soviet factions due to ideological differences. The pro-Soviet faction was criticized for not seriously considering the issue of armed insurrection. Shortly after the PCP's Fourth National Conference in January 1964, the pro-Sino group led by Saturnino Paredes split from the PCP to form the Partido Comunista del Perú–Bandera Roja (PCP-BR) or Red Flag, taking much of the PCP's youth section and members who oversaw party activity in Ayacucho. The PCP-BR split again in 1967 when a faction within the organization felt that the leadership was not initiating armed conflict.[5] Guzmán and his followers were expelled from the organization.

In 1970, Abimael Guzmán, who was active in the Ayacucho regional committee for the PCP-BR, felt that the group was not sufficiently radical and formed the Partido Comunista del Perú–Sendero Luminoso (PCP-SL), the Shining Path, in order to pursue armed struggle.[6] At the time of its founding, Sendero was largely concentrated in the highland town of Ayacucho and had a smaller network in Lima and other areas. Ayacucho was key in Sendero's development for a few reasons: it was isolated and had a high level of poverty, with little government access and almost no communication.[7] Cynthia McClintock argues that Sendero had gained a considerable amount of support in the Ayacucho region.[8] Peasant support for Sendero can be understood within the context of the failure of agrarian reform, environmental disasters, and failures in rural developments.[9] A combination of isolation and a weak repressive capacity in Ayacucho allowed for the emergence of peasant rebellion.[10]

Sendero leadership emerged from and activity was based at the Universidad Nacional de San Cristóbal de Huamanga (UNSCH) in Ayacucho, where Guzmán was a lecturer in philosophy. He eventually became director of personnel, a position from which he was able to hire and fire teachers and non-academic employees. Sendero was critical in the university's development as an institution committed to spreading Marxist principles,[11] and the university in turn was a key base for the growth of Sendero. Guzmán sent his students into different communities in order to begin the process of indoctrination through "popular education," which stressed the need for class struggle.[12] Through this process Sendero "constructed an extensive network of cadres in rural communities throughout Ayacucho."[13]

In 1980, Fernando Belaúnde, who had been deposed by General Juan Velasco Alvarado in a military coup in 1968, was elected president of Peru. He began instituting democratic reforms, and Sendero ended its decade-long process of political organization and began its armed struggle.[14] By the time Sendero escalated its armed campaign, it had well-organized cadres and, according to Degregori, "the power to affect decisively the Peruvian political scene of the 1980s."[15] Its operational capacity was greatly enhanced by the fact that its cadres were highly motivated, ideologically committed, and fueled by the belief that they were changing the nature of Peruvian society.[16] Eglund and Stohl argue that the timing of the armed campaign's commencement presents a puzzle as violence tends to have less appeal in democratic systems, yet Sendero chose a violent path and garnered considerable support. The new reforms were inconsistent with Sendero's Marxist ideology and targeted "both the symbols and representatives of democracy, and eventually also killing leftists with whom they should have been ideological allies."[17] The group saw violence as necessary to bring about a revolution that would allow for the creation of a new revolutionary society.[18]

Sendero was strategic in its attainment of local support, underscoring the centrality of communal support to the movement itself. On May 17, 1980, Sendero initiated its armed campaign when four militants burned ballot boxes and voting lists in the town plaza of the small Andean village of Chuschi.[19] Throughout 1980 and 1981, Sendero carried out bombings of public buildings and private companies, eventually targeting local public figures through attacks and assassinations.[20] During these first public manifestations of Sendero's struggle, they also hung dogs from lampposts in both Lima and Ayacucho.[21] The campaign escalated in August 1981, when eight militants killed two cattle thieves in the Chuschi plaza. Isbell argues that

> Sendero chose Chuschi for its initial military operations precisely because of this absence of haciendas, which allowed SL to experiment with peasant communities that had strong communal structures, autonomy over their resources, and whose experiences with capitalistic market penetration were minimal. . . . It is likely that Sendero viewed these communities as already having the communal structures like those it would establish in the New Peru after the revolution.[22]

By 1981, "Sendero was stronger than assumed. . . . It was established over a wide area, with a basic but effective communications systems and a centralised command structure, which guaranteed unified control over the party apparatus at all times."[23]

The Belaúnde regime underestimated the strength and danger posed by insurgent organizations. The Peruvian central government essentially gave up the Ayacucho countryside to the Shining Path in 1981 and 1982, during which Sendero continued to build a strong base of support and popular infrastructure as it prepared to continue its armed struggle against the Peruvian state.[24] In March 1982, it conducted its first large-scale urban operation in Ayacucho, in which 150 armed militants attacked the prison and freed prisoners, including 50 Sendero militants. In response, the Peruvian government cracked down on Sendero, which temporarily disrupted its operational capacity.[25] On New Year's Day 1983, five provinces declared a state of emergency, resulting in an escalation of counter-violence by the armed forces. Palmer argues that while the military felt that they had regained control of areas under Sendero power, much of Sendero's leadership was still intact.[26]

Social Context

The social context in which Sendero emerged is essential for understanding the group's evolution. The 1961 census figures indicate that in Ayacucho, 90 percent of the population was rural and almost entirely Quechua speaking. Ayacucho was an isolated and poor region, with little government access and limited communication.[27] The illiteracy rate was high at almost 73 percent.[28] Outside of the capital, there were few schools with limited public health facilities. The reopening of the Universidad Nacional de San Cristóbal de Huamanga in 1959 was critical to the revitalization of the city and formed the basis for Sendero's development. Ayacucho further benefited from development programs in the 1960s intended to increase access to education and health and to facilitate temporary migration between urban and rural areas. These changes "upset the balance of power which has rested for more than a century in the hands of a small white and mestizo elite and made others feel that it might be possible after all to improve their historically precarious situation."[29] In the early 1970s, program cutbacks resulted in an increasingly discontented peasantry. Sendero took advantage of this situation by providing paramedical, farming, and literacy services to the Indian community. Rural dissatisfaction formed the basis of much of Sendero's communal support and strengthened the organization.

Frustrated with their lack of social and economic mobility and political influence, both urban and rural youth provided a significant amount of support for Sendero. This frustration was particularly salient among the lower middle class, which according to de Wit and Gianotten formed the majority of Sendero recruits.[30] This group was composed largely of students at the university, who struggled financially and were then unable to advance their careers professionally. These individuals often taught in the villages from which they came and were unable to improve their economic situation. Peru suffered from a weak civil society and a weak state that was unable to respond to the needs of its population.[31] Furthermore, because of this weakness, the state often resorted to coercion and force in order to maintain order. These factors combined to create a climate in which Sendero was able to gain a substantial amount of support.

Sendero's attempt at consolidating power occurred in stages.[32] During the first stage, 1962–1980, Sendero developed its doctrine and leadership through fostering relationships with isolated peasant communities. In the second stage, 1980–1982, Sendero moved into an offensive strategy, in which it began to attack symbols of the state. Sendero sought to destroy communication between the government and the population, and to "begin to create a political vacuum that would allow Sendero Luminoso to become the de facto authority in the areas uncontrolled or abandoned by the state."[33] The third stage, 1982–1983, saw the generalization of violence, beginning with a prison attack in Ayacucho in 1982. During the fourth stage, 1983–1988, Sendero consolidated its politics and logistical support bases. Sendero experienced a substantial territorial expansion that was funded largely through extortion, extraction of agricultural production, and taxes from narcotics traffickers. The fifth stage, 1989–1992, saw the Peruvian government on the verge of collapse. The final stage, starting in 1992, was a continuation of the struggle for state collapse. Counter to the conventional wisdom that the capture of Guzmán resulted in Sendero's demise, Guzmán's arrest was actually beneficial to the group's struggle against the Peruvian state.[34]

It was estimated that by 1992 Sendero activity had killed over 20,000 people and resulted in over $20 billion in damages.[35] By September 1992, at the time of Guzmán's arrest, the Peruvian government "appeared to be on the brink of collapse."[36] Manwaring gives an overview of Sendero capacity at this time:

> An estimated 25,000 people had been killed in "terrorist" actions. Over 500 political figures had been "assassinated"; over 35 percent of voters *did not* vote in elections. At the same time, inflation has reached the staggering rate of 7,600 percent per year, and terrorism had destroyed an estimated equivalent of one-third to one-half of the gross national product (GNP). Businesses were preparing to close, and affluent people were leaving the country and taking their money. One observer commented that, "If *Sendero* had maintained the pressure, the government would have been at their mercy."[37]

He claims that in 1992 Sendero was not strong enough to take advantage of the vulnerability of the Peruvian state, and that Guzmán's arrest provided the group with more time to strengthen itself in order to bring about the collapse of the central government. While the arrest of Guzmán and other key leaders weakened the movement, and the Peruvian government was able to avoid defeat, the organization successfully regrouped and continued its armed struggle. Data from the Global Terrorism Database shows that from 1980 to 2015 the Shining Path carried out 4,548 incidents.[38] While there is variation in the statistics reported, the overall picture is one of a violent organization capable of carrying out a large number of deadly attacks in the face of continued attacks on its leadership.

Peruvian Counterterrorism Policies

This section will broadly examine Peruvian counterterrorism policies with a focus on its strategy of targeting Sendero's leadership. The Peruvian government carried out a number of different counterterrorism measures in an effort to bring about Sendero's collapse. McCormick argues that there were three primary components to Peru's campaign against the Shining Path.[39] First, a military program was implemented to protect key political targets and local populations from guerilla influences and to engage Sendero units directly in the field. Second, the Peruvian government carried out an economic development program to stimulate the rural economy and raise standards of living, undermining a significant source of support for the organization. Finally, a political program was established to increase confidence in the central government with the goal of further undermining support for Sendero. According to McCormick, this policy was destined to

The Shining Path

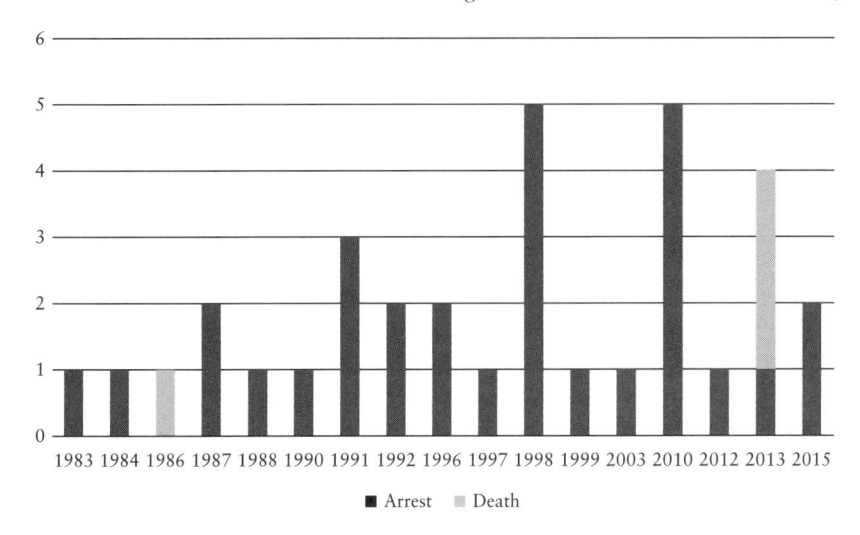

FIGURE 6.1 Leadership decapitation against Shining Path's leadership, 1983–2015

fail as it was insufficient to address the primary source of Sendero's support, lack of reform. In order to defeat Sendero,

> one had to strike at the movement's political base. This, in the end, could be achieved only by attempting to alleviate the source of popular unrest through a broad-based policy of social, economic, and political reform. The military in this scheme would play a secondary role in defeating the insurgency by permitting the government to clear and hold rural areas long enough to "win the hearts and minds" of the local inhabitants.[40]

While the Peruvian policy toward Sendero focused almost exclusively on carrying out a military response, a political response was critical to defeating Sendero. McCormick argues that the army was not well trained and was ill equipped to defeat a rural-based counterinsurgency campaign.[41] Unlike Sendero, which had a strong bureaucracy, the military was weak logistically and did not have a broad base of popular support.

Sendero Luminoso underwent repeated targeting efforts by the Peruvian government since 1983. (See Figure 6.1 for data on the number of the Shining Path leaders that have been arrested and killed from 1983 to 2015.) While the capture of Sendero's top leader, Abimael Guzmán, is often treated as one of the most successful instances of decapitation, this chapter tells a different story. Part of the debate over evaluating the efficacy of Guzmán's arrest can be traced to different standards by which to evaluate the success of counterterrorism measures. Sendero was weakened in 1999 with the arrest of Durand, but the organization regrouped a few years later, with a different focus, different goals, and different tactics. In the years following Durand's arrest, the organization was nearly inactive. The group resumed activities, carrying out more frequent attacks in 2013, but after a series targeting efforts in 2012 and 2013, the organization was nearly defeated. At this point, however, the group was driven less by ideology and more by profit. In this chapter, I examine twenty-three cases of decapitation against Sendero Luminoso in order to understand variation in its efficacy as a counterterrorism policy.[42]

Beginning in 1983, just after the organization began its military operations, Antonio Díaz Martínez, the organization's number three, was arrested. Laura Zambrano Padilla, known as Comrade Miche, believed to have been head of Sendero's military operations in Lima, was arrested in July 1984 and again in 1992 at the time of Guzmán's capture.[43] In October 1986, Claudillo Bellido Huaytalla, number three in the organization's hierarchy, was killed with twelve other leaders who were preparing to hold a regional assembly.[44] After these targeting efforts, many speculated that the group was being run from inside prison. In June 1986, 256 Sendero members were killed in prison uprisings, and Peruvian authorities assumed that the movement would disintegrate. However, Sendero adjusted to these losses and continued its armed campaign. After the events of 1986, authorities began to grasp the complexity of the organization—that the group's leadership was not "limited to a few individuals but extends through a well-trained hierarchical structure."[45] To be promoted, it was essential to exhibit a strong sense of loyalty and love for the organization, which resulted in a leadership cadre with a strong ideological motivation. Leaders were recruited from the large pool of recruits and worked their way up the organizational hierarchy. Through this process, they came to appreciate the significance of local support to the functioning of the organization.[46]

In August 1987, Freddy Rea, a chieftain in four southern states in which some of the most intense fighting occurred, was arrested along with three other rebels. In late 1987, when Sendero commander Tito Roger Valle Travesaño was captured, a number of Sendero documents were seized.[47] Through these arrests, authorities were able to gain information about the organization's structure and identify key members. However, Sendero survived these early arrests as it had developed a strong and clear hierarchy and was undergoing a process of institutionalization, which increased resilience to targeting efforts.

In June 1988, Peruvian authorities achieved a major victory by arresting Sendero's number two in command, Osmán Morote Barrionuevo. He was the highest-ranking Sendero leader to have been captured since the arrest of Martínez in 1983. Barrionuevo's capture was initially viewed as a major blow to the organization. In the aftermath, the organization used his "court appearance as a platform for expounding its views."[48] In March 1990, Julio Cesar Mezich, Sendero's military leader and believed to be the second in command, was arrested. Mezich was reported to be an important figure in Sendero's strategy of creating fear and submission in the Peruvian countryside through violence against the peasantry.[49] As a result, his arrest was believed to be both a strategic and tactical victory in the struggle against Sendero. A year later, in June 1991, Peruvian forces arrested three members of the Central Committee: Yovanka Pardavé Trujillo, Tito Roger Valle Travesaño, and Victor Garcia Castano. In September 1992, Peruvian authorities arrested Abimael Guzmán and found documents, which resulted in the arrest of other Sendero members.[50]

Sendero's command structure was weakened by the events of 1992. In addition to Guzmán, twenty-one Sendero members or sympathizers were arrested, including three senior officials within the movement: Elena Iparraguirre, the organization's number two; Laura Zambrano Padilla, head of the Central Committee in Lima and responsible for operational planning; and Martha Huatay Ruiz, lawyer for the Shining Path. In addition to these high-profile arrests, Peruvian authorities killed or arrested more than twelve members of the Central Committee. At the time, there was a significant amount of optimism regarding the ability of the Peruvian government to defeat Sendero Luminoso, and it was believed that these instances of decapitation would bring about Sendero's demise. The Fujimori and Toledo administrations both claimed that Sendero and the Túpac Amaru Revolutionary Movement (MRTA) had been defeated and that terrorism in Peru had been eradicated.[51] Even in retrospect, many studies have argued that Guzmán's arrest ultimately led to Sendero's decline.[52] However, Sendero continued to carry out terrorist attacks after Guzmán's arrest. Sanchez argues:

> In spite of the capture of several key leaders, the modernization of the armed forces and police, and the massive operations in the Andes, particularly in the province of Ayacucho, the birthplace of the Shining Path, and the Huallaga valley in the Amazon rainforest, Shining Path and the MRTA were not defeated in the 1990s. Major attacks against government institutions and civilian populations slowly ceased, as both insurgent groups turned to isolated, terrorist activities to ensure that their presence continued to be felt.[53]

Despite claims that the organization had been eradicated after the arrests of Guzmán and much of its leadership, a number of leaders remained at large, and violence continued to escalate.[54]

The Shining Path After Guzmán

In the aftermath of Guzmán's capture, the organization carried out a number of high-profile retaliatory attacks. It detonated a bomb on the Pan American Highway, wounding eight people.[55] Later in the day, Sendero guerillas shot and killed a police officer. Immediately following Guzmán's arrest, the *New York Times* reported, "Police and army officials warned repeatedly that the public should expect a wave of such violence as guerillas retaliate for the capture of their 57-year-old leader."[56] Writing three years after Guzmán's capture in 1995, Manwaring argues that "while the government has been able to capture Sendero's key leader and complicate its offensive problem, it has not managed to stop or contain Sendero Luminoso anywhere."[57] By 1995, Sendero had increased its acts of sabotage and terrorism, continued to recruit and indoctrinate militants, maintained a psychological presence with its local base, and consolidated its position within both the rural and urban areas of Peru. Tactically, Sendero continued to carry out activity to signal that it was still strong in spite of the jailed leadership.[58]

This chapter suggests that Sendero successfully regrouped because it had mechanisms in place to withstand attacks on its leadership. However, it is important to acknowledge that while Guzmán's arrest did not result in Sendero's collapse, the group was operationally weakened. One way to analyze Sendero's resilience to counterterrorism policies is to look at changes in the number of attacks and lethality of attacks over time. The Global Terrorism Database reveals that the organization suffered a considerable decline in activity but remained active. Figures 6.2 and 6.3 show the number of terrorist incidents carried out by the Shining Path and the numbers of individuals killed in those attacks, from 1978 to 2015. By 1989 Sendero activity had peaked, carrying out 599 attacks, with 1,294 individuals killed. In 1983 and 1984, Sendero carried out 494 and 502 attacks respectively, with 1,895 killed in 1983 and 2,392 killed in 1984. Sendero then suffered a decline in activity, from over 300 attacks in 1992 to 73 attacks in 1994, indicating that while the group was operationally weakened after Guzmán's arrest, it did not collapse. The number of attacks gradually declined until 1998 when Sendero carried out 3 attacks. While Sendero regrouped after Guzmán's capture, the group was never able to regain the same level of strength after Durand's arrest in 1999. It experienced a slight increase in attacks in 2013, to 10, but the number of attacks has remained remarkably low since Durand's arrest.

The organization did not suffer from succession problems and was able to easily replenish members of the Central Committee through a system in which a standing cadre was able to move into positions of leadership as needed.[59] These succession mechanisms were a major source of the group's resilience. Furthermore, many of the leaders who had been caught or killed were involved mainly in propaganda, political organization, or operational support. A majority of the committee members who were in charge of military operations were not yet apprehended.[60] Thus the insurgency continued to grow despite the capture of many top leaders. Later in this chapter, I will discuss how Sendero's bureaucratic

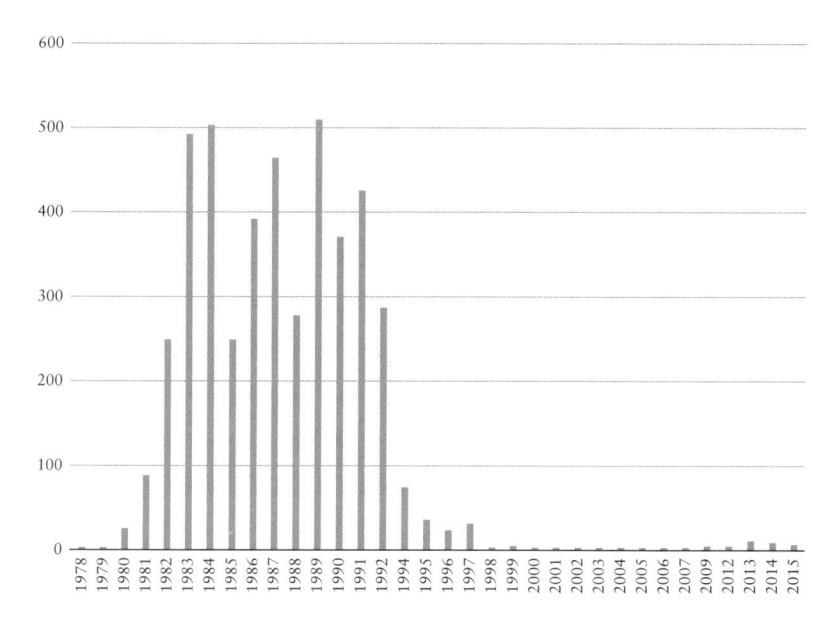

FIGURE 6.2 Shining Path attacks per year, 1978–2015

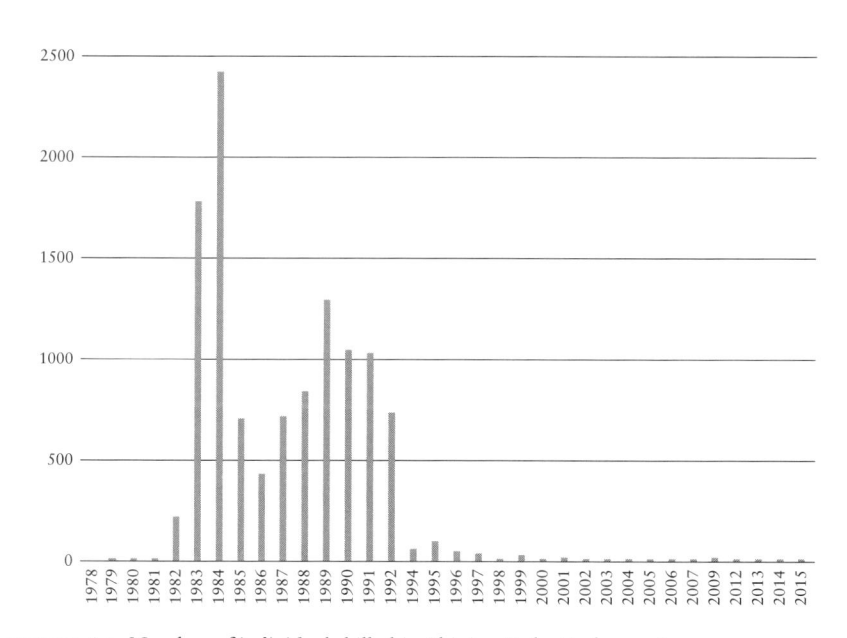

FIGURE 6.3 Number of individuals killed in Shining Path attacks, 1978–2015
SOURCE: National Consortium for the Study of Terrorism and Responses to Terrorism (START), University of Maryland. (2018). The Global Terrorism Database (GTD) [Data file]. Retrieved from https://www.start.umd.edu/gtd.

hierarchy is a key factor in explaining its resilience to over a decade of sustained decapitation attempts.

Sendero's recruitment strategies also played a key role in the ability of the group to sustain itself and recover from a significant loss of leadership. In its early years, the group recruited primarily from the faculty and students at Universidad Nacional de San Cristóbal de Huamanga. However, as the organization grew and adapted in response to counterterrorism measures, its rank-and-file membership was drawn from a diverse group of Peru's dispossessed people, from highland peasants to the urban unemployed. Sendero also made an effort to infiltrate and radicalize the labor force in order to compete with other left-wing Peruvian political movements.[61] It established popular schools aimed at spreading Guzmán's doctrine and recruiting the young.[62] McCormick argues that the recruitment processes were "cautious and methodical," intended to make the organization difficult to infiltrate.[63] A large and diverse base of support provided the group with critical resources needed for it to function, but also provided a large pool of potential recruits from which the leadership could draw.

The group's involvement in the drug trade was also critical in its ability to gain the resources and money necessary to function and withstand counterterrorism policies. In the late 1980s and early 1990s, Sendero obtained control over the coca economy in the Upper Huallaga Valley. The money this generated provided Sendero guerillas with the support necessary for an armed campaign that was strong enough to threaten the Peruvian state.[64] This income was used to pay the salaries of Sendero militants, provide financial support to those whose families were killed in combat, and pay the jail fees of arrested militants.[65] Essentially, income from the cocaine trade provided Sendero with critical resources and an opportunity to carry out violence. This will become important in understanding the significance of communal support in the ability of SL to withstand leadership attacks.

While in prison, Guzmán asked his cadres to lay down their arms. It is frequently argued that Guzmán's arrest damaged organizational morale. This argument is based on the idea that Guzmán had built a mystique, in which his "cult of personality" resulted in a high degree of internal party cohesion and discipline.[66] I argue that this cult of personality explanation cannot account for whether decapitation is successful. Despite Guzmán's capture, the weakened organization was still able to carry out deadly attacks. Moreover, during a lull in activity in the year after Guzmán's capture, Sendero regrouped and continued to carry out deadly and damaging attacks after Óscar Ramírez Durand assumed the leadership. I will look at statistics on the number and frequency of attacks carried out by Sendero after the arrests of 1992. It is important to mention here that not only did Sendero carry out retaliatory attacks in response to Guzmán's arrest, but the number of attacks remained fairly high after Durand became leader.

Under Durand, the organization faced some major setbacks. The high-ranking members of Sendero held a deep ideological commitment to the organization. However, a number of landless and urban unemployed were attracted to the organization by a sense of adventure or because it provided a means by which to earn a living, power, or respect. These members were often loyal fighters and subsequently rose to middle-ranking positions within the organization, yet they lacked the idealistic motives of the upper-level Sendero militants. After the Fujimori government stepped up its military operations against the organization, many of these midlevel operatives were arrested and provided intelligence under interrogation. Further, just before Guzmán's arrest, in May 1992, the Fujimori administration implemented the Repentance Law, which granted amnesty or reduced jail time for anyone who voluntarily abandoned armed struggle and cooperated with authorities by providing information on the identity of their ex-comrades, hideouts, arms caches, and channels of communication.[67] According to Taylor, the Repentance Law offered combatants "a relatively attractive, although far from risk-free, escape route out of the war and proffered the prospect of a more secure future."[68] As a result, the beginning of Durand's tenure was plagued by a declining number of active militants. It was estimated that more than five thousand individuals made deals with the Peruvian government. The information they provided enabled the government to inflict more damage to the organization's political and military structure.[69]

In the first months of 1993, Peruvian authorities captured or killed 15 of the 19 members of the Central Command, 4 of the 5 members of the politburo, about 80 leaders and more than 100 zonal command leaders. These targeting efforts combined with the Repentance Laws to inflict considerable damage on Sendero. But the organization survived, and Durand assumed leadership. The regional committees underwent a smooth process of succession, and a new leadership emerged. While the organization lost members at a rapid rate during this period, the commanders were still able to carry out significant attacks against the Peruvian state. In January 1993, less than three months after Guzmán's arrest, Sendero carried out two attacks, one of which involved raiding and setting fire to a college in Cajabamba. Less than a month later, the group bombed San Marcos's electricity generator. There were other attacks in 1993, which resulted in significant property damage and loss of life. During this period, Sendero moved beyond traditional strongholds and established a presence in new areas. Popular schools were established in these areas in order to garner more support for the group.[70]

In October 1993, Abimael Guzmán announced from prison that the organization should terminate its armed struggle. Despite his plea, a minority continued fighting following either "Linea Liquidacionista de Izquierda" (Left Liquidationist Line) or Sendero Rojo, headed by Durand. Taylor argues that the organization was able to adapt militarily and politically in response to Peruvian counterterrorism policies.[71] Modifying the military was the easier of the two tasks. The organization consolidated its armed groups into a single column, making defense easier. By 1996, when the group was more stable, two military units were reestablished. Rebuilding the political wing was harder and was the group's central concern. The process of political reorganization included reducing contact with the civilian population and increasing secrecy, particularly in areas where the government had successfully captured Sendero militants. In addition, the group became more sensitive to grass-roots complaints and improved its treatment of peasants, reengaging with the Peruvian populace.[72] By 1996, they began holding popular schools in areas they had formally dominated. Taylor argues that through these measures, "regional party leaders successfully restructured the political apparatus, in the process preventing its complete collapse."[73] Sendero was thus able to carry out attacks and made attempts to consolidate its power in local communities.

Alongside this resurgence, Sendero tried to revive the Civil Defense Committees (CDC), which were initially established by mobilizing local labor to protect villages. There was little support for these local committees, as the organization found it was now less able to mobilize the local population.[74] I argue that these mobilization problems reflected a decline in public support. This period of reorganization also saw an increase in targeting efforts by the Peruvian authorities. On June 5, 1995, several members of the Northern Regional Committee were captured and in August 1996, Santos Alberca, a leader in Cajabamba, was arrested. In 1997, fifty lower-level activists were arrested in Cajabamba-Huamachuco, culminating in the arrest of Óscar Ramírez Durand in July 1999.

The organization declined after Durand's capture as it regained neither its size nor the level of support it had achieved in the 1980s and 1990s. Sanchez argues that Sendero's decline was due in part to its failure to obtain support from Peru's indigenous people.[75] Both Sendero and MRTA kidnapped and massacred peasants, alienating a potential base of popular support.[76] The organization also saw an ideological shift during Durand's tenure, developing a more radical ideology that furthered its loss of communal support.

Organizational Resilience

The image of Guzmán behind bars calling upon his followers to renounce violence was seen as a severe blow to the organization. Audrey Kurth Cronin argues that Sendero was "deeply wounded" after the capture of their charismatic leader.[77] However, while Sendero may have been temporarily weakened after Guzmán's capture, the organization continued to carry out a significant number of terrorist attacks and was clearly able to withstand Peruvian efforts at destabilization. While Guzmán was the top leader, the upper echelon of the Central Committee was critical to the organization in terms of regional planning, coordination, and overall control. The narrative and data presented in the previous section demonstrate that while Sendero was weakened by attacks on its leadership, it continued to carry out deadly attacks in the aftermath of Guzmán's arrest.

The group eventually declined, but it did not do so significantly until 1998, a year before Durand's arrest, after which the group was further weakened. Looking at the statistical results presented in this chapter, one would expect that the Shining Path would continue to resist targeting efforts, given that it was large and nearly twenty years of age when it underwent significant targeting efforts. However, the data also show that left-wing organizations are easier to destabilize than other types of organizations. In order to explain variation in the success of decapitation against Sendero, it is necessary to turn to the theory of organizational resilience laid out in Chapter 2. I argue that bureaucracy and communal support can explain why decapitation was unsuccessful in 1992 but more successful after 1999.

Ideology

Sendero's ideology was based largely on a specific understanding of Marxist philosophy, a synthesis of Maoist beliefs about peasant rebellion and the theories of Peruvian Marxist José Carlos Mariátegui.[78] Like Mao, Guzmán saw Peru as a semifeudal and semicolonial society, in which the development of bureaucratic rebellion ran counter to the national interests of the Peruvian people.[79] In addition to emphasizing the importance of class struggle, Sendero provided an important venue for expressing hostility toward the country's failing economy.[80] Sendero's form of Maoism was distinctively violent and centered on armed rebellion. Guzmán envisioned a prolonged peasant guerilla war that spread from a rural base to the cities, ultimately taking over Lima by blocking the city's supply of food, water, and electricity. His ideological doctrine was violent and uncompromising. Violence was an end in itself, a force that could overcome traditional thought and pave the way for the growth of a revolution.[81]

The organization was built from the top down and horizontally.[82] Unlike many separatist or religious organizations, its ideology did not emerge from the beliefs of the community from which it arose. Rather, Sendero's ideology emanated from the group's leadership and specifically from Guzmán's interpretation of Marxism. Given the centrality of Guzmán's philosophy to the movement, the process by which the leadership spread Sendero's doctrine was crucial to gaining supporters and active militants. Moreover, the process of indoctrination that occurred in the universities and local schools resulted in well-organized cadres that were steeped in ideology.[83] The ideological rigidity of the group was critical to its growth and development. According to Guzmán, the organization, as opposed to its activity, was key to its success, and as a result, Guzmán tried to establish "a dedicated cadre, a revolutionary party, a guerilla army, and a support mechanism for the entire organization."[84]

Sendero's ideology and decision-making processes were hierarchical and centralized, originating from Guzmán's radical, autocratic doctrine, and necessitated an extensive process of indoctrination carried out in local schools and rural communities.[85] Guzmán's position at the Universidad Nacional de San Cristóbal de Huamanga allowed him supervision over faculty appointments, and according to McCormick, "Through the establishment of a radical faculty, Guzmán was able to oversee the indoctrination and recruitment of a generation of student supporters, many of whom in turn became teachers themselves, returning to their villages to carry on the movement message and establish a core network of political activists."[86] This process of indoctrination, which was directed at the rural and urban underclasses who had been excluded from the economic mainstream of Peru, was critical in Sendero's recruitment process.[87] Sendero's growth and expansion was based in part on its grassroots political work. During the 1970s, Sendero concentrated on its ideological evolution and on developing its relationship with peasant communities in Ayacucho.

Sendero was able to spread its message through indoctrinating schools with its ideology and providing social services to the rural and urban underclasses. The Peruvian state had failed to address the needs of the rural population, providing an opportunity for Sendero to help the local community and thus gain loyalty. This provided the source for much of the group's support, which was critical to its resilience. Sendero also provided important security mechanisms. Lewis Taylor argues that the group was able to "generate support in the countryside because it brought services that state bureaucracies failed to deliver—personal security, a form of order, an efficient (but summary) system of justice."[88] Initially, Sendero imposed an austere "public morality," which, while reducing individual liberty, still received public acceptance. Essentially, the hierarchical paternalism and authoritarian violence was seen as an acceptable trade-off for the security provided by Sendero.[89] The group delivered security and services to the local communities, which in turn provided Sendero with recruits and support.

There is an important interaction between ideology and communal support in the case of the Shining Path, which can in part explain why decapitation brought about more significant organizational weakening after 1999. Eventually, the imposition of its ideology created hostility between Sendero and the local communities. Taylor writes, "A number of schisms between guerilla organizers and the rural population arose when cadres acted to tighten Party control over the *puna* communities and impose their ideological agenda."[90] There was some support for its tactics, but Sendero's excessive use of violence had a negative impact on local support in certain communities, particularly those that had higher levels of economic development and a history of political participation in peasant unions. Despite these schisms between the activists and the local population, Sendero enjoyed a sufficient amount of support to keep its movement afloat and to continue growing its armed campaign.

The theory developed in this book would predict that as a left-wing organization based upon an ideology that depended upon its leadership, the Shining Path should be more likely to suffer organizational weakening at the hands of a decapitation strategy, but it did not immediately decline. The following two variables on bureaucracy and communal support can account for this variation.

Bureaucracy

The data in Chapter 4 indicate that a group's size and, in some cases, age can account for its ability to survive leadership attacks. Older and larger groups should be more likely to have bureaucratized characteristics, making them more resilient to leadership targeting, while smaller and younger groups are much easier to weaken. In this section, I will look at the relationship between size, age, and Sendero's resilience in the face of repeated instances of decapitation over a thirty-year period.

Sendero was over ten years of age at the time of the 1992 arrest of Guzmán and twelve other leaders. While age was insignificant in the multivariate analyses, generally the data show that older organizations (over twenty years of age) are more resilient, and that decapitation is less effective against larger organizations in a few different ways. In the dataset used in this study, the Shining Path was coded according to a conservative estimate of roughly 1,000 active militants.[91] The data indicate that the largest groups will likely continue carrying out attacks after decapitation, and one of the strongest statistical findings in in this book is that the most resilient organizations have between 1,000 and 5,000 members. Even if we assume that Sendero had under 1,000 members, groups in this category are still quite resilient.

The results of the transition matrix analyses reveal that decapitated groups with over 1,000 members have a higher probability of experiencing an increase in the frequency of attacks than nondecapitated groups. As with all terrorist organizations, there is considerable variation in how to determine a group's size, and estimates can include the number of armed cadres, militants, or the larger base of supporters. According to David Palmer, by 1992, Sendero had gained considerable strength, with between 3,000 and 4,000 armed cadres and over 10,000 militants. This distinction between armed cadres and militants is an important one. Further, Palmer claims that at its height in 1992, just before the capture of Abimael Guzmán, the group had about 50,000 supporters.[92] McClintock reported similar numbers: about 10,000 militants and 50,000–100,000 committed members.[93] This large base of support, or "committed members," provided the group with access to resources and the ability to support and hide its armed cadres in local communities, both urban and rural.

While decapitation did not result in Sendero's collapse, the group was weakened. Many militants took advantage of the Repentance Laws, which significantly reduced the group's membership.[94] The group lost some of its ideological fervor with the arrest of Guzmán and the subsequent rise of Durand.[95] By the time Durand was captured in 1999, it had experienced a decline in the number of armed militants and supporters, and membership dropped to only a few hundred active members. While organizations with between 100 and 500 members are still fairly resistant to decapitation, generally, as a group becomes smaller, decapitation is more likely to be effective.

As an organization grows in size and/or age, it is more likely to have developed bureaucratic features: an organized administrative staff, a division of labor, a hierarchy of authority, and a stable structure of rules, policies, and procedures. A bureaucratic hierarchy, particularly at the upper levels of the organization, can facilitate a clear process of succession and increase organizational efficiency and stability. These bureaucratic elements can strengthen a group's ability to resist leadership decapitation. Changes in Sendero's bureaucratic consolidation provide an explanation for variation in the effectiveness of leadership targeting. While Sendero was highly bureaucratized in 1992, its bureaucratic consolidation began to decline after Guzmán's arrest, and in 1999 when Durand was arrested, the organization did not have the clear and rigid bureaucratic hierarchy necessary to withstand another removal of a key leader.

Sendero built an elaborate political and military apparatus.[96] The organization was structured hierarchically, with responsibility divided into five distinct levels.[97] The largest group, which rarely participated in armed violence, formed the base of the movement and was composed of a nationwide body of *sympathizers*, many of whom were not full party members. These individuals had an interest in the group's ideology, took part in demonstrations, and provided support in the form of money, medicine, clothes, food, arms, and explosives. The second level, the *activists* or *local forces*, comprised students, workers, and members of the urban and rural underclass. Within this group, there were four units. The logistical cell was responsible for collating information for transmission to the upper levels of the organization. The propaganda unit engaged in the distribution of leaflets, set up popular education programs, and organized demonstrations. A third unit provided material support and legal advice to combatants, while the fourth unit carried out assassinations.[98] The third level of the hierarchy, *militants*, which formed the popular guerilla army, were directly involved in militant violence. The fourth level, the *commanders*, were responsible for military and political activity by region. Finally, the *Central Committee* was composed of a small number of the group's elite members.

The upper level of Sendero's leadership comprised the Central Committee.[99] By 1989, it had about nineteen regular members and was headed by Guzmán.[100] The committee was responsible for setting the group's ideology, strategy, and policy. There were six regional committees under the National Central Committee. While each regional committee functioned independently, they followed the directives of the National Committee.[101] The Metropolitan Central Committee, under the National Central Committee, was designed to capitalize on Sendero's increasingly urban strategy. The organization also created a separate Metropolitan Regional Central Committee. There were four "special squads," responsible for assault and assassination, that answered directly to the Metropolitan Central Committee.[102] It is important to underscore that while these regional and metropolitan committees had a considerable amount of autonomy, they were ultimately supervised by, and had direct contact with, the National Central Committee.

While Sendero was structured hierarchically, its basic operational unit was the cell.[103] Each cell had between five and nine members, including a leader, an explosives expert, a physical training instructor, and a person responsible for ideological training. Only one member had contact with leadership at the next level.[104] Cells were organized by leaders of a subsector, who answered to a regional committee, of which there were six in Peru. The regional subcommittees carried out specific operations. Control of the organization rested firmly with the central command and, until 1992, primarily with Guzmán. The cellular structure provided the movement with greater flexibility. The group functioned on a cellular level on the regional and local level, but overall, was structured as a bureaucratic hierarchy. Guzmán had a significant amount of authority over the Central Committee and met frequently with regional leaders. While he coordinated nationwide attacks, regional and local leaders planned local attacks. Similar to the case of Hamas, this hybrid organizational structure, a combination of a decentralized and hierarchical organization, increased Sendero's organizational strength and resilience.

At the time of Guzmán's capture in 1992, Sendero was operationally decentralized, with a clear hierarchical structure at the upper level of the organization, characterized by a hierarchy of authority, a well-organized administrative staff, and a division of labor. This organizational structure provided the group with resilience. Despite Guzmán's plea for nonviolence, the group continued to carry out attacks. However, by Durand's arrest in 1999, the splintered group was unable to sustain its bureaucratic strength, which increased its susceptibility to counterterrorism measures such as leadership decapitation. Durand could not sustain the group's ideological focus and membership. At the time of Durand's capture, the organization was only operating in a few rural areas in eastern Peru.

Communal Support

Groups with a higher degree of communal support are less dependent upon leadership for the acquisition of resources necessary to function. Groups with local support have an easier time building organizational infrastructure, carrying out attacks, and avoiding detection, as the community can provide places for leaders and operatives to hide. Groups with more support also have a larger resource pool to supply recruits, further increasing their ability to carry out effective campaigns. This degree of support for ideological groups can vary considerably.

Given the statistical finding that left-wing organizations are the easiest types of organizations to destabilize through decapitation, Sendero should have succumbed to leadership decapitation after Guzmán's arrest in 1992. It was, however, a highly bureaucratized organization and, unlike many other left-wing organizations, had acquired a significant amount of local communal support, which contributed to its ability to withstand its leader's arrest. The group's decline in later years can be attributed to a decrease in institutionalization and waning support in the Peruvian communities.

Sendero had a much larger base of communal support in 1992 than at the time of Durand's capture in 1999, which explains the failure of decapitation in 1992 and its success in 1999. The remainder of this section will examine trends in support for Sendero. While there is little data on public opinion and surveys about views of the Shining Path during this time period, it is possible to get a sense of attitudes toward the government and political violence in general, and specific polls are referenced when available.[105]

As discussed earlier in the chapter, the social context in which Sendero emerged is an essential component of the group's evolution and support. The organization emerged from the Peruvian Communist Party in the rural department of Ayacucho, an area that was plagued by high rates of poverty and a lack of government services. Sendero drew upon a sizeable base of peasant support through the provision of social services in the Ayacucho region. In addition to peasant support, much of the rural and urban youth, who believed that they lacked social and economic mobility and political influence, were attracted to Sendero. The lower middle class felt the same frustrations due to the lack of economic mobility within Peruvian society.[106] De Wit argues that this frustration over the lack of infrastructure, resource shortages, poor communication, and limited energy production was strongest among the lower middle class. This group, recruited largely from the universities, eventually formed the bulk of Sendero militants. Much of the frustration stemmed from the failure of education to enable social mobility. Many Sendero recruits, who were students at the universities, came from poor families, went to school, graduated as teachers, and were then unable to advance. They usually ended up in low-paying jobs, often in the villages from which they came. Many of these teachers were attracted to the Leninist philosophy, which offered an important role to intellectuals.[107]

In addition to economic and social frustration, Sendero support was bolstered by the weakness of the local administration. Initially, Sendero did not carry out acts of violence against citizens of Ayacucho, while the police arbitrarily arrested and tortured residents in the city. As a result, "by 1982 many local citizens had lost all faith in government processes."[108] A poll from 1989 reported that "60 percent of those surveyed did not trust the police, and 43 percent said that they felt fear—as opposed to security—when they saw a police officer."[109] In fact, between 1987 and 1994 public opinion polls carried out by the Instituto APOYO showed that the police were "consistently ranked as one of the most ineffective of government institutions."[110] This occurred within the context of a breakdown of organized politics, which created political power vacuums that insurgent groups such as SL were able to exploit.

Outside of Ayacucho, there was more peasant resistance to Sendero, especially after the organization targeted peasant and other community leaders. However, the inability of the central government to provide for the rural areas afforded Sendero an opportunity to gain support among rural Peruvian populations by addressing their economic and social needs. McClintock argues that, while Sendero initially succeeded in gaining a significant amount of rural support, over time the movement lost some appeal.[111] Initially, Sendero militants did not try to impose their beliefs upon the peasant populations and supported their local causes. McClintock notes that Sendero would gather intelligence about individuals who were seen as "wrongdoers in a community" and would threaten or assassinate these individuals if they did not submit to Sendero's demands. Often these assassinations increased support for the movement, as the targeted were often rich peasants or leaders of cooperatives, who were resented by the local populations.[112] In Lima, Sendero targeted individuals who were seen as the cause of local problems.[113]

There was local support for Sendero, but participation in the movement could also be coerced. Eglund and Stohl argue that while there was sympathy for the group's goals and ideology, "The SL used violence to force non-participants to essentially choose sides, to intimidate Peruvians to join in their struggle."[114] Whether it was coerced or voluntary, this local, grassroots support was critical to Sendero's organizational strength and its resilience to repeated leadership attacks. In some instances, Sendero's violence against peasants and local leaders resulted in a decline in support, yet the organization was able to convince many peasants in Ayacucho that its selective assassinations were only targeting "bad" people. Not only were people willing to accept its brutal policies, but Sendero's assassinations were actually a selective incentive aimed at individuals reluctant to support and join the movement.[115] Essentially, assassination and terror were used recruitment mechanisms and can account for regional variation in Sendero's assassination campaign. In areas with fewer assassinations, support for Sendero should be higher, and accordingly a large number of assassinations should be correlated with lower levels of support. While Ron argues that this study overlooks the difference between individuals who were afraid to join the movement due to fear of government reprisals and those who did not join because they were already aligned with other left-wing groups in Peru, Marks's work highlights the importance of understanding variation in support for Sendero.[116]

Sendero also provided material benefits, such as money, livestock, and other goods as another means of increasing support and participation. By the late 1980s, Sendero was paying a salary of $250 to $500 per month, about three to eight times higher than the salaries of many Peruvian teachers. McClintock references a study by the Osores research team showing that 57 percent of Senderistas received salaries and 36 percent received food, housing, or money for expenses.[117] "Sendero combined the use of force, material benefits, and symbols, to create a sense among many Peruvians that it was a better, and more powerful, alternative than the Peruvian state."[118] McClintock argues that in the early 1980s support for Sendero was substantial, particularly among peasants in the southern highlands. It was estimated that almost 80 percent of Ayacucho's townspeople sympathized with Sendero. By the late 1980s, support continued to be high in Ayacucho and other departments.

Sendero had support in urban communities as well, where it carried out a number of humiliating acts against the central government that increased its support. By 1991, Sendero had made significant inroads in Lima "in terms of its growing organizational influence in specific districts and its growing military presence."[119] By 1992, Lima was under siege, and the group had developed considerable influence in the *barriadas*, low-income, largely illegal squatter developments in urban areas. A poll carried out in metropolitan Lima revealed that 17 percent of individuals believed that subversion was justified. Burt argues that this poll was startling to those who felt that the Shining Path would not garner enough support. In fact, 17 percent of individuals from the lowest socioeconomic level held favorable views toward Guzmán.[120]

By December 1991, 57 percent of Peru's provinces were reported to be in a state of emergency. Gustavo Gorriti and Simon Strong estimated that from 1991 to 1992, Sendero controlled about 40 percent of Peru. Overall, these numbers indicate a large amount of public support.[121] Burt argues in her study of political violence in Peru that state institutions were collapsing in the late 1980s and early 1990s, which is why the Shining Path's use of violence as a deterrent to criminal activity received high approval. Polls conducted in 1993 and 1994 found that almost half of Lima's population, and 60 percent of the poorest sections, approved of the group's lynching as a form of punishment and tool of coercion.[122]

In many ways, Sendero was able to function as a state-like entity by taking advantage of the weakness of the Peruvian government and institutions. This is a common trend for terrorist organizations seeking support. Hamas was able to take advantage of this vacuum and provide important resources for the Palestinian people, and al-Qaeda franchises were able to do the same. ISIS used the weakness of the state in Iraq and Syria to gain support.[123] The Shining Path's ability to launch a violent and coercive struggle was reinforced by the inability of the Peruvian central government to fight a successful counterterrorism campaign against it.

Sendero's control of a significant amount of the coca production and trade in Peru's Upper Huallaga Valley generated some support for the organization. Bruce Kay examines how the rise and fall of the coca market in the Upper Huallaga Valley played a part in the rise and eventual fall of the Shining Path.[124] He argues that the money from "'King Coca' afforded the guerillas both support and resources with which to project such a formidable national presence that, by 1992, they could credibly claim to be on the verge of 'a strategic equilibrium' with the state."[125] Sendero was able to take advantage of the power vacuum in the Upper Huallaga Valley and by June 1987 took control of the coca trade.[126] The lack of national presence allowed the organization to "perform statelike functions, from protection and 'law' enforcement to conscription and taxation."[127] Kay argues that its relationship with the local community was mutually beneficial. Because of this relationship, Sendero had to rely less upon coercion or indoctrination in developing support. This drug money ultimately financed Sendero's advancement into Lima and other urban areas.

After its peak in the early 1990s, Sendero began to experience a decline in communal support and, ultimately, a serious organizational weakening. Changes in the level of support can be identified in four areas: (1) decline in coca prices and production, (2) the end of the Soviet Union, (3) the Repentance Laws, and (4) disillusionment with its increasingly brutal tactics. First, while the rise of coca prices was correlated with increases in support for Sendero, falling coca prices in the 1990s, along with a process of state strengthening by the Fujimori government, resulted in a loss of popular support and a substantial weakening of the organization. Kay writes that "the opportunity structure that afforded Sendero support and resources in the Upper Huallaga Valley during the 1980s changed in the 1990s through a combination of market forces and the antidrug policies enacted during President Alberto Fujimori's two terms."[128] The major decline in coca prices led to a reduction in coca cultivation and an increase in other legal crops. Kay estimates that the coca bust, Sendero's loss of control over the Upper Huallaga Valley, and the decline of its relationship with Colombia resulted in a loss of tens of millions of dollars. By 1997, it was incapable of holding territory for any length of time, though it did occasionally occupy small villages. Kay argues that the decline of support for the movement after the coca crash "illustrates the pragmatic and ephemeral nature of support for guerilla movements in an age in which Marxist ideologies have lost much of their resonance as revolutionary principles."[129] This decline coincides with a drop in Sendero activity, suggesting that a loss of support weakened the group to such an extent that the arrest of Durand in 1999 would be likely to have much more an impact on organizational strength than Guzmán's arrest had in 1992.

Second, the fall of the Soviet Union resulted in a significant reduction in the popularity and relevance of Marxist ideology. In identifying the different causal pathways by which organizations end, Audrey Kurth Cronin argues that as an ideology loses relevance, its base of support declines.[130] This is particularly apparent in the case of Sendero. After Guzmán's arrest, two years after the collapse of the Soviet Union, support for the organization declined. By the time Durand was captured in 1999, Marxist ideology was largely irrelevant, translating into low support for the organization. Durand had been unable to maintain its ideological cohesion, a major driving force of Guzmán's leadership. Durand actually changed the ideological focus of the organization, which may have alienated many of its former members who believed in Guzmán's doctrine. Ultimately, this decline in support can be traced to disillusionment with the movement itself, which was already in decline at the time of Durand's arrest.

Third, the group also suffered losses in membership. The Repentance Laws, which were used as an intelligence-gathering device to weaken Sendero (and MRTA), led thousands of cadres to make deals with the Peruvian government, depleting Sendero's ranks of militants. This loss of membership should also have contributed to a significant loss of local support for the organization.

Finally, Sendero's increasingly brutal tactics resulted in a loss of popular support. Initially, many peasants were willing to accept the group's rigid ideological agenda and repressive measures in exchange for security and the provision of important services that the central government was unable to provide in many rural areas. But over time Sendero's increasingly brutal tactics undermined its support, particularly in areas that had a history of political participation and higher levels of economic development.[131]

Conclusion

The case of Sendero is somewhat of an outlier. It was a larger and older group that eventually succumbed to sustained efforts at leadership decapitation. Sendero was also a left-wing organization, which should increase the likelihood of its decline after decapitation. While a religious or separatist doctrine has a foundation in the local community and usually represents the goals of the majority, a left-wing group tends to espouse a more radical set of beliefs with a smaller base of support that can alienate potential supporters. Because the doctrine of religious and separatist groups is more rooted in the local communities and less dependent upon the leader for articulation, the loss of a leader will be less disruptive. In the case of the Shining Path, the organization was dependent upon Guzmán's specific interpretation of Marxism, and his capture should have weakened the appeal of the group's goals and the motivating force behind the organization. Durand rejected Guzmán's specific interpretation and advanced his own understanding, motivating a core of activists who believed in the group's larger revolutionary principles. Both bureaucratization and communal support can thus explain why Sendero withstood not only Guzmán's arrest in 1992 but also repeated targeting efforts after 1993. The group then underwent a period of reorganization, with the support and resources provided at the local level proving critical in allowing the group to continue carrying out attacks and pursue its ideological mission. When the group eventually declined, it suffered from organizational weakness and a loss of communal support.

First, communal support can provide one way to understand variation in group resilience to decapitation. Sendero's popularity peaked in 1991 and 1992, which can explain, in part, its ability to withstand the arrest of Guzmán. At the time of his arrest, support for the organization was high and continued to be so through the mid-1990s, despite Guzmán's call for nonviolence. Given that the group's ideology was specific to Guzmán's interpretation of Maoism, it would be reasonable to assume that his arrest and calls for a renunciation of violence would result in the decline of the group's ability to continue its cause. On the other hand, it can be argued that Guzmán successfully institutionalized his ideology, as bin Laden did with al-Qaeda, and was able to retain a cadre of committed members. Moreover, Durand assumed leadership of a faction advancing his own ideology, which lacked the appeal of the original movement. Regardless, a lack of support for the group, its message, and its goals combined with bureaucratic weakness to play a part in the group's eventual degradation. By 1997, the group was losing support due to a number of factors, including disillusionment with the overall struggle and frustration with Sendero's increasingly brutal tactics. The group had also become weakened organizationally, resulting in a further decline in strength after Durand's arrest in 1999. A loss of group support meant fewer resources to carry out an effective campaign that continued to challenge the government in Lima, ultimately increasing susceptibility to collapse.

Second, bureaucratic stability can also account for the variation in Sendero's success. At the time of Guzmán's capture, the organization had a well-institutionalized structure with bureaucratic features in place that should have increased its resilience to targeting. While the organization should have become stronger over time, as older groups are more likely to withstand leadership attacks, the organization became smaller and institutionally weaker. By the time of Durand's arrest, the group's bureaucracy was weakened, caused, in part, by a significant decline in membership and the beginning of organizational splintering, which also undermined its institutionalized structure.

While the case of Sendero is often treated as a great decapitation success, I argue that this claim is flawed on two fronts. First, Guzmán's capture did not result in the collapse of the group he led; it carried out attacks immediately after his arrest, then suffered a period of inactivity, and was ultimately able to regroup and continue its armed campaign. Second, Durand's capture is also treated as a targeting success. While I code his arrest as a success, the group was so severely weakened at the time that it is unclear whether it would have been able to survive even if Durand had not been captured. Nevertheless, Durand's capture is treated as a success that can be explained by the Shining Path's weakness, as seen in its diminished level of bureaucratization and local support.

7

Al-Qaeda
Religious Ideology and Organizational Resilience

Both before and after the targeted killing of Osama bin Laden on May 11, 2011, many experts, scholars, and policy makers assumed that his capture or death would result in the demise of the organization. In June 2011, President Barack Obama claimed that al-Qaeda was "on a path to defeat."[1] The following month, Secretary of Defense Leon Panetta said that the United States was "within reach of strategically defeating al-Qaeda."[2] While bin Laden's death was clearly a tactical victory, in the immediate aftermath it was not clear how it would impact al-Qaeda. Would the organization adapt, become stronger and emboldened, or become operationally ineffective? While optimism regarding this attack was based on the belief that bin Laden was critical to the operational capacity of the organization, al-Qaeda did not fall apart; the organization underwent a process of succession, and subsequently many Islamist groups declared their affiliation with and loyalty to it.

This chapter will consider whether targeting al-Qaeda's leadership affected its strength and operational capacity. In doing so, it will examine data on al-Qaeda and affiliated organizations. More broadly, the organizational structure, communal support, and ideological cohesion of the organization will be examined and analyzed through the theoretical model developed earlier in the book. It is critical to highlight that al-Qaeda is not a single organization, which can complicate analysis. While it began as one group, al-Qaeda Central (AQC), a larger organization, evolved over time, and from it emerged a number of affiliated organizations or franchises.[3] In some cases, AQC wielded considerable control over, or attempted to control, an affiliate, while in other cases, the affiliates operated much more as independent organizations. In this way, al-Qaeda can be thought of as a "metaorganization" composed of many different and independent organizations and individuals characterized by their level of autonomy and their pursuit of shared goals. These networks of organizations and individuals have their own "motivations, incentives, and cognition."[4] Accordingly, each agent may not be linked by formal authority but instead display a range of linkages across boundaries. Within this framework, al-Qaeda is the metaorganization, and the affiliates are the autonomous organizations with shared goals. I argue that both the core organization and its affiliates have been resilient to leadership targeting. In some cases, the organizations have become even more active and have adapted in important ways, strengthening the ideological groups.

The theory of organizational resilience will be examined by looking at the organizational structure and communal support of AQC and al-Qaeda in Iraq (AQI), which eventually became the Islamic State of Iraq and Syria (ISIS). This chapter will underscore how for all three affiliates, variation in the extent to which decapitation impacts a group's operational capacity and resilience can be explained by its level of popular support, degree of bureaucratization, and ideology.

ISIS's territorial gains and successes in summer 2014 diverted attention from al-Qaeda, with many in the press, academic communities, and policy circles operating under the assumption that al-Qaeda was declining, largely inactive, and posed much less of a threat. Bin Laden was seen as a leader with both operational and inspirational authority,[5] essential to the cohesion and functioning of the organization and its ability to broadcast its message and attract new recruits. The raid on bin Laden's compound in Abbottabad, Pakistan, code-named Operation Neptune Spear, resulted in the capture of a large amount of intelligence, with one senior military intelligence official calling it "the single largest collection of senior terrorist materials ever."[6] A year after the raid that killed bin Laden, the Obama administration claimed that al-Qaeda's demise was imminent. On May 1, 2012, President Obama stated, "The goal that I set—to defeat al-Qaeda and deny it a chance to rebuild—is now within our reach."[7] As reported in the *Wall Street Journal*, the White House provided seventeen of the hundreds of captured documents to show that bin Laden was a powerless and isolated individual within an organization that was falling apart. The Obama administration "sought to promote a message that the terrorist organization was essentially defunct."[8] Barak Mendelsohn argues that this message was essential in bringing about an end to the military campaigns in Iraq and Afghanistan. However, the administration continued with counterterrorism policies, such as expanding the use of drones in targeting militants and continued use of the National Security Agency for surveillance and intelligence gathering. Moreover, a closer examination of the documents reveals a different reality, one where bin Laden was involved in the day-to-day functioning of a robust organization that had plans to continue expanding even further in West Africa, the Islamic Maghreb, and East Africa. Despite the threat that al-Qaeda and its many franchises still posed, much of the public discussion was focused on the weakening of AQC in the aftermath of the 2003 invasion of Afghanistan, the 2006 Surge in Iraq, and bin Laden's death. This chapter will show that despite the focus that has been placed upon the threat that ISIS poses to US national security and global security, al-Qaeda remains an active organization.

This chapter will begin with a brief discussion of al-Qaeda's history and current literature on counterterrorism policy, with a focus on AQC and AQI. This will be followed by an examination of data on targeting efforts against AQC and its affiliates that will show how decapitation has been and will continue to be ineffective against them. Finally, the chapter will look at both AQC and AQI through the lens of the theory of organizational resilience in order to explain why the groups have been so resilient and why targeting has the potential to result in counterproductive consequences.

Background

Al-Qaeda, which began in 1988 as a more hierarchically structured organization, has become an expansive transnational movement, or metaorganization, with franchises in Saudi Arabia, Iraq, Algeria, Yemen, Somalia, Syria, and the Indian subcontinent.[9] These affiliates emerged from the original core organization, which for the remainder of this chapter will be referred to as AQC. Al-Qaeda is often treated as a single entity, yet each affiliate is a separate organization with its own structure. Further, each group has its own particular interpretation of al-Qaeda's goals and mission, often simultaneously pursuing local goals. Counterterrorism measures differ depending on the location and group being targeted, and as a result it is useful to consider al-Qaeda as a larger social movement and each affiliate as a separate organization. Mendelsohn characterizes the formal organizational expansion of al-Qaeda as "the reorganization of a terrorist group through publicly announced structural changes, involving formal relationships with other groups."[10]

AQC was formed in Peshawar, Pakistan, in 1988 as the mujahedeen were defeating Soviet forces in Afghanistan. Al-Qaeda, which means "the Base" in Arabic, then moved its operation to Sudan, during which time they planned the 1993 attacks on the World Trade Center in New York City. In 1996, bin Laden moved the group's operations to Afghanistan when he issued a fatwa against the United States. Later that year, al-Qaeda carried out bombings on US embassies in Kenya and Tanzania, resulting in 224 deaths. After the attacks of September 11, 2001, US and British forces launched an invasion in Afghanistan, toppling the Taliban's regime, after which al-Qaeda moved its base of operations to Pakistan. After a period of decline, the group reorganized itself and began planning and executing further attacks, including the 2002 attacks in Bali and the 2004 attacks in Madrid. Bin Laden's calls for global jihad resulted in the formation of numerous affiliates that escalated their own campaigns. An affiliated branch in Yemen was responsible for bombing the USS *Cole* in the Yemeni port of Aden in 2000. In 2009, the Yemeni branch merged with the Saudi branch to form al-Qaeda in the Arabian Peninsula (AQAP). Franchise organizations now span the globe with affiliates in, but not limited to, Somalia, Syria, Iraq, Mali, Nigeria, Indonesia, the Philippines, and the Sinai Peninsula.

Al-Qaeda in Iraq emerged from Jama'at al-Tawhid wal-Jihad (JTJ), an organization formed in Jordan in 1999 under the leadership of Abu Musab al-Zarqawi. JTJ eventually moved to Iraq after the US invasion in 2003, where it fought against coalition forces and their Iraqi allies. In addition to Iraqis, the organization attracted a large number of foreign fighters opposed to the US occupation of Iraq. The group was also composed of members of Ansar al-Islam, a Sunni Kurdish organization. In 2004, al-Zarqawi formally declared loyalty to bin Laden, and the group changed their name to Tanzim Qaidat al-Jihad fi Bilad al-Rafidayn and became known as al-Qaeda in Iraq. In addition to targeting US and coalition forces, it carried out a brutal campaign against Iraqi Shi'ite civilians and politicians, calling for war against the Shi'ite community. Its tactics, such as beheadings, were seen as excessively brutal by bin Laden and the leadership of AQC. In 2005, Ayman al-Zawahiri (who would assume leadership of al-Qaeda after bin Laden's death), sent a letter to al-Zarqawi praising him for his dedication to the movement while urging him to temper his campaign of killing Shi'ite civilians. Al-Zawahiri argued in the letter that popular support from the Muslim community is critical for the group's larger goals, and killing Shi'ite civilians would undermine that support.[11] Similarly, bin Laden later urged al-Shabaab to refrain from killing civilians.[12]

The period from 2004 to 2007 was extremely violent, with over 1,500 civilian and almost 100 US military fatalities per month by August 2006.[13] By 2006, AQI was estimated to have nearly a thousand active militants. In January 2006, it created an umbrella organization called the Mujahedeen Shura Council with the goal of unifying Sunni insurgents in Iraq. Later that same year, AQI merged with several smaller organizations and became known as Islamic State of Iraq

(ISI). AQI all but disintegrated over the next few years. Biddle, Friedman, and Shapiro note that by the end of 2007, US military fatalities had declined to 23 by December, and averaged fewer than 11 from June 2008 to June 2011. Civilian fatalities also saw a dramatic decline, from 1,700 in May 2007 to nearly 500 by December.[14]

There has been a considerable amount of debate over the causes of this decline. Many analyses point to "the surge," a reinforcement of nearly 30,000 soldiers, along with a new strategy for the operation of the US forces. Others have pointed to the "Anbar Awakening," the Sunni tribal uprising against AQI. Biddle, Friedman, and Shapiro argue that it was a combination of both policies that resulted in the decline of AQI.[15] During this time period, coalition forces gained a considerable amount of intelligence on the structure, membership, capabilities, and location of AQI operations.

AQI was nearly wiped out as a result of the surge, the Anbar Awakening, and the death of al-Zarqawi by a US drone strike in 2006.[16] In fact, analysts frequently cite AQI as having undergone an organizational demise. But despite a period of decline, the group reemerged. As Cronin observed, "the defeat was temporary; AQI renewed itself inside US-run prisons in Iraq, where insurgents and terrorist operatives connected and formed networks—and where the group's current chief and self-proclaimed caliph, Abu Bakr al-Baghdadi, first distinguished himself as a leader."[17] The Syrian War broke out in 2011, in the aftermath of protests calling for democratic reforms and the ouster of President Assad. At al-Zawahiri's urging AQI took advantage of the chaos and uncertainty of the civil war, and al-Baghdadi built an organization in Syria. Abu Mouhammed al-Joulani was sent to Syria by al-Baghdadi and would eventually establish Jabhat al-Nusra (JN) in 2011. While originally under the control of AQI, JN eventually broke off ties with AQI and al-Qaeda completely. Many JN members are Syrians who fought in Iraq with AQI against the US occupation.[18] From these networks, jihadists were sent back to fight in Iraq. Like other rebel groups, JN sought to overthrow Assad, but they also wanted to establish an Islamic State in Syria and the Levant.

Establishing a base in Syria proved to be a relatively easy task for al-Baghdadi. The Syrian government allowed jihadists transit and bases in Syria during the Iraq war in order to oppose US and coalition forces.[19] AQI also took advantage of existing JN networks and the uncertainty of the civil war in its attempt to gain more control and establish a base of operations in northeast Syria.[20] In Iraq the group capitalized on the departure of US forces and Prime Minister Nuri al-Maliki's exclusion of and crackdown on Sunnis, which led to an increase in support and legitimacy for the group. This support from local communities allowed AQI to bolster recruitment and capabilities. The group also carried out attacks against government targets in Iraq and "launched several high-profile prison breaks that humiliated the Iraqi government and freed many of the group's most experienced cadre."[21] ISI was gaining strength and momentum leading up to its successes in 2014.

AQI was concerned about JN during this period. Al-Baghdadi felt that JN was too focused on Syria and in 2013 declared that JN was officially part of AQI. JN asserted its independence, resulting in a conflict with AQI, who wanted to be the official al-Qaeda affiliate in Syria. Al-Zawahiri sided with JN and urged AQI to retreat to Iraq and focus its efforts there. Al-Baghdadi refused, and a clash between AQI and JN ensued. In February 2014, al-Zawahiri claimed that ISI was no longer a branch of al-Qaeda and had no organizational ties.[22] ISI captured Fallujah and Ramadi in January 2014, and, as Cronin observes, "most analysts predicted that the US-trained Iraqi security forces would contain the threat."[23] In June 2014, emboldened by desertions from the Iraqi army and grievances among the Sunni population, ISI captured Mosul, Tikrit, al-Qaim, and territory in Northwest Syria, and changed its name to the Islamic State. Essentially, AQI, an affiliate focused on opposition to the US occupation of Iraq, became an independent organization, establishing de facto control in many parts of Iraq and Syria. This chapter will seek to explain how AQI was able to withstand the loss of al-Zarqawi and eventually reemerge as one of the most dangerous terrorist organizations.

Existing Literature

Current research on the susceptibility of al-Qaeda to leadership attacks can be divided into two camps: those who are optimistic about the ability of decapitation to result in organizational decline or defeat and those who are more pessimistic or skeptical of its efficacy. Both political leaders and local populations have argued in favor of targeting terrorist leaders and particularly bin Laden. Targeting terrorist leaders can provide a retributive function. For example, Avery Plaw argues that targeting terrorists provides a "way for the government to combat the social and psychological effects of terrorism—to give the population a sense of efficacy in the face of a relentless threat."[24] Peter Bergen, who ultimately finds that targeting bin Laden will not result in the group's demise, argues that eliminating the top leadership of al-Qaeda "will be useful in terms of seeking justice for the victims of 9/11."[25] This is similar to the case of Hamas, in which targeting leaders has a psychological function and provides the population with a sense of success in countering the terrorist threat and reinforces faith in the government.[26] Plaw looks at American public opinion polls from before and after 9/11 and finds that in 1986, 46 percent responded that that the CIA should not assassinate known terrorists. In 1998, 54 percent favored targeting terrorists, and after 9/11 seven out of eight Americans claimed that bin Laden should be captured or killed.[27]

After 9/11, the United States devoted a great deal of resources to capturing and killing al-Qaeda leaders, particularly bin Laden, including, according to Cronin, "a 'surge' of CIA agents into Pakistan in 2006."[28] The view that capturing bin Laden was a worthwhile priority continued to dominate the counterterrorism agenda. In 2007, President Obama stated, "It was a terrible mistake to fail to act when we had a chance to take out an al-Qaeda leadership meeting in 2005. . . . If we have actionable intelligence about high-value terrorist targets and President Musharraf won't act, we will."[29] On November 12, 2008, he argued that the Bush administration understated the importance of catching bin Laden, reassuring his audience that, "We will kill bin Laden. We will crush Al-Qaeda. That has to be our biggest national security priority."[30]

Echoing these priorities, the Senate Foreign Relations Committee released a report in 2009 entitled, *Tora Bora Revisited: How We Failed to Get Bin Laden and Why It Matters Today*. The report finds:

> Removing the al-Qaeda leader from the battlefield eight years ago would not have eliminated the worldwide extremist threat. But the decisions that opened the door for his escape to Pakistan allowed bin Laden to emerge as a potent symbolic figure who continued to attract a steady flow of money and inspire fanatics worldwide.[31]

While removing bin Laden would not have eliminated the threat from al-Qaeda, the US failure in sending troops to prevent bin Laden's escape to Pakistan had significant consequences. The report continues:

> The failure to finish the job represents a lost opportunity that forever altered the course of the conflict in Afghanistan and the future of international terrorism, leaving the American people more vulnerable to terrorism, laying the foundation for today's protracted Afghan insurgency and inflaming the internal strife now endangering Pakistan.[32]

Despite the conclusion that bin Laden's capture would not have resulted in the demise of al-Qaeda, counterterrorism policies continued to advocate that his removal should be a priority.

The pessimists claimed that removing bin Laden was unlikely to result in al-Qaeda's collapse. Their studies challenged the conventional wisdom regarding the effectiveness of killing or capturing bin Laden or Ayman al-Zawahiri. In a 2004 study of global Salafi jihad, Marc Sageman argues that social networks provide a way for isolated and alienated individuals to join a community. The social bonds that are created within these communities can foster ideological commitment and ultimately the decision to join the jihad. The decentralized and local nature of these groups makes them difficult to target, particularly as current targeting policies focus on the central organizational leaders. Rather, Sageman argues, it is necessary to identify key hubs within the organization, individuals that are often not the group's top leaders.[33]

Audrey Kurth Cronin also challenges the conventional wisdom regarding the effectiveness of decapitation against al-Qaeda. Cronin, who argues that decapitation can be an effective strategy, wrote in 2009, "Past experience with terrorism indicates that al-Qaeda will not end if Osama bin Laden is killed."[34] She identifies key characteristics that has made al-Qaeda resistant to counterterrorism measures, particularly decapitation. While the hierarchy in place on 9/11 was ultimately dismantled with the invasion of Afghanistan and the subsequent dispersal of the core this attack on the upper levels of the organizational hierarchy did not cause the group to collapse.[35] Instead it evolved and was forced to rely on the Internet and alternate means of communication, increasing its ability to withstand future attacks. Cronin argues that "starting in late 2004, the core began to reconstitute itself in the tribal region between Pakistan and Afghanistan, especially North Waziristan, rebuilding the ability to direct operations."[36] By 2007, al-Qaeda had again rebuilt its core, a decentralized network, and a following.

In evaluating the failure of past attacks against al-Qaeda, Cronin identifies four factors that make decapitation unlikely to be effective against al-Qaeda. First, its organizational structure has elements of both a hierarchy and a decentralized network of individual cells. I refer to this as a quasi-bureaucratic structure. Second, like many other organizations, al-Qaeda is not a cult of personality. Bin Laden has "deliberately avoided allowing the movement to revolve around his own persona."[37] Third, killing bin Laden could create a martyrdom effect, ultimately increasing group strength. Fourth, al-Qaeda has a succession plan in place, which should decrease the likelihood of organizational instability following bin Laden's removal.[38]

Peter Bergen has also argued that al-Qaeda is likely to withstand the capture or death of key leaders. Its resilience stems from the fact that group members believe that they are carrying out a holy mission.[39] Writing just before the actual event, Bergen claimed that in the short term, bin Laden's death would lead to anti-American attacks around the globe, and in the medium term would be a major blow to the organization. In the long term, the group would ultimately be strengthened, as his death would bolster the power of his ideas. He compares this to the growth in popularity of Sayid Qutb's writings after his execution by the Egyptian government in 1966.[40] In fact, Qutb's ideology was critical to the evolution of al-Zawahiri's belief system.[41] While bin Laden's capture or death may appeal to the desire for justice, Bergen claims that this "will not end the war of the terrorists. Bin Laden's ideas have circulated widely and will continue to attract adherents for years to come."[42]

While extant work makes important claims about the ability of decapitation to affect organizational capacity, many of these studies do not have strong theoretical foundations upon which their predictions are based. Moreover, they tend to focus on whether decapitation will result in the collapse or serious weakening of the organization, and, as discussed elsewhere in the book, efficacy can be evaluated in a number of different ways.

Targeting Al-Qaeda's Leadership

This section will examine data on targeting efforts against al-Qaeda and will conclude with an examination of ideology, bureaucracy, and popular support for AQC and AQI. The data examined in the remainder of this section begins in 1995 and ends in 2016.[43] It is important to note that this is by no means an exhaustive list. Rather, I wish to show the frequency with which these groups have been targeted, track changes in their activity, and identify whether the theory of organizational resilience accurately explains their ability to withstand attacks on their leadership. Figure 7.1 displays decapitation against al-Qaeda and affiliated organizations from 1995 to 2016, during which al-Qaeda and its affiliated organizations were targeted 288 times. Consistent with the Obama administration's pledge to utilize targeted operations and special operations forces in place of

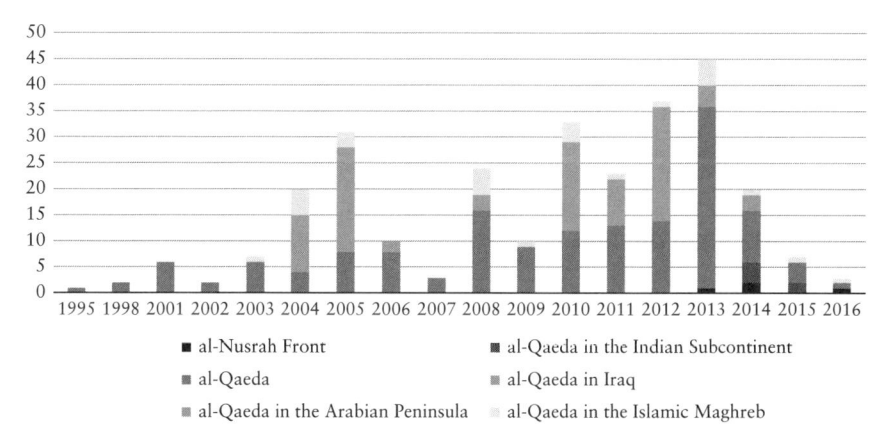

FIGURE 7.1 Decapitation against al-Qaeda and affiliates, 1995–2016

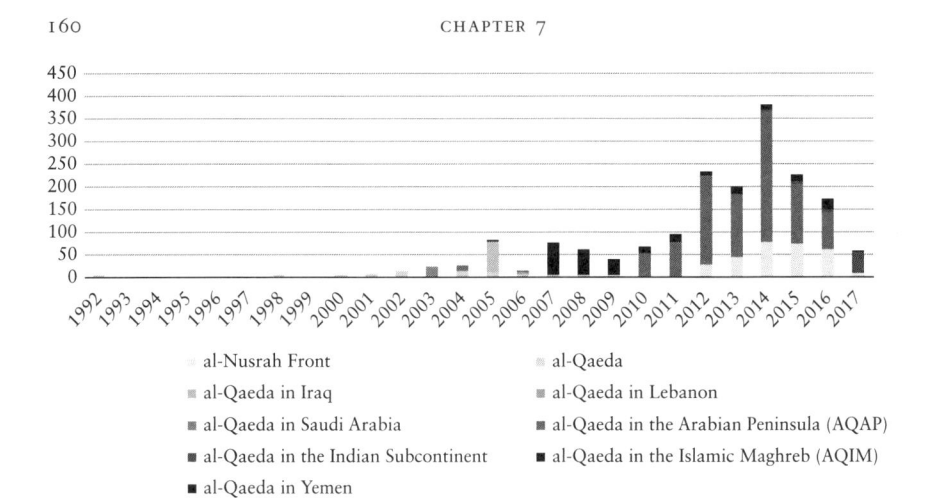

[Bar chart showing attack counts by year from 1992 to 2017, with bars colored by group]

- al-Nusrah Front
- al-Qaeda
- al-Qaeda in Iraq
- al-Qaeda in Lebanon
- al-Qaeda in Saudi Arabia
- al-Qaeda in the Arabian Peninsula (AQAP)
- al-Qaeda in the Indian Subcontinent
- al-Qaeda in the Islamic Maghreb (AQIM)
- al-Qaeda in Yemen

FIGURE 7.2 Attacks carried out by al-Qaeda and affiliates, 1992–2017
SOURCE: National Consortium for the Study of Terrorism and Responses to Terrorism (START), University of Maryland. (2018). The Global Terrorism Database (GTD) [Data file]. Retrieved from https://www.start.umd.edu/gtd.

large-scale military operations, in 2008 there was a significant increase in targeting efforts from the year prior. The idea was that kinetic operations with a lighter footprint would be more effective and result in less backlash against the United States. There was another large spike in the frequency of targeting efforts in 2012, with many of these attacks occurring in Iraq.

Figure 7.2 displays the number of attacks carried out by al-Qaeda and its affiliates from 1992 to 2016. There are two important caveats to mention here. First, this data does not include attacks that are coded in the GTD as having been carried out by AQI after 2006. The Global Terrorism Database, from which all attack data for this book is drawn, codes AQI as having conducted a considerable amount of activity in 2012 and 2013. In fact, according to the GTD, AQI was one of the most active affiliates in those two years, carrying out 303 attacks in 2012 alone. However, at this point, AQI was essentially operating as ISI and very soon after as ISIS, and as a result, I recoded the data to reflect this evolution of AQI. At this point, I think it is more useful to consider these as ISI and then ISIS attacks, which will be discussed in the following chapter. As a result, I included a separate graph (Figure 7.3) of attacks carried out by AQI and ISI; ISIS attacks will be examined in the conclusion. Second, I also removed three affiliated al-Qaeda groups that only carried out five attacks between them.[44]

The data reveals that overall, al-Qaeda has undergone a significant decline in activity, and while some affiliates have become less active, others have increased activity. Figure 7.2 shows that AQC experienced a decline in attacks after the US

Al-Qaeda

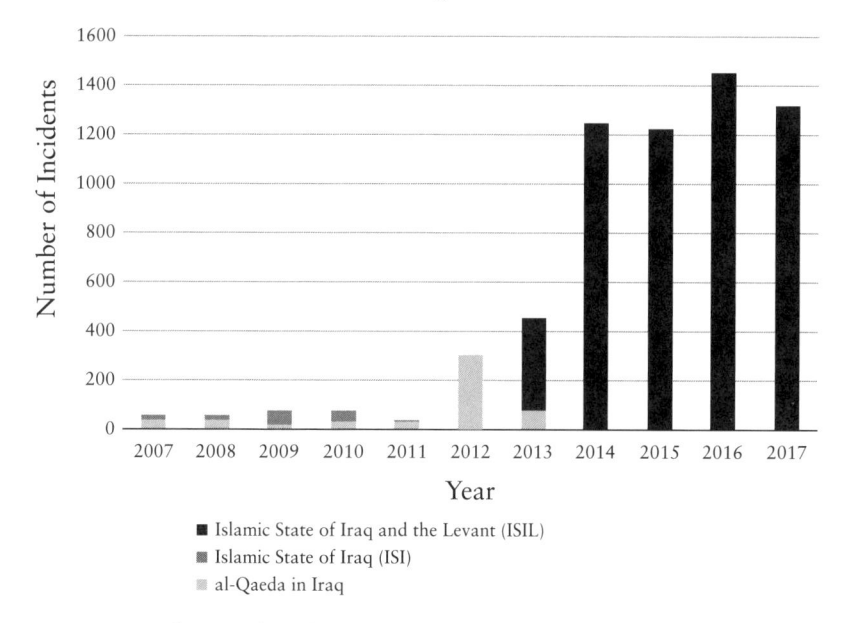

FIGURE 7.3 Attacks carried out by AQI and ISI, 2007–2017
SOURCE: National Consortium for the Study of Terrorism and Responses to Terrorism (START), University of Maryland. (2018). The Global Terrorism Database (GTD) [Data file]. Retrieved from https://www.start.umd.edu/gtd.

invasion of Afghanistan in 2003, but still continued to carry out attacks. While this was occurring, other affiliates became more active, including AQI, AQIM (al-Qaeda in the Islamic Maghreb), and AQAP. AQI experienced 36 instances of leadership targeting, and there were an additional 17 attacks against the organization in 2010, which at that point is coded as ISI. In spite of these attacks, AQI remained exceedingly active, as did ISI after that. Despite considerable targeting efforts, particularly in 2005, AQI carried out 6 attacks in 2004, 68 in 2005, 5 in 2006, and 41 in 2007. While the organization suffered serious setbacks, I would argue that this was not solely due to the death of al-Zarqawi but rather a combination of factors, including the surge and the Anbar Awakening. The rise in attacks continued as ISI, despite 17 instances of decapitation in 2010 alone, carried out 26 attacks in 2010, 31 in 2011, 304 in 2012, and 82 in 2013. This level of activity is indicative of a highly resilient organization that seemed to become even more active after sustained decapitation efforts.

Figures 7.4 and 7.5 plot instances of decapitation against the number of al-Qaeda attacks and fatalities. In these graphs, each point represents data from a single year and each year is plotted according to the number of decapitations and

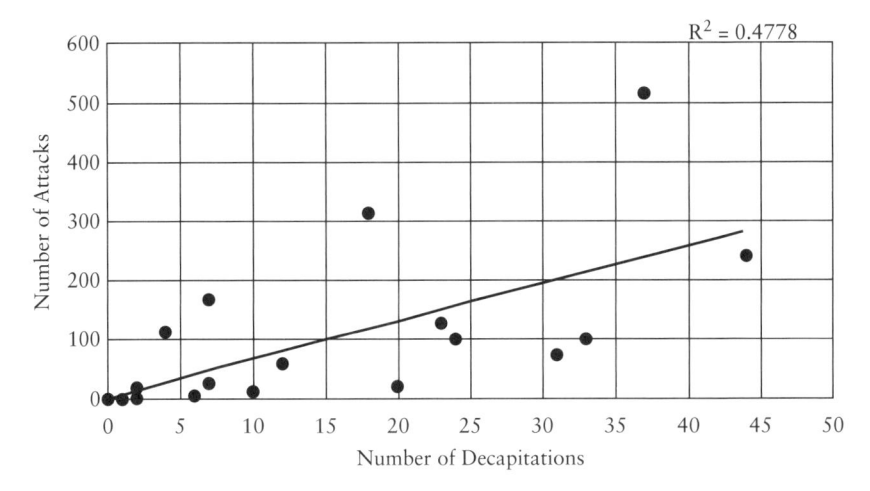

FIGURE 7.4 Relationship between decapitation and terrorist attacks
SOURCE: National Consortium for the Study of Terrorism and Responses to Terrorism (START), University of Maryland. (2018). The Global Terrorism Database (GTD) [Data file]. Retrieved from https://www.start.umd.edu/gtd.
NOTE: This data excludes al-Shabaab and the al-Nusra Front.

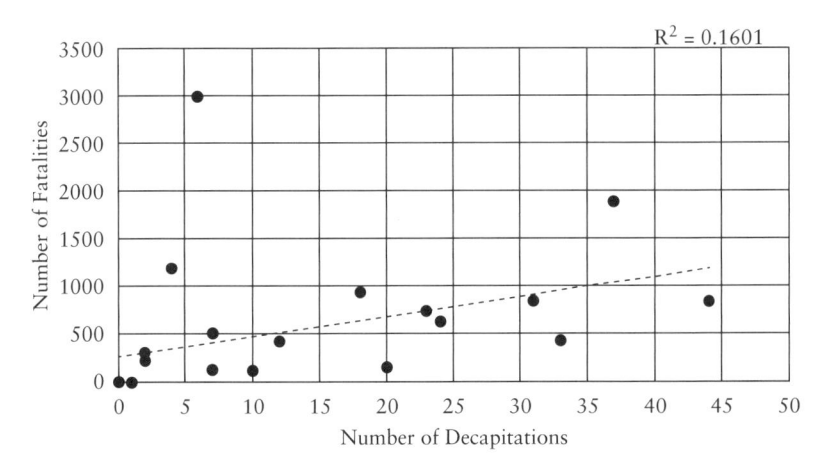

FIGURE 7.5 Relationship between decapitation and fatalities
SOURCE: National Consortium for the Study of Terrorism and Responses to Terrorism (START), University of Maryland. (2018). The Global Terrorism Database (GTD) [Data file]. Retrieved from https://www.start.umd.edu/gtd.
NOTE: This data excludes al-Shabaab and the al-Nusra Front.

number of fatalities/attacks. Figure 7.4 suggests that, aside from a few outliers, there seems to be a relationship between the number of attacks and instances of decapitation. Figure 7.5 highlights a similar trend for fatalities, that as al-Qaeda has been targeted, its fatalities increase. These trends will be unpacked within the context of AQC and AQI in the remainder of this chapter.

Organizational Resilience of Al-Qaeda Central

The statistical findings presented in Chapter 4 support the argument that targeting the leadership of al-Qaeda and its affiliates is unlikely to be effective and may actually have counterproductive consequences. The data indicates that large, religious, Islamist, and sometimes older organizations are highly resistant to leadership targeting. Groups in more autocratic countries are also harder to destabilize. First, al-Qaeda is a religious and Islamist organization; its goals include the establishment of a pan-Islamic caliphate, overthrowing non-Islamic regimes, and expelling infidels from Muslim countries.[45] Second, AQC, formed in 1988, is over twenty years of age; while not as a strong a finding as size, in the bivariate analyses older organizations were often more likely to withstand targeting efforts. Third, decapitation is less successful in more autocratic countries. Fourth, time series data reveals that an organization's prior level of activity has an impact on the frequency of attacks, indicating that decapitation does not necessarily lead to a decrease in attacks and could account for variation in trends in attacks over time. These findings would apply to the cases of AQI as well.

Finally, size was one of the strongest statistical findings, with the data showing that groups with between 1,000 and 5,000 members were the most resilient. Once a group crosses the threshold of 100 active members, it is quite difficult to destabilize. There is considerable disagreement over the size of al-Qaeda stemming from the fact that scholars often measure different aspects of the organization: AQC, its network of decentralized fighters, or its affiliates.[46] Furthermore, al-Qaeda cooperates with other organizations, sharing resources and militants. In a report of the Bipartisan Policy Center's National Security Preparedness Group, Bruce Hoffman and Peter Bergen argue that:

> Al-Qaeda's ideology and tactics have spread to a wide range of militant groups in South Asia, all of which are relatively large. The Taliban in Afghanistan alone is estimated to number 25,000 men, while Lashkar-e-Taiba has thousands of fighting men in its ranks. Finally, al-Qaeda Central has seeded a number of franchises around the Middle East and North Africa that are now acting in an al-Qaeda like manner with little or no contact with al-Qaeda Central itself.[47]

While I do not advocate determining the size of al-Qaeda by measuring affiliated organizations, this passage highlights two points: the intertwining of these diverse networks makes determining size difficult, and the threat posed by al-Qaeda emerges not only from its core but from groups with which al-Qaeda has ties, which creates challenges for counterterrorism policy. The size of an organization can fluctuate and change over time, causing coding problems, especially when data is aggregated. In order to address this, the data compiled uses a group's peak size, putting al-Qaeda in the size category of between 5,000 and 10,000 members.[48] This data estimates that al-Qaeda consisted of several hundred to several thousand members in 2002, 1,000 members in 2004, and 500 to 1,000 members in 2012. Other estimates place the peak number of al-Qaeda operatives at over 10,000. However, once a group crosses a threshold of 500 members, it is quite stable, and it is certainly reasonable to assume that al-Qaeda Central has over 500 members (some sources estimate that it has at least 1,000 members).[49] The numbers for AQI are similar. The database used for this project estimates AQI to have approximately 4,000 members although, as with AQC, there is little agreement on size. However, even with modest estimates of strength similar to AQC, it is still safe to assume that these organizations are also likely to continue carrying out terrorist activity after losing their leadership. The remainder of the chapter will focus on the theoretical argument regarding group resilience and will examine the communal support and level of institutionalization and bureaucracy of AQC and AQI.

Before looking at each affiliate separately, it is important to understand al-Qaeda's original and current overarching organizational structure. Al-Qaeda can be seen as a social movement, with franchises or affiliated groups as social movement organizations that emerged from the overarching group of al-Qaeda. Barak Mendelsohn has examined this process of franchising, an intentional strategy that is based on the creation of:

> a two-tier structure with a central command and below it, branched, each responsible for a particular geographical area. While the center sets its ideological orientation and concomitant broad political goals and the strategy to realize them, the affiliates have considerable organizational and operational autonomy. By introducing franchises, a transnational terrorist organization strongly communicates its intentions as well as confidence in its ability to bring change to the selected arenas.[50]

Franchising is one of many options available to terrorist groups; it is a flexible approach that reflects the importance of the unique particularities of different areas, local autonomy, and the group's desire to continue.[51] It involves a formal relationship between al-Qaeda and its franchises in which the franchise must take a pledge or oath of allegiance (*bay'a*) to al-Qaeda's leader, the acceptance of that oath, and a public announcement of affiliation.[52] In the remainder of this chapter (consistent with Mendelsohn's definition) "al-Qaeda" will refer to the organization's central command and accompanying apparatus (located primarily in Afghanistan and Pakistan) and to its formal branches.[53] "AQC" will refer specifically to the group's central command.

Al-Qaeda is often mischaracterized. Mendelsohn notes that defining it has become problematic. In some cases, analysts conflate the affiliates and analyze al-

Qaeda as one entity. In other cases, any attack by an Islamist group or individual actors who hold a sympathetic view of the organization or bin Laden is attributed to al-Qaeda.[54] By treating al-Qaeda as one organization, it is possible to misunderstand the group's nature and the threat that it poses, undermining counterterrorism efforts. Each affiliate has its own goals, structure, political messages, and strategy, so it is essential that policy makers recognize these differences in order to develop effective counterterrorism policies. In some instances in this chapter, I aggregate data on all of the franchises to get a sense of overall activity because policy makers often conflate this data when discussing the overall threat. However, it is possible to look at specific data for each affiliate.

The remainder of this section will examine the ideology, bureaucratic structure, and communal support of AQC in order to demonstrate how it has been able to resist repeated and frequent targeting efforts. Other than ISI and ISIS, AQC has been targeted more than any other organization in the dataset, and while it has been weakened, as evidenced by a decline in the frequency of attacks, the organization remained active in its messaging and franchising efforts, expanding its jihad to East Africa, the Maghreb (AQIM), Arabian Peninsula (AQAP), and Indian subcontinent. Its strength and resistance, despite a near demise, can be attributed to the strength of its ideology, bureaucratic capabilities, and communal support. While its approval has varied considerably over time, the group has been able to sustain sufficient support from communities in which it is active.

Ideology

Religious and separatist organizations do not usually depend upon an ideological doctrine specific to the group's leader, and al-Qaeda, a Salafist organization, is no exception. A new wave of Islamist movements emerged in the aftermath of two critical events in 1979: the Islamist revolution in Iran and the Soviet invasion of Afghanistan. Abdullah Azzam, a Palestinian Jordanian scholar and theologian who was a founding member of al-Qaeda and mentor to bin Laden, says al-Qaeda's founders built the organization on Islamist principles. In 1987, he wrote that the organization should serve as a vanguard for these principles and developed a pan-Islamic ideology that served as a model to other Islamists.[55] The success of the mujahedeen in the Soviet Afghan War in 1989 contributed to al-Qaeda's internationalization and the growth of its appeal. By the mid-1990s, bin Laden reoriented its focus to fighting the United States, which was seen as supporting corrupt local regimes.[56] While al-Qaeda's goals have shifted over time, from emphasizing its struggle against Israel, to the establishment of an Islamic emirate, to its struggle against apostate regimes, its overarching goal has focused on establishing an Islamic government. To achieve this goal, the group's leaders emphasized the necessity of violent struggle in order to challenge the influence of Western countries, Israel, and the Arab regimes that were at odds with their vision. They were successful at establishing control over a number of Islamist terrorist organizations who pledged allegiance to bin Laden in exchange for access to money, weapons, logistical support, and training.[57] Al-Qaeda worked to create a global organization, expanding its operations and training to Sudan, Yemen, Chechnya, Tajikistan, Somalia, and the Philippines and inviting representatives of Islamist political and terrorist groups to join its Shura Council.[58]

Under bin Laden's leadership, al-Qaeda was successful in extending the group's struggle and its specific interpretation of Islamist thought beyond the organization itself. Al-Qaeda's ideology is not dependent upon bin Laden's charisma or his specific interpretation of Islam, and this was intentional. He was an activist who succeeded in developing and broadening the appeal of al-Qaeda's ideology to attract a broad base of support. As Gunaratna observes, initially most Islamic struggles against non-Muslim governments were engaged in territorial campaigns. Even the guerilla or terrorist groups did not subscribe to a "universalistic brand of Islam."[59] In fact, Robert Pape argues that much of al-Qaeda's appeal was the result of Western occupation of Muslim lands and that a great deal of their support stems from broader opposition to these policies.[60] However, bin Laden's anti-Western and anti-Israeli message attracted widespread support, based on religious ideology, not territorial control. Bin Laden succeeded in broadening the group's appeal and message; charisma was not necessary to propagate the group's ideological message. Bin Laden also created a multiethnic movement, further broadening the organizational base. It is this broad ideological position that has made al-Qaeda's support and infrastructure both global and resilient.

Small groups and individuals with no formal ties to al-Qaeda, but who have claimed allegiance to it, have been responsible for a number of attacks, including the July 7, 2005, attacks on the London Underground; the 2009 Christmas Day bombing attempt; and the 2010 cargo airplane bomb plot. It is the ideology to which these individuals adhere. The rise of these small networks, or "homegrown terrorists," has two implications. First, these groups are hard to target, as they have little if any contact with AQC. Second, they show the appeal of al-Qaeda's ideology, and that contact with bin Laden is certainly not a prerequisite to action, although most of these local networks traveled to Pakistan to receive training. These are groups that have tried to gain notoriety by using al-Qaeda's name:

> In terms of the new al-Qaeda in Islamic Maghreb, little "al-Qaedas" have sprung up everywhere in the world. They are just al-Qaeda in name trying to acquire the reputation of al-Qaeda by using its name. There is strong evidence that the acquisi-

tion of the name by some leaders of the old Algerian GSPC (Group Salafiste pour la Predication et le Combat) has generated a lot of debate in the jihadi chat rooms, with many of the traditional leaders rejecting this move.[61]

Sageman calls these homegrown networks part of the third wave of global Islamist terrorism. Many of them emerged in response to the disruption of AQC. Old and new networks became disconnected from one another, functioning on their own.[62]

The threat emerging from these decentralized networks is further exacerbated by the growth of al-Qaeda's propaganda operations. The use of the Internet has improved communication between AQC and peripheral members and "is potentially dangerous especially in the context of regrouping of al-Qaeda leadership."[63] Given the appeal of al-Qaeda's ideology, the growth of decentralized networks, and the regrouping of al-Qaeda's leadership, it was unlikely that bin Laden's death would have resulted in the group's demise or even a substantial weakening. After his death, al-Zawahiri, who many claimed lacked the charisma of bin Laden,[64] easily assumed the position of leadership, and the group's ideological message was uncompromised.

Bureaucracy

To understand AQC's bureaucratic capabilities, it is necessary to step back and look at al-Qaeda as a whole. Most scholars have characterized its structure as composed of distinct layers, with AQC at the top. Cronin portrays the group as consisting of three main elements: (1) a core central group of leaders and strategists (bin Laden and al-Zawahiri's direct associates), (2) traditional groups that are aligned with the core and can respond to central guidance (sometimes referred to as the "network"), and (3) localized factions that have no contact with the center but who want to be associated with al-Qaeda.[65] Bruce Hoffman argues that al-Qaeda is a decentralized movement, which retains elements of a well-organized group with a central command:

> It is now a more loosely and connected movement that mixes and matches organizational and operational styles whether dictated by particular missions or imposed by circumstances. Nonetheless, it would be mistaken to believe that al-Qaeda does not retain some important characteristics or aspects of a more organized entity with a central command and control structure, however weakened and reduced.[66]

Hoffman describes al-Qaeda as having four layers. These organizational divisions are important when understanding al-Qaeda's bureaucratic features. Hoffman argues that al-Qaeda exercises both top-down and bottom-up planning and operational capabilities.[67] First, al-Qaeda Central consists of the core leadership, which still exerts "some coordination, if not command capability, in terms of commissioning attacks, directing surveillance and collating reconnaissance, planning operations, and approving their execution."[68] The second level, al-Qaeda affiliates and associates, is made up of insurgent or terrorist groups that have received some form of assistance, material or spiritual, from al-Qaeda. These include terrorist and insurgent groups in Uzbekistan, Indonesia, Chechnya, the Philippines, Bosnia, and Kashmir, among other places. The third level, al-Qaeda locals, are adherents to al-Qaeda's ideology who have had experience with terrorism and previously had some kind of connection with al-Qaeda. Finally, the al-Qaeda network is made of home-grown Islamic radicals and local converts to Islam who have no direct contact with al-Qaeda but are prepared to carry out attacks in support of its agenda.[69]

According to Hoffman, this organizational structure highlights the importance of AQC and its hierarchy. He argues that while al-Qaeda has a large and decentralized network of affiliates and operatives, many of the group's threats emanate directly from AQC, now based primarily in Federally Administered Tribal Areas of Pakistan. Hoffman writes, "The most salient threat . . . continues to come from al-Qaeda Central and then from its affiliates and associates."[70] Second, despite its dispersed and decentralized network of affiliates and operatives, "Al-Qaeda remains a hierarchical organization: capable of ordering, planning and implementing bold terrorist strikes."[71] Hierarchical command structures tend to have clear operating procedures, division of labor, and guidelines for succession, mitigating the effects of decapitation. This hybrid structure of decentralization and hierarchy can be referred to as quasi-bureaucratic and is a primary source of al-Qaeda's resilience.

Al-Qaeda was originally a single, hierarchical organization. After the attacks of 9/11, the organization began franchising and became a two-tier group with AQC as the central command and the affiliates below. A strong bureaucratic structure, through which it is able to provide guidance and operational support for its franchises and maintain succession mechanisms in the event of leadership decapitation, has contributed to AQC's robustness and endurance through repeated leadership attacks. Part of al-Qaeda's initial decision to franchise can be traced to its weakening position after the Surge and Anbar Awakening of 2007. This process has strengthened the group's bureaucratic capabilities in that it has to formally manage and maintain relationships with its many franchises. Mendelsohn argues that this strategy did not increase the threat al-Qaeda posed, but it helped the group's political objective. In fact, he argues, the organization incurred costs, such as undermining its goal to create a transnational religious entity. This strategy places its fate in the hands of its affiliates, and the actions of some franchises, particularly those in Iraq and Somalia, have resulted in a considerable amount of damage to the "al-Qaeda brand name."[72] I do not disagree with this assessment; the franchising strategy and the creation of affiliates may have weakened the group's larger political goals, but it created a structure over which a clear and institutionalized bureaucracy was essential, and which played an important part in its ability to withstand leadership attacks.

AQC's central command is a well-organized bureaucracy, with a hierarchy of authority and administrative functions necessary to manage its many affiliates (albeit to varying degrees of success). AQC comprises the leadership structure for al-Qaeda writ large (including its affiliates) and "determines the organization's interests and the strategy to promote those interests."[73] Documents captured after bin Laden's death and released by the Office of the Director of National Intelligence in early 2017 highlight the extent to which the group had developed bureaucratic features. These documents show that AQC was a highly institutionalized organization with stated operating procedures and clear guidelines for administrative duties. For example, documents reveal that administrators met regularly and were responsible for duties such as coordinating deployments and visits between brigades, visiting families, receiving mail, budgeting, securing connections with supporters, and searching for homes. Administrators had a deputy, all personal requests were made through administrators, and disciplinary actions were taken against individuals who did not comply with standard operating procedures.[74] This level of organization is consistent with documents captured in Iraq, and will be discussed in the next section of this chapter. Essentially, these documents reveal that AQC developed a strong bureaucracy in order to effectively manage the organization.

Communal Support

Support from local populations is necessary for organizations to function clandestinely and effectively, and groups with strong local support are more likely to withstand attacks on their leadership. While al-Qaeda has a substantial amount of support for its goals and less support for its tactics, this varies considerably based on location and the specific branch of the organization. Al-Qaeda has support from its local communities, its global community, and individuals with no formal ties to AQC or its affiliates. The basis of this support is largely ideological, and the strength of these ideological claims makes the group more likely to withstand leadership targeting.

In this section, I look at data on public opinion towards al-Qaeda, with a focus on AQC, in order to evaluate the strength of its support. It is important to acknowledge the limitation of public opinion polls. First, there are a number of different ways to evaluate support for terrorist organizations. Schmid identifies three categories of support, both legal and illegal: (1) empathetic understanding of terrorism, (2) sympathy and positive attitudes towards a group's objectives and tactics, and (3) behavioral support and assistance. While it is possible to get a sense of the number of individuals who have traveled to Iraq or Syria to join IS, for example, public opinion polls do not provide a way to distinguish between these levels of support. Second, public opinion polls are often faced with significant methodological challenges: Was the sample large or representative enough? Were the questions biased? Was there government censorship? Were the interviewees under fear of persecution or coercion for providing certain answers? Third, in some cases, large groups of people are excluded from the sample, as was the case with the exclusion of disenfranchised workers in Saudi Arabia, Kuwait, or the United Arab Emirates. Fourth, audiences can be influenced in a number of different ways. In spite of the challenges, according to Alex Schmid, public opinion remains "the second most important instrument for assessing popular support—surpassed only by official and honest election balloting—to assess the strength of endorsement for one or another social cause, political party, religious movement or armed group."[75]

Public opinion polls indicate that there is variation in support for the tactics employed by al-Qaeda and other militant organizations. While support for their overall goal has declined over time, considerable minorities have expressed favorable views of the organization and global jihad in general. Even if the percentage of individuals that have expressed favorable views of al-Qaeda is declining, given the size of the communities, the number of individuals that sympathize with and support the organization is actually considerable. These trends support the argument that al-Qaeda was able to broaden the group's ideological appeal, resulting in more and consistent support. It is important to note that some of the polls mentioned in this section refer to al-Qaeda more broadly, which is consistent with the organizational goal, to create a universalist ideology, overarching the many different affiliated organizations.

A study by World Public Opinion in February 2009 found that people in majority-Muslim countries expressed support for al-Qaeda's goals and disapproval of their tactics. They report: "Views of al-Qaeda are complex. Majorities agree with nearly all of al-Qaeda's goals to change US behavior in the Muslim world, to promote Islamist governance, and to preserve and affirm Islamic identity."[76] Ambivalence towards al-Qaeda is based on public discomfort with attacking civilians. Across eight countries, 66 percent of those polled said that US naval forces in the Persian Gulf was a bad idea, and large majorities approved of attacks on US troops in Egypt, the Palestinian territories, and Jordan.

It is also important to consider Pakistani support for al-Qaeda, given that Pakistan was the primary base of operations for AQC, especially after the 2001 invasion of Afghanistan.[77] The group initially settled in Karachi, after which Khalid Sheikh Mohammed was captured in 2003 along with a significant amount of information on al-Qaeda. In the five years after 9/11, hundreds of lower-level operatives were arrested in Pakistan's cities.[78] As a result, a weakened al-Qaeda fled to the Federally Administered Tribal Areas, primarily in North Waziristan. Given the importance of Pakistan to al-Qaeda's operational capacity, it is worth taking a closer look at Pakistani public opinion on al-Qaeda and jihad.

In order to understand support for militancy in Pakistan, C. Christine Fair, Neil Malhotra, and Jacob Shapiro conducted a survey of 6,000 Pakistanis in April 2009. This study was designed to analyze "beliefs about Islam, Sharia, the legitimacy and efficacy of jihad, and attitudes towards specific militant organizations."[79] They found significant support for jihad, especially when carried out by nonstate actors. The authors also asked respondents about the goals of specific militant groups: Pakistani militant groups fighting in Kashmir, militant groups fighting in Afghanistan, al-Qaeda, and sectarian violence.[80] The survey showed substantial variation in attitudes towards the goals of militant organizations. The majority of respondents (81 percent) believed that Kashmiri groups are fighting for justice. They found that despite "al Qa-ida's vigorous marketing efforts to depict its activities as seeking justice for the world's Muslims," only 47 percent believe that al-Qaeda is fighting for justice.[81] While this number is less than those who believe that other groups are fighting for justice, according to Fair, Malhotra, and Shapiro, it is still a substantial minority. Moreover, a large minority also believed that al-Qaeda stood for democracy: 37 percent. Finally, 47 percent of respondents felt that al-Qaeda is protecting Muslims.[82] This survey also looked at opinions towards how militants achieve their goals. The authors claim that "jihad has a considerable legitimacy among Pakistanis."[83] They cite other polls conducted after 9/11, which have shown that substantial minorities of Pakistan's population support militants and their actions. Overall, these results shed light on variation in Pakistani opinion regarding militancy. This study provides support for the claim that there is considerable support for al-Qaeda's goals and, in some cases, for its tactics.

In an earlier survey of urban Pakistanis in September 2007, Shapiro and Fair look at support for militant organizations. Contrary to the view that economics and religion contribute to militancy, they find that economic poverty and religiosity are poor predictors of support. In fact, respondents from more prosperous areas were more likely to support militant organizations. They also find no relationship between support for democratic rights and disapproval of the Taliban or al-Qaeda. Shapiro and Fair argue that "urban Pakistanis support small militant organizations when two conditions hold: (1) those organizations are using violence in support of political goals the individual cares about; and (2) violence makes sense as a way to achieve those goals, given the respondent's understanding of the strategic environment."[84] Taken together, these surveys indicate a few important trends regarding support for militancy in Pakistan. While there is some variation, it is clear that considerable minorities support al-Qaeda. A substantial percentage of those interviewed believe that al-Qaeda is fighting for justice, stands for democracy, and that jihad is legitimate. There is support not only for militants' goals, but in some cases for their tactics as well. These studies highlight the existence of support for Islamist militancy and for al-Qaeda in particular.

The percentage of individuals expressing favorable views of al-Qaeda has declined over time. A report from early 2017 by Alex Schmid examines these changes. There is regional- and country-level variation in support for al-Qaeda, but overall the trends point to a rise in unfavorable views of the organization, with a decline in support between 2013 and 2014. Schmid points out that

> a Pew opinion survey published in 2013 found that 57 percent of Muslims worldwide disapproved of al-Qaeda. However, one in four respondents refused to answer the question and 13 percent admitted support for al-Qaeda. 57 percent of all Muslims polled having an unfavorable view of al-Qaeda is a majority, but not a large majority.[85]

Moreover, when looking at how those percentages are translated into actual numbers, it appears that a substantial number of individuals support al-Qaeda. Schmid concludes that, "based on such opinion surveys, it is hard to avoid the conclusion that there is a sizeable undercurrent of sympathy and support in both Muslim-majority countries and in Western Muslim diasporas where jihadist propaganda is accepted and a certain freedom of action for recruitment and mobilization continues to be present."[86] Brynjar Lia reaches a similar conclusion regarding public opinion polls on support for al-Qaeda and ISIS. He finds that

> with an estimated 355 million inhabitants in the Middle East and North Africa, the polls . . . actually suggest that several million people in the region may be very supportive of ISIS and/or al-Qaida. . . . That is, the level of popular support is so extensive that the local population in certain areas is willing to go to some length to aid, abet and even glorify "the mujahidin" hiding in their midst. Hence, far from being an isolated terrorist underground or an extremist fringe, hated and despised by the surrounding populations, the jihadi movement has managed to insert itself as an insurgent movement with a foothold among the masses.[87]

These findings suggest that al-Qaeda has managed to create an ideology that appeals to millions of individuals around the globe. This support allows the organization to continue to grow and to attract new adherents, fomenting its strength and organizational resilience.

Gunaratna notes, "The key to fighting al-Qaeda effectively is to engage both the military organization and the support base."[88] Al-Qaeda's lifespan will be determined in part by the ability to destroy its leadership, marginalize its support, and disrupt its recruitment.[89] In the next section of this chapter, I will look at the 1998 cruise missile attacks on al-Qaeda in order to understand the potentially adverse consequences of targeting policies. I argue that these attacks actually increased bin Laden's visibility and generated more support and sympathy for the movement, ultimately enhancing its ability to recruit and keep the organization going.

Counterproductive Outcomes

Decapitation is often not a successful counterterrorism strategy, and it can have unintended consequences. It has the potential to result in civilian death, which can cause a significant amount of outrage, ultimately increasing support for the targeted organization, which can bolster recruitment. Moreover, killing leaders can result in retaliatory attacks, and it can have a martyrdom effect, increasing sympathy and support for the organization. So even if it is not likely to result in the death of al-Qaeda, it has the potential to increase group mobilization.

The CIA concluded that until bin Laden was killed, he would continue to dominate the anti-Western terrorism agenda. President Clinton claimed there was evidence that the bin Laden network was planning to carry out further attacks against the United States. This led Clinton to argue that Executive Order 12333, which was originally intended to ban assassination, does not prevent the President from targeting terrorists, specifically bin Laden, in covert action.[90]

In 1998, the United States ordered cruise missile strikes on terrorist bases in the Khost province of Afghanistan, in retaliation for the August 7 bombing of US embassies in Tanzania and Kenya, which killed 224 people and wounded 4,500.[91] Clinton claimed the United States had intelligence that a meeting of key terrorist leaders, including bin Laden, was going to take place at the training camp in Afghanistan. Plaw argues that although the strikes were intended to degrade terrorist infrastructure, "Clinton cited the presence of terrorist leaders as underlining the 'urgency' of US action."[92] On August 20, 1998, the United States launched dozens of missile strikes on these training camps. The cruise missiles hit six targets, killing over twenty people and wounding thirty. Most of those killed were Pakistani and Afghan members of Harkat ul Mujahidin, primarily Kashmiri militants. In addition to destroying the camps, the United States had hoped the attacks would kill bin Laden.

The missile attacks did not kill bin Laden, who had escaped the training camps. Moreover, the attacks had adverse consequences. The Taliban were outraged and organized demonstrations in Afghan cities to protest the attacks. Mobs attacked UN offices in several towns. The attacks brought bin Laden to prominence. Gunaratna argues: "Both in Afghanistan and in the Muslim world, the US cruise missile response provided Osama with unprecedented international publicity. Overnight the failed assassination attempt propelled him to preeminence as the leading *jihadist* among the many Asian and Middle Eastern Islamist organizations."[93] Gunaratna found that after the attacks, bin Laden's popularity peaked.[94] The attacks mobilized latent support for the organization.

The 1998 cruise missile attacks against al-Qaeda bases did not result in the killing of any of the group's leaders. However, this example shows how targeting terrorist leaders can actually result in counterproductive outcomes such as increasing visibility, prominence, and ultimately support for the group.

Organizational Resilience of AQI

AQI is a particularly interesting case as it exhibited high levels of both bureaucracy and communal support. After 2007, AQI essentially reemerged as ISI, an organization that developed an even greater and more institutionalized bureaucracy and broader base of support that spans the globe. This bureaucratic structure created the conditions for the almost state-like qualities of ISI and later ISIS. Support from disenfranchised Sunnis in Iraq played a significant part in its ability to effectively capture major cities in Iraq and Syria in the summer of 2014. The data on attack frequency reflects these trends. The group's activity declined after decapitation, and it then lost support after it employed tactics that alienated its base of support. ISI underwent significant targeting in 2010 but remained active in the two to three years following, coinciding with a rise in support from Sunnis who felt excluded and discriminated against by the al-Maliki regime. It is important to note that while much of this support is likely coerced and grows out of fear, it sustains an organization's ability to function. It provides resources, recruits, and allies around the globe.

Ideology

AQI differed from AQC in important ways. AQI grew out of the 2003 US invasion of Iraq, during which bin Laden gave al-Zarqawi money to start the organization. While al-Zarqawi initially refused to swear loyalty to bin Laden, he eventually did, and then took on the name "al-Qaeda in Iraq" in 2004.[95] While AQI shared many of the same goals as al-Qaeda's core, al-Zarqawi's interpretation of how the organization should bring about its ideological goals varied in important ways. Many of its direct goals were related to the Iraq war and the group's opposition to the US occupation. Byman notes that while bin Laden and al-Zawahiri urged the groups to focus on US targets, al-Zarqawi emphasized sectarian war and attacking apostate Sunnis, including those who collaborated with Iraq's Shi'a-led regime.[96] The organization targeted Shi'ite Muslims and destroyed important religious and historical Shi'ite sites in Iraq. Al-Zarqawi and his followers used incredibly brutal tactics, including public beheadings, a tactic later used by its successor group, ISIS. As mentioned earlier in the chapter, al-Zawahiri wrote a letter to al-Zarqawi indicating that while he was grateful for his dedication to jihad and the movement, he was concerned that his tactics would undermine support for the organization.

Al-Zarqawi's specific local goals enabled the group to gain support based on a significant amount of anti-American sentiment in Iraq at that time. However, the organization eventually declined, and while this was due to a combination of factors, including the 2007 US Surge and Anbar Awakening, al-Zarqawi's indiscriminate killing of Shi'as and Sunnis undermined much of the group's support. In 2008, Brian Fishman wrote that AQI was in decline due to Zarqawi's divisive politics and brutal tactics:

> Zarqawi's divisive legacy continued after his death. AQI continued to alienate other Sunni groups in Iraq with its religious bullying and bloody attacks. These operational mistakes have undermined AQI's position in Iraq—it is weaker today than at any time since 2003—but the United States is not leveraging the mistakes effectively to attack al Qaeda's ideology and thus disrupt its global operations.[97]

While the resilience of Islamist organizations stems from the fact that a group is not dependent upon a leader's specific religious beliefs, in the case of al-Zarqawi, his views on how to wage jihad stood in opposition to that of the group's core.

Bureaucracy

From the time of its formation through the US invasion of Iraq and the creation of ISI, the organization developed a strong bureaucratic structure, with a clear division of labor and administrative procedures. Jacob Shapiro has examined AQI's bureaucratic structure, drawing upon documents from AQI's successor organization, ISI, to show that the group exhibited a "non-trivial" level of bureaucracy despite risks to its security.[98] An examination of documents from the Department of Defense's Harmony database, captured during the US invasion of Iraq in 2003, provides a glimpse into al-Qaeda's inner workings and reveals a high level of bureaucratic organization.[99] The "Harmony documents" show "how explicit al-Qaida has been in its internal discussions covering a range of organizational issues, particularly regarding the internal structure and functioning of the movement as well as with tensions that emerged within the leadership."[100] Forest, Brachman, and Felter argue that the Harmony collection offers insight into how al-Qaeda developed "Western-styled bureaucratic structures."[101] The documents also identify recruitment criteria, training programs for new hires, and tactics.

Al-Qaeda's bylaws clearly explain their goals, principles, voting laws, organizational structures, membership duties, leadership responsibilities, financial policies, budgetary requirements, and policies for military, political, and security committees.[102] Employment contracts require a member's oath and list their duties, holidays, salaries, travel details, rewards, and punishments.[103] Al-Qaeda also kept membership rosters and lists of martyred individuals.[104]

Documents retrieved by coalition forces in Sinjar, Iraq, during the Iraq war also provide valuable information about AQI's bureaucracy. The 109 documents analyzed in a report by West Point's Combating Terrorism Center include signed contracts, policy memos, press releases, and managerial reports on personnel, finances, and equipment.[105] Examining these documents, Shapiro focuses on the managerial challenges facing terrorist organizations. He observes that leaders have to delegate duties, which can result in preference divergence between principles and agents. To deal with these organizational dilemmas, leaders must monitor their agents. Shapiro finds that "leaders typically exercise control over their agents through a standard set of bureaucratic tools including policy memoranda, reporting requirements, and tracking spreadsheets."[106] This process by which leaders monitor their agents is part of the bureaucratic procedure. Peter Bergen also finds that, like its parent organization, AQI was highly bureaucratized. The organization required that its non-Iraqi recruits fill out application forms that included demographic information, and it kept detailed information on battle plans, pay sheets, minutes of meetings, prisoners, rosters, and vehicle records.[107]

The adoption of bureaucratic structures can make a group more efficient and better able to manage a large, growing, and even increasingly decentralized organization. While I argue that bureaucracies are more resistant to destabilization through leadership targeting, the adoption of policies and procedures intrinsic to a bureaucracy can also make a group more vulnerable to detection, undermining its security. Jacob Shapiro argues that adopting bureaucratic features can actually result in a tradeoff between security and control.[108] In this context, Shapiro understands bureaucracy as a "way of communicating critical facts up and down the chain of command to reduce agency loss."[109] He argues that a diverse subset of terrorist organizations generate organizational minutiae and paperwork that point to the presence of bureaucratic mechanisms. Terrorist organizations almost all face some sort of preference divergence, and bureaucracy provides one way for groups to mitigate the effects of these divergences. While I do not dispute Shapiro's claim that bureaucracy can cause problems for a group's ability to remain clandestine, it can increase its ability to withstand the weakening that could befall a less institutionalized group lacking clear succession mechanisms.

Communal Support

Communal support played a significant role in the ability of AQI, not only to resist targeting efforts, but also in its future expansion and territorial successes in its later incarnation as ISIS, which I will discuss in the conclusion. There are many factors that have contributed to changes in support for AQI, but I will focus on two events that contribute to its resilience and ability to become stronger and continue expanding: the US invasion of Iraq in 2003 and the marginalization of Sunnis from Iraqi society that began with the policy of de-Baathification.

Much of AQI's support emerged from widespread Sunni opposition to the US invasion of Iraq and fears of a Shi'ite government takeover.[110] After the 2003 invasion of Iraq, the Coalition Provisional Authority (CPA) issued orders barring members of the Baath Party from almost all government posts and disbanding the Iraqi Army.[111] The occupation and ensuing policies created a permissive environment of support for what became AQI. In 2004, local mujahedeen pledged their loyalty to al-Zarqawi, who was known as the emir of the "Islamic caliphate in Al-Fallujah." Al-Zarqawi's prominence increased, and he reached an agreement with bin Laden, pledging his loyalty and changing the name of the group to AQI. Abu Maysara al-Iraqi, the chief spokesman of AQI, stated that in addition to establishing a caliphate and waging jihad against infidels and apostates, one of the group's original goals was removing US and coalition forces from Iraq.[112] At this time, Sunnis in Iraq were sympathetic to its goals, this last one in particular. The group had broader regional support as well, with foreign fighters traveling from Syria, Yemen, Sudan, Egypt, and Saudi Arabia to join the insurgency.

Not long after, the organization's tactics became increasingly brutal, targeting Shi'as and other civilians and alienating it from much of its support base.[113] As mentioned earlier, al-Zarqawi ignored orders from AQC to refrain from such brutality and continued to alienate potential supporters with his tactics.[114] In one example, he was responsible for coordinating the bombing of a hotel in Amman that resulted in many civilian deaths. Many Iraqis, including Sunnis, were troubled by AQI's use of suicide bombing and other tactics and felt that it was intentionally inciting sectarian conflict.

During this same time, a majority of the Iraqi public opposed the US occupation. A 2006 poll from World Public Opinion found that "a large majority of Iraqis—71 percent—say they would like the Iraqi government to ask for US-led forces to be withdrawn from Iraq within a year or less. Given four options, 37 percent take the position that they would like US-led forces withdrawn 'within six months,' while another 34 percent opt for 'gradually withdraw[ing] US-led forces according to a one-year timeline.'"[115] Despite this widespread sympathy for the group's objective to remove occupying forces, the organization still managed to lose a significant amount of support, making it susceptible to targeting and other counterterrorism efforts. Al-Zarqawi was killed in 2006, and the decline in support coincided with a decline in activity in 2006, 2007, and 2008. In April 2010, much of the group's senior leadership was killed. Consistent with trends regarding the importance of support, the organization was still active but significantly less so until 2012, when it carried out more than three hundred attacks.

The United States and its allies were successful in severely degrading and nearly crushing AQI in 2006 and 2007, a consequence of the surge in US troop presence and the group's waning support.[116] A number of Sunnis and tribal leaders who were initially sympathetic toward AQI's objectives participated in the "Awakening," a 2006–7 uprising against al-Qaeda in Iraq.[117] Once the surge was under way, members of the Sunni insurgency abandoned AQI in order to receive payments of $300 from the United States as "Sons of Iraq."[118] However, the al-Maliki government failed to deliver on its promises of paying the Sons of Iraq and providing jobs in the Iraqi security forces.[119] Further, al-Maliki eliminated Sunnis from politics, the military, and security services. This feeling of marginalization drove many Sunnis back to the organization they had fought so fiercely during the Awakening and increased support for ISI and eventually ISIS.[120]

Conclusion

Leadership targeting has been an ineffective strategy against al-Qaeda. The organization has proven to be exceedingly resilient in spite of repeated attacks on its leadership over the past twenty years. Islamist and religious groups are very hard to weaken through decapitation. Larger groups and those in autocratic countries are also more resistant to targeting efforts. Data on the frequency of terrorist attacks has shown that over time, al-Qaeda actually experienced an uptick in attacks after targeting efforts. The theoretical framework presented in this book would suggest that over time, a targeting strategy is even more unlikely to result in a significant decline in al-Qaeda's activity after decapitation. Al-Qaeda's ideology continues to grow and reach a larger audience, becoming stronger and more entrenched. Groups also tend to become more bureaucratized or institutionalized over time. In the case of AQI, as the organization grew in size and function, a strong bureaucracy was required to efficiently manage its activities.

Generally, as groups grow and become stronger, communal support increases as well, be it coerced or voluntary. There is also an important relationship between bureaucracy and support. In many cases, organizations can gain support and a sense of legitimacy through the provision of resources, particularly in areas where the government is unwilling or unable to provide for certain communities. In order to distribute and manage the provision of services, bureaucracy is often required. Groups can also acquire more communal support over time, but there are ebbs and flows which can correlate with variation in the ability of targeting to weaken the group. Decapitation has been unable to significantly degrade and defeat al-Qaeda or any of its franchises, and barring the complete breakdown of the group's structure or support, is unlikely to bring about its defeat.

One of the most important mechanisms in a group's ability to resist temporary or short-term destabilization after the removal of a leader is having succession mechanisms in place, an essential part of a bureaucracy. Bureaucracies depend upon clear and transparent organizational features to manage a succession process. No one would expect that the removal of a company's CEO, for example, would result in its demise. While the analogy of the firm is helpful in trying to understand the organizational dynamics of terrorist organizations, the ability to quickly and easily replace leadership is even more important to clandestine organizations. Al-Qaeda's bureaucratic functioning allowed for the quick appointment of al-Zawahiri and minimized the potential for chaos and uncertainty regarding the future of the organization after bin Laden was killed. Many individuals have noted that al-Zawahiri is not as charismatic as bin Laden, and that he lacks the ideological passion and ability to inspire. While it may be true that bin Laden had a unique ability to inspire participation, charisma was not necessary; the organization was bureaucratized, and the ideological message was institutionalized. Bin Laden succeeded in broadening the group's appeal and message; charismatic qualities were not necessary. However, it is important to consider whether charisma, legacy, or some other nonorganizational qualities can make a group even harder to weaken.

Documents seized after the 2011 raid of bin Laden's compound indicate that Hamza bin Laden was poised to become the next leader of al-Qaeda. Hamza is one of Osama bin Laden's twenty-three children and was first seen in al-Qaeda propaganda videos holding a gun. Recognizing the risk posed by Hamza bin Laden's reemergence in propaganda videos, the US Department of State officially listed him as a global terrorist. Ali Soufan, a former FBI agent who has tracked al-Qaeda, stated: "He was that kid who exhibited leadership skills early on. . . . In a way, he was a poster kid for al-Qaeda. They featured him in so many of their propaganda. And for members of al-Qaeda who were indoctrinated with these propaganda videos, he means a lot to them."[121] Hamza's appearance in an al-Qaeda propaganda message in May 2017 suggests that the group is trying to renew itself and its image. Soufan has further stated that he is "being prepared for senior leadership in al-Qaeda, to play a role down the road in leading the organization, and probably in unifying the global jihadi movement."[122] It was clear that al-Zawahiri would take over after bin Laden, and now it seems likely that Hamza might assume leadership following al-Zawahiri.

Hamza has charismatic qualities that Soufan said were present even as a child. He has been "trying to copy his dad" in tone, terminology, and messages. While I have argued that having a charismatic leader does not make decapitation more successful, it can result in a stronger and more unified ideological message, attracting more support and recruits and strengthening the organization. Peter Bergen says that Hamza is "stepping up to the plate as a new face of al-Qaeda."[123] This is an important development for an organization whose notoriety has been overtaken by ISIS, which uses flashier and more sophisticated propaganda and is able to reach a broader audience. Hamza could provide some important recognition for the organization. He is also utilizing his father's martyrdom as a mobilizing tool. He has said that the organization will take revenge for Osama bin Laden's death and the occupations of Iraq and Afghanistan. Revenge is a strong motivator and can create the conditions for more support, particularly given the strength of a revenge narrative and the large number of people, globally, who opposed the 2003 US invasion of Iraq.

This is not to say that al-Qaeda is a small or weak organization. There seems to be a widespread belief that ISIS has grown steadily while al-Qaeda has stepped to the sidelines. This is not an accurate portrayal of al-Qaeda. As the figures earlier in the chapter demonstrated, it is still quite active. Al-Qaeda has been more clandestine than ISIS, drawing less attention to its activities.[124] However, the growing prominence of Hamza might signal that al-Qaeda is willing to conduct a more public and visible campaign. A more visible al-Qaeda, with more recruits and a stronger message, would not only make decapitation less likely to be effective; it could also increase the occurrence of retaliation for the death of its leadership.

8

Conclusion

Leadership decapitation is not a silver bullet in the war on terrorism, and yet, since 9/11, targeting a terrorist group's leadership has remained a critical component in US counterterrorism policy. Over the past four years, in addition to its efforts at killing and capturing leaders of al-Qaeda and its affiliated organizations, the United States has killed and arrested hundreds of ISIS leaders, including members of the Shura Council, commanders, local and regional leaders, military and media leaders, emirs, and others. These efforts are not limited to Iraq and Syria; ISIS leaders have been targeted in Lebanon, Afghanistan, Egypt, Indonesia, Nigeria, and Turkey, a trend that shows no sign of abatement. The findings in this book demonstrate that targeting the leadership of ISIS is not likely to destabilize and weaken the organization and may, in fact, make things worse.

Leadership targeting has been largely ineffective against groups that are religious, Islamist, separatist, and/or large—characteristics of organizations that are the focus of current decapitation efforts. ISIS, al-Qaeda, Hamas, al-Shabaab, and PKK, among others, have experienced repeated attacks on their leadership and have been remarkably resilient to them. Moreover, decapitation does not increase the mortality rate of terrorist groups, and in certain cases, it leads to a rise in activity. This is not to say that decapitation never works. In certain cases, it has weakened organizations and brought about their decline. This book is an effort to account for when decapitation works and when it does not, and to explain this variation.

The susceptibility of terrorist organizations can be explained by three variables: (1) bureaucratization, (2) communal support, and (3) ideology. Organizations that are bureaucratized, that have considerable amounts of communal support, or that are religious, and particularly Islamist, tend be much harder to weaken through the removal of their leadership. In order to determine whether decapitation is an effective counterterrorism policy, the book evaluates whether groups fell apart or experienced a change in the frequency of terrorist attacks after experiencing a loss of leadership. It also examines whether decapitation impacted the survival rate of terrorist organizations.

Bureaucratized terrorist groups are diversified, with a division of administrative responsibilities and functions, standard operating procedures, and clear succession mechanisms, which contributes to their ability to withstand the sudden removal of a leader or multiple leaders. A bureaucratic structure can provide groups with the organizational redundancy necessary to survive leadership attacks. Ideology can also impact a group's resilience in the face of leadership decapitation. Religious, particularly Islamist, groups and separatist groups should be more resilient to targeting efforts as the ideology upon which they are based does not depend upon the leader for its articulation. Ideology can be representative of a significant portion of the local community from which the group emerges, and in these cases, it is not dependent upon a leader but is instead pervasive within the communities. In other cases, a leader can broaden and institutionalize a group's ideological doctrine. Additionally, these groups often have more popular support, which is essential to their ability to acquire the resources necessary to maintain organizational strength and capacity following an attack on their leadership. Groups with lower levels of local support should have fewer resources, increasing their vulnerability to destabilization. Furthermore, groups with significant levels of communal support are frequently seen as more legitimate to the community in which they operate, further increasing their chances of survival in the face of external shocks.

In order to quantitatively examine the relationship between decapitation and a terrorist group's operational capacity and overall rate of survival, I created a dataset of nearly 1,000 cases of decapitation from 1970 to 2012. Statistical analyses examined the effect of organizational size, age, and type, GDP of the group's home country, population, regime type, and variables on the incident of decapitation itself, including whether the attack was an arrest or death and the rank of the leaders targeted. These analyses reveal that larger organizations are more likely to remain active and less likely to fall apart after targeting. In some cases, size has a stronger effect on decapitation in the long term. Islamist and separatist groups are also less likely to experience a cessation of activity in both one- and two-year periods after decapitation. Right-wing groups are more susceptible to targeting, and left-wing groups are more resilient. Finally, organizations in countries with a larger population are also less likely to be negatively impacted by leadership targeting.

The data was also analyzed in order to determine whether decapitation had an impact on the frequency of terrorist attacks. A transition matrix analysis reveals that decapitated groups have a higher probability of increasing the frequency of their attacks than nondecapitated groups, indicating that, overall, decapitation is a counterproductive strategy. However, the probability of experiencing an increase or decrease in activity after decapitation depends on a group's prior level of activity. Islamist, large, and separatist groups tend to be much more active after decapitation than other kinds of organizations.

Finally, a survival analysis shows that decapitation does not shorten a group's life span. The finding that there is no statistically significant relationship between decapitation and a group's survival rate challenges much of the optimism regarding the efficacy of decapitation as a counterterrorism strategy. The data indicates that a group's overall survival rate is significantly impacted by a number of other conditions, including size, type, GDP, regime type, and the average number of attacks and injuries carried out. For example, the largest organizations have a 30 percent lower hazard rate of group mortality than smaller organizations. Separatist groups, religious groups, and left-wing groups also have a lower hazard rate, while organizations in countries with a higher GDP or more autocratic governments have a higher rate. Looking at decapitated and nondecapitated organizations reveals that the life span of decapitated organizations is also influenced by the average number of injuries carried out by each group. In other words, a group's ability to inflict damage is one factor in its resilience or susceptibility to destabilization after decapitation; the higher the average number of injuries caused, the higher the survival rate. This data suggests that groups tend to survive despite decapitation.

These findings are consistent with the theoretical explanations and hypotheses developed in Chapters 2 and 3. First, the finding that as an organization becomes older and larger, it is more likely to withstand attacks on its leadership is consistent with the argument that bureaucracies help groups survive the loss of their leadership. As an organization ages and grows in size, it is more likely to become bureaucratized and to develop a division of labor based on specialization, which allows most of the organization to continue operating even after other organizational components are removed. Second, ideology is an important predictor across all measures of counterterrorism efficacy. Islamist and separatist groups are highly resilient, as are left-wing organizations to a slightly lesser degree. The susceptibility of right-wing organizations was more variable, as they were resilient in some models and not in others. Finally, communal support is essential in understanding the resilience of terrorist groups to leadership targeting. This argument that groups with more support are more resilient is consistent with the finding that separatist and Islamist groups have a lower probability of organizational decline after decapitation. Separatist organizations are often representative of the views of their local communities, more so than other types of organizations, and are thus more likely to have local support. The public opinion polls examined in the case studies support this finding. Moreover, the ideology upon which separatist groups and religious groups recruit and inspire individuals is not dependent upon their leaders; in many cases, their ideologies and doctrines have become institutionalized.

Case studies of Hamas, al-Qaeda, and the Shining Path examine the theoretical assumptions regarding the resilience of terrorist groups to the sudden removal of their leadership. Hamas experienced numerous leadership attacks, which have resulted in neither collapse nor a substantial weakening of its operations. Hamas's ability to continue carrying out attacks was consistent with theoretical predictions regarding the resilience of separatist or Islamist groups with communal support. While the number of attacks increased, the lethality of those attacks decreased over time. This decline can be explained, in part, by other factors that impacted Hamas's ability to carry out more lethal attacks, including the building of the separation wall and an increase in the number of rocket attacks, which result in fewer casualties. Hamas's resilience can be explained largely by its bureaucratic structure, communal support, and ideology.

Hamas has developed an extensive infrastructure for the provision of religious, social, and educational resources, which can influence the ideological and religious beliefs of the community. After Israeli attempts to kill Hamas leaders, the subsequent retaliatory attacks on Israel led to more public support among Palestinians and increased Hamas's political legitimacy. The outrage that often follows the killing of a high-profile leader, particularly an inspirational one like Sheikh Yassin, can increase support for the movement and provide a new mechanism for recruitment. Targeting religious leaders can strengthen a group's operational capacity by increasing group support and recruitment.

The second study, on the Shining Path, demonstrated variation in the effectiveness of decapitation. Abimael Guzmán, the organization's founder and leader, was captured in 1992 and sentenced to life imprisonment. Sendero was weakened in 1999 with the arrest of Guzmán's successor Óscar Ramírez Durand, but regrouped a few years later with a different focus, different goals, and different tactics. After a major decline in the wake of Durand's arrest in 1999 and another series of targeting efforts in 2012 and 2013, the organization was nearly defeated. Sendero was a left-wing organization, which, according to the theory, should make it easier to destabilize through decapitation. This outcome can be explained by organizational changes in the 1990s when the group's bureaucracy began to crumble and it lost much of its support. In Chapter 6, I argued that as Sendero became less bureaucratic in structure and experienced a loss in communal support, it became more susceptible to destabilization after decapitation. When Guzmán was arrested in 1992, the organization had a large amount of communal support and an organized bureaucratic authority structure. The organization was thus able to withstand the 1992 capture of Guzmán and other leaders. By 1999, when Durand was arrested, the organization was already in a state of decline. It had lost a considerable number of its members, and its bureaucratic structure was severely weakened. Moreover, levels of support were lower than at the time of Guzmán's arrest. Finally, I argue that left-wing organizations are not as durable as religious or territorially motivated groups, as their ideology tends to be more dependent upon the group's leadership. These factors played a part in Sendero's inability to survive the capture of its top leader. In the aftermath of Guzmán's capture in 1992, the organization carried out retaliatory attacks. This provides support for the claim that decapitation can also increase the desire and motivation for retaliatory attacks; it is important to recognize that decapitation has the potential to increase attacks by generating a desire for revenge.

The al-Qaeda case is slightly different, in that al-Qaeda is not only one organization. The core of the organization, al-Qaeda Central (AQC), operates as a distinct organization with a number of affiliates that operate globally. After the death of Osama bin Laden in 2011, al-Qaeda was able to easily and swiftly appoint a successor, Ayman al-Zawahiri, which minimized the potential for chaos and uncertainty regarding the future of the organization. Bin Laden had previously succeeded in broadening the group's appeal and message, and the ideology that had inspired so many to join al-Qaeda survived. While the group's support declined over time, its message still resonated with many, inspiring both lone wolves and the growth of other affiliated organizations, which themselves were able to generate support by providing resources and services that the states in which they operated were often unable to provide.

Comparing all three cases, bureaucracy accounts for much of a group's resilience to decapitation. Bureaucracies are not only able to easily replace leaders that have been arrested or killed but also have operating procedures and rules in place that enable organizations to recover from the chaos and confusion that might follow the sudden and high-profile loss of top or very high-level leaders. Lower-level leaders are even more easily replaced. Second, consistent with the theoretical claim that religious and separatist groups are harder to weaken through decapitation, both Hamas and al-Qaeda not only were able to withstand attacks on their leadership but also adapted and in certain cases increased their activity. In both cases, the ideology upon which the groups depended did not rely upon the leadership for its articulation; it transcended leadership. In contrast, the Shining Path was a left-wing organization, and while communal support allowed it to initially withstand Guzmán's arrest, the group eventually fell apart due, in part, to its inability to revive its ideology.

Finally, in all three cases, there is evidence that communal support played a large part in understanding a group's resilience to decapitation. Both Hamas and al-Qaeda managed to gain broad communal support. In the case of al-Qaeda this enlarged the larger movement and helped the franchising process and the development of its affiliated organizations. Likewise, Hamas offered important social and religious services to Palestinians, providing the group with legitimacy and enabling it to win seats in the Palestinian Legislative Council. In contrast, the Shining Path was unable to maintain its support, which, along with its decline in organized administrative structures, contributed to its decline after Durand's arrest in 1999. While decapitation was initially unsuccessful, the group eventually succumbed. Ideology was the primary variable that differed in these three cases. The ideological doctrines upon which religious and separatist groups are based are essential. If a group's ideology does not become institutionalized and remains a function of the leadership, the group will ultimately be unlikely to survive.

Overall, the evidence suggests that decapitation is not an effective counterterrorism strategy, that it is especially unlikely to be effective in the cases of bureaucratized Islamist organizations, and that it is especially ineffective against groups those have managed to amass popular support. Even more problematically, decapitation can, in certain cases, result in an increase in group activity. These findings are central for evaluating current counterterrorism policies. Decapitation is not likely to be effective against the organizations that the United States (and other countries) are currently targeting. This book suggests that such attempts are doomed to fail in a wide range of cases, including ISIS.

ISIS

ISIS is an important case to consider, given that it has occupied a significant amount of US counterterrorism resources. However, the analysis in this book suggests that targeting the leaders of ISIS is not likely to have adverse impacts on the group's capacity. Abu Bakr al-Baghdadi, who became the leader of the Islamic State of Iraq (ISI) in 2010, has been notoriously elusive. He delivered a notable public sermon at a mosque in Mosul on July 4, 2014, declaring himself emir of the Islamic State. Since then, he has made sporadic statements through writings, videos, and audio recordings. The infrequency with which al-Baghdadi has been seen in public has led to a number of claims that he has been killed or is incapacitated in some way.[1] There have been a number of reports of his death. As an example, in June 2016 the Russian military claimed that they had killed al-Baghdadi. This secrecy and elusiveness is an intentional effort to avoid his killing or capture.

According to theories of charismatic leadership, which have underscored much of the early optimism regarding the ability of decapitation to weaken a group, al-Baghdadi's death should cause weakening of the organization, if not its demise. Al-Baghdadi is a scholar of Islamic law and scripture and is often described as a persuasive speaker with a calm and pious demeanor. The assumption is that al-Baghdadi's charisma, which gives him a sense of mystique and authority, inspires recruits and attacks and serves as the basis of the group's operational capacity. However, ISIS is not a cult of personality, and al-Baghdadi has been successful in ensuring that the group is institutionalized to such a degree that it is not dependent upon his leadership. Furthermore, in the wake of losing substantial amounts of territory in Iraq and Syria, al-Baghdadi, and Abu Muhammad al-Adnani before his death, focused on the group's ideological message, just as al-Qaeda's message remained strong following bin Laden's death. While al-Baghdadi's death or capture would certainly have an important symbolic impact, it is crucial to determine whether it would actually hinder ISIS's ability to carry out attacks and expand the reach of its ideological message and mission, both within the region and beyond.

Given ISIS's organizational structure and its significant, albeit declining, territorial control, decapitation should have even less impact than against more "traditional" terrorist groups such as al-Qaeda or Hamas. ISIS is perhaps less straightforward than the other cases examined in this book. It is a terrorist organization, that is, a nonstate actor that targets civilians in pursuit of its political goals. However, the organization also resembles a state-like entity. The governance structures that have allowed ISIS to control a considerable amount of territory have created something that resembles a quasi-state. I do not mean to claim that ISIS is not a terrorist organization, but it has developed state-like characteristics during its process of territorial consolidation and governance. While not the central focus, these state-like features have implications for ISIS's likely resilience to repeated attacks on its leadership.

To govern as a state, ISIS developed bureaucratic structures to manage its finances and military capabilities, and to govern the territory it sought to control. The organization also has clear succession mechanisms in place, so that in the event of al-Baghdadi's removal, his successor should likely be chosen easily and swiftly. These bureaucratic features should strengthen ISIS's ability to withstand the loss of a leader. Second, as argued throughout this book, Islamist organizations

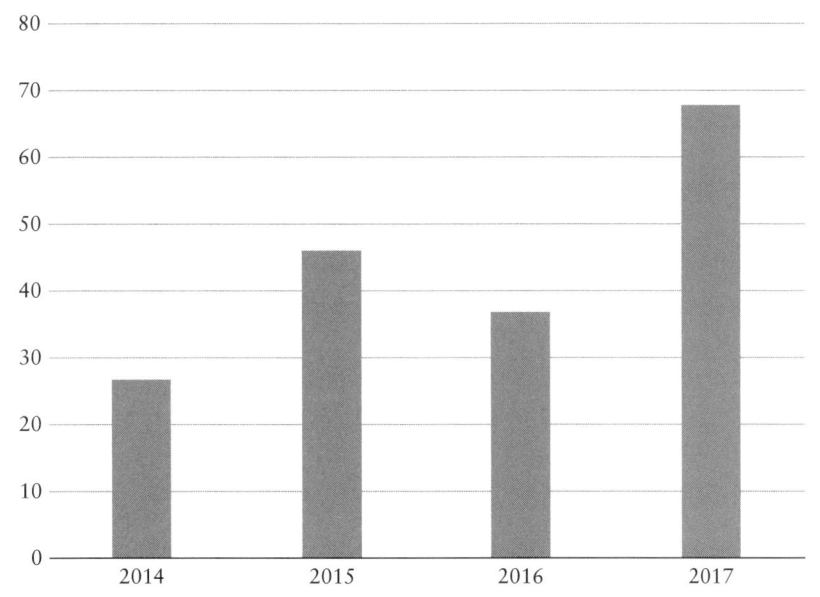

FIGURE 8.1
Leadership decapitation against ISIS, 2014–2017

are especially hard to destabilize through removing a leader. The leadership of the group is not necessary for recruitment, inspiring attacks, or ensuring that the group's message stays relevant. The ideology upon which the group is based is self-sustaining in many ways, and the organization's efforts at propaganda and social media have been effective at broadening the base of support transnationally. While ISIS coerced much of its local support, it was able to consolidate its control in large part through the support of individuals who felt disenfranchised by the Iraqi government and felt that ISIS would represent their interests.

To examine ISIS's resilience to leadership targeting, this chapter will look at decapitation efforts against it and also at ISIS attacks from 2014 through 2017, and will argue that decapitation is likely to have a detrimental impact on the organization.[2] The previous chapter included data on the organizations from which ISIS emerged, AQI and ISI. I coded 198 incidents of leadership targeting against ISIS beginning in 2014 (see Figure 8.1). Of these 198 leaders, 24 were arrested and the rest were killed. This large number of individuals targeted includes a wide variety of members of the organization's upper echelon, including top military and operations commanders, local leaders, leaders of recruitment, governors, emirs, and others.

Abu Muhammad al-Adnani, believed to be the second most important leader after Abu Bakr al-Baghdadi, was killed by an airstrike in Aleppo, Syria, in August

2016. A spokesperson for the group, al-Adnani was in charge of ISIS operations outside of Syria and Iraq and responsible for the recruitment of foreign fighters. He was also one of the longest-serving top commanders. Thomas Joscelyn, a senior fellow at the Foundation for Defense of Democracies and senior editor of the *Long War Journal*, states that Adnani was one of the most senior officials in ISIS, and probably the most visible.[3] His death was claimed by many analysts and policy makers to be a major blow to the organization.[4] Immediately following his death, Adam Deen, a senior researcher at the Quilliam Foundation, said that ISIS would be "scrambling to find a replacement." He argued that ISIS was dependent upon personality cults and the charisma of its leaders, and as such, the death of a figure such as Adnani would be destabilizing.[5] The theory and the findings of this book would have predicted that Adnani's death was unlikely to disrupt the group's operations in any significant way. While he was a skilled propagandist for the organization, there are others who could take his place. Moreover, as a spokesperson who led the group's external operations, Adnani was successful in expanding ISIS's reach globally.[6] According to Gerges, in a communiqué Adnani "demanded that all jihadist factions everywhere pledge allegiance to the new caliph, Baghdadi, as the legality of all emirates, groups, states, and organizations now null and void. . . . Adnani made it clear that there is only one Islamic state and one caliphate, with no room for dissent."[7] Through his propaganda and organizing efforts, Adnani inspired individuals and attacks around the globe, which has the added effect of further advancing ISIS's ideological coherence and reach.

ISIS began operating in Afghanistan in 2015, and there have been a considerable number of attacks carried out by the US, coalition forces, and Afghani security forces against it. An ISIS leader in northern Afghanistan, Qari Hekmatullah, was killed in April 2018. The targeted killing was a joint operation between American Special Operations troops and Afghan Special Security forces. In response to the operation, General Nicholson said, "IS-K will be eliminated."[8] There was internal fighting among rival factions regarding succession, but there are a number of different leaders and the organization survived. In August 2018, another ISIS leader in Afghanistan, Abu Saad Erhabi, was killed in a series of airstrikes in eastern Nangarhar province.[9]

Citing ISIS setbacks and loss of considerable amounts of territory in Syria and Iraq, there has been a sense of optimism regarding the efficacy of targeting and other military operations against ISIS. In the past year, there have been a number of reports that ISIS has suffered serious setbacks and is on the decline.[10] It lost its control over Mosul in July 2017 and its last Iraqi stronghold in October 2017. These losses in territory also translate into fewer financial resources.[11] By the end of the year, ISIS had also lost control of its Syrian capital, Raqqa. While ISIS has lost control of a considerable amount of territory, including prior strongholds, it is important to examine the manner in which territorial control is assessed and evaluated. It recently regrouped and carried out operations in areas it previously controlled, including Diyala, Salah ad-Din, and Kirkuk in Iraq.[12] Aaron Y. Zelin of the Washington Institute for Near East Policy has argued that this loss of control does not signal ISIS's demise. He has stated that "I.S. has a plan, and that is to wait out their enemies locally in order to gain time to rebuild their networks while at the same time provide inspiration to followers outside to keep fighting their enemies farther away."[13]

There were concerns that a loss of territory in Iraq and Syria would result in an increase in presence and activity in Afghanistan. In fact, ISIS released a video praising the virtues of fighting for the struggle in Afghanistan.[14] However, it has been reported that government forces are more firmly in control in the Nangarhar province in eastern Afghanistan, an area in which ISIS has suffered setbacks.[15] Given ISIS's loss of territorial control, its weakness in key strategic areas, and the rate at which its leaders are being targeted, decapitation is likely to remain a primary tool in the counterterrorism arsenal of the United States and other countries battling the group.

Despite a large number of attacks against ISIS, the group is still active. Figure 8.2 shows the number of attacks carried out by ISIS between 2013 and 2017.[16] The Global Terrorism Database finds that the organization has carried out at least 1,000 attacks every year for the past four years. While there was a 10 percent decline in attacks, from 1,454 in 2016 to 1,315 in 2017, and a 40 percent decline in fatalities, the group is still remarkably active despite the loss of a considerable amount of territory. Most ISIS attacks have occurred in the Middle East and North Africa; a smaller amount have occurred in Southeast Asia and even fewer in Western Europe. As ISIS loses ground in Iraq and Syria, it is increasing its efforts to target the West. After a long period of silence and questions about whether he was alive, a recording of al-Baghdadi was released in August 2018 during the holiday of Eid al-Adha. In it, al-Baghdadi called for the organization to regroup, and, as reported by Hassan, "called for lone-actor attacks in Western countries, including bombings, car-rammings, and gun and knife attacks. Previously, such calls only came from ISIS's former spokesman; coming from the self-styled caliph himself, they're likely to carry more weight." Baghdadi actually quantified these actions. Hassan continues, "One attack in the West equals a thousand in the Middle East."[17]

The speech further signaled the emergence of a shift in the organization from a caliphate, a state-like entity, to a classic insurgency. Al-Baghdadi referenced ISIS's history as a "network of insurgent groups waging war against Americans."

FIGURE 8.2
ISIS attacks, 2013–2017

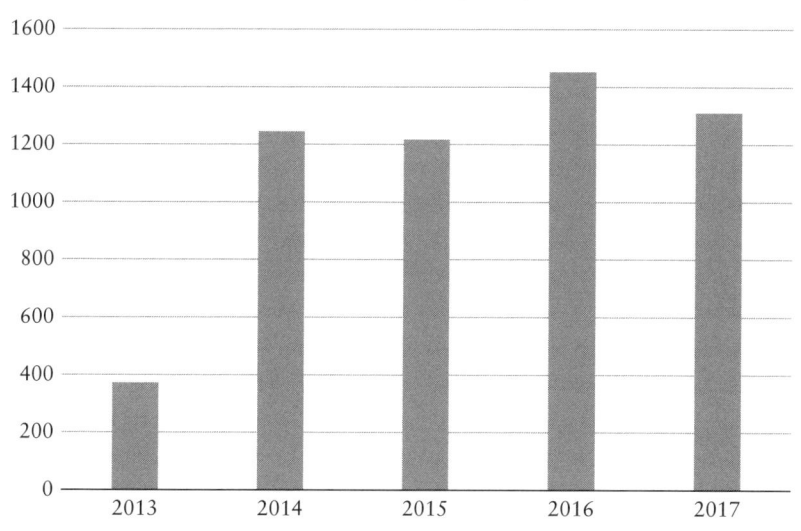

Year	Attacks (approx.)
2013	~370
2014	~1250
2015	~1210
2016	~1450
2017	~1310

SOURCE: National Consortium for the Study of Terrorism and Responses to Terrorism (START), University of Maryland. (2018). The Global Terrorism Database (GTD) [Data file]. Retrieved from https://www.start.umd.edu/gtd.

He also cited al-Zarqawi's statement about the fight against Crusaders in Dabiq, a reference to a town in northern Syria that will be the site of a millennial battle between Muslims and Christians that will bring about the true caliphate.[18] Hassan argues that in his speech, Baghdadi referred to Dabiq as the source of this renewed battle, which has followed their loss of territory. Al-Baghdadi also referenced the success of the initial insurgency in reorganizing after the losses sustained by AQI in 2007. While the organization has suffered territorial losses, it has proposed a way to adapt and continue its struggle. Reports in 2017 argued that after suffering considerable territorial losses, ISIS was seeking a return to its guerrilla roots.[19] Its ability to adapt and reorient its strategy is indicative of the kind of terrorist organization that is capable of withstanding counterterrorism efforts, such as decapitation. This speech reflects Adnani's statement that while organizations can be weakened, the movement and ideology cannot be eliminated.

Theory of Organizational Resilience

The theory of organizational resilience suggests that targeting is not likely to result in the end or even a significant weakening of ISIS. It is an Islamist organization, bureaucratized (albeit decentralized) and with considerable amounts of support (in many cases coerced). Even if al-Baghdadi is captured or killed and the organization undergoes a brief period of disruption, given the group's hierarchy of authority and chain of command, it should ultimately choose a successor easily and recover quickly. Furthermore, the statistical results regarding the resilience of large and Islamist organizations are consistent with ISIS's resilience.

First, ISIS is an Islamist organization, which is one of the strongest predictors of organizational resistance to decapitation. Gerges describes ISIS's ideology as follows: "ISIS was born of a marriage between an Iraq-based AQI (Salafi-jihadism) and an identity frame of politics. The group's ideological lineage of Salafi-jihadism forms part of the ideological impetus; the other part of its ideological nature is a hyper-Sunni identity driven by an intrinsic and even genocidal anti-Shia ideology."[20] He suggests that its development of a "pure ideology" is integral to its strategy and its ability to recruit individuals to fight on its behalf, including as suicide bombers. This brand of Salafist ideology is used to justify its strategy, tactics, and policies. ISIS has been highly effective at broadening its message. Its ideology and messaging have been used to inspire foreign fighters, lone-wolf attacks, and other terrorist organizations to join ISIS's struggle. Some reports have argued that approximately 40,000 foreign fighters went to fight in Iraq and Syria after the declaration of the caliphate in June 2014.[21] There have also been a number of attacks inspired by or carried out on behalf of ISIS. A report by the House Homeland Security Committee examined 243 ISIS-linked attacks that targeted the West. The report found that from February 2014 to July 2016, 54 attacks were "inspired by ISIS" and from July 2016 to July 2018, there were 89 attacks.[22] These attacks can elicit feelings of fear and insecurity on the part of domestic audiences. The ability to carry out attacks and continue to generate fear on the part of the public are both indicative of an active and influential organization.

Another indicator that points to ISIS's resilience is that the organization transcends its material capabilities and territorial control. Prior to Adnani's death, he stated quite prophetically that while ISIS may experience periods of weakening, the movement is more than its capacity or amount of control. He states, "O America. Would we be defeated and you be victorious if you were to take Mosul or Sirte or Raqqa? Certainly not! We would be defeated and you victorious only if you were able to remove the Koran from Muslims' hearts."[23] This statement reflects Gerges's assessment of ISIS. He writes, "Ideology is a superglue that binds Salafi-jihadist activists and combatants to each other and allows the movement to renew and revitalize itself after suffering setbacks."[24] The group's ideology is not dependent upon leadership or even territorial control. ISIS's ideology has provided the group with the ability to recruit, gain supporters globally, and regroup and reorient its strategy after territorial losses.

Second, ISIS has a well-organized structure with features of a bureaucracy. The leadership is made up of a clear command structure, with al-Baghdadi at the top, surrounded by advisors, deputies, and the Shura Council, which technically has the ability to appoint a new leader. The civilian bureaucracy is overseen by twelve administrators who govern territory in Iraq and Syria and manage a council that handles religious, security, military, media, and economic affairs.[25] The leadership has direct control over its fighters in Iraq and Syria.[26]

The organization is large, with estimates of about 30,000 fighters at its height.[27] Granted, size is a difficult variable to code. But when groups become this large, they often require standard operating procedures and organized administrative functions to operate. Moreover, as an organization that is determined to function as a state, bureaucratic structures are critical. Roles and procedures were necessary to govern and to administer the sort of services upon which a state's citizens depend. At its height, ISIS controlled territory roughly the size of Britain, with an estimated population of 12 million people, in addition to a large coastline in Libya, territory in Nigeria, a city in the Philippines, and areas in thirteen other countries.[28] Controlling such a large amount of territory requires sophisticated administrative capabilities to manage finances, provide services, control administrative functions, and engage in taxation.[29]

The organization has developed an extensive bureaucracy. Audrey Cronin has argued that ISIS resembles a state more than it does a terrorist organization,[30] signaling the presence of a sophisticated bureaucracy necessary for a group to perform state-like functions. ISIS developed a complex and efficient organization in order to perform administrative functions, such as a court system with a bureaucratic chain of command; the ability to collect taxes on real estate, clothing, food, and vehicles; and laws related to conduct and war.[31] These mechanisms provide ISIS with the capacity to withstand frequent and repeated decapitation attempts. Consistent with the conclusion of this book, Cronin argues, "Although it is hardly the model government depicted in ISIS' propaganda videos, this pseudo-state would carry on quite ably without Baghdadi or his closest lieutenants."[32] Due to the elaborate bureaucracy necessary to sustain a state-like entity, ISIS is not dependent upon al-Baghdadi for its ideological or organizational cohesion.

Finally, ISIS has widespread support from local populations; indeed, the support of Sunnis and former Baathists was critical for ISIS's ability to claim such a considerable amount of territory in the summer of 2014.[33] Jessica Stern notes that in May 2010 after al-Baghdadi assumed leadership of what was then ISI, he sought to rebuild an organization that was in "shambles." ISIS was committed to creating an Islamic state, and to do so allied with the former Baathists, who were unemployed and held a low status in Iraqi society as a result of de-Baathification.[34]

They "brought military and organizational skills and a network of experienced bureaucrats that AQI and then ISI lacked."[35] Many of the Baathists occupied top positions within the organization. Their importance underscores the critical role that local support and institutionalized structures played in the ability of the group to grow, increase its activity, and withstand frequent attacks on its leadership.

Public opinion polls can shed light on attitudes toward ISIS and the larger movement. First, polls can provide a sense of how ISIS relied upon frustration with the Iraqi government to amass the support necessary to gain control of significant amounts of territory in the summer of 2014. A Gallup poll from 2014 indicated that the number of Sunnis that had faith in al-Maliki's government declined from 2013 to 2014, with the largest decline in Sunni-dominated regions.[36] The poll indicates that prior to the 2014 survey, "those living in predominantly Sunni areas were as likely as those in predominantly Shia regions to express confidence in the national government."[37] As confidence in the government held steady in other regions, this loss of faith in the government occurred in the Sunni-dominated northern and western provinces; these were the same areas seized by ISIS. This is an important shift and reflects the notion that support is essential to a group's ability to succeed. Many of those who expressed disapproval of al-Maliki's regime were located in the region in which ISIS was able to establish control; this support, in part, enabled ISIS's successes in 2014.

Further polls indicated a negative view of the United States and its support of the Iraqi regime and treatment of Sunnis in the aftermath of the invasion. Polls carried out through the Arab Barometer project in Iraq in 2014 demonstrate that a majority of respondents expressed disapproval of US military operations.[38] For example, a majority of both Shi'as and Sunnis agreed that American interference in the region justified armed operations against the United States everywhere. Even further, a majority of respondents felt that the United States had a negative influence in the development of democracy in Iraq. This data does not shed light on support and attitudes toward ISIS, but it does show a dissatisfaction with the United States and its policies, which could be seen as a factor in aiding ISIS's ability to consolidate control. It also suggests a lack of support for al-Maliki (who was supported by the United States) and increasing support for organizations such as ISIS, whose goals included targeting the United States.

Negative attitudes towards ISIS are also considerable. A public opinion poll carried out by the PEW research center in 2015 in eleven countries found that in countries with a majority Muslim population, with the exception of Pakistan, the majority of respondents expressed unfavorable views of ISIS in Iraq and Syria.[39] Another set of polls conducted in Egypt, Saudi Arabia, and Lebanon found little support for the organization.[40] In polls carried out in 2014, only 3 percent of respondents expressed favorable views of ISIS, though it should be noted that even this small percentage still amounts to more than one and a half million individuals in Egypt and half a million in Saudi Arabia. While recent polls indicate unfavorable and negative views of ISIS, it is essential to consider whether the group is gaining strength. The large number of foreign fighters that have gone to Iraq and Syria and the organization's large social media presence are potential sources of future support.[41]

While ISIS has much less local support than other organizations examined for this project, its ability to gain followers and support for its cause globally contributed to its ability to gain territorial control in Iraq and Syria. In addition, its bureaucracy and ideological strength play a critical role in ISIS's resilience to leadership attacks. It is essential to consider these factors when evaluating counterterrorism policies.

Policy Implications

The findings of this book have important implications for the future of counterterrorism policy. Decapitation is not likely to weaken or ultimately result in the demise of the groups the United States is currently targeting, al-Qaeda and ISIS. The data indicates that overall, decapitation does not have an effect on a group's mortality rate. Furthermore, decapitation can have counterproductive consequences, resulting in a rise in terrorist activity or, in certain circumstances, actually increasing a group's survival rate. It can also create martyrs and increase sympathy and support for the organization from local and international communities. Killing a terrorist leader can inspire members or supporters to carry out retaliatory attacks to avenge their leader's death. Revenge is a powerful motivator that can be intensified when civilians are killed during an attack. As an example, after bin Laden's death demonstrators congregated outside the White House, cheering and celebrating his death. In the days following the attack, through jihadist forums, al-Qaeda called upon its followers to carry out retaliatory attacks.[42] In the case of Hamas, retaliatory suicide attacks were not uncommon following the killing of leaders of the organization. After the assassination of Yahya Ayyash, Hamas's chief bomb maker, the group carried out four retaliatory bus bombings that killed more than fifty people. The assassinations of Hamas leaders Sheikh Ahmed Yassin and Abdel Aziz al-Rantisi in 2004 triggered local and international outrage. There was considerable sympathy for Hamas within the Palestinian society after the death of Yassin, who played a spiritual role within the organization. The death of al-Rantisi, who held more of an operational role, resulted in less international condemnation.

Heavy-handed counterterrorism polices can generate organizational support. Policies that are seen as unreasonably severe and that result in civilian casualties can result in outrage toward the government employing them. Atran argues that coercive tactics do not diminish popular support for jihadist movements.[43] A state's counterterrorism policies can affect militant sentiments, the local population, and the international community. Bloom has argued that overly heavy-handed counterterrorism policies can generate support for violence in local communities, which can create the condition for the occurrence of suicide attacks. In response to the 9/11 attacks, the United States launched ground invasions in Afghanistan and Iraq, both of which generated sympathy for the militants and the emergence of territorial groups dedicated to ending the US occupation of Muslim lands in Iraq, Saudi Arabia, and elsewhere.

It is essential that the United States consider whether decapitation is an effective counterterrorism strategy that actually reduces the frequency of attacks, weakens terrorist organizations, and undermines a group's ability to operate and gain new recruits. While decapitation is seen as a low-cost tactic that results in fewer civilian casualties, the findings in this book suggest that current targeting policies need to be reevaluated. Groups currently targeted by the United States and others, such as ISIS, al-Qaeda, Hamas, PKK, and al-Shabaab, are likely to resist continued targeting efforts. They also suggest that decapitation will not adversely impact these groups' life spans, reduce the frequency of their attacks, or bring about their demise. In fact, dependent upon the group's prior level of activity, decapitation could actually *increase* the frequency of their attacks. It could also create sympathy for terrorist organizations, ultimately enhancing their ability to recruit and gain support within local communities and abroad. It is thus essential that states consider these counterproductive consequences of counterterrorism policies. What can states do to combat terrorism? That question is beyond the scope of this project, but states could consider dedicating more resources to counterterrorism policies, such as counterideological efforts, targeting a group's funding, public diplomacy, education, aid, and providing services for individuals in failing states.

Appendix

APPENDIX TABLE I
Transition matrix for groups with over 1,000 members

A. CONTROL GROUP

	Decreasing	Flat	Increasing
Decreasing	0.3388	0.2951	0.3661
Flat	0.0617	0.6872	0.2511
Increasing	0.6289	0.0515	0.3196

B. EXPERIMENT GROUP BEFORE DECAPITATION

	Decreasing	Flat	Increasing
Decreasing	0.3115	0.2213	0.4672
Flat	0.0067	0.8433	0.1500
Increasing	0.5444	0.0500	0.4056

C. EXPERIMENT GROUP AFTER DECAPITATION

	Decreasing	Flat	Increasing
Decreasing	0.2840	0.2654	0.4506
Flat	0.0874	0.7330	0.1796
Increasing	0.5484	0.0591	0.3925

APPENDIX TABLE 2
Transition matrix for Islamist groups

A. CONTROL GROUP

	Decreasing	Flat	Increasing
Decreasing	0.3731	0.3134	0.3134
Flat	0.0645	0.7661	0.1694
Increasing	0.5942	0.0725	0.3333

B. EXPERIMENT GROUP BEFORE DECAPITATION

	Decreasing	Flat	Increasing
Decreasing	0.1948	0.3506	0.4545
Flat	0.0462	0.8000	0.1538
Increasing	0.5963	0.0642	0.3394

C. EXPERIMENT GROUP AFTER DECAPITATION

	Decreasing	Flat	Increasing
Decreasing	0.2742	0.3145	0.4113
Flat	0.0466	0.7754	0.1780
Increasing	0.6074	0.0889	0.3037

APPENDIX TABLE 3
Transition matrix for separatist groups

A. CONTROL GROUP

	Decreasing	Flat	Increasing
Decreasing	0.3136	0.3273	0.3591
Flat	0.0449	0.7275	0.2275
Increasing	0.6923	0.0588	0.2489

B. EXPERIMENT GROUP BEFORE DECAPITATION

	Decreasing	Flat	Increasing
Decreasing	0.3152	0.2667	0.4182
Flat	0.0452	0.8005	0.1543
Increasing	0.6021	0.0860	0.3118

C. EXPERIMENT GROUP AFTER DECAPITATION

	Decreasing	Flat	Increasing
Decreasing	0.2386	0.3466	0.4148
Flat	0.0949	0.6898	0.2153
Increasing	0.5904	0.1117	0.2979

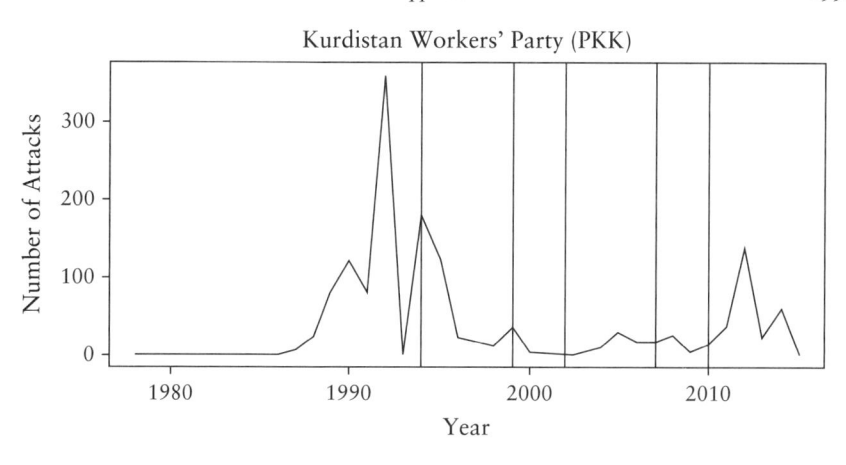

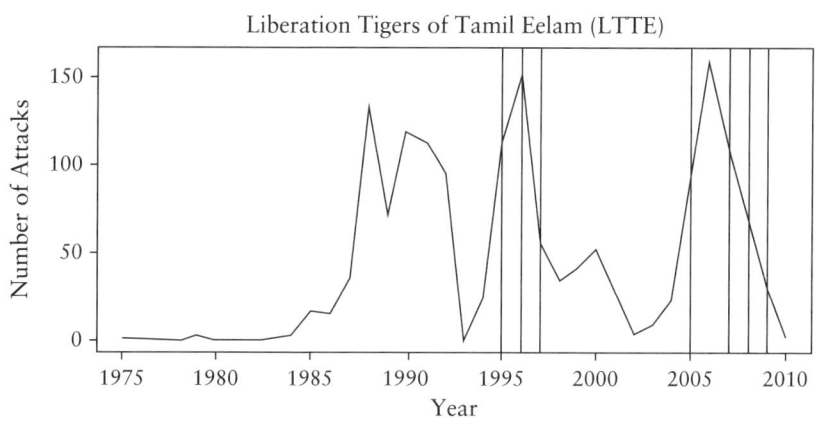

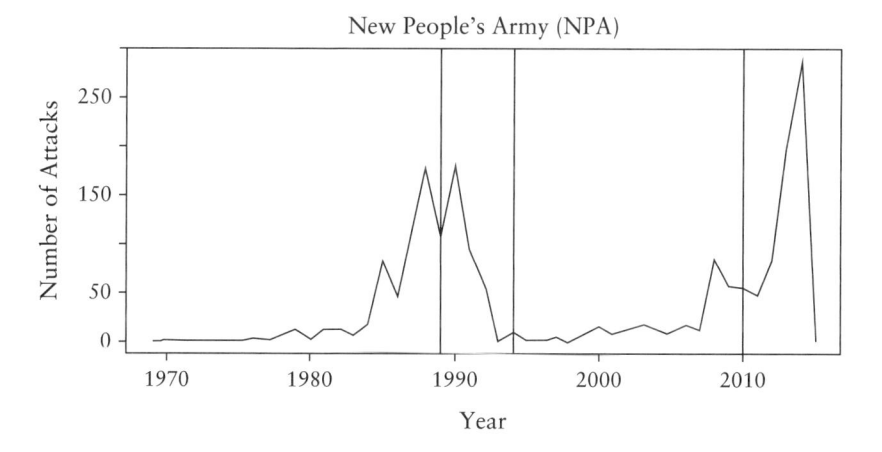

APPENDIX FIGURE A1 Time series analysis on attack frequency

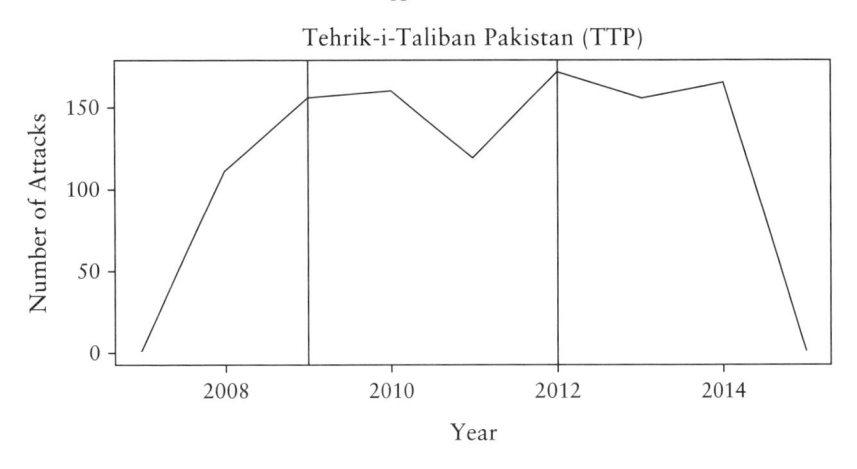

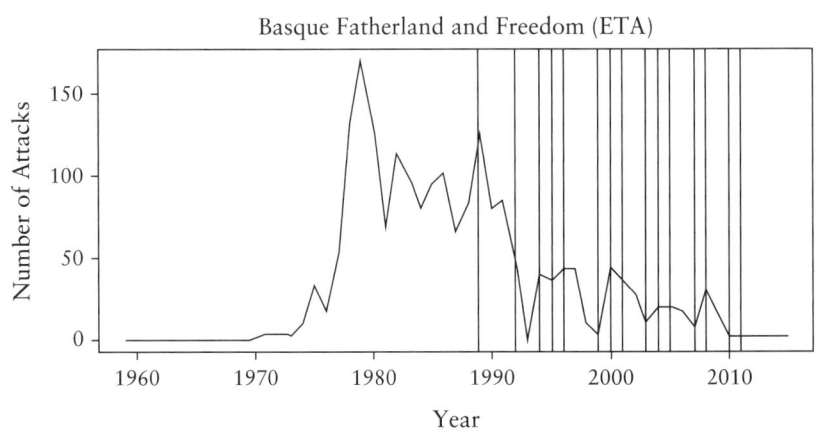

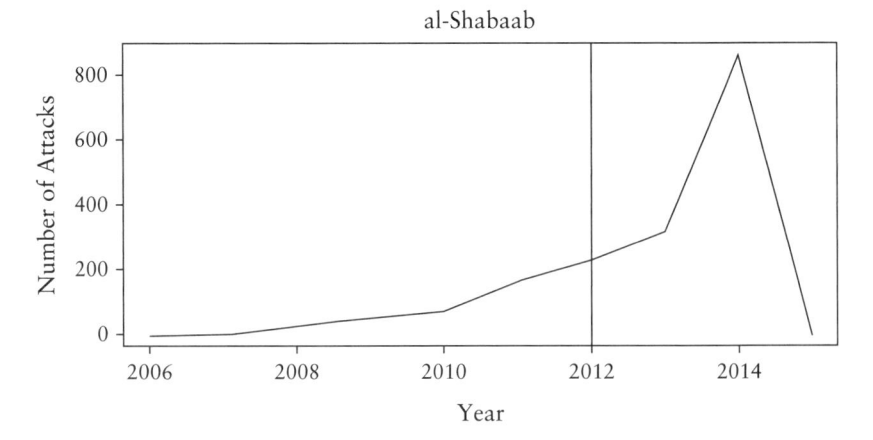

APPENDIX FIGURE A1 *(continued)*

Appendix

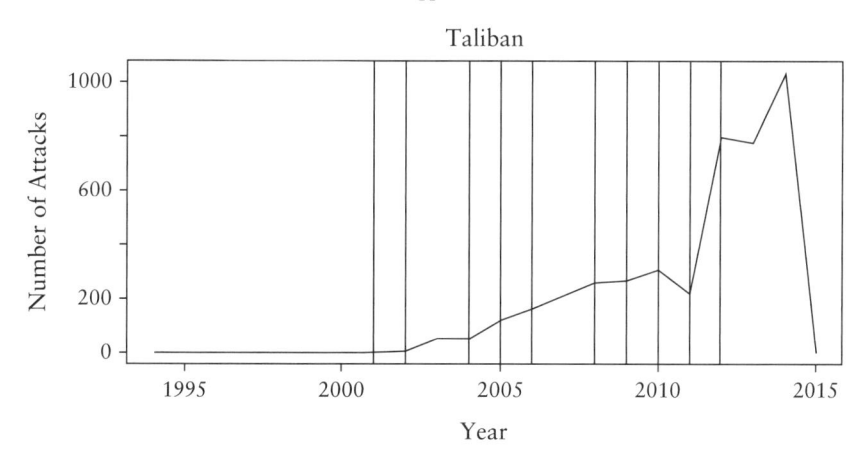

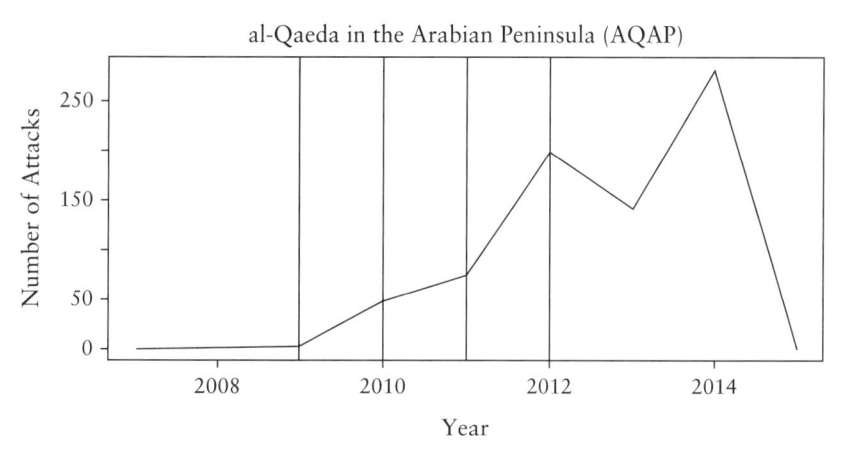

Taliban

al-Qaeda in the Arabian Peninsula (AQAP)

Boko Haram

APPENDIX FIGURE A1 (*continued*)

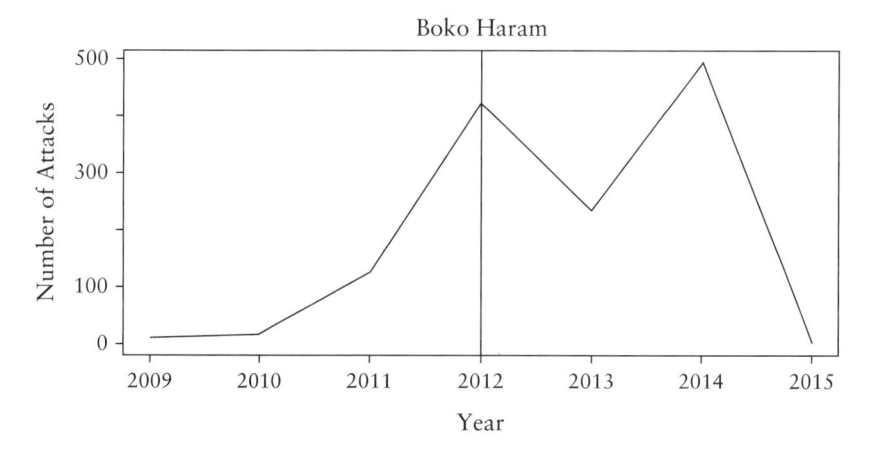

Notes

CHAPTER 1

1. Schmidle, "Getting Bin Laden." There are discrepancies in the accounts of the raid, especially with respect to who actually killed bin Laden. The two primary accounts come from two of the Seals, Mark Owen and Robert O'Neill, and the main difference between these two narratives is over who initially shot bin Laden. See Owen and Maurer, *No Easy Day*. In O'Neill's narrative, the point man who initially shot at bin Laden missed, and then O'Neill fired two shots, hitting bin Laden in the head both times. See Bronstein, "The Man Who Killed Osama Bin Laden. . . . Is Screwed." This contrasts the claim of an unnamed Seal, still active in Seal Team 6, who claimed the point man shot and injured, maybe even killing, bin Laden, and that O'Neill's shots were mere "insurance." See Kulish, Drew, and Naylor, "Another Ex-Commando Says He Shot bin Laden." Bissonnette's narrative matches that of the unnamed source that the point man shot bin Laden and then Bissonnette and other assaulters entered the room and shot bin Laden in the chest.

2. Phillips, "Osama Bin Laden Dead."

3. Ibid.

4. Bakshi, "Former CIA Officer Bruce Riedel on bin Laden Death, Pakistan-U.S. Ties and the Afghan War."

5. The 2006 document also advocates advancing democracy, cutting off sources of funding, and denying the use of a nation as a base of operations. National Security Council, "National Strategy for Combating Terrorism."

6. The disputes about the effect of drone strikes are varied and divisive. I will explore this debate in much greater detail in the chapter on al-Qaeda. See Jordan, "Data on Leadership Targeting and Potential Impacts for Communal Support." and Barela, *Legitimacy and Drones*.

7. For Peter Bergen and Katherine Tiedemann's data at the New American Foundation, "International Security Data Site." There are other datasets on drone strikes. For

data from the Bureau of Investigative Journalism, see Bureau of Investigative Journalism, "Covert War on Terror." For data from the Center for the Study of Targeted Killings at the University of Massachusetts, Dartmouth, Institute for the Study of Counterterrorism & Unconventional Warfare, "States Against Nonstate Actors."

8. Mazzetti, Schmitt, and Worth, "Two-Year Manhunt Led to Killing of Awlaki in Yemen."

9. Walsh and Schmitt, "Drone Strike Killed No. 2 in Al Qaeda, US Officials Say." In the aftermath of al-Libi's death, Peter Bergen wrote that according to senior U.S. counterterrorism officials, Ayman al-Zawahiri was likely the only remaining influential leader in al-Qaeda. See Bergen, "And Now, Only One Senior Al Qaeda Leader Left."

10. Mazzetti, "C.I.A. Drone Is Said to Kill Al Qaeda's No. 2."

11. This book does not address the legal and moral issues related to the use of drone strikes, but rather evaluates whether targeting leaders, through drones strikes or other means, can weaken terrorist organizations.

12. While *leadership targeting* is often used to refer to the killing of a leader, in this book, *leadership targeting* and *leadership decapitation* are used synonymously. Both refer to either the arrest or killing of a leader.

13. David, "Fatal Choices: Israel's Policy of Targeted Killing."

14. See Price, "Targeting Top Terrorists: How Leadership Decapitation Contributes to Counterterrorism"; Johnston, "Does Decapitation Work? Assessing the Effectiveness of Leadership Targeting in Counterinsurgency Campaigns"; Langdon, Sarapu, and Wells, "Targeting the Leadership of Terrorist and Insurgent Movements: Historical Lessons for Contemporary Policy Makers"; Mannes, "Testing the Snake Head Strategy: Does Killing or Capturing Its Leaders Reduce a Terrorist Group's Activity?"; Byman, "Do Targeted Killings Work?"; David, "Fatal Choices"; Freeman and McCormick, "Leadership Targeting of Terrorist Groups: A Strategic Assessment"; Hafez and Hatfield, "Do Targeted Assassinations Work? A Multivariate Analysis of Israel's Controversial Tactic During Al-Aqsa Uprising"; Honig, "Explaining Israel's Misuse of Strategic Assassinations"; or Wilner, "Targeted Killings in Afghanistan: Measuring Coercion and Deterrence in Counterterrorism and Counterinsurgency." Tominaga argues that the results are uncertain, but that in certain cases, targeted killings can have a deterrent effect; see Tominaga, "Killing Two Birds with One Stone? Examining the Diffusion Effect of Militant Leadership Decapitation," 54–68.

15. Langdon, Sarapu, and Wells, "Targeting the Leadership of Terrorist and Insurgent Movements"; Mannes, "Testing the Snake Head Strategy?"; and Honig, "Explaining Israel's Misuse of Strategic Assassinations." See Jordan, "When Heads Roll: Assessing the Effectiveness of Leadership Decapitation," 719–55, and Jordan, "Attacking the Leader, Missing the Mark: Why Terrorist Groups Survive Decapitation Strikes," 7–38.

16. BBC, "Osama Bin Laden's Death: Political Reaction in Quotes."

17. https://www.state.gov/documents/organization/195768.pdf, 5.

18. King and Hennigan, "Why Islamic State's Abu Muhammad Adnani Was Much More Than a Spokesman."

19. Dearden, "ISIS Dealt a 'Major Blow' by Death of Spokesman Abu Muhammad al-Adnani in Air Strike Claimed by US and Russia."

20. https://www.independent.co.uk/news/world/middle-east/isis-abu-muhammad-al-adnani-killed-dead-us-air-strike-syria-intelligence-aleppo-victory-impact-a7218061.html

21. Wright, "After the Islamic State."
22. This dataset includes only cases in which a leader was successfully arrested or killed; it does not include failed decapitation attempts.
23. In this book, the terms *terrorist group* and *terrorist organization* are used interchangeably.
24. It is important to note that there are exceptions to this, but generally this is the expectation.
25. See for example Weinberg, Pedahzur, and Hirsch-Hoeffler, "The Challenges of Conceptualizing Terrorism"; Schmid and Jongman, *Political Terrorism*; Hoffman, *Inside Terrorism*; Crenshaw, *Terrorism in Context*; and Erienbusch, "The Analytical Study of Terrorism: Taking Stock."
26. United States Department of State, *Patterns of Global Terrorism*.
27. US Department of Justice and Federal Bureau of Investigation, "Terrorism: 2002–2005," iv.
28. Joint Chiefs of Staff DOD, "Department of Defense Dictionary of Military and Associated Terms," 236.
29. Schmid and Jongman, *Political Terrorism*.
30. Laqueur, *The Age of Terrorism*.
31. Hoffman, *Inside Terrorism*.
32. Ibid., 40.
33. While this definition does not exclude state-sponsored terrorist organizations, I do not include such cases.
34. Hoffman, *Inside Terrorism*, 34.
35. See ibid., 35. Hoffman also discusses guerilla groups as yet another type of organization. I would like to thank Matthew Kocher for suggesting that the difference between the two groups is grounded in strategic choice. Terrorist organizations employ a strategy of punishment, while insurgencies use a strategy of denial. Of course, this definition allows for potential overlap. For example, the PKK uses denial in rural areas and punishment in urban areas. For work on the distinction between terrorist and insurgent groups see Moghadam, Berger, and Beliakova, "Say Terrorist, Think Insurgent: Labeling and Analyzing Contemporary Terrorist Actors"; Metz, "Rethinking Insurgency"; Hoffman, *Inside Terrorism*, 35.
36. Hoffman, *Inside Terrorism*, 35.
37. Moghadam, Berger, and Beliakova, "Say Terrorist, Think Insurgent."
38. Ibid., 12.
39. Ibid., 3.
40. This book deals exclusively with the effectiveness of leadership targeting and does not address issues of legality and morality. See Barela, *Legitimacy and Drones*; Plaw, *Targeting Terrorists*.
41. Warden III, "Employing Air Power in the Twenty-First Century," 65.
42. Pape, *Bombing to Win*, 79.
43. Pape also makes this claim in his op-ed piece "Wars Can't Be Won Only from Above."
44. Pape, "The Strategic Logic of Suicide Bombing," 356.
45. Hosmer, *Operations against Enemy Leaders*, 1.
46. Ibid., 19.
47. For a good overview of the literature see Carvin, "The Trouble with Targeted Killings."

48. For a more detailed response to these studies see Jordan, "Review of 'Does Decapitation Work? Assessing the Effectiveness of Leadership Targeting in Counterinsurgency Campaigns.'" See also Price, "Targeting Top Terrorists."
49. See Price, "Targeting Top Terrorists."
50. Ibid., 37.
51. Jordan, "When Heads Roll," 719–55.
52. Price, "Targeting Top Terrorists," 14.
53. Ibid., 20.
54. Ibid., 17.
55. Johnston, "Does Decapitation Work?" 50.
56. Ibid., 75. These findings run counter to my own and Price's. However, Johnston's analysis uses ten years as a dividing point in analyzing organizational life span. Had he divided groups over eleven years of age into a few more categories, these results may have changed. Both Price and I found that once a group crosses a twenty-year threshold, decapitation becomes much less effective.
57. Ibid., 60.
58. Ibid., 68.
59. This study examines the targeting of both top leaders and members of the upper echelon.
60. See Langdon, Sarapu, and Wells, "Targeting the Leadership of Terrorist and Insurgent Movements."
61. Mannes, "Testing the Snake Head Strategy."
62. Ibid., 43.
63. Tominaga, "Killing Two Birds with One Stone?"
64. Michael Freeman, "A Theory of Terrorist Leadership (and Its Consequences for Leadership Targeting)," 668.
65. Ibid.
66. Johnston, "Does Decapitation Work?" 48.
67. McClintock, *Revolutionary Movements in Latin America: El Salvador's FMLN and Peru's Shining Path*, 92.
68. Drozdiak, "Avowed 'Decapitation' of Basque Group in Doubt as Olympics Near."
69. Cronin, *How Terrorism Ends*, 17.
70. Ibid., 17.
71. Carvin, "The Trouble with Targeted Killings," 532.
72. Byman, "Do Targeted Killings Work?" 104.
73. Carvin, "The Trouble with Targeted Killings," 532.
74. Bloom, *Dying to Kill*.
75. Ibid.
76. See Brooks, "Societies and Terrorist Violence: How Social Support Affects Militant Campaigns."
77. Ibid., 27–28.
78. See Byman, "Do Targeted Killings Work?" 95–111; Carley, Lee, and Krackhardt, "Destabilizing Networks," 79–92; and Thompson, *Organizations in Action*.
79. See Carley, "A Theory of Group Stability"; Carley, Lee, and Krackhardt, "Destabilizing Networks."
80. See Sageman, *Understanding Terror Networks*.
81. Cronin, *How Terrorism Ends*, 177.

82. Lindelauf, Borm, and Hamers, "Understanding Terrorist Network Typologies and Their Resilience against Disruption."

83. Jacob Shapiro argues that highly bureaucratized terrorist organizations face a trade-off between maintaining security and exercising organizational control. See Shapiro, *The Terrorist's Dilemma,* and Shapiro and Siegel, "Moral Hazard, Discipline, and the Management of Terrorist Organizations."

84. Lindelauf, Borm, and Hamers, "Understanding Terrorist Network Typologies," 3.

85. Ibid., 9.

86. Jordan, "When Heads Roll."

87. Bergen, "Should We Still Fear Al Qaeda?"

88. Bergen, *The Longest War,* 547.

89. Ibid., 549. Qutb's ideology was critical to the evolution of Zawahiri's belief system. See also Riedel, *The Search for Al Qaeda.*

90. Bergen, *The Longest War,* 349.

91. David, "Fatal Choices."

92. Dear, "Beheading the Hydra? Does Killing Terrorist or Insurgent Leaders Work?."

93. Ibid., 325.

94. Abrahms and Mierau, "Leadership Matters: The Effects of Targeted Killings on Militant Group Tactics." Abrahms and Potter make a similar case regarding the impact that leadership deficits have upon the tactical choices that groups make to target civilians. See Abrahms and Potter, "Explaining Terrorism: Leadership Deficits and Militant Group Tactics."

CHAPTER 2

1. Cronin finds that much extant research has focused on single groups, specifically al-Qaeda, and has been "largely concerned with root causes and narrow questions having to do with the weapons and methods being used." Cronin, *How Terrorism Ends: Understanding the Decline and Demise of Terrorist Campaigns,* 2.

2. Cronin, "Behind the Curve: Globalization and International Terrorism," 8.

3. Specifically, Cronin argues that targeting bin Laden will not kill al-Qaeda. Despite bin Laden's charisma, she argues that al-Qaeda is not driven by a cult of personality. Consistent with the results in this study, Cronin also argues that decapitation is unlikely to be effective against nonhierarchical organizations, but her conclusions are based on a limited amount of evidence. See Cronin, "How Al-Qaida Ends: The Decline and Demise of Terrorist Groups," 40.

4. Weber, *The Theory of Social and Economic Organization,* 358. For a detailed analysis of charismatic leadership theory see Ingram, *The Charismatic Leadership Phenomenon in Radical and Militant Islamism.*

5. Weber, *From Max Weber: Essays in Sociology,* 246.

6. Ibid., 249.

7. Nelson, *Cults, New Religions and Religious Creativity,* 117.

8. See Dawson, "Crises in Charismatic Legitimacy and Violent Behavior in New Religious Movements."

9. Cornwell, "Campaign against Terror: A Justifiable Tool in the War against Terrorism."

10. The case of Aum Shinrikyo seems to provide some evidence for the claim that groups depend upon the charisma of their leaders. While the group reemerged as an

organization called Aleph after the arrest of its leader, Shoko Asahara, it had become a nonviolent organization.

11. Due to the difficulties in identifying whether a leader is in fact charismatic, this study does not determine whether the removed leader possessed charismatic qualities. Instead, I test the strength of the charisma claim by evaluating leadership decapitation in general.

12. Nelson, *Cults, New Religions and Religious Creativity*, 120.

13. Weber, *From Max Weber: Essays in Sociology*, 297.

14. See Freeman, "A Theory of Terrorist Leadership (and Its Consequences for Leadership Targeting)." Freeman argues that the likelihood of success can be determined by looking at the interaction of operational and inspirational leadership.

15. Mayer, "Cults, Violence, and Religious Terrorism: An International Perspective."

16. The data in this study indicates that religious groups are the hardest to weaken. See also Langdon, Sarapu, and Wells, "Targeting the Leadership of Terrorist and Insurgent Movements: Historical Lessons for Contemporary Policy Makers."

17. See Nelson, *Cults, New Religions and Religious Creativity*; Carlton-Ford, *Cults and Non-Conventional Religious Groups: The Effects of Ritual and Charisma*; and Galanter, *Cults: Faith, Healing, and Coercion*.

18. Aum Shinrikyo, a large organization that is usually classified as both a terrorist group and a doomsday cult, is notable in this regard. After the arrest of its leader, Shoko Asahara, the group ceased to exist as a terrorist group, renounced violence, and became known as Aleph. It seems plausible that terrorist organizations, which are also classified as cults, would be more susceptible to collapse.

19. For work on the dynamics and effects of organizational groups splintering, see Staniland, *Networks of Rebellion: Explaining Insurgent Cohesion and Collapse*; Bueno de Mesquita, "Terrorist Factions"; Asal, Brown, and Dalton, "Why Split? Organizational Splits among Ethnopolitical Organizations in the Middle East"; Kenny, "Structural Integrity and Cohesion in Insurgent Organizations: Evidence from Protracted Conflicts in Ireland and Burma"; Siqueira, "Political and Militant Wings within Dissident Movements and Organizations," 219; Crenshaw, "Mapping Terrorist Organizations"; and Jones and Libicki, *How Terrorist Groups End: Lessons for Countering Al-Qa'ida*.

20. See Bloom, "Palestinian Suicide Bombing."

21. See Arquilla and Ronfeldt, *Networks and Netwars: The Future of Terror, Crime, and Militancy*; Zanini, "Middle Eastern Terrorism and Netwar"; Pedahzur and Perlinger, "The Changing Nature of Suicide Attacks: A Social Network Perspective."

22. Perrow, *Complex Organizations: A Critical Essay*, 167.

23. While Oots claims that leadership is important, he argues that little is known about the leadership of terrorist organizations. As a result, he does not take a stance on the success of leadership decapitation. Oots, "Bargaining with Terrorists: Organizational Considerations."

24. Oots, "Organizational Perspectives on the Formation and Disintegration of Terrorist Groups," 143.

25. Horgan, "From Profiles to Pathways and Roots to Routes: Perspectives from Psychology on Radicalization into Terrorism"; Horgan and Taylor, "Disengagement, De-Radicalization and the Arc of Terrorism: Future Directions for Future Research."

26. Crenshaw, "Theories of Terrorism: Instrumental and Organizational Approaches."

27. Olson, *The Logic of Collective Action: Public Goods and the Theory of Groups*, 50.

28. Ibid.

29. I expand on the comparison to social movement organizations in the following chapter.

30. Olson, *The Logic of Collective Action: Public Goods and the Theory of Groups*, 51.

31. Ibid.

32. Oots, "Organizational Perspectives on the Formation and Disintegration of Terrorist Groups," 141.

33. See Crenshaw, "How Terrorism Declines."

34. For work on the strategic explanations for terrorist activity see Kydd and Walter, "The Strategies of Terrorism"; Crenshaw, "The Logic of Terrorism"; Abrahms, "Why Terrorism Does Not Work"; Crenshaw, "Theories of Terrorism: Instrumental and Organizational Approaches."

35. See Crenshaw, "An Organizational Approach to the Analysis of Political Terrorism"; Crenshaw, "Theories of Terrorism: Instrumental and Organizational Approaches"; Crenshaw, "The Causes of Terrorism."

36. It is important to note that just following this, Crenshaw discusses the importance of leaders to understanding organizational survival, as "their personal ambitions are tied to the organization's viability and political position." Further, she argues that leaders provide incentives to group members and that the rewards may further or diminish the pursuit of the group's goals. Crenshaw has also argued that terrorist groups can be seen as strategic actors. See Crenshaw, "Theories of Terrorism: Instrumental and Organizational Approaches," 19.

37. Berman, *Radical, Religious and Violent: The New Economics of Terrorism*.

38. Shapiro, *The Terrorist's Dilemma: Managing Violent Covert Organizations*.

39. Within this context, terrorist groups can be understood as strategic actors, conditioned by organizational dynamics. Peter Krause has argued that insurgencies must be understood through a two-level framework in which groups for example pursue both strategic objectives and objectives that benefit the group itself. This book will draw upon these theories of organizations, focusing on both strategy and organizational dynamics in developing a theory of resilience. Krause, "The Political Effectiveness of Non-State Violence: A Two-Level Framework to Transform a Deceptive Debate."

40. It is important to note that these types of authority are ideal types.

41. Weber, *The Theory of Economic and Social Organization*, 341.

42. Ibid., 295.

43. Weber, *From Max Weber: Essays in Sociology*, 296.

44. Weber, *The Theory of Economic and Social Organization*, 56.

45. See ibid.

46. Ibid., 330.

47. Weber, *Max Weber on Charisma and Institution Building*, chapter 7.

48. For a discussion the ideal types on Weber's theory, see Rudolf and Rudolf, "Authority and Power in Bureaucratic and Patrimonial Administration: A Revisionist Interpretation of Weber on Bureaucracy."

49. Baron, Burton, and Hannan, "Engineering Bureaucracy: The Genesis of Formal Policies, Positions, and Structures in High-Technology Firms," 2.

50. Parsons in the introduction of Weber, *The Theory of Social and Economic Organization*, 58.

51. From this perspective terrorist organizations can be thought of as firms, which require succession mechanisms, standard operating procedures, and clear administrative functions.

52. Cronin, "How Al-Qaida Ends: The Decline and Demise of Terrorist Groups," 40.
53. It is important to note that decentralization and bureaucracy are not mutually exclusive, as is commonly assumed. An organization can be highly bureaucratized at the upper levels and still maintain a largely decentralized operational structure.
54. Weber, *From Max Weber: Essays in Sociology*, 79.
55. Crozier, *The Bureaucratic Phenomenon*.
56. Crozier also discusses the pathologies of bureaucracy and how a system of routine and rules contribute to a "vicious cycle" in which individuals are trying to avoid face-to-face relationships. Ibid., 54.
57. Ibid., 187.
58. Weber, *From Max Weber: Essays in Sociology*, 295.
59. Weber, *The Theory of Economic and Social Organization*, 58.
60. Weber, *From Max Weber: Essays in Sociology*, 246.
61. Ibid., 54.
62. In many cases, charismatic authority or a leader's extraordinary qualities inspired new recruits and dedication to the cause. For example, originally members of al-Qaeda pledged *bay'a* or loyalty to bin Laden, not to the organization. However, his charisma became routinized, intentionally so. Bin Laden sought to broaden the appeal of the groups and created an ideology that did not depend upon his leadership or particular qualities. In fact, over time, new al-Qaeda affiliates pledged loyalty to the organization, not to an individual.
63. See Stinchcombe, "Organizations and Social Structure"; Bruderl and Schussler, "Organizational Mortality: The Liabilities of Newness and Adolescence"; Freeman, Carroll, and Hannan, "The Liability of Newness: Age Dependence in Organizational Death Rates"; Hager et al., "Tales from the Grave: Organizations' Accounts of Their Own Demise"; Hager, Galaskiewicz, and Larson, "Structural Embeddedness and the Liability of Newness among Nonprofit Organizations"; Hannan and Freeman, "The Population Ecology of Organizations"; Keohane, "The Demand for International Regimes"; Singh, Tucker, and House, "Organizational Legitimacy and the Liability of Newness"; Ranger-Moore, "Bigger May Be Better, but Older Is Wiser? Organizational Age and Size in the New York Life Insurance Industry."
64. I make a distinction between efficiency and stability. While *efficiency* refers to how well the organizations functions, *stability* refers to how well a group can respond to counterterrorism challenges and other challenges to its existence.
65. Feldman and Pentland, "Reconceptualizing Routines as a Source of Flexibility and Change," 94. See also March and Simon, *Organizations*. and Thompson, *Organizations in Action: Social Sciences Bases of Administrative Theory*.
66. Hager, Galaskiewicz, and Larson, "Structural Embeddedness and the Liability of Newness among Nonprofit Organizations." 162.
67. Levitt and March argue that routines increase stability by making organizations capable of surviving turnover in individual actors; Levitt and March, "Organizational Learning," 320.
68. See Crozier, *The Bureaucratic Phenomenon*; Weber, *The Theory of Social and Economic Organization*; Hannan and Freeman, "Structural Inertia and Organizational Change."
69. See Feldman and Pentland, "Reconceptualizing Routines as a Source of Flexibility and Change."
70. See Cyert and March, *A Behavioral Theory of the Firm*.

Notes to Chapter 2

71. See Feldman and Pentland, "Reconceptualizing Routines as a Source of Flexibility and Change, "95.
72. Ibid.
73. See Shapiro, *The Terrorist's Dilemma: Managing Violent Covert Organizations.* and Shapiro, "Bureaucratic Terrorists: Al-Qa'ida in Iraq's Management and Finances."
74. Shapiro, "Bureaucratic Terrorists: Al-Qa'ida in Iraq's Management and Finances," 75.
75. Zald and Ash, "Social Movement Organizations: Growth, Decay, and Change," 328. I would like to thank Mia Bloom for reminding me that the factionalization and splintering of terrorist organizations is an important process in organizational development and a potential consequence of counterterrorism policies such as leadership targeting.
76. Bueno de Mesquita, "Conciliation, Counterterrorism, and Patterns of Terrorist Violence," 172.
77. Cronin, "How Al-Qaida Ends: The Decline and Demise of Terrorist Groups," 26.
78. Mansfield, "Bureaucracy and Centralization: An Examination of Organizational Structure," 478.
79. Ibid.
80. Kenney, *From Pablo to Osama: Trafficking and Terrorist Networks, Government Bureaucracies, and Competitive Adaptation,* 149.
81. In a study on the effects of leadership targeting, Max Abrahms and Philip Potter argue that leadership targeting can result in more civilian casualties as organizations face a principal-agent problem between leaders and foot soldiers. They demonstrate in a sample of groups in the Middle East and North Africa that those lacking centralized leadership are prone to targeting civilians. See Abrahms and Potter, "Explaining Terrorism: Leadership Deficits and Militant Group Tactics."
82. Uhl-Bien and Marion, "Complexity Leadership in Bureaucratic Forms of Organizing: A Meso Model."
83. Bloom, *Dying to Kill: The Allure of Suicide Terror*; Cronin, *How Terrorism Ends: Understanding the Decline and Demise of Terrorist Campaigns,* 104.
84. Pape, *Dying to Win: The Strategic Logic of Suicide Terrorism,* 81.
85. Ibid.
86. Ibid.
87. Ibid., 81.
88. Bloom, *Dying to Kill: The Allure of Suicide Terror.*
89. Cronin, *How Terrorism Ends: Understanding the Decline and Demise of Terrorist Campaigns,* 104.
90. Cronin uses the Weather Underground, the Red Army Faction, and 17 November as examples of groups whose ideology became irrelevant, leading to their decline. She also includes groups that were supported by the Soviet Union and thus became historically irrelevant in this category. See ibid., 105–6.
91. See Brooks, "Societies and Terrorist Violence: How Social Support Affects Militant Campaigns."
92. Ibid., 27–28.
93. See Petersen, *Resistance and Rebellion.*
94. Ibid., 15–16.
95. The case of Hamas will be discussed more extensively in Chapter 5.
96. Crenshaw, "The Psychology of Terrorism: An Agenda for the 21st Century." On social movement organizations see McCarthy and Zald, "Social Movement

Organizations." and Zald and Ash, "Social Movement Organizations: Growth, Decay, and Change."

97. For studies that utilize the literature on social movements as a tool in understanding terrorist organizations see: Leheny, "Terrorism, Social Movements, and International Security: How Al Qaeda Affects Southeast Asia"; della Porta, *Social Movements, Political Violence, and the State: A Comparative Analysis of Italy and Germany*; Crenshaw, "The Psychology of Terrorism: An Agenda for the 21st Century."

98. See McCarthy and Zald, "Resource Mobilization and Social Movements: A Partial Theory." Neil Smelser also questions the strength of the deprivation model in accounting for the occurrence of terrorist movements. See Smelser, *The Faces of Terrorism: Social and Psychological Dimensions*.

99. Goodwin, *No Other Way Out: States and Revolutionary Movements*, 57.

100. See McAdam, *Political Process and the Development of Black Insurgency, 1930–1970*.

101. McCarthy and Zald, "Resource Mobilization and Social Movements: A Partial Theory," 1220.

102. Zald and Ash, "Social Movement Organizations: Growth, Decay, and Change."

103. McCarthy and Zald, "Social Movement Organizations," 1234.

104. McCarthy and Zald have found that older organizations should be more likely to have stable structures, which can help them to reach a larger and more diversified resources base; see ibid.

105. McAdam, *Political Process and the Development of Black Insurgency*, 58.

106. See ibid., 29.

107. Ibid., 33–34.

108. Ibid., 45.

109. For a discussion on how classification is a useful tool for understanding the dynamics of terrorist organizations, see Wilkinson, *Political Terrorism*. Schultz makes an attempt to refine Wilkinson's study and refers to repressive terrorism and "establishment terrorism." See Schultz, "Conceptualizing Political Terrorism: A Typology." For further analysis on these categories see Wardlaw, *Political Terrorism: Theory, Tactics, and Counter-Measures*; Whittaker, *The Terrorism Reader*; and Anderson and Sloan, *Historical Dictionary of Terrorism*. Sloan and Anderson reference Schultz in identifying different types of actors.

110. Kahler, "Collective Action and Clandestine Networks"; Knoke and Yang, *Social Network Analysis*.

111. Knoke and Yang, *Social Network Analysis*, 4.

112. See Wasserman and Faust, *Social Network Analysis: Methods and Applications*.

113. See Hafner-Burton, Kahler, and Montgomery, "Network Analysis for International Relations," 570; Knoke, *Political Networks: The Structural Perspective, Structural Analysis in the Social Sciences*.

114. Pedahzur argues that horizontal networks can operate within or independently of a group. While focusing on decentralized organizations, he is specifically concerned with local networks that operate under the framework of a larger movement. See Pedahzur and Perlinger, "The Changing Nature of Suicide Attacks: A Social Network Perspective."

115. See Mardsen, "Egocentric and Sociocentric Measures of Network Centrality," 410; Freeman, "Centrality in Social Networks: Conceptual Clarification"; Bonacich and Lloyd, "Calculating Status with Negative Relations"; and Maoz, *Networks of Nations: The Evolution, Structure, and Impact of International Networks, 1816–2001*, 53.

116. Arquilla and Ronfeldt argue that location or degree of an actor's centrality is essential to understanding the structure and function of a network. Arquilla and Ronfeldt, *Networks and Netwars: The Future of Terror, Crime, and Militancy.*

117. Pedahzur and Perliger, "The Changing Nature of Suicide Attacks: A Social Network Perspective."

118. Ibid.

119. He claims that the arrests of key hubs have been successful in breaking up smaller networks, and if key hubs within the global Salafi jihad networks were removed, they would be unable to carry out large-scale attacks. Sageman, *Understanding Terror Networks*, 140. Sageman defines a small-world network as having dense interconnectivity. He juxtaposes this structure to a hierarchically structured organization. Further, Sageman finds that while hierarchical networks can be eliminated through leadership decapitation, small-world networks require the elimination of hubs.

120. Deibert and Stein, "Hacking Networks of Terror," 71.

121. Cronin, "How Al-Qaida Ends: The Decline and Demise of Terrorist Groups."

122. Ibid.

123. See Sageman, *Understanding Terror Networks.*

124. Ibid.; Sageman, *Leaderless Jihad: Terror Networks in the Twenty-First Century.*

125. An important caveat needs to be added here. I assume that religious groups tend to be decentralized in structure. However, there are a number of religiously motivated terrorist organizations that are centralized. For example, Hamas's leadership is more centralized, while other aspects of the organization are more decentralized. Lashkar-e-Taiba in Pakistan/Kashmir is highly centralized. For the purposes of theory building, I assume that religious groups tend toward decentralization.

126. See Cronin, "Behind the Curve: Globalization and International Terrorism," 40. For a discussion of the decline of different types of terrorist organizations see Jones and Libicki, *How Terrorist Groups End: Lessons for Countering Al-Qa'ida.*

127. See Cronin, "Behind the Curve: Globalization and International Terrorism," 40.

128. Bhattacharya, "Comparing Civilian Support for Terrorism."

129. Ibid., 2.

130. Ibid., 18.

131. Fair and Shepherd, "Who Supports Terrorism? Evidence from Fourteen Muslim Countries," 52; Bueno de Mesquita, *Correlates of Public Support for Terrorism in the Muslim World.*

132. Bhattacharya, "Comparing Civilian Support for Terrorism."

133. Hoffman, "Holy Terror: The Implications of Terrorism Motivated by a Religious Imperative."

134. Drake, "The Role of Ideology in Terrorists' Target Selection," 53.

135. Hegghammer, for example, argues that the foreign fighter phenomenon is the result of a larger social movement that began in the 1970s. It is thus a larger social movement that is not dependent upon the actions of individual leaders. See Hegghammer, "The Rise of Muslim Foreign Fighters: Islam and the Globalization of Jihad."

136. See Cronin, "How Al-Qaida Ends: The Decline and Demise of Terrorist Groups," 23.

137. Hroub, "Hamas after Shaykh Yasin and Rantisi," 21.

138. Ibid., 31.

139. Hamas claims that the attacks were carried out in retaliation for Ayyash's killing. Plaw, *Targeting Terrorists*, 167.

140. See Rapoport, "Fear and Trembling: Terrorism in Three Religious Traditions."

CHAPTER 3

1. Jordan, Kosal, and Rubin, "The Strategic Illogic of Counterterrorism Policy."

2. Organizations formed before 1945 were excluded. Data on incidents through 2016 was used in the case studies on al-Qaeda, Shining Path, and Hamas. The data used in the statistical analyses in Chapter 4 ended in 2014 in order to have a long enough time period over which to evaluate the impact of decapitation.

3. See LexisNexis. An earlier version of the database drew from cases referenced in encyclopedias on the history of terrorist organizations, LexisNexis searches of newspapers, the Memorial Institute for the Prevention of Terrorism's (MIPT) database, and the US State Department's *Patterns of Global Terrorism*. See Anderson and Sloan, *Historical Dictionary of Terrorism*. The MIPT's Terrorism Knowledge Base (TKB) was shut down in March 2008 and is no longer active.

4. Some studies include terrorist groups, such as Price, "Targeting Top Terrorists: How Leadership Decapitation Contributes to Counterterrorism"; others look at insurgencies, such as Johnston, "Does Decapitation Work? Assessing the Effectiveness of Leadership Targeting in Counterinsurgency Campaigns"; while others look at groups of a certain size and type, such as Mannes, "Testing the Snake Head Strategy: Does Killing or Capturing Its Leaders Reduce a Terrorist Group's Activity?"

5. Even in the aftermath of 9/11, there were few clear measures by which to evaluate the success of counterterrorism policies. See Goepner, "Measuring the Effectiveness of America's War on Terror."

6. Garamone, "Dunford Lists Ways to Measure Counter-ISIL Success."

7. Jordan, Kosal, and Rubin, "The Strategic Illogic of Counterterrorism Policy."

8. Hudson, "President Obama: 'We Will Degrade and Ultimately Destroy ISIL.'"

9. For a fuller discussion on realistic expectations regarding counterterrorism policy see Jordan and Rubin, "An ISIS Containment Doctrine."

10. START (National Consortium for the Study of Terrorism and Responses to Terrorism), "Global Terrorism Database."

11. Office of the Coordinator for Counterterrorism, US Department of State, "2001 Report on Foreign Terrorist Organizations."

12. The US Department of State does not require that an organization be inactive for two years in order to be removed from the list of FTOs.

13. During the coding process, the decision about whether the group was still in existence was usually quite clear.

14. See Kilcullen and Exum, "Death from Above, Outrage Down Below."

15. Abizaid and Brooks, "Recommendations and Report of the Task Force on US Drone Policy."

16. Harris, "Drone Attacks Create Terrorist Safe Havens, Warns Former Cia Official."

17. Cavallaro, Sonnenberg, and Knuckey, *Living under Drones: Death, Injury and Trauma to Civilians from US Drone Practices in Pakistan*.

18. Fair, "Drones over Pakistan—Menace or Best Viable Option?"

19. See Williams, *Predators: The CIA's Drone War on Al Qaeda*. For figures on casualties of drone strikes, see databases held at the New America Foundation, the *Long War Journal*, and the University of Massachusetts Dartmouth.

20. Johnston and Sarbahi, "The Impact of U.S. Drone Strikes on Terrorism in Pakistan"; Smith and Walsh, "Do Drone Strikes Degrade Al Qaeda? Evidence from Propaganda Output"; Walsh and Schmitt, "Drone Strike Killed No. 2 in Al Qaeda, U.S. Officials Say."

21. Walsh and Schulzke, *Drones and Support for the Use of Force*.

22. For more information on terrorist group factionalization see Jones and Libicki, *How Terrorist Groups End: Lessons for Countering Al-Qa'ida*; Bueno de Mesquita, "Conciliation, Counterterrorism, and Patterns of Terrorist Violence" and "Terrorist Factions."

23. Anderson and Sloan, *Historical Dictionary of Terrorism*, 415–16.

24. Cronin, "How Al-Qaida Ends: The Decline and Demise of Terrorist Groups," 22.

25. See ibid.

26. Anderson and Sloan, *Historical Dictionary of Terrorism*, 415.

27. Hoffman, *Inside Terrorism*, 71.

28. See Zawodny, "Infrastructures of Terrorist Organizations."

29. See Post, Ruby, and Shaw, "The Radical Group in Context: 1. An Integrated Framework for the Analysis of Group Risk for Terrorism," and Post, Ruby, and Shaw, "The Radical Group in Context: 2. Identification of Critical Elements in the Analysis of Risk for Terrorism by Radical Group Type."

30. See Post, *Leaders and Their Followers in a Dangerous World*.

31. See for example, Piazza, "Is Islamist Terrorism More Dangerous? An Empirical Study of Group Ideology, Organization, and Goal Structure"; Berman and Laitin, "Religion, Terrorism, and Public Goods." For a discussion of the effect of Muslim states, see Conrad and Milton, "Unpacking the Connection between Terror and Islam." For a discussion of the role of sectarian religious violence, see Iannaccone and Berman, "Religious Extremism: The Good, the Bad, and the Deadly."

32. Crenshaw, "How Terrorism Declines," 79. Her study focuses on organizations that were active in the post–World War II period and that used terrorism as a strategy of opposition to regimes in power.

33. Chapter 2 discusses the liability of newness, which offers a theoretical explanation for why younger organizations should be easier to destabilize through decapitation.

34. March and Simon, *Organizations*, 89.

35. Ranger-Moore, "Bigger May Be Better, but Older Is Wiser? Organizational Age and Size in the New York Life Insurance Industry"; Freeman, Carroll, and Hannan, "The Liability of Newness: Age Dependence in Organizational Death Rates."

36. Kristof, "Behind the Terrorists."

37. See Collier and Hoeffler, "Greed and Grievance in Civil War"; Alesina et al., "Political Instability and Economic Growth"; Miguel, Satyanath, and Sergenti, "Economic Shocks and Civil Conflict: An Instrumental Variables Approach."

38. See Meierrikes and Gries, "Causality between Terrorism and Economic Growth"; Piazza, "Rooted in Poverty? Terrorism, Poor Economic Development, and Social Cleavages."

39. Krueger and Maleckova, "Education, Poverty, and Terrorism: Is There a Causal Connection?"

40. See Piazza, "Poverty Is a Weak Causal Link"; Piazza, "Rooted in Poverty? Terrorism, Poor Economic Development, and Social Cleavages."

41. Piazza, "Poverty Is a Weak Causal Link," 52.

42. See Piazza, "Incubators of Terror: Do Failed and Failing States Promote Transnational Terrorism?"; Piazza, "Draining the Swamp: Democracy Promotion, State Failure, and Terrorism in 19 Middle Eastern Countries"; Atzili, "State Weakness and 'Vacuum of Power' in Lebanon."

43. Stohl and Stohl, "Networks of Terror: Theoretical Assumptions and Pragmatic Consequences."

44. Ibid., 103.

45. Flanigan, Asal, and Brown, "Community Service Provision by Political Associations Representing Minorities in the Middle East and North Africa."

46. Berman, *Radical, Religious, and Violent: The New Economics of Terrorism*.

47. Ibid., 16.

48. Ibid.

49. Ibid., 18.

50. Flanigan, Asal, and Brown, "Community Service Provision by Political Associations Representing Minorities in the Middle East and North Africa."

51. Marshall and Jaggers, *Polity IV Project: Political Regime Characteristics and Transitions, 1800–2006: Dataset Users' Manual*.

52. Crenshaw, "The Theories of Terrorism"; Schmid, "Terrorism and Democracy"; Eubank and Weinberg, "Does Democracy Encourage Terrorism?"; Li, "Does Democracy Promote or Reduce Transnational Terrorist Incidents?"

53. Erica Chenoweth argues that since 9/11 terrorism is more prevalent in nondemocratic countries. Chenoweth, "Terrorism and Democracy."

54. Brooks, "Researching Democracy and Terrorism: How Political Access Affects Militant Activity."

55. In an early study on the relationship between terrorism and democracy, Tedd Gurr found that democracies encourage violent conflict. Gurr, "Terrorism in Democracies: Its Social and Political Bases." See also Schmid, "Terrorism and Democracy"; Eubank and Weinberg, "Does Democracy Encourage Terrorism?"; and Ross, "Structural Causes of Oppositional Political Terrorism: Towards a Causal Model."

56. Li, "Does Democracy Promote or Reduce Transnational Terrorist Incidents?" 294.

57. Ibid.

58. Ibid., 283.

CHAPTER 4

1. There are a few cases from the 1950s, but most of the data is from 1970–2016.

2. See START, Global Terrorism Database, https://www.start.umd.edu/gtd/; START, Big, Allied and Dangerous (BAAD), https://www.start.umd.edu/baad/database; Center for Systemic Peace, "The Polity Project," systemicpeace.org/polityproject.html; World Bank, https://data.worldbank.org/indicator/ny.gdp.mktp.cd, and https://data.worldbank.org/indicator/sp.pop.totl.

3. See, for example, Cronin, *How Terrorism Ends*; Jones and Libicki, *How Terrorist Groups End*.

4. See Johnston, "Does Decapitation Work?"

5. See Jordan, "Attacking the Leader, Missing the Mark" and "When Heads Roll"; David, "Fatal Choices."
6. Arsu, "Jailed Leader of the Kurds Offers a Truce with Turkey."
7. Yeginsu, "Turkey Attacks Kurdish Militant Camps in Northern Iraq."
8. McDonald and Cowell, "Sri Lanka Says Leader of Rebels Has Died"; McDonald, "Tamil Tigers Confirm Death of Their Leader."
9. Pape and Feldman, *Cutting the Fuse*, 286.
10. Price, "Targeting Top Terrorists," 37.
11. Ibid., 25.
12. See for example, ibid.; Johnston, "Does Decapitation Work?"; Johnston and Sarbahi, "Impact of U.S. Drone Strikes."
13. Perrow, *Complex Organizations*.
14. Pape, "Wars Can't Be Won Only from Above," 47.
15. As noted earlier, this is not true in all cases. There are a number of religious groups that take on a more centralized structure.

CHAPTER 5

1. See Byman, "Do Targeted Killings Work?" David, "Fatal Choices"; Luft, "The Logic of Israel's Targeted Killing"; Hroub, "Shaykh Yasin and Rantisi."
2. See Jordan, "When Heads Roll."
3. The morality and legality of targeting terrorists are exceedingly important issues. Avery Plaw and Yael Stein have both written on the morality and legality of targeted killings. There is widespread condemnation of targeted killings on both legal and moral grounds, a criticism that I feel is justified. In practice these important concerns should precede debates about the effectiveness of targeted killings; however, I bracket these concerns to understand the long-term implications of leadership targeting against Hamas and to focus on its value and possible consequences as a counterterrorism policy. See Plaw, *Targeting Terrorists*; Stein, "By Any Name Illegal and Immoral." See also, Barela, *Legitimacy and Drones*.
4. David, "Fatal Choices," 2.
5. Ibid.
6. Ibid., 16.
7. David does, however, offer four improvements to Israel's current policy of targeted killings. See ibid., 21.
8. Byman, "Do Targeted Killings Work?" 102.
9. Ibid., 103.
10. Ibid., 100. Byman references Khaled Hroub, who argues that targeted killings increase the popular legitimacy of the movement. See Hroub, *Hamas: Political Thought and Practice*, and "Hamas after Shaykh Yasin and Rantisi."
11. Kaplan, Mintz, and Mishal, "Tactical Prevention of Suicide Bombing in Israel."
12. Ibid., 557.
13. See Hafez and Hatfield, "Do Targeted Assassinations Work?"
14. Ibid.; Kaplan, Mintz, and Mishal, "Tactical Prevention"; Zussman and Zussman, "Assassinations: Evaluating the Effectiveness of an Israeli Counterterrorism Policy Using Stock Market Data"; Plaw, *Targeting Terrorists*.
15. Zussman and Zussman, "Assassinations."

16. There is a debate in the literature regarding whether it is appropriate to refer to the policy of targeting terrorists as assassination.
17. Plaw, *Targeting Terrorists*, 165.
18. Thomas, *The Ethics of Destruction*.
19. Luft, "Israel's Targeted Killing," 3.
20. Hamas claims that the attacks were carried out in retaliation for Ayyash's killing. Plaw, *Targeting Terrorists*, 167.
21. Ibid., 166.
22. Ibid., 175.
23. Abu-Amr, "Hamas : A Historical and Political Background," 10.
24. These leaders were Sheikh Ahmed Yassin, Dr. Abdel Aziz al-Rantisi, Salah Shehada, Abd al-Fattah Dukhan, Muhammed Sham'ah, Ibrahim al-Yazuri, and 'Isa al-Nashar. Ibid. 10.
25. Ibid., 10.
26. Tamimi, *Hamas: A History from Within*, 10.
27. Ibid., 14.
28. *Ikhwan* refers to the full name of the Muslim Brotherhood, Jamial al-Ikhwan al-Muslimeen, a religious and political organizations founded in Egypt in 1928. See Levitt, *Hamas: Politics, Charity, and Terrorism in the Service of Jihad*.
29. Mishal and Sela, *The Palestinian Hamas: Vision, Violence, and Coexistence*, 15.
30. Mishal, "The Pragmatic Dimension of the Palestinian Hamas: A Network Perspective," 19.
31. Tamimi, *Hamas: A History*, 21.
32. The Islamic Center was a voluntary association that became the base for the development and control of religious and education institutions in Gaza. Tamini, *Hamas: A History*, 36.
33. Mishal and Sela, *The Palestinian Hamas*, 34.
34. *Majd* is Arabic for "praise" or "glory."
35. In fact, in its charter, Hamas was described as a "wing of the MB." Mishal, "The Pragmatic Dimension," 35.
36. Mishal and Sela, *The Palestinian Hamas*, 41.
37. Ibid., 5.
38. See https://cpost.uchicago.edu/. See also Pape, *Dying to Win*.
39. For more discussion on coding leadership, see Chapter 3.
40. These figures on yearly Hamas attacks are from the Global Terrorism Database (GTD). The GTD uses three criteria for inclusion: "Criterion I: The act must be aimed at attaining a political, economic, religious, or social goal. Criterion II: There must be evidence of an intention to coerce, intimidate, or convey some other message to a larger audience (or audiences) than the immediate victims. Criterion III: The action must be outside the context of legitimate warfare activities." Hundreds of rockets fired nearly daily from Gaza into Southern Israel are not included in the GTD attack count as they occurred within the context of Operation Cast Lead in Gaza in 2008. The Israeli Security Agency reported similar numbers of major attacks and reported that overall there was a decline in both the frequency and lethality of attacks carried out by Palestinian militants and rockets and mortars fired from Gaza in 2009 and 2010.
41. Mishal and Sela, *The Palestinian Hamas*, 61.
42. Greenberg, "Peres and Arafat."

43. Byman, "Do Targeted Killings Work?"
44. Pedahzur, "The Changing Nature of Suicide Attacks."
45. Hroub, "Shaykh Yasin and Rantisi," 21.
46. Ibid., 31.
47. Plaw, *Targeting Terrorists*, 73. Hroub reports that fifteen civilians were killed. See Hroub, "Shaykh Yasin and Rantisi," 28.
48. Kifner, "Death on the Campus: The Bombers; Hamas Says It Regrets American Toll in Attack, but Hails Bombing as Success."
49. Plaw, *Targeting Terrorists*, 73.
50. Ibid., 77.
51. Bennet, "Israeli Strike in Gaza Kills a Hamas Leader and 14 Others."
52. Ibrahim, "Arafat's Forces Push Crackdown on Gaza Radicals."
53. In addition to cases of decapitation against senior Hamas leaders, I also discuss large-scale arrests and deportations. However, the dataset excludes these cases, unless a specific senior figure was included. By looking at them, I can get more information about how the organization has responded to counterterrorism efforts.
54. Tamimi, *Hamas: A History*, 55–56.
55. Mishal and Sela, *The Palestinian Hamas*, 56.
56. Abu-Amr, "Hamas," 14.
57. Ibid.
58. Mishal and Sela, *The Palestinian Hamas*, 56.
59. Tamimi, *Hamas: A History*, 58.
60. Ibid., 59.
61. Amman became the primary headquarters once the US listed Hamas as a Foreign Terrorist Organization (FTO) in 1993. Mishal and Sela, *The Palestinian Hamas*, 58.
62. Tamimi, *Hamas: A History*, 61.
63. Abu-Amr, "Hamas," 10.
64. Tamimi, *Hamas*, 61.
65. Mishal and Sela, *The Palestinian Hamas*, 66.
66. Tamimi, *Hamas: A History*, 75.
67. Bloom, *Dying to Kill*, 25.
68. Pape, *Dying to Win*.
69. See Bloom, *Dying to Kill*; "Palestinian Suicide Bombing."
70. Mishal and Sela, *The Palestinian Hamas*.
71. Roy, "Hamas and the Transformation(s) of Political Islam in Palestine," 15.
72. Ibid., 15.
73. Bloom, *Dying to Kill*, 20.
74. Tamimi, *Hamas: A History*, 107; Plaw, *Targeting Terrorists*, 58.
75. Tamimi, *Hamas: A History*, 107.
76. Ibid.
77. Bloom, *Dying to Kill*, 25.
78. Ibid., 26.
79. Plaw, *Targeting Terrorists*; Pedahzur, *The Israeli Secret Services and the Struggle against Terrorism*.
80. Plaw, *Targeting Terrorists*.
81. Pedahzur, *The Israeli Secret Services*, 117.
82. Plaw, *Targeting Terrorists*, 73.

83. Pedahzur, *The Israeli Secret Services*, 121.
84. Ibid., 122.
85. Byman and David argue that a decline in the lethality of attacks during this period is often attributed to the creation of the separation fence.
86. Pedahzur, *The Israeli Secret Services*, 123.
87. Plaw, *Targeting Terrorists*, 76.
88. Ibid., 77.
89. Tamimi, *Hamas: A History*, 206.
90. Hroub, "Shaykh Yasin and Rantisi," 33.
91. Tamimi, *Hamas: A History*, 218.
92. Proportional list voting indicated that Hamas received 44.5 percent of the vote and Fatah 41.43 percent. It is often argued that the electorate voted for Hamas in order to punish Fatah. Tamimi argues that only a fraction of votes were actually protest votes.
93. Tamimi, *Hamas: A History*, 220–21.
94. Ibid., 221.
95. Hamas was not the only organization firing rockets and mortars; other Palestinian militant organizations were also carrying out attacks against Israel.
96. Mishal, "The Pragmatic Dimension," 580–81.
97. Abu-Amr, "Hamas," 13.
98. Ibid.
99. McAdam, *Political Process and the Development of Black Insurgency, 1930–1970*, 43.
100. Ibid., 44.
101. Ibid. See also Oberschall, *Social Conflict and Social Movements*.
102. Pedahzur and Perlinger, "The Changing Nature of Suicide Attacks."
103. Mishal, "The Pragmatic Dimension," 582.
104. Ibid.
105. See Carley, "A Theory of Group Stability"; Byman, "Do Targeted Killings Work?"; Arquilla and Ronfeldt, *Networks and Netwars*; Zanini, "Middle Eastern Terrorism and Netwar."
106. See Siggelkow and Levinthal, "Temporarily Divide to Conquer: Centralized, Decentralized, and Reintegrated Organizational Approaches to Exploration and Adaptation."
107. Mishal, "The Pragmatic Dimension," 581.
108. For further information on organizational learning, see Carley, "Organizational Adaptation"; Fiol and Lyles, "Organizational Learning"; Jackson, *Aptitude for Destruction*; Levitt and March, "Organizational Learning"; Meyer, "Adapting to Environmental Jolts."
109. Mishal and Sela, *The Palestinian Hamas*, 152.
110. Mishal, "The Pragmatic Dimension," 582.
111. Abu-Amr, "Hamas," 14.
112. See McCarthy and Zald, "Resource Mobilization and Social Movements: A Partial Theory," and "Social Movement Organizations."
113. Pape, *Dying to Win*, 81.
114. Ibid.
115. Ibid.
116. Ibid.
117. Zammuto, *Assessing Organizational Effectiveness*, 17.
118. Ibid., 53.
119. Ibid., 161.

120. Hroub, *Hamas*, 234.

121. Like Hamas, the LTTE (Liberation Tigers of Tamil Eelam) has provided social and educational services to their community as a means by which to increase communal support. It has been argued that the LTTE used charitable services as a way to gain acceptance within their community and acceptance, if not participation, in violent acts. See Flanigan, "Nonprofit Service Provision by Insurgent Organizations: The Cases of Hizballah and the Tamil Tigers."

122. Roy, *Hamas and Civil Society in Gaza : Engaging the Islamist Social Sector*, 79.

123. Hroub, *Hamas*.

124. Roy, *Hamas*, 5.

125. Ibid.

126. Abu-Amr, "Hamas," 15.

127. Quoted in Roy, *Hamas*, 3–4.

128. See JMCC, "Tracking Palestinian Support for Armed Resistance During the Peace Process and Its Demise," 5. http://www.jmcc.org/documents/JMCC_Armed_Resistance_December2011.pdf.

129. Ibid. 11.

130. Birzeit University Center for Development Studies, "Opinion Polls."

131. Seitz, "Tracking Palestinian Public Support," 5.

132. Ibid., 11.

133. Ibid., 5.

134. Nusse, *Muslim Palestine: The Ideology of Hamas*, 49–52.

135. Bondokji, "Peace with Hamas."

CHAPTER 6

1. After Guzmán's arrest, the Fujimori government spoke of Sendero's collapse. Current studies of leadership decapitation frequently cite Guzmán's arrest, in which images of him behind bars were publicly shown, as a key factor in facilitating the decline of the organization. However, Cronin argues that granting amnesty to militants and the military's counterterrorism policies played a part on the weakening of Sendero and the decline in violence. See Cronin, "How Al-Qaida Ends."

2. Wilson, "Peru Fears Reemergence of Violent Rebels."

3. It is important to note that the organization was still active at this point, but it was in remnants and most of the activity was related to drugs.

4. McCormick, *The Shining Path and the Future of Peru*.

5. Ibid., 4.

6. Taylor, *Shining Path: Guerilla War in Peru's Northern Highlands, 1980–1997*, 3.

7. Palmer, "The Revolutionary Terrorism of Peru's Shining Path," 253.

8. McClintock, "Why Peasants Rebel: The Case of Peru's Sendero Luminoso," 48.

9. Ibid.

10. Taylor, *Shining Path: Guerilla War*, 23.

11. Palmer, "The Revolutionary Terrorism," 253.

12. See Tarazona-Sevillano, "The Organization of Shining Path"; Weinstein, *Inside Rebellion: The Politics of Insurgent Rebellion*; Palmer, *The Shining Path of Peru*.

13. Weinstein, *Inside Rebellion*, 81.

14. The initiation of violence just as Peru was undergoing a transition to democracy seems puzzling. James Ron examines why Sendero Luminoso began its armed campaign just as the Peruvian military ceded powers to an elected civilian president, the eve of democratic reforms in Peru. See Ron, "Ideology in Context: Explaining Sendero Luminoso's Tactical Escalation"; Weinstein, *Inside Rebellion*, 81.

15. Degregori, "The Origins and Logics of Shining Path: Two Views," 35.

16. McCormick, *The Shining Path*, 45.

17. Eglund and Stohl, "Violent Political Movements: Comparing the Shining Path to the Islamic State," 25.

18. Ron, "Ideology in Context," 575.

19. Isbell, "Shining Path and Peasant Responses in Rural Ayacucho," 65.

20. Ibid., 129.

21. Palmer, "The Revolutionary Terrorism," 129.

22. Isbell, "Shining Path and Peasant Responses," 60.

23. Taylor, *Shining Path: Guerilla War*, 8.

24. Palmer, "The Revolutionary Terrorism," 293.

25. Ibid.

26. Palmer, "Rebellion in Rural Peru: The Origins and Evolution of Sendero Luminoso," 129.

27. Palmer, "The Revolutionary Terrorism"; "Rebellion in Rural Peru," 133; de Wit and Gianotten, "The Center's Multiple Failures."

28. Palmer, "Rebellion in Rural Peru," 133.

29. Ibid., 134.

30. de Wit and Gianotten, "The Center's Multiple Failures," 51.

31. Ibid., 55.

32. Manwaring, "Peru's Sendero Luminoso: The Shining Path Beckons," 162.

33. Ibid.

34. Ibid.

35. Smith, "Taking the High Ground: Shining Path and the Andes," 16. Philip Mauceri finds similar statistics regarding deaths. He estimates that as of 1991, Sendero violence has resulted in 20,000 deaths, 3,000 disappearances, and $10 billion in damages. See Mauceri, "Military Politics and Counter-Insurgency in Peru," 84.

36. Manwaring, *Shadows of Things Past and Images of the Future: Lessons for the Insurgencies in Our Midst*, 20.

37. Ibid., 20–21.

38. See START, "Global Terrorism Database," http://www.start.umd.edu/gtd/. This number should actually be higher, but the GTD has lost data for 1993. This data will be examined in much greater detail later in the chapter.

39. See McCormick, *The Shining Path*, 31.

40. Ibid.

41. Ibid., 33.

42. This sample does not include every instance of leadership decapitation during this time period, but it gives a sense of the trends in the targeting efforts of the Peruvian authorities and how Sendero responded.

43. Andreas and Fokkema, "Women at War," 20.

44. *New York Times*, "Peruvian Army Kills 39 Rebels in Skirmishes"; Leger, "Surviving Amid Peru's Guerilla War. Peasants Seek to Rebuild Lives in War-Torn Villages."

45. Tarazona-Sevillano, "The Organization of Shining Path," 184.
46. Ibid.
47. Palmer, "The Revolutionary Terrorism," 275.
48. Riding, "Peruvian Guerrillas Emerge as an Urban Political Force," 1.
49. *Sydney Morning Herald*, "Suspected Shining Path Leader Held."
50. McClintock, *Revolutionary Movements in Latin America*, 92.
51. Sanchez, "The Rebirth of Insurgency in Peru," 189.
52. There were, however, studies at the time that argued that Guzmán's arrest did not result in the group's decline. Other studies at the time of his arrest also questioned whether it would have the intended effect of group decline. See Nash, "Peru Rebels."; Manwaring, "Peru's Sendero Luminoso" and *Shadows of Things Past*.
53. Sanchez, "Rebirth of Insurgency," 188.
54. Nash, "Peru Rebels to Remain Potent."
55. Ibid.
56. Ibid., 1.
57. Manwaring, "Peru's Sendero Luminoso," 164.
58. Ibid.
59. Tarazona-Sevillano, "The Organization of Shining Path," 183. As of 1992, Tarazona-Sevillano did not think that Sendero would succumb to Peruvian countermeasures.
60. Nash, "Peru Rebels."
61. McCormick, *The Shining Path*, 11.
62. Palmer argues that the recruitment of a young people was one of seven primary factors contributing to Sendero's growth. Palmer, "The Revolutionary Terrorism," 275.
63. McCormick, *The Shining Path*, 12.
64. Kay draws on resource mobilization theory in order to understand the importance of the cocaine industry to a group's capacity for armed conflict. See Kay, "The Rise and Fall of 'King Coca' and Shining Path."
65. Palmer, "The Revolutionary Terrorism," 275.
66. Taylor, *Shining Path: Guerilla War*, 173.
67. Ibid., 169.
68. Ibid., 174.
69. Ibid.
70. Ibid., 192.
71. Ibid.
72. Ibid., 193.
73. Ibid.
74. Ibid.
75. Sanchez, "Rebirth of Insurgency," 187.
76. Ibid., 188.
77. See Cronin, "How Al-Qaida Ends," 18.
78. McCormick, *The Shining Path*.
79. McClintock, *Revolutionary Movements in Latin America*, 65.
80. Tarazona-Sevillano, "The Organization of Shining Path," 168.
81. Ron, "Ideology in Context," 575.
82. Degregori, "Origins and Logics of Shining Path," 36.
83. Children were also a key aspect of the indoctrination process. See Tarazona-Sevillano, "The Organization of Shining Path," 184.

84. Manwaring, "Peru's Sendero Luminoso," 159.
85. Gorriti, *The Shining Path: A History of the Millenarian War in Peru*, 168.
86. McCormick, *The Shining Path*, 5.
87. Tarazona-Sevillano, "The Organization of Shining Path," 168.
88. Taylor, *Shining Path: Guerilla War*, 29–30.
89. Ibid., 29.
90. Ibid., 30.
91. This data is consistent with the BAAD dataset at GTD.
92. Palmer, "The Revolutionary Terrorism," 267.
93. McClintock, *Revolutionary Movements in Latin America*.
94. As part of the amnesty deal, militants had to turn in themselves and other members of the organization.
95. I will discuss this aspect of group strength in the next section on communal support.
96. Palmer, "The Revolutionary Terrorism," 267.
97. Tarazona-Sevillano, "The Organization of Shining Path," 181.
98. Taylor, *Shining Path: Guerilla War*, 134.
99. Tarazona-Sevillano, "The Organization of Shining Path," 182.
100. McClintock, *Revolutionary Movements in Latin America*, 71.
101. Tarazona-Sevillano, "The Organization of Shining Path."
102. Ibid., 175.
103. Palmer, "The Revolutionary Terrorism," 267.
104. Ibid.
105. Burt makes this point and supplements her research with ethnographic research in order to develop a fuller sense of attitudes toward Shining Path in the 1980s and 1990s. Burt, *Political Violence and the Authoritarian State in Peru*.
106. de Wit and Gianotten, "The Center's Multiple Failures," 51.
107. Ibid., 52.
108. Ibid.
109. Burt, *Political Violence*, 46.
110. Ibid.
111. McClintock, *Revolutionary Movements in Latin America*, 291.
112. Ibid.
113. Ibid., 292.
114. Eglund and Stohl, "Violent Political Movements," 25.
115. See Marks, "Making Revolution with Shining Path."
116. Ron, "Ideology in Context: Explaining Sendero Luminoso's Tactical Escalation."
117. McClintock, *Revolutionary Movements in Latin America*, 292.
118. Ibid., 292–93.
119. Burt, *Political Violence*, 100.
120. Ibid.
121. McClintock, *Revolutionary Movements in Latin America*, 79–81.
122. Burt, *Political Violence*, 111.
123. For a discussion on parallels between the state-like capacities of Shining Path and ISIS see Eglund and Stohl, "Violent Political Movements."
124. See Kay, "King Coca."
125. Ibid., 97.

126. Ibid., 103.
127. Ibid.
128. Ibid., 106.
129. Ibid., 122.
130. This is discussed further in Chapter 3. See Cronin, *How Terrorism Ends*, 105.
131. See Taylor, *Shining Path: Guerilla War*, 30.

CHAPTER 7

1. Obama, "Remarks by the President on the Way Forward in Afghanistan."
2. Bumiller, "Panetta Says Defeat of Al Qaeda is Within Strategic Reach," A11.
3. For a discussion of Al Qaeda's expansion, see Mendelsohn, *The Al-Qaeda Franchise: The Expansion of Al Qaeda and Its Consequences*. Mendelsohn's theory of al-Qaeda's organizational evolution will be discussed in greater detail in the following section.
4. Gulati, Puranam, and Tushman, "Meta-Organization Design: Rethinking Design in Interorganizational and Community Contexts," 573.
5. For a study that discusses the difference between operational and inspirational authority, see Freeman, "Theory of Terrorist Leadership."
6. Hayes and Joscelyn, "How America Was Misled on Al Qaeda's Demise."
7. Obama, "Remarks by President Obama in Address to the Nation from Afghanistan."
8. Mendelsohn, *Al-Qaeda Franchise*, 1.
9. Ibid., 2.
10. Ibid., 6.
11. Combating Terrorism Center, "Zawahiri's Letter to Zarqawi." https://ctc.usma.edu/harmony-program/zawahiris-letter-to-zarqawi-original-language-2/.
12. Bergen, "Bin Laden: Seized Documents Show Delusional Leader and Micromanager."
13. Biddle, Friedman, and Shapiro, "Testing the Surge: Why Did Violence Decline in Iraq in 2007?" 7.
14. Ibid.
15. Ibid.
16. Cronin, "ISIS Is Not a Terrorist Group: Why Counterterrorism Won't Stop the Latest Jihadist Threat."
17. Ibid.
18. Byman, *Al Qaeda*.
19. Ibid., 167.
20. Cronin, "ISIS Is Not a Terrorist Group."
21. Byman, *Al Qaeda, the Islamic State, and the Global Jihadist Movement: What Everyone Needs to Know*, 167.
22. Ibid., 167.
23. Cronin, "ISIS Is Not a Terrorist Group."
24. Plaw, *Targeting Terrorists*, 182.
25. Bergen, *The Longest War*, 349.
26. See Byman, "Do Targeted Killings Work?" David, "Fatal Choices."
27. Plaw, *Targeting Terrorists*.
28. Cronin, *How Terrorism Ends*, 179.

29. BBC, "Obama Warns Pakistan on al-Qaeda."
30. Arena, "Obama Administration to Ratchet up Hunt for bin Laden."
31. Committee on Foreign Relations, *Tora Bora Revisited: How We Failed to Get Bin Laden and Why It Matters Today*, 1.
32. Ibid.
33. See Sageman, *Understanding Terror Networks*.
34. Cronin, *How Terrorism Ends*, 177.
35. Ibid., 170.
36. Ibid., 171.
37. Ibid., 177.
38. Ibid., 178.
39. Bergen, *The Longest War*, 547.
40. Ibid., 549.
41. See Riedel, *Search for Al Qaeda*.
42. Bergen, *The Longest War*, 249.
43. The data in Chapter 4 ends in 2012, in order to have a long enough time frame in which to evaluate the effect of attacks over time. In this chapter, I will look at targeting instances through 2016.
44. The excluded groups include al-Qaeda Kurdish Battalions, al-Qaeda Network for Southwestern Khulna Division, and al-Qaeda Organization for Jihad in Sweden.
45. Cronin, *How Terrorism Ends*, 182.
46. Pape and Feldman, *Cutting the Fuse*, 178–80.
47. Bergen and Hoffman, *Assessing the Terrorist Threat*, 6.
48. This coding in consistent with the BAAD dataset, which places al-Qaeda in a category of organizations with between 1,000 and 10,000 members.
49. See Bergen and Tiedemann, "Almanac of Al Qaeda."
50. Mendelsohn, *Al-Qaeda Franchise*, 8.
51. Ibid.
52. Ibid., 14.
53. Ibid.
54. Ibid., 13.
55. Gunaratna, *Inside Al Qaeda: Global Network of Terror*, 4.
56. Byman, "Comparing Al Qaeda and ISIS: Different Goals, Different Targets."
57. Ibid.
58. Gunaratna, *Inside Al Qaeda*, 5.
59. Ibid.
60. See Pape and Feldman, *Cutting the Fuse*; Pape, *Dying to Win*.
61. Sageman, *Leaderless Jihad*, 129.
62. Ibid. According to Sageman, these networks dominate the current threat. Risa Brooks, on the other hand, argues that homegrown terrorism does not present a serious threat, nor is there sufficient evidence to indicate that it will become one in the near future. See Brooks, "Muslim 'Homegrown' Terrorism in the United States: How Serious Is the Threat?"
63. Sageman, *Leaderless Jihad*, 130.
64. Bajoria and Teslik, "Profile: Ayman Al-Zawahiri."
65. Cronin, *How Terrorism Ends*, 170.
66. Hoffman, "Combating Al Qaeda and the Militant Islamic Threat," 3.

67. See Hoffman, "The Myth of Grass-Roots Terrorism: Why Osama Bin Laden Still Matters."
68. Hoffman, "Combating Al Qaeda," 3.
69. See ibid. For a debate about the intensity of the threat from home-grown terrorism, see Hoffman, "Grass-Roots Terrorism"; Hoffman and Sageman, "Does Osama Still Call the Shots?: Debating the Containment of Al Qaeda's Leadership."
70. Hoffman, "Combating Al Qaeda," 6.
71. Hoffman, "Challenges for the U.S. Special Operations Command Posed by the Global Terrorist Threat: Al Qaeda on the Run or on the March," 11.
72. Mendelsohn, *Al Qaeda Franchise*, 201.
73. Ibid., 13.
74. bin Laden, "Administrative Instructions." https://www.dni.gov/files/documents/ubl2017/english/Administrative%20instructions.pdf.
75. Schmid, "Public Opinion Survey Data to Measure Sympathy and Support for Islamist Terrorism: A Look at Muslim Opinions on Al Qaeda and IS," 4–5.
76. Kull et al., "Public Opinion in the Islamic World on Terrorism, Al Qaeda, and US Policies," 3.
77. Bergen, *The Longest War*, 248.
78. Ibid., 253.
79. Fair, Malhotra, and Shapiro, "Islam, Militancy, and Politics in Pakistan: Insights from a National Sample," 495. For other studies on support for militancy in Pakistan see Fair, "Militant Recruitment in Pakistan: Implications for Al Qaeda and Other Organizations"; Shapiro and Fair, "Understanding Support for Islamist Militancy in Pakistan."
80. Fair, Malhotra, and Shapiro, "Islam, Militancy, and Politics," 510.
81. Ibid., 511.
82. Ibid.
83. Ibid.
84. Shapiro and Fair, "Understanding Support for Islamist Militancy in Pakistan," 83.
85. Schmid, "Public Opinion Survey."
86. Ibid., 25.
87. Lia, "Jihadism in the Arab World after 2011: Explaining Its Expansion," 8.
88. Gunaratna, *Inside Al Qaeda*, 221.
89. Ibid., 223–24.
90. Plaw, *Targeting Terrorists*, 115.
91. Rashid, *Taliban: Militant Islam, Oil and Fundamentalism in Central Asia*, 75.
92. Plaw, *Targeting Terrorists*, 112.
93. Gunaratna, *Inside Al Qaeda*, 32–33.
94. Ibid., 208.
95. Byman, "Comparing Al Qaeda and ISIS."
96. Ibid.
97. Fishman, "Using the Mistakes of Al Qaeda's Franchises to Undermine Its Strategies," 48.
98. Shapiro, *The Terrorist's Dilemma*.
99. Harmony documents (originals and translations) are available through the Combating Terrorism Center website, https://ctc.usma.edu/harmony-program/.
100. Forest, Brachman, and Felter, *Harmony and Disharmony: Exploiting Al-Qa'ida's Organizational Vulnerabilities*, 2.

101. Ibid. According to Shapiro and Siegel, this level of bureaucratization not only lessens the effect of preference divergence, but it can also increase efficiency and signal legitimacy to local populations. See Shapiro and Siegel, "Moral Hazard."

102. Combating Terrorism Center, "Al-Qaida's Structure and Bylaws (English Translation)," Harmony #AFGP-2002–600048. https://ctc.usma.edu/app/uploads/2013/10/Al-Qa%E2%80%99ida%E2%80%99s-Structure-and-Bylaws-Translation1.pdf.

103. Combating Terrorism Center, "Al Qaida Constitutional Charter (Original Language)," Harmony #AFGP-2002–600045. https://ctc.usma.edu/app/uploads/2013/10/Al-Qaida-Constitutional-Charter-Translation.pdf.

104. Combating Terrorism Center, "Names of Al-Qaida Members (Original Language)," Harmony #AFGP-2002–600046. https://ctc.usma.edu/app/uploads/2012/05/AFGP-2002-600046-Trans.pdf.

105. Fishman et al., *Bombers, Bank Accounts, and Bleedout: Al-Qa'ida's Road in and out of Iraq.*

106. Shapiro, "Bureaucratic Terrorists," 75.

107. Bergen, *The Longest War*, 169.

108. Shapiro and Siegel, "Moral Hazard."; Shapiro, *The Terrorist's Dilemma.*

109. Shapiro, "Bureaucracy and Control in Terrorist Organizations," 4.

110. Al-Jabouri, Abed, and Jensen, "The Iraqi and AQI Roles in the Sunni Awakening."

111. Kirdar, *Al Qaeda in Iraq.*

112. Hashim, "The Islamic State: From al-Qaeda Affiliate to Caliphate."

113. Al-Jabouri, Abed, and Jensen, "Iraqi and AQI Roles in the Sunni Awakening."

114. Daniel Byman has argued that atrocities committed by AQI went further than undermining the group's support; they were also used to discredit the core. He also argues that ties to foreigners, of which AQI had many, can alienate insurgents who are often motivated more by nationalism than religion. Byman, "Al Qaeda's M&A Strategy."

115. World Public Opinion, "U.S. Troops."

116. Ibid.

117. Long, "The Anbar Awakening."

118. Biddle, Friedman, and Shapiro, "Testing the Surge."

119. Nordland and Rubin, "Sunni Fighters Say Iraq Didn't Keep Job Promises."

120. Hashim, "The Islamic State."

121. Master, "FBI Investigator Warns: 'We're Not Done with the Bin Ladens Yet.'"

122. McConnell and Todd, "Latest Al Qaeda Propaganda Highlights Bin Laden's Son."

123. Ibid.

124. Simcox, "The Perils of Forgetting About Al Qaeda."

CHAPTER 8

1. Warrick and Mekhennet, "New Clues Bolster Belief That ISIS Leader Is Still Alive—and Busy with a Chilling New Mission."

2. ISIS was not included in the larger quantitative analysis because there was an insufficient timeframe in which to evaluate the consequences that leadership decapitation has had upon the group's activity.

3. King, Bulos, and Hennigan, "Why Islamic State's Abu Muhammad Adnani Was Much More Than a Spokesman."

4. Dearden, "ISIS Dealt 'Major Blow' by Death of Spokesman Abu Muhammad Al-Adnani in Air Strike Claimed by US and Russia."

5. Dearden, "Isis Dealt 'Major Blow' by Death of Spokesman Abu Muhammad al-Adnani in Air Strike Claimed by US and Russia."

6. De Luce, Groll, and Hudson, "Going after the ISIS Propaganda Mastermind."

7. Gerges, *ISIS: A History*, 28.

8. IS-K refers to the Islamic State of Khorasan, which is the Afghan and Pakistani branch of the organization. Nordland and Ghazi, "ISIS Leader in Afghanistan Is Killed in U.S. Airstrike."

9. Al Jazeera, "ISIL Leader in Afghanistan Killed in Air Raids."

10. See Coker, Schmitt, and Callimachi, "With Loss of Its Caliphate, ISIS May Return to Guerrilla Roots." Callimachi, "Fight to Retake Last ISIS Territory Begins."

11. al-Habib, "For ISIS, Losing Territory Means Losing Revenue."

12. Hassan, "ISIS Is Ready for a Resurgence."

13. Coker, Schmitt, and Callimachi, "Guerrilla Roots," A1.

14. Nordland and Ghazi, "ISIS Leader."

15. Ibid.

16. START, Global Terrorism Database [Data file]. Retrieved from https://www.start.umd.edu/gtd.

17. Hassan, "ISIS Is Ready for a Resurgence."

18. Ibid. See also McCants, *The ISIS Apocalypse: The History, Strategy, and Doomsday Vision of the Islamic State*.

19. See Coker, Schmitt, and Callimachi, "Guerrilla Roots."

20. Gerges, *ISIS: A History*, 24.

21. See Barrett, *Beyond the Caliphate: Foreign Fighters and the Threat of Returnees*. See also Soufan Group, *Foreign Fighters: An Updated Assessment of the Flow of Foreign Fighters into Syria and Iraq*.

22. House Homeland Security Committee Majority Staff, *Terror Gone Viral: Overview of the 243 ISIS-Linked Incidents Targeting the West*.

23. Wright, "After the Islamic State."

24. Gerges, *ISIS: A History*, 23.

25. Cronin, "ISIS Is Not a Terrorist Group," 91.

26. Hassan, "Ready for a Resurgence."

27. Ibid. See also Cronin, "ISIS Is Not a Terrorist Group," 87.

28. Jones et al., *Rolling Back the Islamic State*.

29. See Revkin, "Taxation by Resource-Rich Rebels."

30. See Cronin, "ISIS Is Not a Terrorist Group."

31. March and Revkin, "Caliphate of Law: ISIS' Ground Rules."

32. Cronin, "ISIS Is Not a Terrorist Group," 91.

33. Stern and Bereger, *ISIS: The State of Terror*, 38.

34. Ibid.

35. Barrett, "The Islamic State," 19.

36. Crabtree, "Faith in Iraqi Government."

37. Ibid.

38. Arab Barometer, "Arab Barometer Wave II."

39. Poushter, "In Nations with Significant Muslim Populations, Much Disdain for ISIS."

40. Pollock, "ISIS Has Almost No Popular Support in Egypt, Saudi Arabia, or Lebanon."
41. Studies of Twitter accounts have examined the number of accounts that support and oppose ISIS. See Bodine-Baron et al., *Examining ISIS Support and Opposition Networks on Twitter*.
42. Miller, "Al-Qaeda Confirms Osama Bin Laden's Death, Vows Retaliation."
43. Atran, "Mishandling Suicide Terrorism"; Bloom, *Dying to Kill*.

Bibliography

Abizaid, Gen. John P., and Rosa Brooks. "Recommendations and Report of the Task Force on US Drone Policy." Washington, DC: Stimson Center, 2014.
Abrahms, Max. "Why Terrorism Does Not Work." International Security 31, no. 2 (Fall 2006): 42–78.
Abrahms, Max, and Jochen Mierau. "Leadership Matters: The Effects of Targeted Killings on Militant Group Tactics." Terrorism and Political Violence 29, no. 5 (2017): 830–51.
Abrahms, Max, and Philip B. K. Potter. "Explaining Terrorism: Leadership Deficits and Militant Group Tactics." International Organization 69, no. 2 (2015): 311.
Abu-Amr, Ziad. "Hamas: A Historical and Political Background." Journal of Palestine Studies 22, no. 4 (Summer 1993): 5–19.
Alesina, Alberto, Sule Ozler, Nouriel Roubini, and Phillip Swagel. "Political Instability and Economic Growth." Journal of Economic Growth 1, no. 2 (1996): 189–211.
Al Jazeera. "ISIL Leader in Afghanistan Killed in Air Raids." August 26, 2018. https://www.aljazeera.com/news/2018/08/isil-leader-afghanistan-killed-air-strikes-180826134946305.html.
Anderson, Sean K., and Stephen Sloan. Historical Dictionary of Terrorism. Lanham, MD: Scarecrow, 2002.
Andreas, Carol, and Anita Fokkema. "Women at War." NACLA Report on the Americas 24 (1990).
Arab Barometer. "Arab Barometer Wave II." 2010. http://www.arabbarometer.org/waves/arab-barometer-wave-ii/.
Arena, Kelli. "Obama Administration to Ratchet Up Hunt for bin Laden." CNN, November 12, 2008.
Arquilla, John, and David Ronfeldt. Networks and Netwars: The Future of Terror, Crime, and Militancy. Santa Monica, CA: RAND, 2001.
Arsu, Sebnem. "Jailed Leader of the Kurds Offers a Truce with Turkey." New York Times, March 21, 2013.

Asal, Victor, Mitchell Brown, and Angela Dalton. "Why Split? Organizational Splits among Ethnopolitical Organizations in the Middle East." Journal of Conflict Resolution 56, no. 1 (February 2012): 94–117.

Atran, Scott. "Mishandling Suicide Terrorism." Washington Quarterly 27, no. 3 (Summer 2004).

Atzili, Boaz. "State Weakness and 'Vacuum of Power' in Lebanon." Studies in Conflict and Terrorism 33 (2010): 757–82.

Bajoria, Jayshree, and Lee Hudson Teslik. "Profile: Ayman Al-Zawahiri." Council on Foreign Relations, 2011. https://www.cfr.org/backgrounder/profile-ayman-al-zawahiri.

Bakshi, Amar C. "Former CIA Officer Bruce Riedel on bin Laden Death, Pakistan-U.S. Ties and the Afghan War." CNN, May 4, 2011.

Barela, Stephen J., ed. Legitimacy and Drones: Investigating the Legality, Morality and Efficacy of UCAVS. Abingdon, UK: Routledge, 2016.

Baron, James N., M. Diane Burton, and Michael T. Hannan. "Engineering Bureaucracy: The Genesis of Formal Policies, Positions, and Structures in High-Technology Firms." Journal of Law, Economics, and Organization 15, no. 1 (1999).

Barrett, Richard. Beyond the Caliphate: Foreign Fighters and the Threat of Returnees. Soufan Center, 2017. https://thesoufancenter.org/wp-content/uploads/2017/11/Beyond-the-Caliphate-Foreign-Fighters-and-the-Threat-of-Returnees-TSC-Report-October-2017-v3.pdf.

———. The Islamic State. Soufan Group, 2014. http://soufangroup.com/wp-content/uploads/2014/10/TSG-The-Islamic-State-Nov14.pdf.

BBC. "Obama Warns Pakistan on al-Qaeda." August 1, 2007.

BBC. "Osama Bin Laden's Death: Political Reaction in Quotes." May 3, 2011.

Bennet, James. "Israeli Strike in Gaza Kills a Hamas Leader and 14 Others." New York Times, 2002.

Bergen, Peter. "And Now, Only One Senior Al Qaeda Leader Left." CNN, June 6, 2012.

———. "Bin Laden: Seized Documents Show Delusional Leader and Micromanager." CNN, May 3, 2012.

———. The Longest War: The Enduring Conflict between America and Al-Qaeda. New York: Free Press, 2011.

———. "Should We Still Fear al Qaeda?" CNN, February 6, 2013.

Bergen, Peter, and Bruce Hoffman. Assessing the Terrorist Threat. Bipartisan Policy Center, 2010. https://bipartisanpolicy.org/library/assessing-terrorist-threat/.

Bergen, Peter, and Katherine Tiedemann. "The Almanac of Al Qaeda." Foreign Policy (May/June 2010).

Berman, Eli. Radical, Religious and Violent: The New Economics of Terrorism. Cambridge, MA: MIT Press, 2009.

Berman, Eli, and David D. Laitin. "Religion, Terrorism, and Public Goods." Journal of Public Economics 92 (2008): 1942–67.

Bhattacharya, Srobana. "Comparing Civilian Support for Terrorism." Journal of Strategic Security 10, no. 2 (2017): 1–32.

Biddle, Stephen, Jeffrey A. Friedman, and Jacob N Shapiro. "Testing the Surge: Why Did Violence Decline in Iraq in 2007?" International Security 37, no. 1 (2012): 7–40.

Bloom, Mia. Dying to Kill: The Allure of Suicide Terror. New York: Columbia University Press, 2007.

———. "Palestinian Suicide Bombing: Public Support, Market Share, and Outbidding." Political Science Quarterly 119, no. 1 (2004): 61.

Bodine-Baron, Elizabeth, Todd C. Helmus, Madeline Magnuson, and Zev Winkelman. *Examining ISIS Support and Opposition Networks on Twitter.* Santa Monica, CA: RAND, 2016.

Bonacich, Phillip, and Paulette Lloyd. "Calculating Status with Negative Relations." *Social Networks* 26 (2004).

Bondokj, Neven. "The Nationalist versus the Religious: Implications for Peace with Hamas." Brookings, March 18, 2014.

Bronstein, Phil. "The Man Who Killed Osama bin Laden . . . Is Screwed." *Esquire*, February 11, 2013.

Brooks, Risa. "Muslim 'Homegrown' Terrorism in the United States: How Serious Is the Threat?" *International Security* 36, no. 2 (Fall 2011): 7–47.

———. "Researching Democracy and Terrorism: How Political Access Affects Militant Activity." *Security Studies* 18 (2009): 756–88.

———. "Societies and Terrorist Violence: How Social Support Affects Militant Campaigns." Milwaukee, WI: Marquette University, 2011.

Bruderl, Josef, and Rudolf Schussler. "Organizational Mortality: The Liabilities of Newness and Adolescence." *Administrative Science Quarterly* 35 (1990): 530–47.

Bueno de Mesquita, Ethan. "Conciliation, Counterterrorism, and Patterns of Terrorist Violence." *International Organization* 59, no. 1 (2005): 145–76.

———. *Correlates of Public Support for Terrorism in the Muslim World.* United States Institute of Peace, 2007. https://www.usip.org/sites/default/files/May2007.pdf.

———. "Terrorist Factions." *Quarterly Journal of Political Science* 3 (2008): 399–418.

Bureau of Investigative Journalism. "Covert War on Terror." 2012. http://www.thebureauinvestigates.com/category/projects/drones/.

Burt, Jo-Marie. *Political Violence and the Authoritarian State in Peru.* New York: Palgrave Macmillan, 2007.

Bumiller, Elisabeth. "Panetta Says Defeat of Al Qaeda is 'Within Reach.'" *New York Times*, July 9, 2011.

Byman, Daniel. "What Happens When ISIS Goes Underground." Brookings, January 18, 2018.

———. *Al Qaeda, the Islamic State, and the Global Jihadist Movement: What Everyone Needs to Know.* Oxford: Oxford University Press, 2015.

———. "Al Qaeda's M&A Strategy." Brookings, 2010. https://www.brookings.edu/opinions/al-qaedas-ma-strategy/.

———. "Comparing Al Qaeda and ISIS: Different Goals, Different Targets." Brookings, 2015. https://www.brookings.edu/testimonies/comparing-al-qaeda-and-isis-different-goals-different-targets/.

———. "Do Targeted Killings Work?" *Foreign Affairs* (March/April 2006).

Callimachi, Rukmini. "Fight to Retake Last ISIS Territory Begins." *New York Times*, September 11, 2018.

Carley, Kathleen. "Organizational Adaptation." *Annals of Operations Research* 17 (1997): 25–47.

———. "A Theory of Group Stability." *American Sociological Review* 56, no. 3 (June 1991): 331–54.

Carley, Kathleen, Ju-Sung Lee, and David Krackhardt. "Destabilizing Networks." *Connections* 24, no. 3 (2002): 79–92.

Carlton-Ford, Steven Lewis. *Cults and Non-Conventional Religious Groups: The Effects of Ritual and Charisma.* New York: Garland, 1993.

Carvin, Stephanie. "The Trouble with Targeted Killings." Security Studies 21, no. 3 (2012): 529–55.

Cavallaro, James, Stephan Sonnenberg, and Sarah Knuckey. Living under Drones: Death, Injury and Trauma to Civilians from US Drone Practices in Pakistan. International Human Rights and Conflict Resolution Clinic of Stanford Law School (Stanford Clinic), Global Justice Clinic at New York University School of Law (NYU Clinic), 2012. https://www-cdn.law.stanford.edu/wp-content/uploads/2015/07/Stanford-NYU-Living-Under-Drones.pdf.

Center for the Study of Targeted Killings at the University of Massachusetts, Dartmouth, Institute for the Study of Counterterrorism & Unconventional Warfare, "States Against Nonstate Actors." https://iscuw.org/.

Chenoweth, Erica. "Terrorism and Democracy." Annual Review of Political Science 16 (2013): 355–78.

Coker, Margaret, Eric Schmitt, and Rukmini Callimachi. "With Loss of Its Caliphate, ISIS May Return to Guerrilla Roots." New York Times, October 17, 2017.

Collier, Paul, and Anke Hoeffler. "Greed and Grievance in Civil War." Oxford Economic Paper 56, no. 4 (2004): 563–95.

Committee on Foreign Relations. Tora Bora Revisited: How We Failed to Get Bin Laden and Why It Matters Today. 111th Congress, 1st Session, November 30, 2009. https://www.foreign.senate.gov/imo/media/doc/Tora_Bora_Report.pdf.

Conrad, Justin, and Daniel Milton. "Unpacking the Connection between Terror and Islam." Studies in Conflict and Terrorism 36, no. 4 (2013): 215–336.

Cornwell, Rupert. "Campaign against Terror: A Justifiable Tool in the War against Terrorism." The Independent, November 6, 2002. https://www.independent.co.uk/news/world/politics/rupert-cornwell-a-justifiable-tool-in-the-war-against-terrorism-133198.html.

Counterterrorism Strategy Initiative. "The Year of the Drone." New America Foundation. http://counterterrorism.newamerica.net/drones.

Crabtree, Steve, "Faith in Iraqi Government Falls Sharply in Sunni Regions." Gallup, June 27, 2014. https://news.gallup.com/poll/171959/faith-iraqi-government-falls-sharply-sunni-regions.aspx.

Crenshaw, Martha. "The Causes of Terrorism." Comparative Politics 13, no. 4 (July 1981): 379–99.

———. "Theories of Terrorism: Instrumental and Organizational Approaches." In Inside Terrorist Organizations, edited by David Rapaport, 13–30. London: Frank Cass, 2001.

———. "How Terrorism Declines." Terrorism and Political Violence 3, no. 1 (Spring 1991): 69–87.

———. "The Logic of Terrorism." In Origins of Terrorism, edited by Walter Reich, 7–24. Washington DC: Woodrow Wilson Center Press, 1998.

———. "Mapping Terrorist Organizations." Center for International Security and Cooperation: Stanford University, 2010. https://cisac.fsi.stanford.edu/research/mapping_militant_organizations.

———. "An Organizational Approach to the Analysis of Political Terrorism." Orbis 29, no. 3 Fall (1985): 465–89.

———. "The Psychology of Terrorism: An Agenda for the 21st Century." Political Psychology 21, no. 2 (June 2000): 405–20.

———, ed. Terrorism in Context. University Park: Pennsylvania State University Press, 1995.

Cronin, Audrey Kurth. "Behind the Curve: Globalization and International Terrorism." International Security 27, no. 3 (2002–2003): 30–58.

———. "How Al-Qaida Ends: The Decline and Demise of Terrorist Groups." International Security 31, no. 1 (Summer 2006): 7–48.

———. How Terrorism Ends: Understanding the Decline and Demise of Terrorist Campaigns. Princeton, NJ: Princeton University Press, 2009.

———. "ISIS Is Not a Terrorist Group: Why Counterterrorism Won't Stop the Latest Jihadist Threat." Foreign Affairs (March/April 2015). https://www.foreignaffairs.com/articles/middle-east/2019-02-18/isis-not-terrorist-group.

Crozier, Michel. The Bureaucratic Phenomenon. Chicago: University of Chicago Press, 1963.

Cyert, R. M., and J. G. March. A Behavioral Theory of the Firm. Englewood Cliffs, NJ: Prentice-Hall, 1963.

David, Steven R. "Fatal Choices: Israel's Policy of Targeted Killing." Mideast Security and Policy Studies 51 (September 2002).

Dawson, Lorne L. "Crises in Charismatic Legitimacy and Violent Behavior in New Religious Movements." In Cults, Religion, and Violence, edited by David G. Bromley and J. Gordon Melton. Cambridge: Cambridge University Press, 2002.

Dear, Keith P. "Beheading the Hydra? Does Killing Terrorist or Insurgent Leaders Work?" Defence Studies 13, no. 3 (2013).

Dearden, Lizzie. "ISIS Dealt 'Major Blow' by Death of Abu Muhammad al-Adnani in Air Strike Claimed by US and Russia." Independent, August 31, 2016.

Deibert, Ronald J., and Janice Gross Stein. "Hacking Networks of Terror." Dialog-IO (2002): 71.

Degregori, Carlos Ivan. "The Origins and Logics of Shining Path: Two Views." In The Shining Path of Peru, edited by David Scott Palmer. New York: St. Martin's, 1992.

della Porta, Donatella. Social Movements, Political Violence, and the State: A Comparative Analysis of Italy and Germany. Cambridge: Cambridge University Press, 1995.

De Luce, Dan, Elias Groll, and John Hudson. "Going after the ISIS Propaganda Mastermind." Foreign Policy (August 31, 2016).

de Wit, Ton, and Vera Gianotten. "The Center's Multiple Failures." In The Shining Path of Peru, edited by David Scott Palmer. New York: St. Martin's, 1992.

Drake, C.J.M. "The Role of Ideology in Terrorists' Target Selection." Terrorism and Political Violence 10, no. 2 (2007): 53–85.

Drozdiak, William. "Avowed 'Decapitation' of Basque Group in Doubt as Olympics Near." Washington Post, May 3, 1992.

Eglund, Scott, and Michael Stohl. "Violent Political Movements: Comparing the Shining Path to the Islamic State." Perspectives on Terrorism 10, no. 4 (2016): 21–31.

Erienbusch, Verena. "The Analytical Study of Terrorism: Taking Stock." Journal of Peace Research 51, no. 2 (March 2014): 257–71.

Eubank, William Lee, and Leonard Weinberg. "Does Democracy Encourage Terrorism?" Terrorism and Political Violence 6, no. 4 (1994): 417–35.

Fair, C. Christine. "Drones over Pakistan—Menace or Best Viable Option?" Huffington Post, August 2, 2010.

———. "Militant Recruitment in Pakistan: Implications for Al Qaeda and Other Organizations." Studies in Conflict and Terrorism 27 (2004): 489–504.

Fair, C. Christine, Neil Malhotra, and Jacob N Shapiro. "Islam, Militancy, and Politics in Pakistan: Insights from a National Sample." Terrorism and Political Violence 22 (2010): 495–521.
Fair, C. Christine, and Bryan Shepherd. "Who Supports Terrorism? Evidence from Fourteen Muslim Countries." Studies in Conflict and Terrorism 29 (2006): 51–74.
Feldman, Martha S., and Brian T. Pentland. "Reconceptualizing Routines as a Source of Flexibility and Change." Administrative Science Quarterly 48, no. 1 (2003): 94–118.
Fiol, C. Marlene, and Marjorie A. Lyles. "Organizational Learning." Academy of Management Review 10, no. 4 (1985): 803–13.
Fishman, Brian. "Using the Mistakes of Al Qaeda's Franchises to Undermine Its Strategies." Annals of the American Academy of Political and Social Science 618 (July 2008): 46–54.
Fishman, Brian, Jacob Shapiro, Joseph Felter, Peter Bergen, and Vahid Brown. Bombers, Bank Accounts, and Bleedout: Al-Qa'ida's Road in and out of Iraq. West Point, NY: Combating Terrorism Center, 2008. https://ctc.usma.edu/bombers-bank-accounts-and-bleedout-al-qaidas-road-in-and-out-of-iraq/.
Flanigan, Shawn Teresa. "Nonprofit Service Provision by Insurgent Organizations: The Cases of Hizballah and the Tamil Tigers." Studies in Conflict and Terrorism 31, no. 6 (2008): 499–519.
Flanigan, Shawn Teresa, Victor Asal, and Mitchell Brown. "Community Service Provision by Political Associations Representing Minorities in the Middle East and North Africa." VOLUNTAS: International Journal of Voluntary and Nonprofit Organizations 26, no. 5 (2015): 1786–804.
Forest, James J. F., Jarret Brachman, and Joseph Felter. Harmony and Disharmony: Exploiting Al-Qa'ida's Organizational Vulnerabilities. West Point, NY: Combating Terrorism Center, 2006.
Freeman, John, Glenn R. Carroll, and Michael T. Hannan. "The Liability of Newness: Age Dependence in Organizational Death Rates." American Sociological Review 48, no. 5 (October 1983): 692–710.
Freeman, Linton C. "Centrality in Social Networks: Conceptual Clarification." Social Networks 1, no. 3 (1979).
Freeman, Michael. "A Theory of Terrorist Leadership (and Its Consequences for Leadership Targeting)." Terrorism and Political Violence 26, no. 4 (2014).
Freeman, Michael, and Gordon McCormick. "Leadership Targeting of Terrorist Groups: A Strategic Assessment," 2007.
Galanter, Marc. Cults: Faith, Healing, and Coercion. New York: Oxford University Press, 1999.
Garamone, Jim. "Dunford Lists Ways to Measure Counter-ISIL Success." DoD News, Defense Media Activity, July 25, 2016.
Gerges, Fawaz A. ISIS: A History. Princeton, NJ: Princeton University Press, 2016.
Goepner, Erik W. "Measuring the Effectiveness of America's War on Terror." Parameters 46, no. 1 (Spring 2016): 107–20.
Goodwin, Jeff. No Other Way Out: States and Revolutionary Movements, 1945–1991. Cambridge: Cambridge University Press, 2001.
Gorriti, Gustavo. The Shining Path: A History of the Millenarian War in Peru. Chapel Hill: University of North Carolina Press, 1999.
Greenberg, Joel. "Peres and Arafat, After Talks, Agree to Revive Peace Efforts." New York Times, April 19, 1996.

Gulati, Ranjay, Phanish Puranam, and Michael Tushman. "Meta-Organization Design: Rethinking Design in Interorganizational and Community Contexts." Strategic Management Journal 3, no. 6 (2012): 571–86.

Gunaratna, Rohan. Inside Al Qaeda: Global Network of Terror. New York: Columbia University Press, 2002.

Gurr, Ted Robert. "Terrorism in Democracies: Its Social and Political Bases." In Origins of Terrorism: Psychologies, Ideologies, Theologies, States of Mind, edited by Walter Reich, 86–102. Washington, DC: Woodrow Wilson Center Press, 1990.

al-Habib, Maria. "For ISIS, Losing Territory Means Losing Revenue." Wall Street Journal, October 18, 2017.

Hafez, Mohammed M., and Joseph M. Hatfield. "Do Targeted Assassinations Work? A Multivariate Analysis of Israel's Controversial Tactic During Al-Aqsa Uprising." Studies in Conflict and Terrorism 29 (2006): 359–82.

Hafner-Burton, Emilie M., Miles Kahler, and Alexander M. Montgomery. "Network Analysis for International Relations." International Organizations 63, no. 3 (2009): 559–92.

Hager, Mark A., Joseph Galaskiewicz, Wolfgang Bielfeld, and Joel Pins. "Tales from the Grave: Organizations' Accounts of Their Own Demise." American Behavioral Scientist 39 (August 1996): 975–94.

Hager, Mark A., Joseph Galaskiewicz, and Jeff A. Larson. "Structural Embeddedness and the Liability of Newness among Nonprofit Organizations." Public Management Review 6, no. 2 (2004): 159–88.

Hannan, Michael T., and John Freeman. "The Population Ecology of Organizations." American Journal of Sociology 82, no. 5 (1977): 929–64.

———. "Structural Inertia and Organizational Change." American Sociological Review 49, no. 2 (April 1984): 149–64.

Harris, Paul. "Drone Attacks Create Terrorist Safe Havens, Warns Former CIA Official." The Guardian, June 5, 2012.

Hashim, Ahmed S. "The Islamic State: From al-Qaeda Affiliate to Caliphate." Middle East Policy Council 21, no. 4 (2015).

Hassan, Hassan. "ISIS Is Ready for a Resurgence." The Atlantic, August 26, 2018. https://www.theatlantic.com/international/archive/2018/08/baghdadi-recording-iraq-syria-terrorism/568471/.

Hayes, Stephen F., and Thomas Joscelyn. "How America Was Misled on Al Qaeda's Demise." Wall Street Journal, March 5, 2015. https://www-wsj-com.prx.library.gatech.edu/articles/stephen-hayes-and-tomas-joscelyn-how-america-was-misled-on-al-qaedas-demise-1425600796.

Hegghammer, Thomas. "The Rise of Muslim Foreign Fighters: Islam and the Globalization of Jihad." International Security 35, no. 3 (Winter 2011): 53–94.

Hoffman, Bruce. "Challenges for the U.S. Special Operations Command (SOCOM) Posed by the Global Terrorist Threat: Al Qaeda on the Run or on the March." Testimony submitted to the House Armed Services Subcommittee on Terrorism, Unconventional Threats and Capabilities, 2007. https://www.govinfo.gov/content/pkg/CHRG-110hhrg37980/html/CHRG-110hhrg37980.htm.

———. "Combating Al Qaeda and the Militant Islamic Threat." Testimony submitted to the House Armed Services Subcommittee on Terrorism, Unconventional Threats, and Capabilities, U.S. Congress, 2006. https://www.rand.org/content/dam/rand/pubs/testimonies/2006/RAND_CT255.pdf.

———. "Holy Terror: The Implications of Terrorism Motivated by a Religious Imperative." Studies in Conflict and Terrorism 18, no. 4 (1995): 271–84.

———. Inside Terrorism. London: Victor Gollancz, 2006.

———. "The Myth of Grass-Roots Terrorism: Why Osama Bin Laden Still Matters." Foreign Affairs (May/June 2008).

Hoffman, Bruce, and Marc Sageman. "Does Osama Still Call the Shots? Debating the Containment of Al Qaeda's Leadership." Foreign Affairs (July/August 2008).

Honig, Or. "Explaining Israel's Misuse of Strategic Assassinations." Studies in Conflict and Terrorism 30 (2007): 563–77.

Horgan, John. "From Profiles to Pathways and Roots to Routes: Perspectives from Psychology on Radicalization into Terrorism." Annals of the American Academy of Political and Social Science 618, no. 1 (2008): 80–94.

Horgan, John, and Max Taylor. "Disengagement, De-Radicalization and the Arc of Terrorism: Future Directions for Future Research." In Jihadi Terrorism and the Radicalisation Challenge, edited by Rik Coolsaet, 173–86. Farnham, UK: Ashgate, 2011.

Hosmer, Stephen T. Operations against Enemy Leaders. Santa Monica, CA: RAND, 2001.

Hroub, Khaled. "Hamas after Shaykh Yasin and Rantisi." Journal of Palestine Studies 33, no. 4 (Summer 2004).

———. Hamas: Political Thought and Practice. Washington DC: Institute for Palestine Studies, 2000.

Hudson, David. "President Obama: We Will Degrade and Ultimately Destroy ISIL." September 10, 2014. https://obamawhitehouse.archives.gov/blog/2014/09/10/president-obama-we-will-degrade-and-ultimately-destroy-isil.

Iannaccone, Laurence R., and Eli Berman. "Religious Extremism: The Good, the Bad, and the Deadly." Public Choice 128 (2006): 109–29.

Ibrahim, Youssef M. "Arafat's Forces Push Crackdown on Gaza Radicals." New York Times, July 10, 1995.

Ingram, Haroro J. The Charismatic Leadership Phenomenon in Radical and Militant Islamism. Farnham, UK: Ashgate, 2013.

Isbell, Billie Jean. "Shining Path and Peasant Responses in Rural Ayacucho." In The Shining Path of Peru, edited by David Scott Palmer. New York: St. Martin's, 1992.

al-Jabouri, Najim Abed, and Sterling Jensen. "The Iraqi and AQI Roles in the Sunni Awakening." Prism 2, no. 1 (2010): 3–18.

Jackson, Brian A. Aptitude for Destruction: Organizational Learning in Terrorist Groups and Its Implications for Combating Terrorism. Santa Monica, CA: RAND, 2005.

Johnston, Patrick. "Does Decapitation Work? Assessing the Effectiveness of Leadership Targeting in Counterinsurgency Campaigns." International Security 34, no. 6 (Spring 2012).

Johnston, Patrick B., and Anoop Sarbahi. "The Impact of U.S. Drone Strikes on Terrorism in Pakistan." Belfer Center for Science and International Affairs, John F. Kennedy School of Government, Harvard University, 2011.

Joint Chiefs of Staff DOD. Department of Defense Dictionary of Military and Associated Terms. Washington, DC: DOD, 2008.

Jones, Seth, James Dobbins, Daniel Byman, Christopher S. Chivvis, Ben Connable, Jeffrey Martini, Eric Robinson, and Nathan Chandler. Rolling Back the Islamic State. Santa Monica, CA: RAND, 2017.

Jones, Seth G, and Martin C. Libicki. How Terrorist Groups End: Lessons for Countering Al-Qa'ida. Santa Monica, CA: RAND, 2008.

Jordan, Jenna. "Attacking the Leader, Missing the Mark: Why Terrorist Groups Survive Decapitation Strikes." International Security 38, no. 4 (Spring 2014): 7–38.

———. "Data on Leadership Targeting and Potential Impacts for Communal Support." In Legitimacy and Drones: Investigating the Legality, Morality and Efficacy of UCAVs, edited by Steven Barela, 217–42. Farnham, UK: Routledge, 2016.

———. "Review of 'Does Decapitation Work? Assessing the Effectiveness of Leadership Targeting in Counterinsurgency Campaigns,' and 'Targeting Top Terrorists: How Leadership Decapitation Contributes to Counterterrorism.'" H-Diplo | ISSF (October 24, 2012).

———. "When Heads Roll: Assessing the Effectiveness of Leadership Decapitation." Security Studies 18, no. 4 (October 2009): 719–55.

Jordan, Jenna, Margaret E. Kosal, and Lawrence Rubin. "The Strategic Illogic of Counterterrorism Policy." Washington Quarterly 39, no. 4 (2016): 181–92.

Jordan, Jenna, and Lawrence Rubin, "An ISIS Containment Doctrine." The National Interest. June 14, 2016.

Kahler, Miles. "Collective Action and Clandestine Networks." In Networked Politics: Agency, Power, and Governance, edited by Miles Kahler. Ithaca, NY: Cornell University Press, 2009.

Kaplan, Edward H., Alex Mintz, and Shaul Mishal. "Tactical Prevention of Suicide Bombing in Israel." Interfaces 36, no. 6 (2006): 553–61.

Kay, Bruce H. "The Rise and Fall of 'King Coca' and Shining Path." Journal of Interamerican Studies and World Affairs 41, no. 3 (Autumn 1999).

Kenney, Michael. From Pablo to Osama: Trafficking and Terrorist Networks, Government Bureaucracies, and Competitive Adaptation. University Park: Pennsylvania State University Press, 2007.

Kenny, Paul. "Structural Integrity and Cohesion in Insurgent Organizations: Evidence from Protracted Conflicts in Ireland and Burma." International Studies Review 12, no. 4 (December 2010): 533–55.

Keohane, Robert O. "The Demand for International Regimes." International Organization 36, no. 2 (Spring 1982): 325–55.

Kifner, John. "Death on the Campus: The Bombers; Hamas Says It Regrets American Toll in Attack, but Hails Bombing as Success." New York Times, August 2, 2002.

Kilcullen, David, and Andrew McDonald Exum. "Death from Above, Outrage Down Below." New York Times, May 16, 2009.

King, Laura, Nabih Bulos, and W. J. Hennigan. "Why Islamic State's Abu Muhammad Adnani Was Much More Than a Spokesman." Los Angeles Times, August 30, 2016.

Kirdar, M. J. Al Qaeda in Iraq. Washington, DC: CSIS, 2011.

Knoke, David. Political Networks: The Structural Perspective, Structural Analysis in the Social Sciences. Cambridge: Cambridge University Press, 1990.

Knoke, David, and Song Yang. Social Network Analysis. Thousand Oaks, CA: SAGE, 2007.

Krause, Peter. "The Political Effectiveness of Non-State Violence: A Two-Level Framework to Transform a Deceptive Debate." Security Studies 22, no. 2 (2013): 259–94.

Kristof, Nicholas. "Behind the Terrorists." New York Times, May 7, 2002. https://www.nytimes.com/2002/05/07/opinion/behind-the-terrorists.html.

Krueger, Alan B., and Jitka Maleckova. "Education, Poverty, and Terrorism: Is There a Causal Connection?" Journal of Economic Perspectives 14, no. 4 (2003): 119–44.

Kulish, Nicholas, Christopher Drew, and Sean D. Naylor. "Another Ex-Commando Says He Shot bin Laden." New York Times, November 6, 2014.

Kull, Steven, Clay Ramsay, Stephen Weber, Evan Lewis, and Ebrahim Mohseni. "Public Opinion in the Islamic World on Terrorism, Al Qaeda, and US Policies." WorldPublicOpinion.org, 2009. http://worldpublicopinion.net/wp-content/uploads/2017/12/STARTII_Feb09_rpt.pdf.

Kydd, Andrew, and Barbara Walter. "The Strategies of Terrorism." International Security 31, no. 1 (Summer 2006): 49–80.

Langdon, Lisa, Alexander J. Sarapu, and Matthew Wells. "Targeting the Leadership of Terrorist and Insurgent Movements: Historical Lessons for Contemporary Policy Makers." Journal of Public and International Affairs 15 (Spring 2004): 59–78.

Laqueur, Walter. The Age of Terrorism. Boston: Little Brown, 1987.

Leger, Kathryn. "Surviving Amid Peru's Guerilla War. Peasants Seek to Rebuild Lives in War-Torn Villages." Christian Science Monitor, November 28, 1986.

Leheny, David. "Terrorism, Social Movements, and International Security: How Al Qaeda Affects Southeast Asia." Japanese Journal of Political Science 6, no. 1 (2005): 87–109.

Levitt, Barbara, and James G. March. "Organizational Learning." American Review of Sociology 14 (1988): 319–40.

Levitt, Matthew. Hamas: Politics, Charity, and Terrorism in the Service of Jihad. New Haven, CT: Yale University Press, 2006.

Li, Quan. "Does Democracy Promote or Reduce Transnational Terrorist Incidents?" Journal of Conflict Resolution 49, no. 2 (2005): 278–97.

Lia, Brynjar. "Jihadism in the Arab World after 2011: Explaining Its Expansion." Middle East Policy 23, no. 4 (2016).

Lindelauf, Roy, Peter Borm, and Herbert Hamers. "Understanding Terrorist Network Typologies and Their Resilience against Disruption." Discussion Paper 2009-85, Tilburg University, Center for Economic Research, 2009. https://pure.uvt.nl/ws/portalfiles/portal/1133313/2009-85.pdf.

Long, Austin. "The Anbar Awakening." Survival 50, no. 2 (2008).

Luft, Gal. "The Logic of Israel's Targeted Killing." Middle East Quarterly 10, no. 1 (Winter 2003).

Mannes, Aaron. "Testing the Snake Head Strategy: Does Killing or Capturing Its Leaders Reduce a Terrorist Group's Activity?" Journal of International Policy Solutions 9 (Spring 2008).

Mansfield, Roger. "Bureaucracy and Centralization: An Examination of Organizational Structure." Administrative Science Quarterly 18, no. 4 (December 1973): 477–88.

Manwaring, Max G. "Peru's Sendero Luminoso: The Shining Path Beckons." Annals of the American Academy of Political Science 541 (September 1995).

———. Shadows of Things Past and Images of the Future: Lessons for the Insurgencies in Our Midst. Strategic Studies Institute, 2004. https://ssi.armywarcollege.edu/pubs/display.cfm?pubID=587.

Maoz, Zeev. Networks of Nations: The Evolution, Structure, and Impact of International Networks, 1816–2001. Cambridge: Cambridge University Press, 2011.

March, Andrew F., and Mara Revkin. "Caliphate of Law: ISIS' Ground Rules." Foreign Affairs (April 15, 2015).

March, James G., and Herbert Simon. Organizations. Cambridge: Blackwell, 1993.

Mardsen, Peter V. "Egocentric and Sociocentric Measures of Network Centrality." Social Networks 24, no. 4 (2002): 407.

Marks, Tom. "Making Revolution with Shining Path." In The Shining Path of Peru, edited by David Scott Palmer. New York: St. Martin's, 1992.

Marshall, Monty G. and Keith Jaggers. Polity IV Project: Political Regime Characteristics and Transitions, 1800–2006: Dataset Users' Manual. 2006. Distributed by the University of Maryland. http://www.systemicpeace.org/inscr/p4manualv2017.pdf.

Master, Cyra. "FBI Investigator Warns: 'We're Not Done with the Bin Ladens Yet.'" The Hill, May 14, 2017.

Mauceri, Philip. "Military Politics and Counter-Insurgency in Peru." Journal of Interamerican Studies and World Affairs 33, no. 4 (Winter 1991): 83–109.

Mayer, Jean-François. "Cults, Violence, and Religious Terrorism: An International Perspective." Studies in Conflict and Terrorism 24 (2001).

Mazzetti, Mark. "C.I.A. Drone Is Said to Kill Al Qaeda's No. 2." New York Times, August 27, 2011.

Mazzetti, Mark, Eric Schmitt, and Robert F. Worth. "Two-Year Manhunt Led to Killing of Awlaki in Yemen." New York Times, September 30, 2011.

McAdam, Doug. Political Process and the Development of Black Insurgency, 1930–1970. Chicago: University of Chicago Press, 1982.

McCants, William. The ISIS Apocalypse: The History, Strategy, and Doomsday Vision of the Islamic State. New York: St. Martin's, 2015.

McCarthy, John D., and Mayer N. Zald. "Resource Mobilization and Social Movements: A Partial Theory." American Journal of Sociology 82, no. 6 (1973): 1212–41.

———. "Social Movement Organizations." In The Social Movements Reader: Cases and Concepts, edited by Jeff Goodwin and James Jasper, 159–74. Chichester, UK: Wiley-Blackwell, 2009.

McClintock, Cynthia. Revolutionary Movements in Latin America: El Salvador's FMLN and Peru's Shining Path. Washington, DC: United States Institute of Peace Press, 1998.

———. "Why Peasants Rebel: The Case of Peru's Sendero Luminoso." World Politics 37, no. 1 (1984).

McConnell, Dugald, and Brian Todd. "Latest Al Qaeda Propaganda Highlights Bin Laden's Son." CNN, May 15, 2017.

McCormick, Gordon. The Shining Path and the Future of Peru. Santa Monica, CA: RAND, 1990.

McDonald, Mark. "Tamil Tigers Confirm Death of Their Leader." New York Times, May 25, 2009.

McDonald, Mark, and Alan Cowell. "Sri Lanka Says Leader of Rebels Has Died." New York Times, May 18, 2009.

Meierrikes, Daniel, and Thomas Gries. "Causality between Terrorism and Economic Growth." Journal of Peace Research 50, no. 1 (2013): 91–104.

Mendelsohn, Barak. The Al-Qaeda Franchise: The Expansion of Al Qaeda and Its Consequences. New York: Oxford University Press, 2016.

Metz, Steven. "Rethinking Insurgency." In The Routledge Handbook of Insurgency and Counterinsurgency, edited by Paul B. Rich and Isabelle Duyvestey. London: Routledge, 2012.

Meyer, Alan D. "Adapting to Environmental Jolts." Administrative Science Quarterly 27, no. 4 (1982): 515–37.

Miguel, Edward, Shanker Satyanath, and Ernest Sergenti. "Economic Shocks and Civil Conflict: An Instrumental Variables Approach." Journal of Political Economy 112 (2004): 725–53.

Miller, Greg. "Al-Qaeda Confirms Osama Bin Laden's Death, Vows Retaliation." Washington Post, May 6, 2011.

Mishal, Shaul. "The Pragmatic Dimension of the Palestinian Hamas: A Network Perspective." Armed Forces and Society 29, no. 4 (Summer 2003): 569–89.

Mishal, Shaul, and Avraham Sela. The Palestinian Hamas: Vision, Violence, and Coexistence. New York: Columbia University Press, 2000.

Moghadam, Assaf, Ronit Berger, and Polina Beliakova. "Say Terrorist, Think Insurgent: Labeling and Analyzing Contemporary Terrorist Actors." Perspectives on Terrorism 8, no. 5 (2014).

Nash, Nathanial C. "Peru Rebels to Remain Potent." New York Times, September 15, 1992, 1.

National Security Council. "National Strategy for Combating Terrorism." 2006. https://www.hsdl.org/?view&did=466588.

Nelson, Geoffrey. Cults, New Religions and Religious Creativity. London: Routledge and Kegan Paul, 1987.

New York Times, "Peruvian Army Kills 39 Rebels in Skirmishes." October 26, 1986.

Nordland, Rod, and Zabihullah Ghazi. "ISIS Leader in Afghanistan Is Killed in U.S. Airstrike." New York Times, April 9, 2018.

Nordland, Rod, and Alissa J. Rubin. "Sunni Fighters Say Iraq Didn't Keep Job Promises." New York Times, March 23, 2009.

Nusse, Andrea. Muslim Palestine: The Ideology of Hamas. Amsterdam: Harwood Academic, 1998.

Obama, Barack. "Remarks by the President on the Way Forward in Afghanistan." June 22, 2011. https://obamawhitehouse.archives.gov/the-press-office/2011/06/22/remarks-president-way-forward-Afghanistan.

———. "Remarks by President Obama in Address to the Nation from Afghanistan." May 1, 2012. https://obamawhitehouse.archives.gov/the-press-office/2012/05/01/remarks-president-obama-address-nation-afghanistan.

Oberschall, Anthony. Social Conflict and Social Movements. Englewood Cliffs, NJ: Prentice-Hall, 1973.

Olson, Mancur. The Logic of Collective Action: Public Goods and the Theory of Groups. Cambridge, MA: Harvard University Press, 1965.

Oots, Kent L. "Bargaining with Terrorists: Organizational Considerations." Terrorism 13, no. 2 (1990): 145–58.

———. "Organizational Perspectives on the Formation and Disintegration of Terrorist Groups." Terrorism 12, no. 3 (1989): 139–52.

Owen, Mark, and Kevin Maurer. No Easy Day: The Autobiography of a Navy Seal: The Firsthand Account of the Mission That Killed Osama Bin Laden. New York: Dutton Books, 2012.

Palmer, David Scott. "Rebellion in Rural Peru: The Origins and Evolution of Sendero Luminoso." Comparative Political Studies 18, no. 2 (1986): 127–46.

———. "The Revolutionary Terrorism of Peru's Shining Path." In Terrorism in Context, edited by Martha Crenshaw. University Park: Pennsylvania State University Press, 1995.

———, ed. The Shining Path of Peru. New York: St. Martin's, 1992.

Pape, Robert A. Bombing to Win. Ithaca, NY: Cornell University Press, 1996.

———. Dying to Win: The Strategic Logic of Suicide Terrorism. New York: Random House, 2005.

———. "The Strategic Logic of Suicide Terrorism." American Political Science Review 97, no. 3 (2003): 343–61.

———. "Wars Can't Be Won Only from Above." New York Times, March 21, 2003.
Pape, Robert A., and James K. Feldman. Cutting the Fuse: The Explosion of Global Suicide Terrorism and How to Stop It. Chicago: University of Chicago Press, 2010.
Pedahzur, Ami. The Israeli Secret Services and the Struggle against Terrorism. New York: Columbia University Press, 2009.
Pedahzur, Ami, and Arie Perlinger. "The Changing Nature of Suicide Attacks: A Social Network
Perspective." Social Forces 84, no. 4 (June 2006).
Perrow, Charles. Complex Organizations: A Critical Essay. New York: Mc Graw Hill, 1986.
Petersen, Roger D. Resistance and Rebellion. Cambridge: Cambridge University Press, 2001.
Phillips, Macon. "Osama Bin Laden Dead." May 2, 2011. https://obamawhitehouse.archives.gov/blog/2011/05/02/osama-bin-laden-dead.
Piazza, James A. "Draining the Swamp: Democracy Promotion, State Failure, and Terrorism in 19 Middle Eastern Countries." Security Studies 30 (2007): 512–39.
———. "Incubators of Terror: Do Failed and Failing States Promote Transnational Terrorism?" International Studies Quarterly 52 (2008): 469–88.
———. "Is Islamist Terrorism More Dangerous? An Empirical Study of Group Ideology, Organization, and Goal Structure." Terrorism and Political Violence 21, no. 1 (January 2009): 62–88.
———. "Poverty Is a Weak Causal Link." In Debating Terrorism and Counterterrorism: Conflicting Perspectives on Causes, Contexts, and Responses, edited by Stuart Gottlieb. Thousand Oaks, CA: CQ Press, 2013.
———. "Rooted in Poverty? Terrorism, Poor Economic Development, and Social Cleavages." Terrorism and Political Violence 18 (2006): 159–77.
Plaw, Avery. Targeting Terrorists. Aldershot, UK: Ashgate, 2008.
Pollock, David. "ISIS Has Almost No Popular Support in Egypt, Saudi Arabia, or Lebanon." Washington, DC: Washington Institute, 2014. https://www.washingtoninstitute.org/policy-analysis/view/isis-has-almost-no-popular-support-in-egypt-saudi-arabia-or-lebanon.
Post, Gerald. Leaders and Their Followers in a Dangerous World. Ithaca, NY: Cornell University Press, 2004.
Post, Gerald M., Keven G. Ruby, and Eric D. Shaw. "The Radical Group in Context: 1. An Integrated Framework for the Analysis of Group Risk for Terrorism." Studies in Conflict and Terrorism 25 (2002): 73–100.
———. "The Radical Group in Context: 2. Identification of Critical Elements in the Analysis of Risk for Terrorism by Radical Group Type." Studies in Conflict and Terrorism 25 (2002): 101–26.
Poushter, Jacob. "In Nations with Significant Muslim Populations, Much Disdain for ISIS." Pew Research Center, November 17, 2015. https://www.pewresearch.org/fact-tank/2015/11/17/in-nations-with-significant-muslim-populations-much-disdain-for-isis/.
Price, Bryan. "Targeting Top Terrorists: How Leadership Decapitation Contributes to Counterterrorism." International Security 34, no. 6 (Spring 2012).
———. Targeting Top Terrorists. New York: Columbia University Press, 2018.
Ranger-Moore, James. "Bigger May Be Better, but Older Is Wiser? Organizational Age and Size in the New York Life Insurance Industry." American Sociological Review 62, no. 6 (December 1992): 903–20.

Rapoport, David C. "Fear and Trembling: Terrorism in Three Religious Traditions." American Political Science Review 78, no. 3 (September 1984): 658–77.

Rashid, Ahmed. Taliban: Militant Islam, Oil and Fundamentalism in Central Asia. New Haven, CT: Yale University Press, 2000.

House Homeland Security Committee Majority Staff. Terror Gone Viral: Overview of the 243 ISIS-Linked Incidents Targeting the West. 2018. https://www.hsdl.org/?abstract&did=817196.

Revkin, Mara. "What Explains Taxation by Resource-Rich Rebels? Evidence from the Islamic State in Syria." Journal of Politics, forthcoming.

Riding, Alan. "Peruvian Guerrillas Emerge as an Urban Political Force." New York Times, July 17, 1989.

Riedel, Bruce. The Search for Al Qaeda: Its Leadership, Ideology, and Future. Washington, DC: Brookings Institution, 2008.

Ron, James. "Ideology in Context: Explaining Sendero Luminoso's Tactical Escalation." Journal of Peace Research 38, no. 5 (September 2001): 569–92.

Ross, Jeffrey Ian. "Structural Causes of Oppositional Political Terrorism: Towards a Causal Model." Journal of Peace Research 30, no. 3 (1993): 317–29.

Roy, Sara. Hamas and Civil Society in Gaza: Engaging the Islamist Social Sector. Princeton, NJ: Princeton University Press, 2011.

———. "Hamas and the Transformation(s) of Political Islam in Palestine." Current History 102, no. 660 (January 2003): 13–21.

Rudolf, Lloyd I., and Susan Hoeber Rudolf. "Authority and Power in Bureaucratic and Patrimonial Administration: A Revisionist Interpretation of Weber on Bureaucracy." World Politics 31, no. 2 (January 1979): 195–227.

Sageman, Marc. Leaderless Jihad: Terror Networks in the Twenty-First Century. Philadelphia: University of Pennsylvania Press, 2008.

———. Understanding Terror Networks. Philadelphia: University of Pennsylvania Press, 2004.

Sanchez, Alejandro W. "The Rebirth of Insurgency in Peru." Small Wars and Insurgencies 14, no. 3 (Autumn 2003): 185–98.

Schmid, Alex P. "Public Opinion Survey Data to Measure Sympathy and Support for Islamist Terrorism: A Look at Muslim Opinions on Al Qaeda and IS." International Centre for Counter-Terrorism 8, no. 2 (2017).

———. "Terrorism and Democracy." Terrorism and Political Violence 4, no. 4 (1992): 14–25.

Schmid, Alex P., and Albert J. Jongman. Political Terrorism: A Guide to New Actors, Authors, Concepts, Databases, Theories and Literature. Amsterdam: North-Holland, 1988.

Schmidle, Nicholas. "Getting Bin Laden." New Yorker, August 8, 2011.

Schultz, Richard. "Conceptualizing Political Terrorism: A Typology." Journal of International Affairs 32 (1978): 7–15.

Seitz, Charmaine. "Armed Resistance During the Peace Process and Its Demise." Jerusalem Media and Communications Centre, December 2011.

Shapiro, Jacob N. "Bureaucracy and Control in Terrorist Organizations." Princeton University, 2008. https://www.semanticscholar.org/paper/Bureaucracy-and-Control-in-Terrorist-Organizations-Shapiro/7065507efdf4def81114bf8193a6483113f447eb.

———. "Bureaucratic Terrorists: Al-Qa'ida in Iraq's Management and Finances." In Bombers, Bank Accounts, and Bleedout: Al-Qa'ida's Road in and out of Iraq, edited by Brian

Fishman. West Point, NY: Combating Terrorism Center, 2008. https://ctc.usma.edu/bombers-bank-accounts-and-bleedout-al-qaidas-road-in-and-out-of-iraq/.

———. The Terrorist's Dilemma: Managing Violent Covert Organizations. Princeton, NJ: Princeton University Press, 2013.

Shapiro, Jacob N, and C. Christine Fair. "Understanding Support for Islamist Militancy in Pakistan." International Security 34, no. 3 (2009/2010): 79–188.

Shapiro, Jacob N., and David A. Siegel. "Moral Hazard, Discipline, and the Management of Terrorist Organizations." World Politics 64, no. 1 (2009): 39–78.

Siggelkow, Nicolaj, and Daniel A. Levinthal. "Temporarily Divide to Conquer: Centralized, Decentralized, and Reintegrated Organizational Approaches to Exploration and Adaptation." Organization Science 14, no. 6 (November–December 2003).

Simcox, Robin. "The Perils of Forgetting About Al Qaeda." War on the Rocks, November 9, 2016.

Singh, Jitendra V., David J. Tucker, and Robert J. House. "Organizational Legitimacy and the Liability of Newness." Administrative Science Quarterly 31, no. 2 (June 1986): 171–93.

Siqueira, Kevin. "Political and Militant Wings within Dissident Movements and Organizations." Journal of Conflict Resolution 49, no. 2 (2005).

Smelser, Neil J. The Faces of Terrorism: Social and Psychological Dimensions. Princeton, NJ: Princeton University Press, 2007.

Smith, Megan, and James Igoe Walsh. "Do Drone Strikes Degrade Al Qaeda? Evidence from Propaganda Output." Terrorism and Political Violence 25 (2013): 311–27.

Smith, Michael L. "Taking the High Ground: Shining Path and the Andes." In The Shining Path of Peru, edited by David Scott Palmer. New York: St. Martin's, 1992.

Soufan Group. Foreign Fighters: An Updated Assessment of the Flow of Foreign Fighters into Syria and Iraq. 2015. http://soufangroup.com/wp-content/uploads/2015/12/TSG_ForeignFightersUpdate3.pdf.

Staniland, Paul. Networks of Rebellion: Explaining Insurgent Cohesion and Collapse. Ithaca, NY: Cornell University Press, 2014.

START (National Consortium for the Study of Terrorism and Responses to Terrorism). "Global Terrorism Database." 2015.

Stein, Yael. "By Any Name Illegal and Immoral." Ethics and International Affairs 17, no. 1 (2003).

Stern, Jessica, and J. M. Bereger. ISIS: The State of Terror. New York: Harper Collins, 2015.

Stinchcombe, Arthur. "Organizations and Social Structure." In Handbook of Organizations, edited by J. G. March, 142–93. Chicago: Rand McNally, 1965.

Stohl, Cynthia, and Michael Stohl. "Networks of Terror: Theoretical Assumptions and Pragmatic Consequences." Communication Theory 17, no. 2 (May 2007).

Sydney Morning Herald. "Suspected Shining Path Leader Held." March 5, 1990.

Tamimi, Azzam. Hamas: A History from Within. Northampton, MA: Olive Branch, 2007.

Tarazona-Sevillano, Gabriela. "The Organization of Shining Path." In The Shining Path of Peru, edited by David Scott Palmer. New York: St. Martin's, 1992.

Taylor, Lewis. Shining Path: Guerilla War in Peru's Northern Highlands, 1980–1997. Liverpool: Liverpool University Press, 2006.

Thomas, Ward. The Ethics of Destruction. Ithaca, NY: Cornell University Press, 2001.

Thompson, James D. Organizations in Action: Social Sciences Bases of Administrative Theory. New Brunswick, NJ: Transaction, 2007.

Tominaga, Yasutaka. "Killing Two Birds with One Stone? Examining the Diffusion Effect of Militant Leadership Decapitation." International Studies Quarterly 62, no. 1 (March 2018): 54–68.

Uhl-Bien, Mary, and Russ Marion. "Complexity Leadership in Bureaucratic Forms of Organizing: A Meso Model." Leadership Quarterly 20 (2009): 631–50.

US Department of Justice and Federal Bureau of Investigation. Terrorism: 2002–2005. 2007. https://www.fbi.gov/file-repository/stats-services-publications-terrorism-2002-2005-terror02_05.pdf.

US Department of State. Patterns of Global Terrorism. 2004. http://www.state.gov/j/ct/rls/crt/2003/c12153.htm.

US Department of State. Office of the Coordinator for Counterterrorism. 2001 Report on Foreign Terrorist Organizations. 2001. https://20012009.state.gov/s/ct/rls/rpt/fto/2001/5258.htm.

Walsh, Declan, and Eric Schmitt. "Drone Strike Killed No. 2 in Al Qaeda, U.S. Officials Say." New York Times, June 5, 2012.

Walsh, James Igoe and Marcus Schulzke. Drones and Support for the Use of Force. Ann Arbor, MI: University of Michigan Press, 2018.

Warden, John A., III. "Employing Air Power in the Twenty-First Century." In The Future of Air Power in the Aftermath of the Gulf War, edited by Richard Shultz Jr. and Robert Pfaltzgraff Jr., 57–82. Maxwell Air Force Base, AL: Air University Press, 1992.

Wardlaw, Grant. Political Terrorism: Theory, Tactics, and Counter-Measures. Cambridge: Cambridge University Press, 1989.

Warrick, John, and Souad Mekhennet. "New Clues Bolster Belief That ISIS Leader Is Still Alive—and Busy with a Chilling New Mission." Washington Post, May 19, 2018.

Wasserman, Stanley, and Katherine Faust. Social Network Analysis: Methods and Applications. Cambridge: Cambridge University Press, 1994.

Weber, Max. From Max Weber: Essays in Sociology. Translated by H. H. Gerth and C. Wright Mills. New York: Oxford University Press, 1946.

———. Max Weber on Charisma and Institution Building. Edited by S. N. Eisenstadt. Chicago: University of Chicago Press, 1968.

———. The Theory of Economic and Social Organization. New York: Free Press, 1964.

———. The Theory of Social and Economic Organization. Translated by Talcott Parsons. New York: Free Press, 1947.

Weinberg, Leonard, Ami Pedahzur, and Sivan Hirsch-Hoeffler. "The Challenges of Conceptualizing Terrorism." Terrorism and Political Violence 16, no. 4 (2004).

Weinstein, Jeremy M. Inside Rebellion: The Politics of Insurgent Rebellion. Cambridge: Cambridge University Press, 2007.

Whittaker, David, ed. The Terrorism Reader. London: Routledge, 2001.

Wilkinson, Paul. Political Terrorism. London: Macmillan, 1974.

Williams, Brian Glyn. Predators: The CIA's Drone War on Al Qaeda. Washington, DC: Potomac Books, 2013.

Wilner, Alex S. "Targeted Killings in Afghanistan: Measuring Coercion and Deterrence in Counterterrorism and Counterinsurgency." Studies in Conflict and Terrorism 33, no. 4 (2010): 307–29.

Wilson, Scott. "Peru Fears Reemergence of Violent Rebels." Washington Post, December 10, 2001.

World Public Opinion. "Most Iraqis Want U.S. Troops Out Within a Year." September 27, 2006. http://worldpublicopinion.net/most-iraqis-want-u-s-troops-out-within-a-year/.

Wright, Robin. "After the Islamic State." New Yorker, 2016. https://www.newyorker.com/magazine/2016/12/12/after-the-islamic-state.

Yeginsu, Ceylan. "Turkey Attacks Kurdish Militant Camps in Northern Iraq." New York Times, July 25, 2015.

Zald, Mayer N., and Roberta Ash. "Social Movement Organizations: Growth, Decay, and Change." Social Forces 44, no. 3 (March 1966): 327–41.

Zammuto, Raymond F. Assessing Organizational Effectiveness. Albany: State University of New York Press, 1982.

Zanini, Michele. "Middle Eastern Terrorism and Netwar." Studies in Conflict and Terrorism 22 (1999): 247–56.

Zawodny, J. K. "Infrastructures of Terrorist Organizations." In Perspectives on Terrorism, edited by Lawrence Zelic Freedman and Yonah Alexander. Wilmington, DE: Scholarly Resources, 1983.

Zussman, Asaf, and Noah Zussman. "Assassinations: Evaluating the Effectiveness of an Israeli Counterterrorism Policy Using Stock Market Data." Journal of Economic Perspectives 20, no. 2 (2006): 193–206.

Index

Page numbers followed by f or t indicate material in figures or tables.

Abrahms, Max, 19, 207n94, 211n81
Abu-Amr, Ziad, 97, 105–106, 118
Abu Hanoud, Mahmoud, 104
adaptation of organizational routines, 33–35, 210n67
Afghanistan: al-Qaeda in, 3, 164; bin Laden in, 153–154; drone strikes in, 19; ISIS in, 189–190; Soviet invasion of, 153, 158, 165; Taliban in, 163, 174; US cruise missile strikes in, 173–174; US invasion of, 153–154, 158, 160, 171, 196
age of organizations and resilience, 8, 69–71 (71t), 73 (73t), 82, 90, 163
al-Adnani, Abu Muhammad, 3, 5–6, 44, 187–189, 191–192
al-Awlaki, Anwar, 4
al-Baghdadi, Abu Umar, 4
al-Baghdadi, Abu Bakr, 5, 155–156, 186–188, 190–191, 193
Alberca, Santos, 138
Aleph, 18, 208nn10. *See also* Aum Shinrikyo
al-Fatah, Amal, 2
al-Iraqi, Abu Maysara, 177
al-Joulani, Abu Mouhammed, 155
al-Kuwaiti, 1
al-Libi, Abu Yahya, 4, 204n9
al-Maliki, Nuri, 155, 174, 178, 194
al-Masri, Abu Ayyab, 4–5

al-Qaeda, 11; attacks by, 83, 154; under bin Laden's leadership, 153–154, 165–166; bureaucratic structure of, 175–177; communal support for, 177–178; cruise missile attacks on, 173–174; dataset on, 63; effects of age, size on, 91; expansion of, 165–166; following bin Laden's death, 6, 18–19, 41–42, 158; founding of, 153, 165; franchises, 163–164, 166, 168; ideological goals, 44; literature on, 156–159; a multiethnic movement, 166; organizational structure of, 18, 151–152, 158; rebuilding of, 158; resistance of to decapitation, 158; September 11 attacks, 154; shifting focus from USSR to US, 165; size of, 163–164; as a social movement, 164. *See also* AQAP (al-Qaeda in the Arabian Peninsula); AQC (al-Qaeda Central) and affiliates; AQI (al-Qaeda in Iraq); bin Laden, Osama
al-Qaim, 156
al-Rahman, Atiyah Abd, 4
al-Rantisi, Abdel Aziz, 46, 99, 102–105, 111, 116, 195
al-Shabaab, 67, 83–84, 154, 181, 196, 200f
al-Sharitha, 106
al-Sinwar, Yahya, 105
al-Wuhayshi, Nasir, 4

al-Zarqawi, Abu Musab: bin Laden and, 154, 174–175, 177, 185; brutal tactics of, 175, 177; and Dabiq, 191; effects of death of, 156, 161; founder of JTJ, 154; killing of, 5, 155, 178. *See also* AQI (al-Qaeda in Iraq)

al-Zawahiri, Ayman: advisability of killing, 157; advising AQI, 155–156; counter-terrorism assessment regarding, 204n9; criticizing al-Zarqawi, 154, 175; Hamza bin Laden a potential successor to, 180; as leader of al-Qaeda, 6, 167, 179–180, 185; and Sayid Qutb, 158–159

Amman bombing, 177

Anbar Awakening, 155, 161, 168, 175, 178

Ansar al-Islam, 154

AQAP (al-Qaeda in the Arabian Peninsula), 83–84; after bin Laden's death, 6; al-Wuhaysi killed, 4; attacks by, 160f, 161, 201f; decapitation attacks against, 159f, 162f; formation of, 154, 165; impact of decapitation on, 67, 84

AQC (al-Qaeda Central) and affiliates: after bin Laden death, 185; and al-Zarqawi, 177; attacks by, 160 (160f); Bali, Madrid attacks, 154; bureaucracy of, 167–169; decapitation attempts against, 159 (159f), 161–162 (161f, 162f), 173–174; embassy bombings, 154; ideology of, 165–167; local public opinion regarding, 169–173; organizational resilience of, 163–174; origins of, 153–154; Pakistan as base of operations for, 153–154, 171; relationship with affiliates, 151–154, 168–169, 174; World Trade Center attacks, 153

AQI (al-Qaeda in Iraq), 228n114; and AQC, 154; attacks by, 160–161 (160f, 161f); brutality diminishing support for, 175, 177; bureaucracy of, 175–177; communal support for, 177–178; decline and reemergence of, 155–156, 191–192; drone strikes against, 4; formation and growth of, 154, 156, 175; and ISIS/Islamic State, 152, 154–156, 160, 174; and JN, 156; leadership targeting of, 161; and Mujahedeen Shura Council, 154; organizational resilience of, 163, 174–178; size of, 164. *See also* al-Qaeda; al-Zarqawi, Abu Musab; ISIS; JTJ

AQIM (al-Qaeda in the Maghreb), 160f, 161, 165

Arab Barometer project, 194

Arafat, Yasser, 102, 104, 108

Armed Islamic Group of Algeria (GIA), 10

Arquilla, John, 213n116

Asahara, Shoko, 18, 25, 208n10

Asal, Victor, 59

Ash, Roberta, 39

Assad, Bashar al-, 155

Atran, Scott, 196

attack frequency post-decapitation, 78–85 (79t–81t)

Aum Shinrikyo, 15, 25, 207–208n10, 208n18

authority, types of, 30–31

Ayacucho, 126–129, 133, 140, 145–146. *See also* Sendero Luminoso

Ayyash, Yahya, 46, 96, 108, 195, 214n139

Azzam, Abdullah, 165

BAAD (Big Allied and Dangerous) database, 57, 63–64

Baader-Meinhoff gang, 34, 45, 53–54

Ba'ashir, Abu Bakar, 26

Baath Party, 177, 193–194

Baghdadi, Abu Bakr al-, 5, 155–156, 186–188, 190–191, 193

Barak, Ehud, 108

Barrionuevo, Osmán Morote, 132

beheadings, 154, 175

Belaúnde, Fernando, 127–128

Beliakova, Polina, 10

Bergen, Peter, 18–19, 156, 158–159, 163, 176, 180, 204n9

Berger, Ronit, 10

Berman, Eli, 29, 59

Bhattacharya, Srobana, 43–44

Biddle, Stephen, 155

bin Laden, Hamza, 179–180

bin Laden, Khalid, 1

bin Laden, Osama: al-Qaeda after death of, 6, 18–19, 41–42, 158; and al-Zarqawi, 154, 174–175, 177, 185; and AQI, 154, 174–175; avoiding cult of personality, 158, 207n3; call for global jihad, 154; escape to Pakistan, 157; expectations after death of, 1–3, 32, 151, 156–158; focus on religion not territory, 166; leadership of al-Qaeda, 153–154, 165–166; missile attacks against, 173–174; Obama on, 2, 4–5, 151–152, 157; raid, killing of, 1–3, 4, 24–25, 152, 157; successfully institutionalizing ideology, 150; succession after, 32, 151; US celebration of death, 4, 195; and US Executive Order 12333, 173. *See also* al-Qaeda

Birzeit University polls, 119–120, 120f, 121f

Bissonnette, Matthew, 203n1

bivariate analyses of targeting, 68–72 (68t, 70t–72t), 163
Black September Organization, 54
Bloom, Mia, 17, 36, 107, 109, 196, 211n75
Boko Haram, 67, 83–84, 201f
Bondokj, Neven, 122
Borm, Peter, 18
Brachman, Jarret, 176
Brooks, Risa, 17, 37, 60, 226n62
Brown, Mitchell, 59
Bueno de Mesquita, Ethan, 34
bureaucracy, 31–36, 38, 57, 114–115
bureaucratization, 29; of al-Qaeda and affiliates, 175–177; of Hamas, 105–106, 113–116; and leader replacement, 32, 91; and reorganization, 22; structure of rules, policies, procedures, 31, 114, 142, 212n104; of terrorist groups generally, 7, 29, 56, 207n83, 210nn53. *See also* division of labor
Burt, Jo-Marie, 147, 224n105
Bush, George W., 5, 49, 58, 157
Byman, Daniel, 17, 95–96, 102, 175, 220n85, 228n114

capture versus death of leader, 54
car bombs, 50, 107
Carroll, Glenn R., 57
Carvin, Stephanie, 17
case studies, 11. *See also* al-Qaeda; Hamas; Sendero Luminoso
CDC (Civil Defense Committees), Sendero, 138
charisma, 24–26, 30–33, 35, 92, 179, 207n10, 208n11
Chechen separatists, 10
Chenoweth, Erica, 216n53
Chicago Project on Security and Threats, 99
Christmas Day 2009 bombing attempt, 166
Chuschi, Peru, 128
civilian deaths, 10–11; after leadership strikes, 19–20; by al-Qaeda, 170; by both side of a conflict, 112; as collateral damage, 95; creating public outrage, 118–119; and definition of terrorism, 9–10, 27; drone strikes and, 3–4, 51–52; in Gaza City, 104; International Crisis Group on, 118; in Iraq, 154; in Israel, 95, 102–103, 118; as retaliation, 5, 104; by Sendero, 133, 138; as strategic decision, 29. *See also* Hamas
clandestine organizations, 13, 26–27, 34, 39
Clinton, Bill, 173

coca trade, 147
collateral damage from attacks, 95
collective action, 25, 27, 39
communal support: for AQI, 152, 177–178; for Hamas, 116–122 (120f, 121f); "indigenous structures," 40; for ISIS, 152, 172; organizational resilience, 22, 30, 116–122 (120f, 121f); over civilian deaths, 17, 36–37, 43; reasons for, 42–44; for Sendero, 141, 144–149; supplying resources to rebellion, 36–38
communication network perspective, 40, 42
Comrade Artemio (Florindo Eleuterio Flores Hala), 125
Comrade Feliciano, 125
Comrade Miche (Laura Zambrano Padilla), 132–133
counterproductive behavior/outcomes, 49–52, 173–174
counterterrorism policies, success and failure of, 48–49
Country Reports on Terrorism (US, 2011), 5
CPA (Coalition Provisional Authority), 177
Crenshaw, Martha, 29, 56, 209n36
Cronin, Audrey Kurth: on al-Qaeda and bin Laden, 3, 32, 158, 207nn1 (ch5), 220n85; on AQC, 167; on AQI, 155–156; on arresting versus killing leaders, 54; on CIA in Pakistan, 157; on communal support, 43; on decapitation, 17–18; on ideology becoming irrelevant, 211n90; on ISIS, 193; patterns of organizational decline, 23, 37, 45; on Sendero after Guzmán arrest, 138–139, 148
Crozier, Michel, 32, 210n56
cruise missile strikes, 173–174
cults, 25–26
cults of personality, 26, 136, 158, 187, 207n3
Cyert, R. M., 33

dataset on leadership targeting, 6–8 (7f), 182–183; attack frequencies, 83–85; bivariate analyses, 68–72 (68t, 70t–72t); and Global Terrorism Database, 50; parameters of, 51–54, 59, 63, 78, 86–87; previous projects, 15, 48, 52, 214n3; results, 63–68 (64f, 65f, 66f); sources for, 50, 57, 60; time period covered by, 15
David, Stephen, 19, 94–96, 217n7 (ch5), 220n85
Dear, Keith P., 19
death, organizational, 77–78, 85–90 (87f, 88t)

decapitated organizations, 12, 56, 63; and communal support, 116–118; effects of size of, 142; frequency of attacks by, 78–85 (79t, 80t, 81t), 183; leader vs. organizational death, 77–78, 85–90 (87f, 88t); lifespan/survival of, 22, 40, 47, 85–91 (87f, 88t), 183. See also AQAP; Hamas; organizational resilience theory; Sendero Luminoso

decapitation hypotheses, 53–61

decapitation strategy, 6–7, 204n12; causing increase in activity, 8; and charismatic leadership, 25; effect of on domestic audience, 4–5, 94–95, 156; evaluating efficacy of, 8, 53–61, 116–117; G. W. Bush on, 5; impact of on activity, existence, 67–78; impact of on attack frequency, 78–85 (79t–81t); impact of on organizational survival, 85–90 (87f, 88t); increasing revenge killings, 104; by Israel against Hamas, 4, 96, 99–104 (100f, 100t, 101f, 103f); killing versus arrest, 74–75, 77; not effective, 90–92; Obama on, 5; over time, 64 (64f), 183; post-2001 increase in, 3; against separatist versus religious groups, 45; types of decapitation, 53–54, 77. See also organizational resilience theory

decentralization, 34–35, 42, 92, 210n53

Declaration of Principles, 101

Deen, Adam, 5, 189

Degregori, Carlos Ivan, 127

Deibert, Ronald J., 41

de Wit, Ton, 129, 145

disruption and resilience, 17, 19, 33, 192

division of labor, 31, 46, 183; within al-Qaeda/ISI, 91, 168, 175; within Hamas, 91, 105, 106, 114; within Sendero, 142, 144

doctrine, 40, 44–45

drone strikes, 3–4, 51–52, 203n6, 204n11

Dunford, Joseph, 49

Durand, Óscar Ramírez: capture of, 131–132, 134, 144, 150, 184–186; consequences of capture, 124–126, 131–132, 134, 138–139, 148–150, 184, 186; death of, 149; Sendero under, 25, 136–139, 142, 144, 148, 150, 185. See also Sendero

East Africa, 153, 165

efficiency versus stability, 210n64

Eglund, Scott, 127, 146

Egypt, 19, 112, 158, 171, 194–195

Erhabi, Abu Saad, 189

ETA (Basque Fatherland and Freedom), 17, 67, 83, 85, 200f

factionalization, 22, 211n75, 215n22; Baader-Meinhof Group, 34, 53; Hamas, 108, 119–120; ISIS, 189; Jemaah Islamiyah, 26; Shining Path, 25, 124, 126, 150; splintering, 15, 26, 34, 53, 144, 150

Fair, C. Christine, 44, 52, 171–172

Fallujah, 156, 177

FARC, 124

Fatah, 108–109, 111, 118–120, 220n92

Felter, Joseph, 176

fence between Palestinian, Israeli territories, 95, 109–110, 220n85

firms, terrorist organizations as, 91, 179, 209n51

First Intifada, 97, 101–102

Fishman, Brian, 175

Flanigan, Shawn Teresa, 59

Flores Hala, Florindo Eleuterio (Comrade Artemio), 125

Foreign Terrorist Organizations (US State Dept.), 67

Forest, James J. F., 176

Freeman, John, 57

Freeman, Michael, 16, 25, 208n14

free-rider problems, 27–28

frequency of terrorist attacks metric, 47, 49–50, 79–82 (80t, 81t)

Friedman, Jeffrey A., 155

FTO (foreign terrorist organizations) designation, 50

Fujimori, Alberto, 133, 137, 148, 221n1

Garcia Castano, Victor, 133

Gaza Strip, 19, 46, 97, 103–104, 114, 116, 119

Gaza War (2008–9), 111

GDP metric, 58–61, 63, 182–183; and activity after decapitation, 8, 71–72 (71t); Model 2 variable, 77, 88–89 (88t); Model 3 variable, 74; source of, 67; survival rate and, 87–91 (88t)

Gerges, Fawaz A., 189, 192

Gerth, H. H., 33

Ghousheh, Ibrahim, 119

GIA (Armed Islamic Group of Algeria), 10

Gianotten, Vera, 129

global Salafi jihad, 18, 42, 157, 192

Global Terrorism Database. See GTD

Gorriti, Gustavo, 147

Grenier, Robert, 51
group activity metric, 50, 53, 57, 86, 95, 186; one-year postdecapitation, 71–73 (71t, 73t); two-year postdecapitation, 75–78 (76t). *See also* organizational/group activity metric
group/organizational existence metric, 48, 51, 53, 67–69, 72, 77–78, 89–90, 117–118
group/organizational strength: after attack, 8, 16, 30, 182; and civilian support, 43, 114; determining, 64, 91; indigenous, 39; martyrdom effect on, 158; redundancy increasing, 42; of Sendero Luminoso, 144, 146, 148
group resilience theory, 23, 29, 42, 82, 113, 150, 164. *See also* organizational resilience theory
group type/ideology, 7, 40–46
GTD (Global Terrorism Database), 48; and AQI activity, 160 (160f); versus BAAD database, 57; data on Hamas attacks, 101–103 (101f, 103f); inclusion criteria used by, 218n40
guerilla groups, 205n35
Gunaratna, Rohan, 166, 173–174
Gurr, Tedd, 216n55
Guzmán, Abimael: arrest of, 17, 20, 25, 125–126, 130–134, 137, 148–150; effects of arrest on Sendero, 124, 136–137, 141, 144, 150, 185–186, 221n1, 223n52; expulsion from PCP-BR, 126; Maoist beliefs of, 150; Marxist beliefs of, 45, 125, 139–140, 149; message from prison, 124, 136, 138–139, 150; popularity of, 147; publicized photos of, 124; at UNSCH, 127, 140. *See also* Sendero Luminoso

Hafez, Mohammed M., 95
Hamas, 93–94, 99, 112–113, 121; Abdel Aziz al-Rantisi, 46, 99, 102–105, 111, 116, 195; adaptation to decapitation, 104–113 (110f); Arafat and, 108; arming of, 98; attacks against leadership of, 11, 94–97, 99–104 (100f, 101f, 103f) (100t), 109, 111–112, 121; attacks by, 99, 101–103 (103f), 107, 109–112; both religious and separatist, 45, 93–94; bureaucratization of, 105–106, 113–116; ceasefire agreement (2008), 112; Charter 1988 and formation of, 122; communal support for, 116–122 (120f, 121f); decapitation effects on, 46, 94, 103, 121, 123; decentralization of, 35, 43; declaring jihad, 97, 105; decline in targeting of, 111–112; effects of age, size on, 91; identifying leaders of, 99–100, 103; ideology of, 97–98, 122–123; international leadership, 106; Israeli temporary ceasefire, 112; and Jordan, 108; justification of violence by, 122; killing of civilians, 95, 102–103, 109–110 (110f), 118; leadership abroad, 116; *majlis shura*, 114; nationalism of, 122; organizational adaptation, 104–113 (110f); origins, early history of, 97–99, 122; and Palestinian Authority, 108; providing education, services, 38, 98, 107–108; public support for, 103, 107, 111, 119; resilience of, 20, 94, 106, 113–123 (120f, 121f); rocket, mortar attacks by, 101–102, 110, 184, 218n40; and Second Intifada, 109, 111, 121; as successor to PLO, 98; use of car bombs, suicide attacks, 107, 110; use of tunnels, 112–113; Yahya Ayyash, 46, 96, 108, 195, 214n139. *See also* Yassin, Sheikh Ahmed
Hamers, Herbert, 18
Hannan, Michael T., 57
Harakat-ul-Jihad al-Islami (HuJI), 4
Harkat ul Mujahidin, 174
"Harmony documents," 176
Hassan, Hassan, 190–191
Hatfield, Joseph M., 95
hazard rates, 51, 63, 85–89, 91–92, 183
Hegghammer, Thomas, 213n135
Hekmatullah, Qari, 189
Hezbollah, 35, 50–51, 58
hierarchical organization, 26, 144, 168
hierarchy of authority. *See* bureaucratization
Hoffman, Bruce, 9, 44, 163, 167–168, 205n35
homegrown networks, 166–168, 226n62
Hosmer, Stephen, 12
Hroub, Khaled, 46, 103, 111, 117, 217n10 (ch5)
Huatay Ruiz, Martha, 133
Huaytalla, Claudillo Bellido, 132
hubs, 18, 41–42, 158, 213n119
HuJI (Harakat-ul-Jihad al-Islami), 4
Hussein of Jordan, 108
hybrid structures, 35, 43, 105, 115, 144, 168
hypotheses on decapitation, 47–48; country GDP, 58–60; evaluating counterterrorism outcomes, 48–53; leader's position, 54–55; organizational type, age, size, 55–58; regime type, 60–61; type of decapitation, 53–54

identity-based organizations, 42
Ikhwan, 97, 218n28
incentives to participation, 27–28
incident of decapitation metric, 50, 54, 69, 72, 182
India, 4, 153, 159f, 160f, 165
indigenous structures, 40, 114
"institutionalization of charisma," 25
insurgency versus terrorism, 9–11, 205n35
intelligence information and resilience, 16–17
International Crisis Group, 52, 118
Internet, terrorist use of, 158, 167
intifadas: First Intifada, 97, 99, 101–102; Second Intifada, 97, 101–102, 107, 109, 111, 113, 119–121
Iparraguirre, Elena, 133
IRA (Irish Republican Army), 34
Iran, Islamist revolution in, 165
Iraq: al-Qaeda affiliates in, 169; killing of Shi'ite civilians, 154–155; Sunnis in, 155; US prisons in, 155
Isbell, Billie Jean, 128
ISI (Islamic State of Iraq), 4, 34, 154–156, 160–161 (160f, 161f), 174–175, 193–194
ISIL (Islamic State of Iraq and the Levant), 161f
ISIS (Islamic State of Iraq and Syria), 3, 228n2; dataset on, 63; decapitation attacks against, 188t, 189, 195–196; effects of age, size on, 91; formed from AQI, 152; hybrid structure of, 43–44; independence of leaders, 187; killing of al-Adnani, 5–6; lacking metric of success against, 49; organizational structure of, 186–187; public attitudes toward, 152, 172, 180, 194–195; public beheadings by, 175; resilience of, 188, 191–194 (191t); state-like qualities of, 174; targeting of, 181; territorial losses by, 189–190. See also AQI
IS-K (Islamic State of Khorasan), 189, 229n8
Islamic Center (al-Mujamma' al-Islami), 98, 218n32
Islamic Jihad, 45, 98–99, 108–109, 119–120
Islamic State, 156. See also ISI; ISIL; ISIS
Israel: decapitation attacks against Hamas, 11, 99–104 (100f, 101f, 103f) (100t), 109, 111; IDF blockades, 110; killing of civilians, children, 104; literature on targeting policies, 94–97; Operations Cast Lead, Pillar of Defense, 112; prisoner exchange freeing Yassin, 98; revenge narrative against Hamas, 4, 106; separation fence against suicide attacks, 109–110; stock market reactions to assassination, 96; use of deportation, 107; withdrawal from Gaza, 110–111. See also West Bank
Izz al-Din al-Qassam, 106

Jabari, Ahmed, 112
JI (Jemaah Islamiyah), 26
JMCC (Jerusalem Media Communications Center), 119–121 (120f, 121f)
JN (Jabhat al-Nusra), 155–156
Johnston, Patrick, 12–15, 79, 87, 206n56
Joscelyn, Thomas, 5, 189
JTJ (Jama'at al-Tawhid wal-Jihad), 154. See also AQI

Kaplan, Edward H., 95
Kashmiri, Ilyas, 4
Kashmiri militants, 11, 174
Kay, Bruce, 147–148, 223n64
Kenney, Michael, 35
Knoke, David, 41
Kocher, Matthew, 205n35
Krause, Peter, 209n39
Krueger, Alan B., 58
Kurdistan Workers' Party (PKK), 25, 45, 67, 83–84, 181, 196, 199f, 205n35

Langdon, Lisa, 15
Laqueur, Walter, 9
"latent" groups, 27–28, 174
leadership: acting from abroad, 106; defined, identified, 99; less important than ideology, 44–45; rank of target, 69, 71t, 77; and resilience, 16; role of, 26–27
Lebanon, 107, 160f, 194
left-wing groups, 45; activity post-decapitation, 69, 70t, 77, 90–91; distribution of, 66f, 67; hazard rate of, 87, 183; resilience of, 182; subject to destabilization, 139, 144, 185–186. See also Sendero Luminoso
legality of decapitation, 5
Levinthal, Daniel A., 115
LexisNexis database, 47–48, 63, 214n3
Li, Quan, 60–61
Lia, Brynjar, 172
life span, 85–86, 89–90; and counterterrorism policies, 48–54; decapitation and, 8, 12, 22, 61; of nondecapitated organizations, 56; religion and, 46; survival of decapitated organizations, 22, 40, 47, 85–91 (87f, 88t),

183. *See also* organizational/group life span metric
Lindelauf, Roy, 18
literature on decapitation, 11–12, 48–49; arguments on resilience, 16–18; consequences of decapitation, 18–20, 79 (79t); Israeli targeting policies, 94; quantitative research, 12–16; toward Hamas, 96
literature on organizational leadership theories, 24–28
local support. *See* communal support
London Underground attacks, 166
"lone wolf" attacks, 29, 192
LTTE (Liberation Tigers of Tamil Eelam), 67, 83–85, 199f, 221n121
Luft, Gal, 96

Majd, 98. *See also* Hamas
majlis shura, 114
Maleckova, Jitka, 58
Malhotra, Neil, 171
Mannes, Aaron, 15
Mansfield, Roger, 35
Manwaring, Max G., 130, 134
Maoist ideology, 139, 150
March, James G., 33, 57, 210n67
Mariátegui, José Carlos, 126, 139
Marion, Russ, 35
Marks, Tom, 146
Martínez, Antonio Díaz, 132
martyrdom: of assassinated leaders, 95, 158, 180; commemoration of, 118, 176; communal support for, 36, 116, 195; and martyrdom effect, 18, 32, 54, 95, 173; suicide attacks, 36
Marxist ideology, 37, 45, 55, 125, 127, 139–140, 148–149
Marzuq, Abu, 106, 107
McAdam, Doug, 39, 114
McCarthy, John D., 39, 212n104
McChrystal, Stanley, 51
McClintock, Cynthia, 127, 142, 145–146
McCormick, Gordon, 130–131, 136, 140
Meinhof, Ulrike, 34, 45, 53, 54
Mendelsohn, Barak, 152, 153, 164, 168
"metaorganizations," 152, 153
metrics for evaluating counterterrorism, 49–53
Mezich, Julio Cesar, 132–133
Mierau, Jochen, 19
millenarian groups, 26
Mills, C. Wright, 33

Mintz, Alex, 95
Mishal, Khaled, 108
Mishal, Shaul, 95, 97, 105, 107, 114–115
MMI (Majelis Mujahidin Indonesia), 26
Moghadam, Assaf, 10
Mohammed, Khalid Sheikh, 171
moral disengagement, 27
"moral framework," 44
morality of decapitation, 5
mosque network, 35, 106
Mosul, 6, 156, 186, 189, 192
Mughniyeh, Imad, 50
Múgica Garmendia, Francisco, 17
mujahedeen, 153, 154, 165, 177
multivariate analyses of targeting, 48, 68–69, 71–78 (73t, 75t, 76t), 113, 141
Munich Olymipics kidnappings, 54
Musharraf, Pervez, 157
Mushtaha, Rawhi, 105
Muslim Brotherhood (MB), 97–99, 105–106, 122. *See also* Hamas

National Strategy for Combatting Terrorism (2006), 3, 49
National Strategy for Counterterrorism (2011), 3, 49
Nelson, Geoffrey, 25
Netanyahu, Benjamin, 108
Netanya suicide attacks, 109
network centrality perspective, 41
Nicholson, John W. Jr., 189
nondecapitated comparison groups, 63, 78–83 (81t), 86–91 (87f), 142, 183
nonhierarchical groups, 207n3
NPA (New People's Army), 67, 83–84, 199f

Obama, Barack: al-Qaeda on "path to defeat," 151–152; on death of bin Laden, 4–5; objectives of regarding ISIS, 49; order to kill/capture bin Laden, 2, 4, 157; use of drone strikes, 4, 87; use of targeted operations, 2, 159
Oberschall, Anthony, 114
Öcalan, Abdullah, 25, 84
Olson, Mancur, 27–28, 57
O'Neill, Robert, 203n1
Oots, Kent Layne, 27–28, 208n23
Operation Cast Lead, 112, 120, 218n40
Operation Defensive Shield, 109
Operation Neptune Spear, 152
Operation Pillar of Defense, 111–112

256   Index

organizational adaptation to decapitation (Hamas), 104–113 (110f)
organizational age metric, 56
organizational collapse, 47
organizational death, 77–78, 85–90 (87f, 88t)
organizational decline, 4, 6, 11, 23, 156, 186
organizational/group activity metric, 48, 50; age and, 69, 71t; and attack frequency, 53, 78, 95, 186; dataset differences and, 86; and decapitation results, 8, 76t; GDP and, 71 (71t); leadership rank and, 54, 69, 71t; multivariate analyses, 72–73 (73t); regime type and, 72; and Shining Path, 11; size of group and, 83–84
organizational/group existence metric, 48, 51, 53, 67–69, 72, 77–78, 89–90, 117–118
organizational/group life span metric, 206n56; decapitation and, 53, 61, 63, 79, 85–86, 89–91, 183; ideology and, 69; leader's position and, 54–55; organizational age and, 56; quantitative measures, 48–53
organizational resilience theory, 11, 22–24, 152; arguments on resilience, 16–20; bureaucracy and, 22, 30–36, 113–116; communal support, 29, 36–40, 43–44; doctrine, 40–46; group ideology, 29, 40–44; and Hamas, 113–123; and leadership decapitation, 29–30; literature on, 24–28; redundancy, 29; and Sendero, 139; size and, 92
organizational size, 56–58, 68t, 73–74 (73t), 76t
organizational structure, 6, 7, 64; of al-Qaeda, 151–152, 158, 164, 168, 176; cellular structure, 35; of Hamas, 105, 114–115; of ISIS, 187; and resilience, 17–18, 29, 42; of Sendero Luminoso, 144; and susceptibility to decapitation, 92
organizational survival metric, 49, 63, 85–90 (87f, 88t), 209n36
organizational theory, 26–28
organizational typology, 55–56, 91–92
organizational weakening, 49
Oslo Accords, 101–102
Owen, Mark, 203n1

Pakistan, 213n125; al Qaeda in, 164, 166, 168, 171; bin Laden escape to, 157; bin Laden killed in, 1–3, 152; CIA "surge" into, 157; drone strikes in, 3–4, 19, 52; Lashkar-e-Taiba in, 163, 213n125; survey on support for al-Qaeda, 171–172, 194. *See also* AQC (al-Qaeda Central) and affiliates
Palestine Liberation Organization (PLO), 97–98, 102, 106–107, 118, 122
Palestinian Authority (PA), 108–109
Palestinian Legislative Council:, 111, 119, 186
Palmer, David, 128, 142, 223n62
Panetta, Leon, 2, 151
Pape, Robert, 12, 36, 99, 107, 116, 166
Pardavé Trujillo, Yovanka, 133
Parsons, Talcott, 31–32
patriotism as motivator, 28
PCP-BR (Red Flag), 126
PCP-SL. *See* Sendero Luminoso
peasant rebellion, 139
Pedahzur, Ami, 41, 102–103, 109, 212n114
Peres, Shimon, 102
Peru. *See* Sendero Luminoso
Petersen, Roger, 37
PFLP (Popular Front for the Liberation of Palestine), 98, 120
Piazza, James, 58
PKK (Kurdistan Workers' Party), 25, 45, 67, 83–84, 181, 196, 199f, 205n35
Plaw, Avery, 96, 104, 156, 173, 217n3
PLO (Palestine Liberation Organization), 97–98, 102, 106–107, 118, 122
political process theory, 38–40
Polity scores, 60, 63, 67, 72 (72t), 74, 76t, 77–78
popular support. *See* communal support
Poraz, Avraham, 104
Post, Gerald, 55
Potter, Philip, 207n94, 211n81
Prabhakaran, Velupillai, 85
preference divergence, 34, 43, 176–177, 228n101
pre-/post-2001 strategy, 3
preventive arrests, 95
Price, Bryan, 12–13, 16, 79, 86–87, 206n56
public opinion on terrorism, 17, 169–172

Qassam rocket attacks, 102
quasi-bureaucratic structure, 35, 158, 168
Qutb, Sayid, 19, 158

Ramadi, 156
Ranger-Moore, James, 57
rational-legal authority, 30–31, 33
Rea, Freddy, 132
rebellion, logic of, 37–38
Red Army Faction, 34, 53, 211n90

Red Brigade, 16
Red Flag (PCP-BR), 126
regime type metric, 60–61, 72 (72t), 74, 77, 91, 182–183
religious groups, 7, 208n16; activity post-decapitation, 70t; communal support, 42–46; decapitation and, 45; distribution of, 66f; hazard rate of, 87; identity-based, 42; and organizational resilience, 22–23, 30, 43, 46; religion supplying legitimacy, 44; susceptibility of, 40; terrorism and, 25–26
resilience: arguments for, 16–20; bureaucracy and, 30–33, 35, 57, 115; in organizations, 42–43, 91–92, 175
resistance versus jihad, 122
resource mobilization theory, 38–40, 116, 223n64
retaliatory responses to decapitation, 5, 18–19; by al Qaeda, 173, 180, 195; bureaucratization and, 7; by Hamas, 46, 96, 103–104, 108–109, 184, 195, 218n20; leading to cycle of violence, 95–96; preventing, 111, 123; by Shining Path, 133–134, 137, 185
revenge as motive: for Hamza bin Laden, 180; for Sendero, 185; for strikes by Israel, 4, 19, 46, 94, 96, 104, 123; US public cheering bin Laden's death, 195
Riedel, Bruce, 2
right-wing groups, 55–56, 90–91; and communal support, 43; dependence on dominant figure, 45; distribution of, 66f; effect of decapitation on, 61, 67, 69, 73–74 (73t), 77, 182–183; targeting of, 66f
rocket, mortar attacks, 101–102, 110, 112, 184, 218n40, 220n95
Ron, James, 146, 222n14
Ronfeldt, David, 213n116
routinization of charisma, 13, 25, 33–34, 210n62
Roy, Sara, 107–108, 117–118
Ruby, Keven, 55

Sa'adon, Ilan, 106
Sageman, Marc, 18, 41–42, 157–158, 167, 213n119, 226n62
Sarapu, Alexander J., 15
Sasportas, Avi, 106
scale-free networks, 42
Schmid, Alex, 9, 170, 172
Schultz, Richard, 212n109

Schulzke, Marcus, 52
Second Intifada, 97, 101–102, 107, 109, 111, 113, 119–121
Sela, Avraham, 107
selective incentives, 28, 146
Sendero Luminoso (PCP-SL, Shining Path), 10–11, 17; and Ayacucho, 126–129, 133, 140, 145–146; bureaucratization, 142–144; Central Committee and structure of, 143; communalism under, 128; communal support for, 141, 144–149; as decapitation example, 125–126, 131–133; under Durand's leadership, 137–138, 142, 144, 148–150; early success of, 129–130; following Durand's arrest, 125, 184–185; following Guzmán's arrest, 124, 133–137, 141, 144, 150, 185–186, 221n1, 223n52; government attacks on, 128; under Guzmán's leadership, 127; organizational resilience and ideology, 138–141; origins and early years of, 126–128; Peruvian counterterrorism against, 127, 130–138 (131f, 136f); popularity of, 140, 147–148; size of, 142; social context of, 128–130; turning to violence, 127–128, 141; typical recruits of, 129. See also Guzmán, Abimael
separatist groups: activity post-decapitation, 70t; distribution of, 66f; hazard rate of, 87; ideology of, 7, 40, 42–43; and organizational resilience, 43–45, 78, 122; resilience of to targeting, 8, 73–74 (73t), 83, 87
Shapiro, Jacob: AQI bureaucratic structure, 175–177; decline in US military fatalities, 155; managerial challenges for terrorists, 29; survey of Pakistanis, 171–172; terrorist efficiency versus secrecy, 18, 34; terrorist security versus organizational control, 207n83
Sharm al-Sheikh summit, 111
Sharon, Ariel, 109–111
Shaw, Eric, 55
Shehada, Salah, 98, 104
Shepherd, Bryan, 44
Shining Path. See Sendero Luminoso
Shiqaqi, Fathi, 98, 108
Siggelkow, Nicolaj, 115
size of organization, 141–143; and bureaucracy, 7–8; and group activity postdecapitation, 73t, 76t; ISIS, 193; largest groups, 83–85; and resilience, 74, 91–92, 163–164, 170, 182–183
Smelser, Neil, 212n98

SMOs (social movement organizations), 38–39
social network analysis, 40–43, 92, 115
social networks, 18, 91, 157
Somalia, 3–4, 153–154, 166, 169
"Sons of Iraq," 178
Soufan, Ali, 180
South Waziristan, 52
Soviet Union, 37, 148, 165
splintering, 15, 26, 34, 53, 144, 150. *See also* factionalization
Sri Lanka, 85
Stein, Janice Gross, 41
Stein, Yael, 217n3
Stern, Jessica, 193
Stimson Center report, 51
Stohl, Cynthia, 42, 58
Stohl, Michael, 42, 58, 127, 146
strategic actors, 39, 209nn36
Strong, Simon, 147
substitution effects, 113
succession mechanisms, 30, 32, 179
suicide terrorism, 17, 107–109; by AQI, 178; counterterrorism generating support for, 196; by Hamas, 99, 104, 107–112, 195; by ISIS, 192; public support for, 36, 109, 116, 119, 121 (121f); targeted assassinations increasing, 95, 97
Sungkar, Abdullah, 26
Sunni "Awakening," 155, 161, 168, 175, 178
"Surge" in Iraq, 153, 155, 161, 168, 175, 178
survival rate, 51, 85–91 (87f, 88t), 182–183
Syria, 155–156, 170, 177, 188–189. *See also* ISIS

Taliban, 67, 83–84, 154, 163, 172, 174, 200f
Tamimi, Azzam, 97, 105–107, 111, 220n92
Tanzim Qaidat al-Jihad fi Bilad al-Rafidayn, 154
targeting of civilians, 207n94
Task Force on US Drone Policy, 51
Taylor, Lewis, 137–138, 140–141
Temple Mount and Second Intifada, 109
territorial control and popular support, 43
terrorism, definitions of, 8–10, 205n23
terrorist groups/organizations, 205n23; activity postdecapitation, 72–77 (73t, 74t, 76t); categories of support for, 170; difficulty of exiting, 27; as firms, 91, 179, 209n51; largest, 83–85; and organizational "death," 77–78; providing social services, 37; as rational actors, 29
third wave of global Islamist terrorism, 167

Thomas, Ward, 96
Tikrit, 156
time series data, 50, 78–79, 83–85, 163, 199f
Toledo administration, 133
Tominaga, Yasutaka, 16, 204n14
Tora Bora Revisited (Senate Foreign Relations Committee), 157
traditional authority, 30
transference of authority, 25, 31
transition matrix analysis, 63, 78–80 (79t), 82, 90, 142, 197–198
transnational terrorism, 43–44, 153, 164, 168, 188
Trump, Donald, 49
TTP (Taliban, and Tehrik-i-Taliban Pakistan), 67, 83–84, 200f

Uhl-Bien, Mary, 35
United States: Bush, George W., 5, 49, 58, 157; Executive Order 12333 and bin Laden, 173; government definitions of terrorism, 9; use of drones, 87; use of special operations forces, 87. *See also* Obama, Barack
UNSCH (Universidad Nacional de San Cristóbal de Huamanga), 127
USS *Cole,* 154

Valle Travesaño, Tito Roger, 132–133
Velasco Alvarado, Juan, 127

Walsh, James Igoe, 52
Warden, John, 11–12
Weber, Max, 24–25, 30–35
Wells, Matthew, 15
West Bank: after Sharon's Temple Mount visit, 109; arrests in, 106; Hamas in, 114, 116, 118, 122; political agreement in, 97; poll results in, 46, 103, 119–120 (120f); separation fence, blockades, 109–112; targeted killings in, 19, 104. *See also* Muslim Brotherhood
West Point's Combating Terrorism Center, 176
Wilkinson, Paul, 212n109
Williams, Brian Glyn, 52
World Bank dataset, 63
World Public Opinion, 170, 178

Yang, Song, 41
Yassin, Sheikh Ahmed: arrest of, 106; assassination of, 46, 103–104, 111, 116,

184, 195; forming Majd, 98; and Hamas, 97–98, 105; identification of, 99; imprisonment and release of, 98, 108. *See also* Hamas

Yemen, 3–4, 51, 153–154, 160f, 166, 177

Zald, Mayer N., 39, 212n104
Zambrano Padilla, Laura (Comrade Miche), 132–133
Zammuto, Raymond, 117
Zelin, Aaron Y., 190
Zussman, Asaf and Noah, 96